D1706936

FROM
CRISIS
TO
CHRIST

PAUL N. ANDERSON

FROM
CRISIS
TO
CHRIST

A Contextual Introduction to the New Testament

Abingdon Press™

Nashville

FROM CRISIS TO CHRIST:
A CONTEXTUAL INTRODUCTION TO THE NEW TESTAMENT

Copyright © 2014 Abingdon Press

All rights reserved.
No part of this work may be reproduced or transmitted in any form or by any means, electronic or mechanical, including photocopying and recording, or by any information storage or retrieval system, except as may be expressly permitted by the 1976 Copyright Act or in writing from the publisher. Requests for permission can be addressed to Permissions, The United Methodist Publishing House, P.O. Box 801, 201 Eighth Avenue South, Nashville, TN 37202-0801, or e-mailed to permissions @umpublishing.org.

This book is printed on acid-free paper.

Library of Congress Cataloging-in-Publication Data   ·

Anderson, Paul N., 1956–
  From crisis to Christ : a contextual introduction to the New Testament / Paul N. Anderson.
    pages cm
  Includes bibliographical references and index.
  ISBN 978-1-4267-5104-2 (binding: soft back, trade pbk. : alk. paper) 1. Bible. New Testament—Introductions. I. Title.
  BS2330.3.A53 2014
  225.6'1—dc23

2014029825

Scripture quotations unless noted otherwise are from the Common English Bible. Copyright © 2011 by the Common English Bible. All rights reserved. Used by permission. (www.CommonEnglishBible .com)

Scripture quotations marked (NRSV) are taken from the New Revised Standard Version of the Bible, copyright 1989, Division of Christian Education of the National Council of the Churches of Christ in the United States of America. Used by permission. All rights reserved.

Scripture quotations marked (NKJV) are taken from the New King James Version®. Copyright © 1982 by Thomas Nelson, Inc. Used by permission. All rights reserved.

14 15 16 17 18 19 20 21 22 23—10 9 8 7 6 5 4 3 2 1

MANUFACTURED IN THE UNITED STATES OF AMERICA

CONTENTS

Contents

FOREWORD

Why do people read the New Testament, and how do they come to grips most effectively with its meaning? After all, the Bible is the most widely published book, and the New Testament is the most valuable resource for understanding the origins of Christianity. It also provides a unique set of insights into first-century Judaism and the rise of the Jesus movement from Judaism into Hellenistic Christianity. As Jesus of Nazareth is the most important figure in human history, the writings that tell his story are foundational to understanding Christian origins and their developments. Beyond Christian readers, though, the New Testament will be of interest to persons of other faiths and concerns, as well as those seeking to understand Christianity from a secular perspective. And a contextual approach to the New Testament provides the best way to understand and engage its meanings, then and now.

From Crises to Christ

The Jesus movement did not arise in a vacuum. At every turn, developments emerged in the contexts of crises—political, social, religious, economic, psychological. Given that the Jewish people had felt called by God as a chosen nation, their tumultuous history produced a good deal of cognitive dissonance from one generation to another. Geographically, Israel is located at the crossroads between three continents: Africa, Europe, and Asia. As a result, whenever one empire expanded, usually at the expense of another, armies tended to trample the settings in which those boundaries were negotiated. Further, as a modest nation among giants, ancient Israel was often courted by Egypt to the south and west, against the Assyrians and Babylonians to the north and east—and vice versa—a buffer zone of one empire against others. As a result, allegiances with other nations brought on retaliatory treatment when the prevailing empire sought to exact its dues, or when the next empire expanded. When Alexander the Great conquered the larger Mediterranean world between 334 and 324 BCE, however, a new crisis emerged. Hellenistic culture and practices became a new threat to Israel's religious ethos.

As Greek architecture, art, and language came to dominate the Mediterranean world, holding on to Jewish religious customs and practices became more of a challenge for Israel. For over a century, the Hellenistic empire ruled Israel from Egypt under the Ptolomaic Dynasty, but when Syria expanded its reach in 198 BCE, the Seleucid Dynasty came to rule the region. As a means of resisting a hostile occupation, Jewish religion provided the staunchest basis of national strength. As a result, Antiochus IV, king of Syria, banned all aspects of Jewish religion, burned copies of the Torah, and set up a statue of Zeus in the Jerusalem temple in 167 BCE. A three-year campaign by Judas Maccabeus and his militant followers brought short relief from Syrian domination, and the temple was rededicated and made available for use again in December of 164 BCE. The Maccabean wars, as they were called, continued for another two decades, and Israel finally garnered a respite of freedom for the first time since the exile to Babylon four and a half centuries earlier. But after eight decades of relative autonomy in the Hasmonean Period, the land once again came under the domination of a foreign empire in 63 BCE: Rome.

It is under the occupation of Rome that all the New Testament writings were produced—indeed, times of crisis prevailed on many levels. But how might God deliver Israel from its new oppressors? That would depend on how redemption was understood, and what group was describing such a vision. As Israel's calling as a people of God was understood in various ways during the previous millennium or more, these multiple visions contributed to diverse messianic and covenantal understandings also during the Roman era. Interpreting the Law of Moses and keeping its statutes faithfully became one central trajectory among Israel's religious leaders. Yearning for the wistful days of Israel's monarchy a thousand years earlier led to visions of God's restoring her glory by means of a king like David, or a figure of internationally noted wisdom, like Solomon. Memories of such holy-war figures as Moses and Joshua became conflated with King Cyrus of Persia, who is described as "the anointed one" (*Mashiach* in Hebrew; *Christos* in Greek) in Isaiah 40–55. Many in Israel dreamed of a military leader, such as Judas Maccabeus, because he was remembered as successfully delivering Israel from Syrian occupation between 167 and 164 BCE and beyond. And yet, other views of God's deliverance advocated the social-justice themes of the Prophets and the non-violent, paradoxical model of the suffering servant as found in Isaiah 40–55. Therefore, ways Israel had dealt with crises in the past presented a diversity of options as to how her leaders might address impending crises during the

Roman occupation, and the New Testament is filled with precisely that diversity of idealism in the light of disconcerting realism.

As a result, Israel's own sense of vocation, her tumultuous history, and the various ways her leaders perceived and addressed impending crises informed the ways followers of Jesus and their contemporaries engaged crises during the New Testament era. From the birth of Jesus of Nazareth, born during the reign of Herod the Great (ca. 4–6 BCE), to the latest canonical writings of his followers a century later, many other crises were also faced and addressed. The deaths of John the Baptist and Jesus then created formidable crises for their followers, as did the later martyrdoms of Stephen, James, Peter, and Paul. But, so did other events, such as the crucifixion of two thousand Jews after the plundering of the Roman armory in Sepphoris in 4 BCE, followed by the tax revolt of Judas the Galilean nine years later. The Romans also captured and killed the followers of such messianic figures as Theudas and "the Samaritan," who envisioned deliverance as renewed expressions of earlier conquests. Then, later, in response to Jewish zealots and terrorist assaults, Rome invaded Judea and destroyed Jerusalem between 66 and 73 CE. And imagine the personal crisis experienced by Saul, on the road to Damascus with the intention of persecuting followers of Jesus, when he was struck by a vision of Christ—blinded and knocked to the ground. As Paul took the gospel to Jewish communities all over the Mediterranean world, known as the diaspora (the dispersion), imagine the crisis of uneven receptions among his Jewish compatriots. Who could have guessed that Gentiles would be so receptive to his message and embrace a Jewish savior, while some Jews rejected Paul's message?

Then, imagine the crises faced by Jewish and Gentile followers of Jesus as they sought to form gathered communities of believers—forced to sort out a host of issues related to diverse matters of faith and practice. If God's saving grace was to be received by grace through faith, not works, did it really matter how "Jewish" the lifestyles of Gentile believers were? What was permissible and what was not for believers in the Jewish Messiah, and who would make such determinations? Then, as the Roman persecution of Jesus followers developed during the reigns of Nero in Rome (54–68 CE) and Domitian throughout the empire (81–96 CE), new sets of crises emerged. His followers had remembered that Jesus promised to return before the eyewitnesses died, but what were they to do when the last of the apostles passed away without witnessing the vindication of the Lord's return? And how could the ministry of Jesus continue among the second and third generations of believers, after all the eyewitnesses were gone? Further, who would evaluate the divergent teachings of various traveling ministers, and how would problematic teachings and behaviors be addressed?

These are the sorts of crises that faced the Jesus movement, so having a sense of the historical backdrop behind the New Testament writings will help us interpret their meanings—then and now. Understanding how God's redemptive work would be accomplished through the earthly ministry of Jesus involved one set of developments, but clarifying the world-changing significance of his redemptive work on the cross is also a subject of interest within the texts of the New Testament themselves. Getting a sense of the different forms of literature by different authors and in different contexts is thus essential for achieving an adequate understanding of the New Testament.

Second Criticality—An Interdisciplinary Approach to the New Testament

Biblical studies in the modern era have faced an ongoing struggle between traditional readings of the New Testament and critical challenges, and one of the primary issues of discussion has been the question of history. This is understandable. When measures of truth came to be argued in terms of "fact" and "historicity" in the scientific era, and when biblical authority came to be debated in those terms, a number of problems ensued, often causing the central meanings of scripture to be lost. As the saying goes, when all one has is a hammer, everything looks like a nail. Therefore, appeals to certainty regarding authorship, dates, and composition have been paramount in New Testament scholarship, and introductory texts must navigate those waters effectively.

Traditionalistic approaches to the New Testament have tended to assert particular interpretations, supporting them with appeals to divine dictation or supernatural claims. Such appeals to certainty might work for a while within an insular faith community, but when subjected to external scrutiny, many claims are found lacking. For instance, attempts to harmonize differences between the Gospels have led to somewhat speculative reconstructions of Jesus's ministry, when some presentations of it were crafted for thematic and narrative reasons rather than chronological ones. And while the New Testament concludes with the warning that any who add or detract from "this book" will be afflicted with plagues and forfeit eternal life, this is not a defense of the canonized New Testament or any of its translations (e.g., Latin Vulgate or the King James Version of the Bible). Rather, the warning was addressing the audiences of Revelation as the scroll was circulated and read among the churches, calling hearers to heed the message and not to water it down. Traditionalistic scholars have also tended to bolster their interpretations on the basis of authorship, although the names of authors were not included in most original manuscripts but were added later. These sorts of operations have understandably led to critical challenges, and rightly so.

Critical challenges of traditional views have thus been the mainstay of New Testament scholarship over the last century or two, and often the work of critical scholarship ("critical" means analytical—using reasoned judgment based on evidence rather than dogma) has sought to provide alternatives to traditional views. Identifying literary relationships between the first three Gospels, for instance, helped scholars understand why there were so many word-for-word similarities (especially between Mark and Matthew) as well as differences. And analyses of the larger set of contemporary writings—Christian, Jewish, and Greco-Roman—have allowed scholars to make considered judgments with greater contextual awareness. In nineteenth-century German and French scholarship, knowledge of dialogues with Gnostics and with Jews in the second century CE led some scholars to push the composition of many New Testament writings into the mid-second century. This also made it easier to view reports of signs and wonders as incorporations of contemporary folklore rather than history-connected memory, although most scholars nowadays see the canonical texts as written within the first century, either by members of the apostolic generation or their followers. Authorship and composition issues thus have been central to critical scholarship, sometimes moving fallaciously from "not necessarily" to "necessarily not."

Second naïveté is a term introduced by Paul Ricoeur, describing the capacity to come back to an earlier understanding in the light of critical scrutiny. As this applies to biblical authority, the question is not "*Is* the Bible true?" but "*How* is the Bible true?" Where theology and meaning may have been the measures of the New Testament's value in previous centuries, they may still be appreciated, even if its historicity is unconfirmed by external verification or if some of the particulars vary between accounts. As Hans Küng put it, "Truth is beyond mere facticity." Therefore, second naïveté allows one to come back to existential meanings of scripture, even if modern critical analyses might call into question particular views of history, authorship, or composition. After all, the early church included these twenty-seven books as inspired and authoritative, and their canonical authority stands regardless of who wrote them or when. Therefore, how the New Testament speaks to readers personally and existentially—individually or in community—is itself a worthy interpretive venture. Is this last consideration, though, the endpoint in seeking to interpret the New Testament adequately?

What I might call *second criticality* also deserves a place within the scientific investigation of the New Testament, as not all critical approaches to interpretation are equally compelling—either in theory or in practice. Some even disagree with each other. Therefore, simply questioning a traditional view is not to overturn it, and upon this fallacy many hermeneutical schemes founder, and critically so. Further, just because a claim is traditional, that does not mean it is wrong or suspect. Diverse critical approaches to interpretation also differ in what they contribute, and an issue is often best perceived through multiple lenses, not just one. Therefore, critical analysis deserves to be applied to critical studies as well as traditional ones, and second criticality allows one to do so programmatically and in interdisciplinary ways. The goal of this approach, however, is neither to confirm nor to disconfirm a traditional or a critical claim, nor is it to establish one methodology over all others. Rather, the goal is to seek the truth about an issue, drawing in the strongest methodologies that are best suited for the particular task at hand. It also keeps in mind that even "scientific" approaches to objectivity may themselves be distortive, as subjective engagement is required for making any sort of aesthetic, historical, or hermeneutical judgment, which is essential for interpreting any text.

Therefore, this introduction to the New Testament will endeavor to build upon the strongest of traditional views and critical methodologies, seeking to apply the best of objective judgments to subjective inferences of meaning and their applications. In that sense, some first- and second-century views will only be abandoned when critical scholarship has compellingly overturned them, not just questioned them. And, gradations of certainty will also be referenced, as all judgments fall within a continuum of plausibility.[1] This more nuanced approach to critical analysis has also led me to propose several new ways forward in seeking to address several of the New Testament's most enduring theological, historical, and literary riddles, convincing me that second criticality is needed now more than ever in biblical studies. There is truth in both traditional and critical scholarship, and in all judgments probing discernment is required.

---

1. Given that 0 percent and 100 percent degrees of probability are elusive, the following gradations are workable: 1–15 percent—probably not, with some certainty; 16–30 percent—unlikely; 31–45 percent—questionable; 46–55 percent—possible, but hard to decide either way; 56–70 percent—plausible; 71–85 percent—likely; 86–99 percent—probably, with some certainty.

Distinctive Features of this Introduction to the New Testament

Indeed, many excellent introductions to the New Testament abound, but the distinctive approach of this work involves three primary features. First, it calls for a reading of New Testament texts in the light of pertinent contexts and crises in every chapter—a total of nearly sixty in all. Second, it considers traditional views in the light of critical analyses, but in a measured way, inviting also personal engagement with the content. Third, it makes use of several new paradigms on the Gospels, Jesus, and the history of early Christianity, which form a basis for some of my approaches. These paradigms are argued more fully elsewhere, but in this book they are succinctly laid out as plausible ways forward in addressing some of the most perplexing of the New Testament's riddles. In that sense, this text is not content simply to describe standard critical approaches to pressing issues; it also advances several robust new paradigms, which on their merits seem compelling. Those interested in state-of-the-art discussions of these paradigms should of course read further, beyond this introductory text.

As a contextual approach to the New Testament, each chapter will therefore outline first the *historical crises and contexts* that are most relevant to each of the books being discussed. That will help one appreciate the historical backdrop of each book in its canonical order. Although Paul's letters were some of the first pieces written and most of the Gospels were among the last New Testament texts to be written, moving from the Gospels to the Epistles nonetheless works well. The ministry of Jesus, after all, becomes the basis for the Acts of the Apostles and the letters of the New Testament. Second, each chapter will highlight *literary features of the text* that seem most characteristic of the particular book being studied. Sometimes literary features will show relationships with writings outside that book; sometimes literary connections will be most evident within that particular book. Third, each chapter will illuminate particular aspects of the *theological message* of each of the books, building upon the historical and literary groundwork laid. That will lead to a brief section at the end of each chapter designed to help the reader *engage* the text personally and existentially in the light of its historical, literary, and theological features. The goal there is to read the New Testament as scripture while also appreciating its contextually informed origins and meanings.

This introduction to the New Testament is thus divided, after an overall introduction, into three parts involving the Gospels and Jesus (Part I), Acts and the Letters of Paul (Part II), and the General Epistles and Revelation

(Part III). Introductions to each of the parts will address aspects of authorship and composition, and excurses along the way will also explore other relevant subjects. Few references will be made to secondary literature, and readers are exhorted to consult other introductions, commentaries, monographs, and Bible reference works as well as online resources, some of which are listed at the end of the book. Most important, readers of this book should stay close to its subject—the text of the New Testament. At the beginning of each chapter, they are encouraged to read first the book(s) of the Bible being discussed in order to get a sense of the issues and themes involved. That will bolster an appreciation for the discussions of issues related to the text. This book cites the Common English Bible translation and recommends the *Common English Study Bible* as a companion text.

ACKNOWLEDGMENTS

No book-length project is conducted in isolation, and I am deeply indebted to many who have contributed to the development and completion of this project. I am especially grateful to Kathy Armistead at Abingdon for her vision of a rather distinctive approach to engaging the New Testament, contextually and meaningfully. Her encouragement to craft an introductory text in ways that break new ground, in keeping with my own approaches to longstanding issues, is greatly appreciated, and I look forward to seeing how it plays out in the classroom and beyond. I also appreciate Kelsey Spinnato, David Teel, and the rest of the fine editorial staff at Abingdon; they've been a delight to work with! I additionally appreciate the permission to publish again slightly revised forms of some of my previously published diagrams and outlines.[1]

I must also thank my students and colleagues at George Fox University, where I've taught since 1989 after completing my doctoral studies at the University of Glasgow. Much of this material follows what I teach in my introductory classes, although reading the New Testament in the light of several dozen crises emerged in a doctoral course I cotaught with Chuck Conniry in our Seminary's DMin program. I especially thank my New Testament colleagues, Tim Tsohantaridis, Kent Yinger, Mary Schmitt, and Nijay Gupta for their input into the process. My writing group involving Brian Doak, Joseph Clair, and Roger Nam was exceptional to work with, as they reviewed and critiqued drafts of various portions of the manuscript. I also want to thank my administrative assistant, Paula Hampton, for her editorial help, as well as the same from my students John Hodges, Jordon Hufford, Harper Swords, Johnny Walker, and Jordan Keagle. I also thank my colleagues and students

---

1. The Bi-Optic Hypothesis chart (p. 126) was first published in Paul N. Anderson, *The Fourth Gospel and the Quest for Jesus: Modern Foundations Reconsidered*, LNTS 321 (London: T&T Clark, 2006), 126; the outline of "Jesus as the Prophet Like Moses" (pp. 159–61) is more fully represented in *Semeia* 85 (1999), 33–57, and Paul N. Anderson, *The Christology of the Fourth Gospel: Its Unity and Disunity in the Light of John 6* (3rd printing, Eugene: Cascade Books, 2010), lxxiv–lxxix.

at Yale Divinity School, where I had the privilege of teaching some of this material as a visiting professor in 1998–99. Likewise, gratitude is expressed to my colleagues at Princeton Theological Seminary, where I served as a visiting scholar in the fall semester of 2004, hosted by James Charlesworth.

I also greatly appreciate my colleagues at other institutions, who have invited me to present on and refine various topics here addressed. Jan Van der Watt hosted me for two Fulbright Specialist visits at the Radboud University of Nijmegen (May/June 2013, and, along with Stephan Joubert, May 2014) as well as inviting me to lecture in the summer of 2010. Ruben Zimmerman invited me to speak on my contextual introduction to the New Testament at the University of Mainz (May 2014) and hosted me for a DAAD visit (summer of 2010), where I also refined my work on the Johannine riddles. On that visit, I also presented my Bi-Optic Hypothesis at the New Testament Seminar at Münster, and a most engaging interaction was hosted by Friedrich Avemarie at Marburg—home of the Bultmannian School; I grieve his untimely passing two years ago. I also appreciate the feedback received in June on this approach from David Lincicum and others at Oxford and from Mark Elliot at St. Andrews. I thank George Fox University for making some of this travel possible, as well as the North West University of Potchefstroom, South Africa, for their support.

I must also thank my colleagues in the SNTS and SBL (regional, national, and international) meetings for receiving my papers over the years, as well as my colleagues in the John, Jesus, and History group and in the Historical Jesus, Synoptic Gospels, and Psychology and Biblical Studies sections at SBL for the privilege of doing good work together. Many of my understandings and approaches have been developed and refined within such venues of inquiry. In particular, I appreciate the feedback received on particular sections of the book from Harold Attridge, Tom Wright, Mark Goodacre, Wayne Rollins, Craig Keener, Steve Mason, and Lee McDonald, although they are not accountable for my own judgments.

Finally, I want to thank other authors of New Testament introductory texts, to whom I am greatly indebted. When Raymond Brown's introduction to the New Testament was being reviewed at the national SBL meetings in 1997, I asked what he'd learned from the exercise. His response was: "I'm amazed at what I've learned from reading the overall literature—primary and secondary—lots of things to think about in coming up with an overall approach." My sentiments now, exactly! And, in addition to his outstanding text, I also appreciate greatly the critical introductions to the New Testament by Edwin Freed and Carl Holladay, the multiauthor introductions by

Achtemeier/Green/Thompson, Köstenberger/Kellum/Quarles, and Spivey/ Smith Black, the historical introductions by Bart Erhman and Helmut Koester, New Testament surveys by Robert Gundry and Stephen Harris, and the interdisciplinary introductions by David de Silva and Bruce Malina, as well as the very fine introductions by Luke Timothy Johnson, Mark Allan Powell, John Drane, and Donald Hagner. I must say, though, that my overall favorite introductory text is *The New Testament: Its Background, Growth, and Content* by Bruce Metzger (3rd ed.; Nashville: Abingdon, 2003). It is to Bruce Metzger that this book is dedicated; I hope he would have approved of its approach.

And, of course, I am indebted to my wife Carla and to our daughters, Sarah, Della, and Olivia, for their support along the way, without which such endeavors would be impossible.

Chapter 1

Introducing the New Testament— The Writings and Their Contexts

How did the New Testament become God's word for the church, and what did it mean to its original writers and audiences? As a collection of diverse writings, the twenty-seven books of the New Testament are gathered into four main groups as distinctive types of literature. The four Gospels tell the story of Jesus, and the Acts of the Apostles continues the story into the history of early Christianity. The next section includes thirteen epistles attributed to Paul and eight other letters attributed to other authors, while Revelation ("the Apocalypse of John") assures believers within the context of a hostile Roman Empire that God and the faithful will triumph in the end. These works are of unequal length, but together they form the most authoritative collection of early Christian writings—the canonical New Testament.

While finalized later than most of the epistles, Matthew begins the gospel record with a genealogy and a birth narrative, connecting the story of Jesus with the Old Testament. John, being the most different and theological among the Gospels, is placed fourth, as it also includes perspectives and reports that the others do not. Acts narrates the rise and progress of the Jesus movement, including the ministries of Peter and Paul, setting the stage for Paul's letters. Among them, Romans represents Paul's fullest articulation of the gospel message, and the Corinthian correspondence represents Paul's fullest engagement with a particular church, followed by shorter letters to congregations. Letters to Timothy, Titus, and Philemon reflect correspondence with individuals, and a general collection of other epistles follows. The authorship of Hebrews is unknown, but it represents a universal understanding of Jewish values that are seen typologically as fulfilled by Christ Jesus. Letters attributed to James, Peter, John, and Jude offer a rich range of contextual perspectives on the emerging Christian movement. Revelation, of course, makes a fitting conclusion, as it calls for faithfulness until the end of the age.

1

In addition to understanding the contexts in which these writings were produced, appreciating their literary features and forms helps the interpreter understand *what* is being said by first considering *how* it is said. One cannot apprehend the literal meaning of a text without determining first its literary form. Therefore, literary analyses will accompany historical inquiry in seeking to discern the writings' literary functions and thus their interpretive implications. These are important aspects of understanding the content of any piece of literature, especially the Bible. Matters of authorship and date will also be considered, but not much weight can be sustained by most claims, whether arguing a traditional view or challenging it. More robust are analyses of the literary features themselves, whoever the authors might have been.

It is fair to say, however, that all the books of the New Testament were written by Jewish believers in Jesus, even though some are crafted for Gentile audiences, such as the writings of Luke and Paul. This also makes it difficult to describe the New Testament's authors as "Christians" because most of them wrote before the Jesus movement separated from Judaism, within a generation or two of the ministry of Jesus. Therefore, it is important for invested readers not to read later Christian developments and views into the more primitive Jewish-Christian situation. After all, Jesus was a Jew, and so were all of his first followers. It was only decades later, and in some cases into the next century, that the Jesus movement fully individuated away from Judaism, and even then many connections remained close. In terms of second criticality, just as New Testament themes should not be confused with later orthodox confessions of Christian theologians (a problematic tendency of some traditionalistic interpretations), writers' adversaries should not be taken simplistically for later Gnostics and heretics (a tendency of some historical-critical interpretations).

Religious Institutions and Groups in Israel— Diverse Messianic Expectations Then and Now

Within the Judaism of Jesus's time two primary institutions provided the backbone of societal structure: the temple and the synagogue. The *temple*, located in Jerusalem, was the center of Jewish religious life. Originally constructed on the traditional site of Mount Moriah, where Abraham is thought to have nearly sacrificed Isaac and where David had built an altar (Gen 22:2;

2 Chron 3:1), Solomon's temple stood for four hundred years until it was plundered by the Babylonians in 587 BCE. Its rebuilding was completed in 515 BCE, just over two decades after the first wave of Jews returned from Babylon. Other than the desecration by Antiochus IV (167–164 BCE), it continued to be in use until destroyed by the Romans in 70 CE. The temple featured several areas with distinctive functions. Around the perimeter was the Court of the Gentiles, in which sacrificial animals and other goods were bought and sold. Further inside was the Court of the Women, leading to the Court of Israel (excluding women), and inside that, on the altar, priests would offer animal sacrifices. Beyond the altar and the sanctuary, the holy of holies was only entered once a year by the high priest on the Day of Atonement (*Yom Kippur*), when the high priest would make sacrifices on behalf of his household and the nation (Lev 16). Observant Jews were expected to travel to Jerusalem at least three times a year to participate in the three pilgrimage festivals (Deut 16:16): Passover (*Pesach*, remembering the exodus from Egypt), Weeks (*Shavuot*, remembering God's giving of the Law to Moses), and Booths (*Sukkot*, following the Day of Atonement, remembering Israel's wandering in the wilderness). The temple and its festivities were managed by the priests and the Sadducees.

Conversely, the *synagogue* provided a gathering place for weekly worship within local cities and villages where Jews lived (*synagōgē* in Greek means "meeting") throughout the Mediterranean world. Sabbath worship included such features as reading scripture, preaching and teaching, and corporate prayers. Within their order of worship the "eighteen benedictions" were recited, affirming Jewish values and faith-related commitments. During the week, synagogues served important functions as schools for Jewish children and as community centers—of special significance for maintaining Jewish identity in settings outside of Palestine. The first synagogues were organized during the Jewish exile in Babylon, and they became increasingly important in discerning and advocating how to keep the Law of Moses. In that sense, the synagogue was more text oriented in contrast to the temple, which was more cultic, or ritual oriented. During this time, synagogues tended to be organized and managed by local Jewish leaders, called the Pharisees. While synagogues became more established after the destruction of the temple in 70 CE, references in literature and archaeological remains show that they were nonetheless in existence before that, albeit in more modest forms.

The *Pharisees* (those who are "separated"—Ezra 6:21; 9:1) embraced the Torah (the five books of Moses) and other Jewish scriptures, and they also developed rich histories of interpretation (the oral Torah—later preserved along with other writings in the Talmud). They were especially concerned with purity laws and scripture interpretation, often engaged corporately in local synagogues. Unlike the priests in Jerusalem, they received no monetary support but made their livings in conventional ways. Going back to the days of the Babylonian captivity (587 BCE and following), the Pharisees built a "hedge" around the Law (*Pirkei Avot* 1:1). In seeking to define the devout keeping of the Sabbath, what was adultery, what was idolatry, and so on, they became what Josephus described as the most accurate and expert interpreters of Mosaic Law, numbering around six thousand in Palestine during the first century CE (*Antiquities of the Jews* 17.2.4). As a result, the Pharisees would have enjoyed local popular support in most Jewish towns and villages. When Rome destroyed Jerusalem in 70 CE, accompanied by the killing of the high priest and the abolition of temple sacrifice and worship, the Pharisaic movement gained the ascendency in both Palestinian and diaspora Judaism.

The *Sadducees* (named after Zadok, the priest who anointed Solomon king) managed the temple and its various affairs in Jerusalem, and they were the closest thing to nobility and a religious aristocracy in Second-Temple Judaism (538 BCE and following). As the wealthier members of Jewish society and owners of land that was passed down within family lines, they were the cultured class within Jewish society. Sadducees were thus invested in maintaining the status quo in Jerusalem and its environs, and it was they whom the Romans engaged in negotiating terms of occupation. As a result, they were resented by other members of Jewish society—by the poor because of their wielding of power and by the religiously devout because they were perceived to have sold out the nation. While theologically conservative (they held the five books of Moses alone to be authoritative), they were politically more open to cooperating with the Roman authorities, which brought on resentment and further distrust from other devout Jews. They were predominant leaders in the Sanhedrin, the high council of Jewish leaders in Jerusalem, and the high priest and other members of the Jewish priesthood would have been associated with this prestigious group.

The *Essenes* are described by Josephus (a Jewish historian who wrote a history of the Jews around the end of the first century CE) as numbering around four thousand adherents in Judea and Syria, populating small towns rather than major cities (*Antiquities* 18.20). Their initiation codes were strict, requiring giving all their possessions to the community and going through a preparatory period before being accepted into membership. Some members of these communities were celibate, though not all; and it is thought that Qumran, on the west side of the Dead Sea, was one of these communities.

4

The Essenes believed in ritual bathing for purification, and they shared sacred meals together. At Qumran several *mikva'ot* (ritual-cleansing baths) can still be seen, the largest of which has four staircases—one for descending into the water, separated by a rail from the others. If impurity was transferred by touch, one who had undergone a purification cleansing would not want to be touched by another coming into the water, and the different staircases might have reflected varying degrees of purity depending on the individual's social status and the type of bathing performed. The Qumran Community is thought to have fled to the wilderness some time during the Hasmonean Period, claiming to be followers of "the Teacher of Righteousness," who had apparently been spurned by "the wicked priest" in Jerusalem. Their *Community Rule* and the *War Scroll* show a strong dualistic thrust, portraying them as "children of light" versus "children of darkness." Qumran was destroyed by the Romans in 68 CE, but the writings produced and/or stored in nearby caves have been a great help in understanding first-century Judaism—especially showing that dualism could be a feature of Judaism as well as Hellenism. Some wonder if John the Baptist might have been a member of the Qumran community, given his ministry in the Judean wilderness and his challenging of Jewish compromises.

The *Zealots* wanted to rid Palestine of its Roman occupiers by any means necessary, including violence, in the traditions of Phinehas, son of Eleazar, and the Maccabean Revolt (Num 25; Sir 45:23-26; 1 Macc 2:1-28). Unlike the other groups, Zealots might have been members of other parties as well; they probably had most in common with the Pharisees, and some of them may even have been Pharisees. Nor were they singularly committed to violence; some of them probably occupied respected roles in Jewish society. Josephus refers to the Zealots as the "fourth philosophy" of the Jews and even blames the Roman backlash and the destruction of the nation upon them (*Antiquities* 18.1-23). One approach they took backfired in particular; the *sicarii* dagger-men would slip through a crowd, stab a Roman official or collaborator, and then slip back into the crowd undetected (Josephus, *Jewish Wars* 2.13). The Romans responded with severe retaliation, and the instability created by the Zealots eventually led to the invasion of Judea in between 66 and 73 CE, wherein the Romans sacked most villages and destroyed Jerusalem and its temple (in 70 CE). They chased insurgents to a final stronghold—the winter palace of Herod, Masada—an impenetrable fortress atop a huge rock. Just before the Romans finally breeched the wall, ten men were chosen to pick lots; each would kill all the members of his family and group, and the last would kill the others before committing suicide himself. Rather than be captured by the Romans, this mass-suicide—with ample supplies of food and water present, so as to make it clear they were not in a state of desperation—insured an ending with honor, rather than subjecting themselves to Roman torture and violation (Josephus, *Wars* 7.9).

Among these groups, a variety of theological disagreements are apparent. Between the Pharisees and the Sadducees, the Pharisees believed in an afterlife and the resurrection, whereas the Sadducees saw God's blessing as temporal; the Pharisees believed in angels and demons, whereas the Sadducees believed in one power in the heavens—God—whereas the Pharisees saw God's action in human history as somewhat determinative, the Sadducees believed outcomes were of human making. Between the Sadducees and the Essenes, the Essenes felt the priests in Jerusalem had compromised with foreign powers all too readily, and they saw themselves as the children of light versus the children of darkness—the compromised priests in Jerusalem; the Essenes gave up all their possessions for the sake of the community, whereas the Sadducees held onto their wealth and property; the Essenes in Qumran (though not all Essenes) separated themselves from worldliness by living in the wilderness, whereas the Sadducees were centered in Jerusalem and were accused of participating in Hellenizing games and events where prayers were offered to pagan deities. The Zealots disagreed with the other groups (especially the Essenes) primarily in their willingness to use violence to bring about the restoration of Israel's glory. They hoped for a restoration of Israel as effected by the ending of Roman occupation, and they were willing to go to extreme measures in the name of Jewish nationalism. Some among them would have opposed paying taxes to Rome, and they would have seen tax collectors as traitors to the cause. Some of these disputes can be seen in the Gospels and Acts, where debates about the afterlife and taxation, for instance, are featured explicitly.

In addition to these main parties or sects, other groups and members of society in first-century Israel are also apparent. *Herodians* supported King Herod and the three Herodian rulers that followed him, seeking to work out a compromise with Rome, which included the paying of taxes. *Tax collectors* were leaders in society whom the Romans chose to do their bidding in collecting taxes from the populace; it was they who also determined the actual amount to be paid, and they were allowed to keep a part of what they gathered—a system susceptible to intimidation and corruption. *Hellenistic Jews* were often members of Jewish synagogues in the diaspora who still felt loyalty to Judaism while not following all Jewish customs or displaying some outward signs. *Scribes and lawyers* worked with Pharisees in keeping tabs on the content of the Jewish scriptures, often researching texts and oral traditions to produce authoritative interpretations of the Law of Moses. *Apocalyptists* believed that God was in control of religious and political events, and they sketched transcendent images of how God would reward the faithful and demolish God's enemies. *Samaritans* occupied the area between Judea and Galilee, and while they also followed the way of Moses (they had their own rendering of the *Torah* and anticipated a prophetic Messiah), they were disregarded by the Jews because the Assyrians had resettled conquered peoples from other lands in that region in the eighth century BCE, resulting in intermarriage between Jews and Gentiles. Tensions between Judean hegemony and the Samaritans and Galileans are palpable in the gospel presentations of Jesus's ministry. The *am ha-aretz* (the people of the land) would have included a strong majority of the populace in Galilee and Judea (as many as 90 percent of the population), and as the poor of the land, they would have worked with subsistence farming or shepherding, striving desperately to make ends meet but with little hope of advancement.

Among these groups, a variety of messianic expectations ensued. Sadducees might have not put much hope in a Messiah but would have favored a leader restoring the political and economic glory of Jerusalem. Pharisees would have looked for a perfect keeper of the Law of Moses—one who influenced others to adhere to the covenant faithfully in order for God to restore glory to Israel. Recorded later in the Talmud, the Pharisees held that if all Israel would keep the Sabbath fully for just one day, then the Messiah would come (*Shemot Rabba* 25:121; *Yerushalmi, Ta'anit* 1:10). Essenes anticipated two Messiahs—a priestly Messiah in the lineage of Aaron (back before the days of the levitical priesthood) and a kingly Messiah in the lineage of David. In their embrace of the Isaiah tradition, they also valued highly the faithful servant motif of Isaiah 40–55. The Zealots would have seen Yahweh's *Anointed One* in the mold of King Cyrus the Great (Isa 40–55; note 46:11), whom God used to deliver the Jews from their Babylonian captivity. Add to that image the warrior victories of Moses, Joshua, and David, as well as the idea of a messianic age, and one can appreciate the diversity of messianic expectations in the world to which Jesus came.

The Canonization of the New Testament— The Authoritative Word

So how did "the writings" become "the Bible," and why did this particular set of twenty-seven early Christian writings get chosen over others? Given the discovery of other ancient Christian writings in recent years—although none of them appear to have been written before the mid-second century—understanding the canonization of the New Testament is essential for interpreting its meaning.

The word *kanōn* in Greek means "rule" or "measuring reed," a standard by which religious writings are held to be authoritative for a community of faith. Following the canonization of the Hebrew scriptures, the Christian scriptures underwent their own history of canonization between the second and fourth centuries CE. The authoritative character of the Jewish scriptures is reflected in 2 Peter, which describes a Jewish impression of their inspired character in this way: "Most important, you must know that no prophecy of scripture represents the prophet's own understanding of things, because no prophecy ever came by human will. Instead, men and women led by the Holy Spirit spoke from God" (2 Pet 1:20-21). Second Timothy also describes the value of Jewish sacred writings as follows:

> But you must continue with the things you have learned and found convincing. You know who taught you. Since childhood you have known the holy scriptures that help you in a way that leads to salvation through faith that is in Christ Jesus. Every scripture is inspired by God and is useful for teaching, for showing mistakes, for correcting, and for training character, so that the person who belongs to God can be equipped to do everything that is good. (2 Tim 3:14-17)

While Paul was probably not here referencing his own writings (indeed, *pasa graphē* simply means "all writing," not necessarily canonized scripture), or gospel narratives that had yet to be written, he does indeed display a representative approach to Jewish religious writings as being inspired by God (*theopneustos*) and thus profitable for teaching and formation among the faithful. One can certainly see this appropriation of—and expansion upon—Hebrew scripture within nearly all the New Testament writings. And 2 Peter disparages "people who are ignorant and whose faith is weak," who fail to understand Paul's writings, which they "twist . . . to their own destruction, just as they do the other scriptures" (2 Pet 3:16), so contention apparently arose quite early over how to interpret early Christian writings as well as Jewish ones. Apparently, Paul's writings were already being gathered by the time this comment was written, although it need not imply a full complement of all the ones that were eventually canonized and attributed to Paul.

And, it is wrong to envision early Christian communities as having in their possession much more than some (probably not all) Jewish scriptures and a few Christian writings. There was a fair amount of traveling ministry within the early Jesus movement, so hearing preachers and teachers in person preceded the primary use of Christian writings by several generations. Interestingly, even in the early second-century Christian movement in Asia Minor, Papias of Hierapolis describes two values in terms of traditional authority. First, he distinguishes the value of eyewitnesses and apostles from that of the elders (presbyters) and other preachers. Second, he distinguishes the "living and abiding voice" of vocal ministry over and against the use of written sources:

> If, then, any one came, who had been a follower of the elders, I questioned him to regard to the words of the elders,—what Andrew or what Peter said, or what was said by Philip, or by Thomas, or by James, or by Matthew, or by any other of the disciples of the Lord, and what things Aristion and the presbyter John, the disciples of the Lord, say. For I did not think that what was to be gotten from the books would profit me as much as what came from the living and abiding voice.[1]

From this description we see a preference for apostolic and eyewitness testimony, followed by ministries of their followers, followed by a valuing of written resources if neither of the above was available. In that sense, it is important to envision New Testament Christianity not as possessing a set of Christian texts but rather as a set of communities that valued the teachings of Jesus and the preaching of the apostles and their associates in ways that helped believers follow the way of Christ in later situations. As Harry Gamble puts it, "Christianity did not begin as a scriptural religion. The faith of the earliest Christians was evoked by and focused on a person, Jesus of Nazareth, and he was apprehended not in written texts but in the preaching about him as the crucified and risen Messiah, and in the charismatic life of the Christian community."[2]

Nonetheless, the formation of the Christian canon included internal and external factors. Internally, the fact that all of Jesus's first followers were Jewish means that they would have been accustomed to using religious texts in their meetings for worship and instruction. Therefore, alongside Jewish scriptures being read within corporate settings, Christian writings also came to be used. The Gospels report Jesus's having spoken or read from Jewish scriptures during

---

1. Papias, quoted in Eusebius, *Ecclesiastical History* 3.39.4, in vol. 1 of *The Nicene and Post-Nicene Fathers*, series 2, ed. Philip Schaff (New York: Christian Literature, 1890).

2. Harry Y. Gamble, *The New Testament Canon: Its Making and Meaning* (Philadelphia: Fortress Press, 1985), 57. Intrinsic and extrinsic factors in the formation of the Christian canon are outlined in fuller detail in Gamble's treatment, pp. 57–72.

his ministry in the synagogues of Nazareth and Capernaum (Matt 4:23; Mark 6:2; Luke 4:15-21; John 6:26-59; 18:20). And after the Jerusalem Council, James instructs a letter to be written to the churches regarding standards of faith and practice (Acts 15:20). Letters attributed to Paul, Peter, James, and John were written to communities and circulated among the churches quite extensively in the third and fourth decades of the movement, and as the first generation of apostles began to die or depart from the scene, some of their narratives were reportedly preserved in written form. In particular, Papias records that John Mark (the former companion of Paul) gathered in written form some of Peter's preaching and teaching about Jesus and his ministry, and an interest in preserving Jesus tradition can be seen to be developing over the next several decades (Eusebius, *Ecclesiastical History* 3.39).

Likewise, external factors reflected the need to select some writings as authoritative over and against others. In addition to the twenty-seven writings chosen to be part of the New Testament canon, a good number of other early Christian writings were used with regularity in early Christian worship—some of them from the late first and early second centuries. The *Didachē* ("the teaching") conveys "the teaching of the Lord to the Gentiles by the twelve apostles," outlining a host of issues related to church order and Christian living, including *the two ways*: one leading to death and the other to life. The Epistles of *1 Clement, Barnabas, Ignatius,* and *The Shepherd of Hermas,* and the *Epistle of Mathetes to Diognetus* also circulated in the early second century CE. Some of these writings (especially *Barnabas* and *Hermas*) were used quite extensively in the early church, at times more so than works that became canonized. Middle to late first-century Christian writings included several works of church history such as *The Martyrdom of Polycarp* and *Interpretations of the Sayings of the Lord* (five volumes, but available only in fragments, mostly preserved by Eusebius) by Papias, several Christian apologies by the likes of Justin Martyr, Irenaeus, and Athenagoras, and additional epistles and other forms of writing.

Discovered in 1945, over fifty additional manuscripts were found in the Nag Hammadi Library. These Coptic-language writings are mostly translations of earlier Greek writings, illuminating a fuller sense of the larger diversity that characterized early Christianity. Within this collection, one can imagine the sorts of writings that Athanasius intended to exclude from his official Christian canon in 367 CE. Those books were officially approved by several regional councils between 363 (Laodicea) and 419 (Carthage), largely establishing a closed canon by the early fifth century CE. Despite this rather late finalization of the canon, however, most of the books were approved by the mid-second century. Eusebius describes the disputed books as James,

2 Peter, 2 and 3 John, Jude, and to some degree Hebrews and Revelation. One of the questions regarding these books had to do with whether letters to individuals should be included among the writings to be used in corporate worship, although questions of authorship and content were also in play.

The earliest unofficial canons emerged in the second century, as around 170 CE the Muratorian Fragment lists as authentic twenty-three of the canonical works, omitting Hebrews, James, and the Petrine Epistles.[3] Smaller lists are mentioned by Polycarp and Papias before the middle of the second century, but it was really Marcion's favoring the Gospel of Luke and the writings of Paul that caused an affirmative canonical backlash. Marcion had also rejected the vindictive God of the Old Testament in favor of the gracious God revealed by Jesus, but mainstream Christians were not prepared to forfeit the Hebrew scriptures. In a direct assault upon Marcion's limiting the Gospels and others' expanding the list, Bishop Irenaeus of Lyons argued for a fourfold gospel that included Matthew, Mark, and John in addition to Luke. Here Irenaeus claims that because there were four corners of the world, four prevailing winds, four faces of cherubs, and four creatures in Revelation (Rev 4:7) that there must be four Gospels—no more and no fewer (*Against Heresies* 3.11.8). He also attributes authorship of the four Gospels to apostles or their followers, but given the rhetorical character of his argument and that this attribution was between 170 and 180 CE and religiously motivated, some scholars question its historical accuracy. Tatian's *Diatesseron*, however, presenting a harmonization of the four canonical Gospels around 160 CE, shows that Irenaeus's work is less than innovative, bolstering their authority over and against other texts or selections in the mid-second century.

Irenaeus also refers to the *Infancy Gospel of Thomas*, a mid-to-late second-century collection of folkloric narratives about Jesus as a young boy, creating live birds out of clay, cursing his playmates when they angered him, causing them to die and then raising them from the dead, and reciting the alphabet backwards to his teacher (diminutive Zacchaeus, just the right size for young Jesus). Of course, there is no connection between this narrative and the set of 114 sayings in the *Gospel of Thomas*, both falsely attributed to the apostle as pseudepigraphal works. In addition to these works and a growing number of Gnostic-Christian writings, the Montanist movement began writing their own set of inspired texts, claiming them to be of equal status as the writings of Paul and the apostles. Montanus, a charismatic Christian leader in Phyrgia in central Asia Minor, sought to recover the spiritual vitality of the apostolic age,

---

3. Some scholars date the Muratorian Canon later, assuming that it was written in support of the canonizing endeavors of the 4th century CE.

believing that the church was growing cold in its institutionalism. Along with his two female ministers, Prisca and Maximilla, Montanus referred to himself as the *Paraklētos*, the term used in the Gospel of John for the Holy Spirit. While this movement later caught the imagination of such leaders as Tertullian, it was experienced as a threat by other Christian leaders. Its advocacy for the Spirit-based authority of its leaders' writings then caused a canonical reaction in a negative direction—limiting authoritative texts to first-century and apostolic sources over and against later writings.

As a result, criteria for determining the Christian canon involved several components. First, authoritative writings were limited to the first generation of apostolic leaders and their followers over and against later writings, even if used and appreciated by later believers. Second, works needed to be catholic (universal) and corporate, rather than representing private letters between individuals. For instance, 2 and 3 John were debated on this account but later were accepted on the basis of their connection with 1 John. Third, writings were selected and rejected on the basis also of their orthodoxy and compatibility with historical and theological integrity. Fourth, some works were included partially because of their use within Christian meetings for worship, made increasingly possible because of advancements in writing materials and codices—bound sheets of papyrus in book-like forms, rather than more expensive scrolls on the hides of animals.

Therefore, according to Gamble, "The NT writings did not become canonical because they were believed to be uniquely inspired; rather, they were judged to be inspired because they had previously commended themselves to the church for other, more particular and practical reasons."[4] That being the case, it might be better to approach the authority of these texts not as being true because they are in the Bible, but inferring them to be in the Bible because they were experienced and perceived as being true by the early church and in subsequent generations. Such may be the grounded measure of their authority today as well.

Interpreting the New Testament— An Overview

The New Testament has been interpreted in many ways over the years, and there are as many approaches as there are interests and methodologies.

---

4. Gamble, *The New Testament Canon*, 72.

However, effective and meaningful interpretation will involve asking the most fitting questions for a particular text, and discerning how to go about that task is helpful at the outset. Following are several approaches to interpreting the New Testament, and considering how to make use of each of these ways of reading is central to reading well and fruitfully.

1. *The Exegetical Task.* The first stage of biblical interpretation involves drawing out the meanings of the text in terms of what it says: *exegesis.* The New Testament was written in Greek—common Greek of the first century, called *Koinē*—so considering what the text was saying to its first audiences in its original settings is the first task of meaningful interpretation. Of course, we might not know whom a text was addressed to, or even who was writing it, but the literary features of the text, combined with noting its structure and design, help one appreciate its message contextually. Here, discerning the genre of the text (the type of literature it is) will help the reader understand how it is designed to communicate its message. A gospel narrative, for instance, will communicate differently from an epistle, and likewise an apocalypse. Books of the New Testament may also have different forms of literature within the same piece of writing, so sensitivity to *how* a text communicates will help us understand *what* it might be saying. Conversely, reading meanings into the text and then attributing it to authoritative scripture is disparagingly referred to as *eisegesis*, although biblical writers did not hesitate in doing so.

2. *The Hermeneutical Task.* As the goal of reading the Bible is to find meaning in its message, so the hermeneutical task follows directly from the exegetical task. At times, however, the Bible speaks to us personally, which is also a fitting way to proceed; that is the way all classic texts function, and that is what makes great literature what it is. So, whether one starts with discerning what a text is saying and moves to asking what it means, or whether one starts with a personal inference of meaning and moves to looking more closely at the text, the exegetical and hermeneutical tasks go hand in hand. For individuals, New Testament hermeneutics may involve existential reflection—how the text "speaks to the condition" of persons in later generations. Or it may compel groups of readers to come to a corporate understanding of what the New Testament means to their communities in terms of

faith and practice. When the text has been engaged meaningfully, applications of biblical content may emerge, either as direct appropriations of the message or in the indirect noting of parallels between meanings back then and meanings today. In all cases, meaningful interpretation of the New Testament calls for discernment in terms of appropriation—rightly dividing the word of truth (2 Tim 2:15)—as a means of engaging the authoritative text personally and corporately.

3. *Interpretive Methodologies.* In service to the important work of biblical interpretation, various methodologies and forms of critical analysis (called "criticism" because they involve critical judgments) will need to be utilized in order to address particular concerns. From the most basic to the more ethereal, some of these disciplines are as follows.

- *Textual Criticism* seeks to establish, as far as is possible, the earliest texts of the New Testament. Within this field, scholars have noted that often families of texts will incline in one direction or another, so discerning more primitive groupings makes this task easier. Also, the shorter and the more problematic renderings often reflect earlier renderings; later editings tend to emend problematic wording and to add explanatory passages so as to fill out the meaning better.

- *Source and Redaction Criticism* seeks to infer how an author made use of earlier sources—either known or hypothetical—noting similarities and differences among texts and making inferences accordingly. The most extensive example of source criticism in New Testament studies involves the likelihood that Matthew and Luke made use of Mark; hundreds of word-for-word similarities make this a strong inference. Additionally, the moves made by later authors suggest their editorial (*redact* means "edit") contributions along the way, as factors of the authors' theological, historical, and literary interests.

- *Form Criticism* focuses on the literary forms of biblical units of material, seeking to infer something about their pre-written history and their earlier function within the life-setting (*Sitz im Leben*) of the tradition. For instance, a parable will function differently from a discourse, and a christological hymn

14

will function differently from exhortation (paraenetic) material. Sometimes the inference of distinctive forms may inform a guess about the pre-history of a unit of material, although the material underlying one passage might not have undergone the same development as other material.

- *History-of-Religions Criticism* seeks to identify parallels with contemporary religious themes and tendencies, inquiring as to possible connections with biblical features. Especially when a narrative reports a supranatural occurrence or a religious motif, this methodology seeks to determine the originative character of the unit of tradition as well as its rhetorical function.

- *Historical-Critical Methodologies* seek to determine the accuracy of a report on the bases of external verification, multiple attestation, coherence, dissimilarity, naturalism, and plausibility. Positivistic approaches favor reluctance to make any historical claim unless it is demonstrably verified by external evidence, so historical-critical analysis seeks to interpret biblical narratives in the light of natural, cause-and-effect assumptions. It also helps one understand a text within its original historical context, facilitating new insights as to its associated meanings.

- *Canonical Criticism* focuses on the place and function of material within the Jewish and Christian canons of religious literature rather than making it subject to comparative-religious factors. Considering the reasons a book was included within the canons of Hebrew and Christian scriptures as inspired and authoritative literature allows the book to be analyzed and interpreted with those values in mind.

- *Narrative and Rhetorical Criticism* seeks to identify the literary anatomy and design of a particular body of writing. It studies settings, plots, characters, irony, chronotope (time/place), dialogues, discourses, and narratological asides to help one come to grips with the form and operation of a text. Whether or not a narrative is historical, or however an epistle is constructed, each text nonetheless possesses rhetorical and literary features that can be noted and employed to appreciate its content and meaning.

- *Social-Scientific Criticism* interprets biblical texts in the light of social-science analyses of the Mediterranean world, noting such features as status within society, family relations, systems of patronage, shame and honor designations, and other socio-anthropological ways of conceiving of relationships in the biblical world. Precedence here is granted to measures of ancient societal realities over and above modern and postmodern constructs.

- *Cognitive-Critical Biblical Analysis*, also referred to as psychological biblical analysis, employs psychological models for understanding cognitive factors in perception, experience, reflection, and memory in the development and dissemination of biblical traditions and writings. Cognitive dissonance, projective association, developmental movement, archetypal symbolization, and psychodynamic analysis are but a few of the models employed to understand how human sources of biblical traditions came to understand and express their content.

- *Ideological Criticism of the Bible* reads biblical texts through the lenses of any number of ideological perspectives including: feminist, Marxist, postcolonial, deconstructionist, postmodern, and globalizing hermeneutics. While the perspective of the interpreter sometimes goes unacknowledged, ideological hermeneutics declare the interest up front and proceed to interpret the text from a declared stance, acknowledging it at the outset.

- *New Literary Theory* and *Reader-Response Analyses* of biblical texts ask how the reader is engaged by the content and form of a passage, connecting literary-rhetorical features of the text with the situation of the reader—ancient and contemporary. They take note of characterization, plot development, irony, and other narrative features as they relate to the text and its effect on readers.

- A *Spiritually Formative Reading* of the Bible concerns itself with the spiritual experience and development of the reader in engaging religious texts. That being the case, reading a text thoughtfully and prayerfully connects understandings and associations with one's existence and situation. Personal

16

meaning is therefore sought, assisted by interpretive tools but not limited to their methodological constraints.

Engaging the New Testament as Scripture— An Experiential Reading of the Text

While distanced and objective appraisals of issues are helpful for rational inquiry, garnering understanding and inferring meaning always requires personal engagement with the subject. Therefore, reading the New Testament as scripture will make good use of all the critical methodologies necessary for conducting critical inquiry, but it will not stop there. It will also be open to spiritually formative processes, which require an experiential reading of the text. Therefore, the most engaging feature of reading the Bible as scripture has less to do with one's views on the inspired writing of the text and more to do with one's openness to an inspiring reading of the text. If that be the case, how might it be approached? This is where crises and contexts become especially relevant.

First, the reader should be encouraged to read the text for herself or himself—noting the flow of the material, its form, and its content, but also reflecting on how it speaks to one's life and situation. We may be familiar with a passage, but how does it speak to us today? After all, the reading of a classic text may speak to a person in one way early in her or his life, while speaking in entirely different ways the next week or several decades later. That's what makes it a classic text! Embracing such encounters with the text is potentially transformative, as it involves an existential reading of the Bible. Second, if the reader is made aware of the contextual backdrops of New Testament texts, that reader will be better enabled to appreciate direct and timely meanings there and then, facilitating fuller understandings of meanings here and now. Third, considering the relevance of meanings for earlier audiences helps one discern their appropriation for later audiences—individually and corporately.

These are the sorts of experiences this introduction to the New Testament is designed to effect for readers today, and they need not be persons of faith or even self-identifying as Christians. The test will be in the experience of reading the New Testament itself, in the light of original crises and contexts; as Jesus and Philip said to the first followers of Jesus, "Come and see!" (John 1:39, 46).

PART I

THE GOSPELS AND JESUS

The four Gospels tell the story of Jesus and his ministry more fully than any other source—ancient or modern. They all were probably finalized before the turn of the first century CE and are attributed either to disciples of Jesus (Matthew and John) or to followers of Paul (Mark and Luke). These writings, however, do not contain direct attributions to their authors within their texts (unlike some of the letters and Revelation) but came simply to be titled "According to . . . " followed by an ascribed name some time later. Therefore, traditional claims regarding authorship have been analyzed critically in the modern era, producing a more nuanced set of views. Of course, these canonical works are held to be authoritative, whoever their authors might have been, and just because a traditional view is questioned or is problematic does not mean the case is solved in one direction or another.

The Gospels are probably among the later writings of the New Testament (between 70 and 100 CE), written after the letters of Paul and some of the other epistles. Reasons scholars date the Gospel narratives and their finalization during this time revolve around several factors. First, Mark is the shortest and the roughest among the four, and Matthew and Luke show clear signs of having incorporated Mark into their texts (more will be said about this in Excursus I). If Mark was written around 70 CE, seeing Matthew and Luke as following a decade or two later makes good sense.

Scholars date Mark as having been written about 70 CE because it reports the "disgusting and destructive thing" in the temple, saying "the reader should understand this" (Mark 13:14). This appears to be a knowing acknowledgment of the Roman destruction of the temple in Jerusalem in 70 CE. In that sense, the memory of what Jesus had predicted makes the finalization of Mark seem acutely relevant in the light of the cataclysmic events in Jerusalem around that time, although Caligula attempted to erect an image of himself in the temple in 40 CE.

When you see the disgusting and destructive thing standing where it shouldn't be (the reader should understand this), then those in Judea must escape to the mountains. Those on the roof shouldn't come down or enter their houses to grab anything. Those in the field shouldn't come back to grab their clothes. How terrible it will be at that time for women who are pregnant and for women who are nursing their children. Pray that it doesn't happen in winter. In those days there will be great suffering such as the world has never before seen and will never again see. If the Lord hadn't shortened that time, no one would be rescued. But for the sake of the chosen ones, the ones whom God chose, he has cut short the time. (Mark 13:14-20)

In addition, the second-century testimony of Papias (ca. 100–130 CE, recorded by Eusebius two centuries later; *Ecclesiastical History* 3.39) argues that Mark recorded in written form the preaching of Peter (who died ca. 65 CE), so moving Mark too late is problematic. Given his criticisms of Mark, this view is unlikely to have been fabricated, and elements of Peter's preaching in Acts and the thrust of the Petrine Epistles cohere with much of what is in the Gospel of Mark, so such a view cannot be easily discarded from a critical standpoint.[1]

Eusebius also locates the death of John the disciple of the Lord as during the reign of Trajan (98–117 CE; *Ecclesiastical History* 3.1.23), so if John was involved with the Gospel bearing his name (although the death of the beloved disciple is indirectly suggested in John 21:24, implying a different final editor) the parameters of the last third of the first century work fairly well as the time period in which the four canonical Gospels were written.

The Four Canonical Gospels

The Gospel of Mark has been described as a Passion narrative with a long introduction, and something similar can be claimed for the other Gospels, as well. The reason is that the entrance to Jerusalem, Last Supper, arrest, trials, death, burial, and resurrection of Jesus constitute the heart of the Christ Events, and these certainly form the backbone of apostolic preaching about Jesus as the Christ. Whether or not the book was written by John Mark, the

---

1. The view of Martin Hengel on the matter still seems compelling; Mark contains at least some of Peter's preaching material. See his *Studies in the Gospel of Mark* (Philadelphia: Fortress, 1985), 47–63. Developed below are several clusters of Petrine sayings and images associated with the pre-Markan tradition, the presentation of Peter's sermons in Acts, and the Petrine Epistles.

companion of Paul (the traditional view), the importance of the death of Jesus and events leading up to it is clearly served by the narrative. Whoever its author was, and whatever his sources were, Mark provides an important service: preserving in written form stories and sayings of Jesus from the generation of the apostles for the benefit of later generations.[2]

Mark thus translates some Aramaic sayings from the early stages of tradition into Greek for more general audiences, and "the way of the cross" is certainly a theme of existential importance for hearers of apostolic preaching in Rome and for other audiences, as well. It could be that Mark was finalized in Rome, although Mark's allusion to the destruction of Jerusalem seems to connect it also with sufferings in Judea. While Mark may have emerged from a community, it was not written for a single community alone. Rather, it was probably circulated as a traveling circular to be read in meetings for worship around the Mediterranean world.[3] Therefore, from 70 CE forward, it likely circulated among the churches, perhaps in several editions, to be performed and engaged in corporate settings of worship.

The Gospel of Matthew is most closely tied to Mark, as it incorporates as much as 90 percent of Mark's account, often in a word-for-word fashion. Matthew presents Jesus as the Jewish Messiah, reaching first "the lost sheep, the people of Israel" (Matt 10:6) and thereby extending the blessings of Abraham and Moses to the rest of the world. Matthew was likely finalized a decade or two after Mark (ca. 85–90 CE), and it seeks to compensate for the deaths of Peter and the apostolic generation by setting up church structures for authority and accountability. It also contains a robust presentation of discipleship-training material, and one can understand why the Gospels of Matthew and John were often used side-by-side in second-century Christianity as resources for training in Christian discipleship. A plausible setting for Matthew's finalization is a center of Jewish-Christian leadership, such as Antioch.

About a quarter of Matthew's and Luke's material is shared in common but not found in Mark, and a slightly smaller amount is unique to Matthew. This suggests that Matthew's final author made use of several sources of gospel-tradition material on the way to its helping its readers make disciples of all nations (Matt 28:18-20). Matthew's extensive dependence on Mark,

---

2. The traditional identification of the author as John Mark also fits his presentation as a companion of Paul and Barnabas in Acts (Acts 12:12, 25; 15:37, 39), to whom Paul also refers in his writings (Col 4:10; 2 Tim 4:11; Phlm 1:24) and to whom Peter refers as "my son Mark" in 1 Peter 5:13 in writing from "Babylon" (i.e., Rome).

3. Richard Bauckham, ed., *The Gospels for All Christians* (Grand Rapids: Eerdmans, 1997).

however, makes it highly unlikely that an apostle such as Matthew was its final author, and the two references to Matthew the tax collector in the Gospel bearing his name (Matt 9:9-10; 10:3) say nothing else about him, nor do they make any claim related to his being an author. Further, the man sitting at the tax collector's booth in Mark 2:14 is Levi son of Alphaeus (cf. Luke 5:27), so Matthew's replacing the name Levi with Matthew (Matt 9:9) may be a factor of conjecture (based upon Matt 10:3?) rather than historical knowledge, and the addition of Matthew's name in that instance may have been the basis for the later authorial connection. Nonetheless Matthew's name is associated with this Gospel in the second century, and his contribution to the forming of its earlier tradition is not, of course, implausible.[4]

The Gospel of Luke also incorporates most of Mark, but not as much of it as Matthew does. Luke is written to "most honorable Theophilus" (as is Acts—Luke 1:3; Acts 1:1) and is the first of a two-volume work providing a "carefully ordered account" of the story of Jesus and his followers. Luke is written in especially fine Greek, and it compares favorably with standard historical works in the Greco-Roman world at the time. Likely written a decade or two after Mark, a date of 85 CE makes sense, and Luke presents the story of Jesus as the savior of the world for Gentile and Jewish audiences alike. Some of its material (especially in Luke 1–2) contains poems and hymns of early Jewish-Christian worship, so a location such as Caesarea Maritima with its emerging libraries makes sense, although no location is certain. In addition to making use of written Mark, Luke shares a considerable amount of material with Matthew that is not in Mark, which implies their using a common source, or perhaps suggesting Luke's familiarity with some stage of the Matthean tradition. Luke also departs from Mark and coincides with John numerous times, so even though John was finalized later, some Johannine influence upon Luke's story of Jesus is a likely inference.

The traditional view of Luke's authorship associates it with Luke the companion of Paul, who is referred to in Paul's letters (2 Tim 4:11; Phlm 1:24) and called "Luke, the dearly loved physician" in Colossians 4:14. The author of Acts also reports events using the first-person plural "we" and "us" as part of the travel narrative (Acts 16:10-17; 20:5-15; 21:1-18; 27:1-37; 28:1-16), bolstering the inference that Luke traveled with Paul on his second

---

4. The names *Matthaios* and *Matthias* (Acts 1:13, 23, 26) were also sometimes confused within the early church traditions; it is interesting that Peter is involved with the selection of Matthias as a late-appointed eyewitness member of "the Twelve," whereas the Gospel of Matthew presents Peter as first-called among the apostles, the one who walked to Jesus (albeit only briefly) on the water and to whom Jesus entrusted authority (Matt 10:2; 14:29; 16:17-19).

and third journeys. While earlier scholars such as William Hobart had sought to show that the "medical language" of Luke-Acts, when compared with ancient medical writings, proved that Luke's author was indeed Luke the beloved physician of Colossians 4:14, Henry Cadbury, in his doctoral studies at Harvard, researched parallels with ancient veterinarian texts.[5] Upon finding many similarities with the latter corpus, Cadbury challenged Hobart's view, claiming that just because many similarities can be found between Luke's writings and those of ancient horse doctors, this does not prove Luke was a horse doctor; likewise, neither should proof that he was a medical doctor be claimed based on similar findings among ancient medical texts.

However, "not certain" does not imply "certainly not," nor does it overturn first-century associations with Paul—direct and indirect. It simply qualifies claims and diminishes their certainty. Nonetheless, the evidence still seems plausible that Paul's reference to Luke as a physician has some basis to it (given Luke's concerns for the poor and sensitivity to the well-being of women—e.g., 4:18; 13:11-13), and it seems highly likely that Luke was an associate of Paul (given his use of Pauline material in his presentation of the Last Supper—cf. 1 Cor 11:25; Luke 22:20—and his featuring of Paul's mission in Acts). Whoever the author might have been, though, the author of Luke-Acts presents the story of Jesus in a compelling and exemplary way, seeking to commend to his audiences in the Mediterranean world Jesus of Nazareth as Lord and Christ, savior of the world.

The Gospel of John is the most problematic of all New Testament writings, and for good reasons. John includes eight miracles, but only one of these is in all four Gospels (the feeding of the five thousand); the sea crossing is in Mark and Matthew but not Luke, and the great catch of fish is in Luke but not the other two. John also has no Synoptic-like parables and only two kingdom sayings, and Jesus's teachings in John include a variety of distinctive I-Am sayings. Further, John's presentation of Jesus's itinerary differs from the Synoptics in conspicuous ways. John features three Passovers instead of one, John's Jesus travels to Jerusalem at least four times instead of once, the Last Supper is on the evening before the Passover instead of being a Passover meal, and the cleansing of the temple happens at the beginning of Jesus's ministry instead of at the end. Instead of short, pithy sayings, John's Jesus speaks in

---

5. William Kirk Hobart, *Medical Language of St. Luke* (Dublin and London: Hodges, Figgis, & Co. and Longmans, Green, and Co., 1882); H. J. Cadbury, "Lexical Notes on Luke-Acts V: Luke Among the Horse Doctors," *JBL* 52 (1933): 55–65. In showing contravening evidence regarding singular proof of Luke's having been a medical doctor, it is thus quipped that Cadbury earned his doctorate at Harvard by depriving Luke of his.

long, extended discourses, and some of them expand theologically upon incidents in the narrative, or miracles of Jesus, which John calls *sēmeia,* or "signs." John's narrative seeks to compel the reader to believe that Jesus is the Jewish Messiah/Christ (John 20:31), and yet like Mark, it translates Jewish words and customs for non-Jewish audiences in the Hellenistic world.

The traditional view of John's finalization locates it at Ephesus, the heart of Paul's mission to the Gentiles, into the reign of Trajan, who became Caesar in 98 CE (therefore, around 100 CE), and an earlier edition is likely (around 80–85 CE). Four other writings are associated with the Johannine corpus in addition to the Gospel, but only one of these claims the name "John" as its author—Revelation—and it is the most distinctive in terms of language, form, and theology.

John's authorship issues are thus exceedingly complex, and the one "assured result of biblical critical scholarship" has been that John cannot have been written by an apostle, especially the one bearing its name. Several features in addition to the riddles mentioned above bolster such a judgment. First, John's final editor claims the author was the beloved disciple—but does so as a third-person reference, explaining also that Jesus never said he would not die—apparently implying his death (John 21:23-24). Second, all the passages in which either or both of the sons of Zebedee are present in the Synoptics are missing from John. Third, John is the most theological of the Gospels, beginning with a *Logos* hymn to the pre-existent Christ—not exactly the stuff of eyewitness historiography. Fourth, John's narrative shares only 15 percent of the Synoptic reports of Jesus's ministry, omitting exorcisms, parables, healings, and other important material. Fifth, much of John's distinctive material reports Jesus's ministry in Jerusalem in quite sophisticated ways—an odd thing if it were written by a Galilean son of a fishing merchant. Sixth, it is argued that John the apostle died early along with his brother James on the basis of two reports in the fifth and ninth centuries. This explains why modern scholars have claimed that the Fourth Gospel cannot possibly have been written by the son of Zebedee.

Then again, challenges to the traditional view are also fraught with new sets of critical problems. First, if not written by John, who might the author have been? If the beloved disciple was an associate of Peter (as presented in the Fourth Gospel), no other figure (Lazarus, Thomas, John the Elder, and so on) has any support for being a companion of Peter, whereas John and Peter are associated together extensively in the Synoptics, Acts, and Galatians. Second, the sons of Zebedee are indeed mentioned in John 21, where the beloved disciple is also featured, so John is not absent from the narrative altogether.

Third, the Gospel of John has more archaeologically attested material and distinctively accurate topographical details than all the other gospels combined—much of it antedating the destruction of Jerusalem in 70 CE. So, a first-hand source for John's narrative fits the character of much of the material. Fourth, claims that John died early on the basis of the views of Philip of Sides (fifth century CE) and George the Sinner (ninth century CE) are totally wrong—they recall that James and John would suffer martyrdom (referring to Mark 10:38-39), but Philip identifies John the Divine as an associate of Papias (late first century or early second century), and George claims that after the death of Domitian (96 CE), John was welcomed back from Patmos to Ephesus, where he later died as the last of the twelve apostles. Therefore, neither of the purported witnesses to "the early death of John" actually said or believed that—at all. Only modern scholars seeking to disparage John's traditional authorship have argued such, and they are factually wrong. Sixth, I have uncovered an overlooked first-century clue to John's apostolic authorship in Acts 4:19-20, where Peter and John speak: one making a Petrine-sounding statement, "whether it's right before God to obey you rather than God" (v. 19; cf. Acts 5:29; 11:17; 1 Pet 3:17), while the second makes an unmistakably Johannine-sounding statement, "We can't stop speaking about *what we have seen and heard*" (v. 20, emphasis mine; cf. 1 John 1:3; John 3:32). While John's author being John the apostle is problematic, so are alternative views, including claims to know whom the author is not.

Attempts to explain John's origin, if not that of an individuated memory of Jesus's ministry, have been attempted, but they also face new critical problems. A highly diachronic approach to John's composition was championed by Rudolf Bultmann, who claimed to identify three major sources underlying John (a signs source, a Revelation-sayings source, and a passion source) that the evangelist arranged into a narrative, but which became disordered and reordered (wrongly) by the final redactor, who was also the author of the epistles. When Bultmann's evidence for different sources is tested, however, it fails to convince overall; John is more of a traditional and textual unity than he allows. Another approach, championed by C. K. Barrett and the Leuven School, seeks to explain John as a theological expansion upon Mark and Synoptic material. Indeed, John does expand upon the mundane theologically, but none of John's similarities with Mark (or any of the other Gospels) is identical (making literary dependence implausible), and the 85 percent of John that has no Markan overlap has no basis for its origin if John has no independent tradition of its own. A third attempt to explain John's origin is to infer that we have here a "mimetic imitation of reality," whereby a novelistic author has sought to create a believable story by adding graphic detail and realistic features—as authors of fictive narratives might have done back then (cf. *The Life of Apollonius of Tyana* by Philostratus).[6] The problem with this view is that when Matthew and Luke incorporate Mark's narrative into their accounts, they most often leave out graphic details, such as names of persons and places and time references, so the ancient literature closest to John in its genre—the Synoptic Gospels—operated in exactly the opposite direction. Again, any of these alternative approaches to John's origin may be true, but each has new sets of critical problems that are worse than a somewhat nuanced form of the traditional view.[7]

The Gospel of John likely developed in more than one edition, with John 20:31 being the original ending of the first edition ("these things are written so that you will *believe* . . . "), plausibly written around 80–85 CE in Ephesus of Asia Minor. At least, there is no other location superior to the unanimous second-century association on that matter. Of all Johannine composition theories, the one addressing most of the *aporias* (perplexities) and riddles most effectively is a two-edition theory, by which such supplementary material as John 1:1-18; 6; 15–17; and 21; and beloved disciple and eyewitness references were added by the final compiler (plausibly the author of the Johannine Epistles) around 100 CE, after the death of the beloved disciple.[8] The dating of the book of John's first edition around 80–85 CE works well for a couple of other reasons. First, the confession of Thomas ("My Lord and my God!" John 20:28) seems to be a direct challenge to the requirement of emperor worship during the reign of Domitian (81–96 CE), and yet the first edition of John seems to have formed a basis for the first Johannine Epistle, which then seems to have been followed by the other two (85, 90, 95 CE). If the later material was added during the reign of Trajan, this would place the Johannine Epistles between the first and final editions of the Gospel, which makes sense of some of John's other features. The prologue, thus, is not the

---

6. Some scholars have applied the work of Erich Auerbach, *Mimesis: The Representation of Reality in Western Literature*, trans. Willard R. Trask (Princeton, NJ: Princeton University Press, 1953) to the subject, although he does not claim the Gospels made use of this device.

7. For a fuller treatment of these and other views, see Paul N. Anderson, *The Riddles of the Fourth Gospel: An Introduction to John* (Minneapolis: Fortress, 2011), 95–124.

8. This is a modification of the view of Barnabas Lindars, *The Gospel of John* (Grand Rapids: Eerdmans, 1972), which John Ashton and I came to agree with independently. Cf. John Ashton, *Understanding the Fourth Gospel* (Oxford: Oxford University Press, 1991); Paul N. Anderson, *The Christology of the Fourth Gospel: Its Unity and Disunity in the Light of John 6*, 3rd printing (Eugene, OR: Cascade Books, 2010). See also my analysis of other views, including Bultmann's and Barrett's, in chapters 1–7 of that book.

first stroke of the authorial quill, but it reflects the worship material of the Johannine community after years of reflecting upon the narrated story of Jesus in the earlier edition and preaching (cf. 1 John 1:1-4). Therefore, John's original beginning was more like that of Mark (more mundane, beginning also with John the Baptist, perhaps written as an alternative complement to Mark), and the "new commandment" to love one another in John 13:34-35 has become the "old commandment that you had from the beginning" in 1 John 2:7. If the first edition of John might have been composed in awareness of Mark, it might have been written as a complement and alternative to Mark and thus is different on purpose.

A chronology of the decades leading up to and including the ministry of Jesus looks something like this:

4 BCE—The birth of Jesus and the death of Herod the Great, followed by the crucifixion of 2,000 Jews by the Roman army in Syria

6 CE—The tax revolt of Judas the Galilean, leading to the Zealot movement

9 CE—Jesus's visit to Jerusalem with his parents for the Passover

26 CE—The ministry of John the Baptist begins

27 CE—The ministry of Jesus begins

30 CE—The death and resurrection of Jesus

Chapter 2

The Gospel According to Matthew

Begin with the text. Read the Gospel of Matthew, and note important themes and details that come to mind.

Author: traditionally Matthew, although its dependence on Mark makes this unlikely

Audience: Jewish Christians and Jews who regard or might come to regard Jesus as their Messiah

Time: 85–90 CE

Place: plausibly Antioch or some other Jewish-Christian center

Message: Jesus is the Jewish Messiah, God with us.

Among the four Gospels, it's easy to see why Matthew was placed first among them. It displays the fullest collection of Jesus's teachings on discipleship and church-community life. It also sets the stage well for understanding the contexts of Jesus's ministry, despite being written several decades later.

I. Crises and Contexts

Matthew comes across as the Gospel of the Jewish Messiah. The genealogy at the beginning makes a fine bridge with the Old Testament, and the lineage of Jesus is traced back to Abraham—descending through the household of King David. Matthew and John are the most Jewish of the Gospels, and both of them take special care to show Jesus as fulfilling Jewish scripture as the prophesied Messiah/Christ. They also present clear patterns for Christian discipleship and models for how to be the church. While most of Mark is replicated in Matthew word-for-word, Matthew's special content has its own way of showing Jesus to be the Jewish Messiah and king of the Jews. At the outset, though, that theme is presented as a threat to King Herod.

Herod—The "King of the Jews"

Some two and a half decades after Pompey conquered the region, Caesar Augustus appointed Herod (later termed "the Great") as its ruler. Son of Antipater the Idumean (Edomite), who had found favor with Augustus by coming to his aid, Herod was first appointed governor of Galilee by his father, and his brother Phasael was appointed governor of Judea. In an attempt to restore the Hasmonean Dynasty to Jerusalem, Antigonus defeated Phasael with the help of the Parthians, and Herod traveled to Rome to appeal directly for support. There the senate named him "King of the Jews" in 40 BCE, and after a three-year struggle Herod became king of Judaea in 37 BCE. In doing so, the Hasmonean Dynasty was replaced by the Herodian Dynasty, although Herod's second wife, Miriamne, was of royal Hasmonean lineage. Because Herod was an Idumean, though, and because he wielded his power in ruthless ways and taxed the people heavily, he was never fully accepted by the Pharisaic and devout Jewish leadership.

Nonetheless, Herod became especially well known for two things. First, he built massive construction projects, of which impressive evidence can still be seen today. In addition to his great winter palace on the Dead Sea (Masada) and his impressive fortress southwest of Jerusalem (the Herodium), Herod built a fine seaport, Caesarea Maritima, complete with an open-sea harbor, amphitheater, aqueduct, and hippodrome. The palace, jutting out into the sea on a promontory point, was known for its impressiveness as a *basileia* (kingdom). Later, over two thousand Christians would be martyred in the sports arena, and the Apostle Paul was imprisoned in Caesarea under Roman custody, according to Acts 24:23-27. As the primary point of entry from the sea to Judea and Syria and other points eastward, Caesarea Maritima became the official residence of the regional Roman Procurator, and the inscription of the name *Pontius Pilatus* was discovered there in the palace in 1961. Pilate's presiding over the death of Jesus in the Gospels reveals a practice of the Roman ruler's being present in Jerusalem during national festivals, such as Passover, evidence of political tensions at such times. In addition to building bathhouses and spas, Herod also built a temple to Roma and Augustus, and the imperial cult continued to be patronized during later administrations as well. Most impressive, however, was Herod's reconstruction of the temple in Jerusalem. Begun in 19 BCE, Herod's temple project was attested as being in process in John 2:20, where its construction at that time was still in its forty-sixth year.

A second distinction of Herod's legacy is his ruthlessness. He killed two of his ten wives and three of his fourteen children—all of them sons destined to succeed him as king. While he had willed his kingdom to Antipater II, his firstborn son, knowing he was anxious to succeed his father, Herod had him killed five days before he himself died. On the concern that his death would not be mourned, he had Jewish leaders in Jericho imprisoned, ordering that they be killed on the day of his death. At least, he thought, there would be some sorrow in Judaea on his passing. Those orders, however, were disregarded, and the prisoners were released. Herod had arranged for his kingdom to be divided upon his death into four tetrarchies to be ruled by his sons. Philip was appointed tetrarch (ruler of a quarter part) of Batanea and other provinces to the north and east (Luke includes Ituraea and Trachonitis, Luke 3:1); Archelaus was appointed ethnarch (ruler of an ethnic grouping) of Judea, Idumea, and Samaria; Antipas was made tetrarch of Galilee and Peraea—two distinct regions separated by the Decapolis (a region of ten cities). The Herodian Dynasty thus continued until 34 CE in Galilee, Peraea, and Batanea, but Archelaus only reigned in Judea, Idumea, and Samaria for a decade.

Herod died in a gruesome way, as described by Josephus (who also had Hasmonean sympathies), but shortly before he died, two pharisaic leaders aroused their students to tear down a golden eagle posted atop the gate leading into the temple area in Jerusalem. While not inside the temple area, so Herod might have reasoned, it still gave tribute to Rome as a means of trying to have things both ways—preserving Jewish monotheism while still honoring Roman rule. Jewish leaders, however, disagreed. Herod charged the rabbis and their forty students with sedition, but they claimed loyalty to God alone; whereupon they were burned alive to deprive them of a painless transition to the eternal reward they hoped for. Herod's legacy of cruel dealings with opposition continued, especially under the reign of Archelaus, his primary successor. Archelaus began his reign promising a more tolerant and measured administration, but as visitors to Jerusalem during Passover demanded an accounting for the deaths of the two teachers and their students during Herod's last days, Archelaus ordered the Roman forces into Jerusalem, and reportedly, over three thousand were killed in the temple area. Passover was canceled, and the memory of this incident led to his being replaced after nine years by the first of fourteen Roman procurators over Judaea. This explains why Pontius Pilate, the fifth Roman Procurator over Judaea, presided over the trial of Jesus.

From this brief sketch of Herodian rule in Judaea, several contextual issues behind the Gospel of Matthew become apparent.

First, in heralding Jesus as the Jewish Messiah, the Gospel of Matthew shows Jesus's birth as fulfilling the glorious memory of the Davidic monarchy a thousand years earlier. Just as the zenith of Solomon's legacy is punctuated by the Queen of Sheba coming from the east, bearing gifts to drink from his internationally renowned wisdom (1 Kgs 10; 2 Chron 9) so *magi* (later associated with Persian astrologers) come bearing gifts of gold, frankincense, and myrrh. While their number is not specified, the bearing of three gifts explains why such a number of kings is inferred. They had seen a celestial sign of a new era, and they had traveled from the east to Jerusalem to pay tribute to "the king of the Jews." Given that Herod's family was from the south and east region of the area, one might infer a bit of territoriality in his being threatened. The memory of the Sheba entourage in Israel's history, signaling the bolstering of trade with Arabia and the elevation of her respect among the nations, would have resonated with readers of the magi visit in Matthew 2:2-12. Another encroachment on Herod's authority would have been signaled by the reference to the Christ child as "the king of the Jews"—a title alone bestowed upon Herod the Great, which Caesar Augustus then denied to his successors. In all four Gospels, Jesus's receiving this title at his trial and crucifixion is presented as Jesus's pretension, which Pilate ironically affirms.

Second, upon learning of their quest for "the newborn king of the Jews" Herod "and everyone in Jerusalem" were troubled (Matt 2:2-3). The chief priests and legal experts cite Micah 5:2 as the birthplace of the prophesied Messiah, information Herod then shares with the magi. Given that Bethlehem is only two or three miles from Herod's palace (the Herodion), the magi's refusal to report back to Herod brings a swift response. Told that that they should do so in a dream (a Jewish presentation of divine direction used five times in Matthew 1–2), the magi return along a different path. Joseph likewise is instructed to take Mary and the baby to Egypt, thus fulfilling the scripture of Hosea 11:1, "Out of Egypt I called my son." Of course, Hosea was referring to the exodus and God's choosing Israel as a "son," but original meanings were not as compelling for Matthew as appropriated meanings. Thus, the events here fulfill scripture, confirming the presentation of Jesus as the Jewish Messiah.

Third, in his anger, Herod is reported to have ordered the killing of all male infants under the age of two, leading to conjecture that Jesus might have been in his second year at the time. This is why scholars estimate the date of Jesus's birth to be between 6 and 4 BCE. The flight to Egypt by Joseph and Mary and the slaughter of infant boys (Matt 2:16-18) being reminiscent of Pharaoh's ordering the killing of Jewish babies in Exodus 1 shows Jesus as fulfilling a Mosaic typology. Given that this report is only mentioned in Matthew, some scholars question its veracity, inferring a theological origin of the report rather than historical incidence. Then again, negative proof from silence is always a weak basis of argumentation, and this report is certainly in keeping with the sort of thing Herod would have had no hesitation in ordering, given his willingness to kill his own sons who threatened his reign. Several centuries later, though, citing Herod's killing of his sons and possibly of the infants in Bethlehem, Macrobius cites a quip by Caesar Augustus: "I would rather be Herod's pig than his son" (*Saturnalia* 2:4:11). Here we see an impression of Herod's cruelty around the time of Jesus's birth, but his family's legacy continues into the ministry of Jesus.

The Gospel of Mark notes two references to "Herodians"—those carrying out the policies of Herod Antipas, the son of Herod the Great (Mark 3:6; 12:13). The first reference notes that upon Jesus's healing people on the Sabbath, Pharisees were offended, and they consulted with Herodians to find a way to put Jesus to death. Here, political powers are presented as being yoked to the carrying out of religious concerns. The second passage (followed by Matt 22:16-22) shows Herodians trying to trap Jesus with the age-old conundrum: should the religiously devout pay a tithe (or a tax) to a foreign occupier, Rome? If not, they would be guilty of sedition and susceptible to punishment; if so, they would alienate the theologically conservative Jews. Either answer would produce a no-win consequence. Note that Jesus rejects the leveraged dichotomy and asks whose image is on the coin (itself a breaking of the third commandment). Given that it is of Caesar, in declaring "Give to Caesar what belongs to Caesar and to God what belongs to God" (Matt 22:21) he also declares to the faithful that God requires our total devotion, not simply our money.

The Herod family comes back onto the scene with John the Baptist challenging the tetrarch of Galilee and Peraea, Herod Antipas (sometimes confused with his father, Herod the Great), over his public marital scandal—divorcing his own wife and marrying Herodias, the wife of his half-brother, Philip. While Mark tells the story in fuller detail (Mark 6:7-31), Matthew 14:1-12 features Herod's worry that this might be a risen John, whom he had killed, back from the dead to haunt him. After promising the daughter of Herodias, who had pleased him greatly with her dancing, up to half his kingdom, she requested on her mother's behalf the head of John on a platter—a promise that Herod did not break.

Luke also adds some distinctive stories about Herod Antipas. Jesus is warned by Pharisees that Herod intends to have Jesus killed—providing the occasion for his departure (Luke 13:31). And as Herod Antipas is in Jerusalem during the final Passover of Jesus's ministry, Pilate sends Jesus to Herod to be tried, as it is in his Galilean jurisdiction that most of Jesus's ministry has taken place. While Herod has been intrigued with Jesus and has wanted to meet him, neither he nor Pilate finds fault with Jesus, and Luke notes that the trial of Jesus becomes the occasion for Herod and Pilate to become friends, whereas before they were enemies (Luke 23:1-16).

The Herodian legacy of taxation and Roman occupation is also thrown into sharp contextual relief in showing the pointedness of John the Baptist's message. Not only does he challenge Herod and the effects of Roman occupation, but John also challenges those who may have partaken in ritual cleansing yet whose lives have not been changed in ways of righteousness. According to Matthew, John challenges Sadducees and Pharisees, calling them "children of snakes" and warning that "the ax is already at the foot of the trees" ready to exact God's judgment on the corrupt (Matt 3:7-12). God requires not religious purity but authentic changes of heart and life for religious leaders, tax collectors, and even soldiers (Luke 3:11-14). This prophetic teaching piqued the moral conscience of the populace, and as he addressed social concerns of the day, many wondered if John was the Messiah/Christ.

Jesus among the Scribes, Pharisees, and Sadducees

In terms of religious groups in first-century Judaism, Matthew's Jesus is closest in association to the Pharisees. He works with Jewish scripture, interpreting the Law of Moses and its implications meaningfully and authoritatively. Matthew's Jesus seems close to the Pharisaic school of Hillel, who was a more liberal interpreter of scripture, in his challenging legalistic approaches to the Law. It might even be said that Jesus sided with critiques of the school of Shammai, which emphasized strict keeping of Sabbath laws and at times was susceptible to relying on violence in the name of religious concern. Then again, Matthew's Jesus shows affinities with the more exacting school of Shammai, in challenging grounds for divorce other than adultery. Given that Jesus is presented as expounding on Jewish scriptures in local synagogues, he would have been associated with various Pharisaic leaders of his day, and that presentation is consistent in all four Gospels.

In the Synoptics, Jesus also is presented as being engaged in the debates between Sadducees and Pharisees, yet as with the Herodians, he refuses to be drawn into their trick questions and rhetorical traps. While these exchanges are also reported in Mark and Luke (Mark 12:18-34; Luke 20:27-40; 10:25-28), it is Matthew that shows the sharpest sensitivities to particular issues debated by the Sadducees, Pharisees, and scribes. While Sadducees would have seen God's blessing in material and social terms, the Pharisees argued for eternal rewards to be actualized in the afterlife. Matthew's Jesus thus accentuates the rhetoric of eternal consequences, turning the tables pointedly upon religious leaders, citing "weeping and grinding of teeth" as their afterlife reward (Matt 8:12; 13:42, 50; 22:13; 24:51; 25:30).

Matthew's Jesus, however, also challenges the Sadducees, who attempt to trap him with a question about the resurrection (Matt 22:23-33). Regarding the status on earthly marriages in the afterlife, God is the God of the living, not the dead. This leads, then, to Jesus's being challenged on which is the greatest commandment of the Law. Of course, any of the Ten Commandments chosen would result in nine counterproposals, so this is another no-win question. Jesus, however, selects two verses from the Torah that serve as summaries of the vertical and horizontal aspects of the Mosaic Law (Deut 6:5; Lev 19:18). After all, the first four commandments in Exodus 20 address humanity's relationship with God, and the remaining six address persons' relations with others. Jesus replies: "*You must love the Lord your God with all your heart, with all your being, and with all your mind.* This is the first and greatest commandment. And the second is like it: *You must love your neighbor as you love yourself.* All the Law and the Prophets depend on these two commands." Here, rather than resorting to a legalistic approach to outer boundaries of the Law, Jesus elevates the center (Matt 22:34-40).

Then Jesus seizes the role of the inquisitor, driving questions at the Pharisees. He first asks whose son the Messiah would be, to which they respond, the Son of David. Jesus then quotes Psalm 110:1, asking "Then how is it that David, inspired by the Holy Spirit, called him Lord when he said, The Lord said to my lord, 'Sit at my right side until I turn your enemies into your footstool'? If David calls him Lord, how can he be David's son?" (Matt 22:41-46). A more pointed discourse follows about the legal experts (the scribes) and Pharisees loving to "sit on Moses' seat" in synagogues and burdening people with legal restrictions that they themselves are unable to keep. Says Jesus, "But the one who is greatest among you will be your servant. All who lift themselves up will be brought low. But all who make themselves low will be lifted up" (Matt 23:1-12). Jesus then launches into a series of seven woes against the scribes and Pharisees (Matt 23:13-36), by which Matthew expands on Mark 12:38-40, where Jesus declares: "Watch out for the legal experts. They like to walk around in long robes. They want to be greeted with honor in the markets. They long for places of honor in the synagogues and at banquets. They are the ones who cheat widows out of their homes, and to show off they say long prayers. They will be judged most harshly."

Imperial Domination and Jesus's Third Way

One of the primary factors in the longevity and reach of the Roman Empire was its capacity to yoke local and regional loyalties to a central government. In contrast to Seleucid attempts to command loyalty by means of Hellenizing Israel at the expense of Judaism, Rome allowed Jewish practices to remain in place as long as they did not interfere with Roman taxation and occupation. As a means of putting down resistance and motivating subservience, however, Rome continued the practice of domination, operative for millennia within the Mesopotamian and Mediterranean worlds. Domination functions by forcing dichotomies involving only two choices: an undesired choice and a worse one. Walter Wink describes the two options as fight and flight. If the dominated individual or group chooses to fight, they will assuredly suffer and be destroyed.[1] Therefore, the goal is to motivate flight, or submission, therefore bringing about acquiescence to the demands of the dominating powers. If a leader of society or a group can be made to follow Roman commands—preferably willingly—the rest of society will more easily follow.

Following the death of Herod the Great, uprisings in Israel were put down by the Roman general Varus, in Syria, who reportedly crucified two thousand Jews in 4 BCE as a disincentive to revolutionaries (Josephus, *Antiquities* 17.10.10; *Wars* 2.5.2). Therefore, it is not surprising that his teaching would have involved the willingness to suffer on a Roman cross if challenging the empire effectively. And yet, in contrast to Maccabean and zealot approaches to foreign occupation, Jesus taught a new way: seeking to end the spiral of violence rather than simply incurring another chapter in its escalation. While Jesus's admonition in Matthew 5 to "turn the other cheek" has been wrongly understood to refer to an impractical form of doormat passivity (do not resist an evildoer), a better reading of the verb *antistēnai* in Greek (v. 39) is as an injunction not to counterstrike an offender; that would simply escalate the violence. Rather, just as Jesus refused legal and religious dichotomies in the interest of posing a third and redemptive alternative, so his teachings on nonviolence offer an alternative to domination-related force as a means of putting an end to the spiral of violence in the ancient world and in later situations as well. Consider the implications of the following three injunctions (Matt 5:38-42; cf. also Luke 6:29-30) within the context of Roman occupation.

- First, "You have heard that it was said, *An eye for an eye and a tooth for a tooth*. But I say to you that you must not oppose those who want to hurt you. If people slap you on your right cheek, you must turn the left cheek to them as well"

1. Walter Wink, *Engaging the Powers: Discernment and Resistance in a World of Domination* (Minneapolis: Fortress, 1992).

(Matt 5:38-39). From a social-sciences perspective, the right hand was used for public exchange, but the left hand was unclean—associated with unhygienic functions. Therefore, being stricken on the right cheek by the right hand of an adversary would have implied a back-handed slap. The function of a back-handed slap is not to injure but to intimidate—creating a fight-or-flight dichotomy. If a Roman soldier were to slap, or even threaten to slap, a member of Jewish society, his goal would have been to remind that person and others of Roman power and occupation—to keep the populace in its subservient place. Given asymmetrical-force capabilities, if the subject responded with violence, the oppressor would take up the challenge and decimate him and others; and justifiably so by the dominator's standards. The subject was expected to cower at the threat of a full-fledged forehand. However, what if the subject put his hands behind his back, looked the soldier in the eye—as a fully equal human being—and called in the threat? "Go ahead, strike with a forehand; here's my other cheek. I am unarmed and nonviolent; is that your demonstration of Roman honor—threatening to strike an unoffending civilian?" Such a creative action would put the intimidator on his heels, creating a new situation instead of furthering a dominator-subject structure of oppression.

- Second, "When they wish to haul you to court and take your shirt, let them have your coat too" (Matt 5:40). Too often this verse has been understood as sacrificial generosity only; it is that, but it also would have involved much more. If one wonders who would ask for a person's clothing in a court case, Luke's rendering adds a helpful insight: "If someone takes your coat, don't withhold your shirt either" (Luke 6:29). Rather than generosity being the main issue here, within a stressed economy suffering from oppressive foreign occupation, those dragged into court and required to give up their clothing would have been those who had no money to repay a loan. According to the Torah, a debtor could be required to offer his cloak as a promise of paying a debt (Exod 22:25-27; Deut 24:10-13), but such a system was not to be abused. Garments of the poor would be returned at nightfall so the homeless person could have something to sleep in, the cloak of a widow could not be required (Deut 24:17), and the creditor was not to sleep in the cloak of the debtor (Amos 2:7-8). As a means of forcing a payment, this system of lending functioned at times to take a person's land or to indenture him or her into slavery. By giving also one's undergarments to the creditor, however, the tables were turned. As nakedness was an offense to the beholder in Jewish society, going without one's clothes enacted a prophetic demonstration of injustice—pointing to an unfair system of crediting, calling for societal change. Rather than forcing the forfeiture of land or liberty, giving also one's undergarments to a creditor exposed the fact of unjust leverage by means of one's bodily exposure.

- Third, "When they force you to go one mile, go with them two. Give to those who ask, and don't refuse those who wish to borrow from you" (Matt 5:41-42). Roman occupation was also justified as a provision of protection; under the banner of the empire, subject states would enjoy peace and prosperity within the empire, invoking gratitude in return. Therefore, the least a subject could be expected to offer is a bit of help with carrying the pack of a Roman soldier for a mere mile; from Rome's standpoint, this modest expectation exhibited the graciousness of Roman restraint. What would happen, though, if the Galilean peasant refused to put the pack down at the first mile marker and carried the pack for an extra mile? On one hand, it would seize the initiative, and it would offer help out of voluntary hospitality and dignity rather than forced compliance. Additionally, who would believe the Roman soldier if called on the carpet by his superiors? Did he really not threaten the peasant or his family? Might he be disciplined because of the unbelievable generosity of the subject? Walter Wink sketches a scenario where the soldier is chasing the Galilean peasant, pleading with him to put down the pack, lest he suffer reprimand or worse. Again, Jesus turns the tables on leveraged domination, instituting a third way as a means of bringing redemptive change and ending the spiral of violence.

A danger, of course, in seeing these injunctions as simply means of seizing the initiative and creating a new playing field with redemptive possibilities is that Jesus's instruction here might be separated from its overall thrust of loving the other—including one's enemies. In his teachings here and elsewhere, Jesus sees as the center of the Law the love of God and neighbor, and that is the primary thrust of his teachings on religion and society. In that sense, love is not a transaction designed to effect a desired return either from God or from others. Rather, it is freely given, whether or not a desired response ensues. Authentic love releases the other from obligation because it is offered liberally, with no expectation of return. That, then, is transformative in its impact precisely because it is an extension of grace. As Jesus closes this section on the heart of the Law, the love of neighbor is extended also to include the love of enemy—even praying for adversaries nearby and far away.

> You have heard that it was said, *You must love your neighbor* and hate your enemy. But I say to you, love your enemies and pray for those who harass you so that you will be acting as children of your Father who is in heaven. He makes the sun rise on both the evil and the good and sends rain on both the righteous and the unrighteous. If you love only those who love you, what reward do you have? Don't even the tax collectors do the same? And if you greet only your brothers and sisters, what more are you doing? Don't even the Gentiles do the same? Therefore, just as your heavenly Father is complete in showing love to everyone, so also you must be complete. (Matt 5:43-48)

II. Features of Matthew

The Gospel of Matthew is crafted to show that Jesus is the Jewish Messiah/Christ. Its opening genealogy features three sets of fourteen generations between Abraham and Jesus, highlighting especially his royal connection with David's lineage and interestingly featuring women in the lineage as well as men (Matt 1:1-17). In a dream, an angel tells Joseph to take Mary as his wife, as her child is conceived of the Holy Spirit, fulfilling the Septuagint (Greek—not necessarily so in the Hebrew) rendering of Isaiah 7:14: "*Look! A virgin will become pregnant and give birth to a son, and they will call him,* Emmanuel." The narrator then explains the meaning of *Emmanuel* as being "God with us"—one of the central themes of the Gospel (Matt 1:20-23). The angel also declares the name of the child to be "Jesus" (*Yeshua* in Hebrew, meaning "the salvation of Yahweh"), which is interpreted as meaning that "he will save his people from their sins." Like bookends, while Jesus's being "the king of the Jews" poses an initial threat to Herod, the story concludes ironically with Pilate's posting precisely such a title on the cross on which Jesus died (2:2-3; 27:37).

After settling in Nazareth, the ministry of Jesus begins with his baptism by John. He is then tempted in the wilderness and calls his disciples to follow him (Matt 3–4). The teaching ministry of Jesus is launched with the Sermon on the Mount (Matt 5–7), the longest single discourse of Jesus anywhere in the Gospels. Jesus then begins his healing ministries and commissions the Twelve—sending them out to minister to others (Matt 8–10). The central part of the narrative includes ongoing teachings and miracles of Jesus, featuring debates with religious leaders and the prediction of his death and resurrection (Matt 11–20). Jesus then travels to Jerusalem, where he cleanses the temple, delivers parables of judgment, declares woes upon the legal experts and the Pharisees, and shares a Passover meal with his disciples. Jesus is arrested in Gethsemane, and Peter denies him thrice. He is tried before a Jewish council and before Pilate and is sentenced to death. Jesus is crucified and buried, and Pilate places a seal over the tomb and a guard at the site (Matt 21–27). The last chapter (Matt 28) relates accounts of women coming to the tomb and the stone being rolled away in an earthquake. An angel instructs the women to tell the disciples that Jesus has risen from the dead, but soldiers are bribed to say that Jesus's disciples stole the body while they were sleeping—a rumor continuing until the time Matthew was finalized. The Gospel concludes with the Great Commission: Jesus sending his followers out to make disciples of all nations, promising to be with them until the end of the age.

Within this larger narrative, Matthew's distinctive material (the M tradition) shows several features worth noting. It is organized as teaching material, which gives the impression that the Gospel of Matthew functioned as a manual for Christian discipleship as well as being an outreach document. Some of these special features include: scripture fulfillments about Jesus's Messiahship, five collections of sayings, and special lists of sayings material.

Scripture Fulfillments about Jesus's Messiahship

In addition to scripture-fulfillment passages in Mark, Matthew has its own set of distinctive references. A plausible inference is that the Matthean evangelist and perhaps other leaders have expanded connections between readings from scripture and elements of Jesus's ministry, listing them as fulfillments of the prophets. In most cases a scripture-fulfillment reference is made: "that the word of the Lord through the prophet . . . might be fulfilled . . . ," and Isaiah and Psalms are clearly favorite resources. In addition, Davidic connections with Micah and Zechariah are also drawn upon to show that Jesus fulfills the kingly typology of David, noted explicitly in the genealogy. Other more subtle fulfillments of scripture abound, such as showing that Jesus also fulfills the typologies of Moses and Joshua, but following are the distinctively Matthean scripture-fulfillment references designed to lead people to faith and to affirm their continuing belief.

Scripture-Fulfillment References in Matthew

1:22-23 (arrows here denote scriptures fulfilled in Matthew)➡Isaiah 7:14—the prediction of the virgin birth and Emmanuel, "God with us"

2:5-6➡Micah 5:2—the Shepherd of Israel will come from Bethlehem

2:15➡Hosea 11:1—out of Egypt Yahweh has called his son

2:17-18➡Jeremiah 31:15—weeping and grieving is heard in Ramah: Rachel weeping for her children

2:23➡Psalm 22:6; Isaiah 53:3—he shall be called a Nazarene

4:14-16➡Isaiah 9:1-2—in Galilee of the Gentiles those who lived in darkness have seen a great light

8:17➡Isaiah 53:4—he bore our illnesses and carried our diseases

12:17-21➡Isaiah 42:1-4—Yahweh's servant will have Yahweh's Spirit upon him; he will neither break a bent stalk nor snuff out a smoldering wick, and the Gentiles will put their hope in his name

13:35➡Psalm 78:2—speaking in parables, that which has been hidden since the beginning of the world will be declared

27:9-10➡Zechariah 11:12-13; Jer. 19:1-3; 32:6-9—thirty pieces of silver is the price for the one whose price has been set by some of the Israelites

Five Main Discourses

Another distinctive feature of Matthew's material is the packaging of sayings material within five key sections. These, of course, are interspersed with miracles and action narrative, which makes for a highly readable progression. Within a Jewish mindset, however, the number five is significant. Might this reflect an intentional designing of the five discourses of Jesus to be reminiscent of the five Books of Moses? Such a design is unlikely to have been accidental. The themes of the discourses also progress in an intensifying way. The Sermon on the Mount lays out the way of the kingdom—how Jesus expects his followers to live (Matt 5–7). Instructions to the Twelve lay out the hardships of discipleship while calling for adherence to the mission (ch. 10). The collections of kingdom parables, then, move from additions to Mark's parables (Matt 13) to implications for community life together as believers (Matt 18) to parables of judgment and discipline (Matt 24–25). Just as Mark locates the most intense confrontations of Jesus with Jewish leaders at the end of the story in Jerusalem, Matthew does the same, while also making pointed admonitions to would-be followers of Jesus along the way.

Five Discourses in Matthew

Chs. 5–7—The Sermon on the Mount

Ch. 10—Jesus's Instructions to "the Twelve"

Ch. 13—Parables of the Kingdom (I, features of the kingdom)

Ch. 18—Parables of the Kingdom (II, community life together)

Chs. 24–25—Parables of the Kingdom (III, judgment now and later)

Various Collections of Sayings

Another distinctive feature of Matthew is that it displays with prominence several smaller collections of sayings that make several points in organized ways. The ordered presentations here reflect teaching material that has been formed into memory-friendly units, likely used in community life before being finalized in written forms.

The Beatitudes (Matt 5:3-12)

Note how the Beatitudes (*beatus* in Latin means "happy" or "blessed"—in Greek, *makarios*) in Matthew lead off the great teaching unit with paradoxical assertions. The way of the kingdom is counter-conventional. It challenges the values of the world diametrically; following that path is what makes Jesus's followers the savory salt of the earth and the illuminative light of the world—despite worldly harassment and rejection (5:11-16). Luke also includes beatitudes, four of them (Luke 6:20-23), but Matthew's list is full and programmatic. Whereas the world sees the hopeless and poor in spirit as dejected, Jesus declares them to possess the kingdom of heaven; whereas the grieving evoke pity, Jesus promises comfort; whereas the meek get trampled by the strong, Jesus bequeaths them the earth; whereas those hungering for righteousness are seen as insatiable idealists, Jesus promises fulfillment; whereas the world advocates score-settling, Jesus promises that it is the merciful who will receive grace; whereas the pure of heart miss out on worldly promise, Jesus promises a divine vision and destiny; whereas the world rewards victors, it is the peacemakers who will enjoy the reward of divine adoption; whereas pursuing righteousness can irritate and evoke harassment, inheriting the kingdom is not a bad trade. Finally, to be insulted and maltreated because of following Jesus promises heavenly rewards—the plight and blessing of prophetic living, both then and now. Matthew's Beatitudes thus display the paradox of the kingdom at the outset of Jesus's teaching ministry in an unmistakable way.

Happy Are . . .

- . . . people who are hopeless, because the kingdom of heaven is theirs. (5:3)

- . . . people who grieve, because they will be made glad. (5:4)

- . . . people who are humble, because they will inherit the earth. (5:5)

- . . . people who are hungry and thirsty for righteousness, because they will be fed until they are full. (5:6)

- . . . people who show mercy, because they will receive mercy. (5:7)

- . . . people who have pure hearts, because they will see God. (5:8)

- . . . people who make peace, because they will be called God's children. (5:9)

- . . . people whose lives are harassed because they are righteous, because the kingdom of heaven is theirs. (5:10)

- . . . you when people insult you and harass you and speak all kinds of bad and false things about you, all because of me. Be full of joy and be glad, because you have a great reward in heaven. In the same way, people harassed the prophets who came before you. (5:11-12)

Fulfilling the Law (Matt 5:17-48)

It might be argued that when Jesus challenged interpretations of the Mosaic Law by Pharisees and Sadducees, he was trying to change the Law or to counter its normative appeal. In his dining with "sinners" and healing on the Sabbath, he apparently threatened conservative interpreters and was regarded as a liberal (11:19). And yet, his approach to the Law was anything but liberal—negotiating boundaries. Instead, it was radical—aiming at the center. Jesus also taught with personal authority. Rather than quoting other Rabbis or Pharisaic leaders, Jesus speaks in the name of God, claiming divine agency for his convictions, and audiences were reportedly divided over such an approach. Jesus speaks with authority in all four Gospels, but Matthew presents it as an occasion for glorifying God (9:8). What we see in Matthew's gathering of six above-and-beyond treatments is not a doing away with the Law, but a means of fulfilling it by getting at the center of its concerns rather than the legalistic boundary. As a radical interpreter, Jesus fulfills the Law by getting at the heart of faith and practice in a contradistinctive way.

You Have Heard That It Was Said . . .

- *Don't commit murder. . . .* But I say to you that everyone who is angry with their brother or sister will be in danger of judgment. (5:21-26)

- *Don't commit adultery.* But I say to you that every man who looks at a woman lustfully has already committed adultery in his heart. (5:27-30)

- Whoever divorces his wife must *give her a divorce certificate.* But I say to you that whoever divorces his wife except for sexual unfaithfulness forces her to commit adultery. (5:31-32)

- *Don't make a false solemn pledge, but you should follow through on what you have pledged to the Lord.* But I say to you that you must not pledge at all. . . . Let your *yes* mean yes, and your *no* mean no. Anything more than this comes from the evil one. (5:33-37)

- *An eye for an eye and a tooth for a tooth.* But I say to you that you must not oppose those who want to hurt you. (5:38-42)

- *You must love your neighbor* and hate your enemy. But I say to you, love your enemies and pray for those who harass you so that you will be acting as children of your Father who is in heaven. (5:43-48)

Matthew's Distinctive Kingdom-of-Heaven Parables

Whereas Mark and Luke describe the kingdom as being "of God," Matthew's Jesus elaborates on the kingdom "of heaven." This feature likely represents Matthew's respect for the name of the deity, as the four times when Matthew does refer to "the kingdom of God" it does so in pointed ways (12:28; 19:24; 21:31, 43). Use of "the kingdom of heaven" also denotes Matthew's distinctive material, and it reflects Matthew's independent tradition as well as its special emphases. First, the kingdom is worth the highest of costs because of its greatness of value; it is worth everything, and that's exactly what it costs. Second, there will be diversity and incompatibility within the community of faith, but judgment must be left up to God at the end of the age. Third, being watchful and ready for the Lord's return is what characterizes faithfulness, and the aggressive steward multiplies the Master's assets commendably.

The Kingdom of Heaven Is Like . . .

- Weeds planted in a field; do not uproot them, but let the Master sort things out at harvest time (13:24-30; interpreted in vv. 36-43)
- A treasure hidden in a field, worth buying (13:44)
- A pearl of great price, worth any cost (13:45-46)
- A drag net, gathering many types of fish, which the angels will sort later (13:47-50)
- A head of a household, who brings things new and old out of the treasure chest (13:51-52)
- Continual forgiveness of monumental debts (18:22-35)
- Late-coming laborers and the graciousness of a full-day's wage (20:1-16)
- A king's wedding banquet with unlikely responses (22:1-14; cf. also Luke 14:15-24)
- Ten young bridesmaids waiting for the bridegroom and keeping lamps lit (25:1-13)
- The faithful steward and investing aggressively (25:14-30)

Second, Matthew also contributes _a pra[...]_ whereby most disputes and grievances within [...] be resolved peaceably if the steps are followe[...] we have Jesus presented as speaking in ways t[...] ing Christian communities ("report it to the c[...] sage is not in the other gospels, it likely repr[...] Matthean Christianity. So, if a brother or sis[...] that person should go to the offender perso[...] rather than feeling bad about it or resorting t[...] work, one or two independent witnesses shou[...] offending party a chance to understand the g[...] not lead to reconciliation, the offending par[...] church and given a third chance to make thir[...] he or she be treated as an outsider. Of course, [...] tax collectors? He dined with them and embr[...]

A third contribution to church life mad[...] _grace, tolerance, and forgiveness._ As noted in [...] thew, the parable of the weeds sown among t[...] leave judgment up to God (13:24-30); likew[...] diversity of the fish at the end of the age, g[...] 50). Despite Peter's being entrusted structu[...] unmerciful servant calls for Peter (and those[...] not just seven times, but seventy-seven or [...] The parable of the workers in the vineyard [...] for "late-comers," as the same day's wage has [...] Therefore, in addition to contributing leader[...] accountability in service to well-functioning [...] thew seasons these with graciousness and f[...] healthy family life and effective leadership w[...]

IV. Engaging N[...]

The rich gathering of material in the Go[...] see why it was the favorite teaching Gospel [...] of John and Matthew have been found am[...] than any of the other New Testament texts, a[...] as sources for church teaching and guidanc[...] original contexts may be helpful to conside[...] ings for today's readers.

20:30-31; 21:9, 15; 22:41-45), Jesus not only is born in the city of David (Mic 5:2; Matt 2:4-6) but also becomes the Davidic shepherd of the flock of Israel (Zech 13:7; Matt 26:31). It is in fulfilling the vocation of Zion (21:5) that the true Israel will become a light to the nations and a source of healing to the world (5:13-16). Therefore, the mission of Jesus will be accomplished in the larger world by his first reaching his own people and then extending the Abrahamic and Davidic promises of blessing to the rest of the world. As Matthean leaders and audiences are still engaged with local Jewish communities, inferences of anti-Semitism are anachronistic; we have here an in-house Jewish struggle, wrestling over the mantle of authentic Judaism. Thus, in Matthean perspective, embracing Jesus as the Jewish Messiah not only fulfills the Jewish vocation, but it also fosters a global theology of presence in his becoming a source of God's blessing and salvation to the entire world.

The Transvaluation of the Kingdom

Imagine the cognitive dissonance faced by first-century Galileans when Jesus came proclaiming the kingdom of God (also in the other Gospels), but in a non-political way. One might even say it was anti-political. In an intentional contrast to the divine sonship claimed by Caesar Augustus and Herod's kingdom-palace at Caesarea Maritima, Jesus spoke of a different _basileia_. In opposition to a political empire, the reign of God is spiritual—without boundaries; in contrast to visible edifices and structures, the kingdom of God is ordered by truth and love; in contrast to position and power, the ways of God's workings are humble and lowly—desiring the elevation of others over oneself; in contrast to legal propositions, the way of the kingdom focuses on love of God and neighbor as the radical center of discipleship. Therefore, the _basileic_ activity of God should be seen as a dynamic and spiritual reality, which followers of Jesus are called to attend, discern, and heed. That will result in changes in the outward world, but it does not depend on them. It is thus powerfully political, because politics is neither its motivation nor operative means; it is ordered by the leadership and righteousness of God alone.

Therefore, the way of the kingdom involves turning the world's values upside down—_transvaluation._ The first will be last, and the last will be first. One who wishes to save one's life will lose it; the only way to find one's life is to release it. Coming into the kingdom hinges upon coming as a child, exercising basic trust. Remaining in the kingdom implies unending forgivingness. The value of the kingdom is priceless, costing no less than all one has and is. Its power is quiet, yet explosive, and living by its values makes one the light of

the world and the salt of the earth. T
naked, visiting the imprisoned, and
least of these so is one's regard for th
of truth rather than coercion; theref
violence or force. The leadership of (
ing for repentance and total dedicati
why it requires a revelation to glimps
it. The dynamic leadership of God is
truth as its king, and eternity as its n

The Foundatic

Matthew is the only Gospel th
Greek, *ekklēsia*—those who are "calle
several passages are key to understan
life and its developments. The Gosp
as shepherd, sheep, and sheepfold (Jc
(John 15:1-8), and these models wer
among discussions of community a
Christian situation. Matthew's contri

First, Matthew contributes *a moa
ter's confession Jesus describes the fou
Consoling later audiences that the de
mean a loss of apostolic leadership ("tr
NRSV] is a promise that his legacy w
Rather, it will continue in terms of st
tion is what is meant by Jesus's building
Peter or his confession? On that matte
Church, which had taught that the Cr
church where Peter last served as a lead
("You are the Christ, the Son of the li
tion of the church is getting one's faith
perhaps the foundational "rock" is the
revelation, as Christ leads the church
Whatever the case, these three verses i
copal (single overseer) form of governa
Ignatius of Antioch called for churche
church as a means of instilling corpora

First, consider Matthew's presentation of Jesus and the way of the kingdom against a backdrop of Roman occupation, the legacy of Herod, and incitements either to cower and submit to dominating forces or to stand up and fight. Herodians and some members of the establishment would have advocated the former; the Zealots would have advocated the latter. But what did Jesus say and do within such a setting, and how might those reflections affect ways we deal with empire, power, violence, and domination in the world today? There's lots there to consider!

Second, consider Matthew's approach to the Law of Moses in the light of how Sadducees, Pharisees, Essenes, and even early believers in Jesus might have conceived of righteous living. What difference does it make to aim at the heart of a concern or a teaching rather than focusing on the outward boundaries of acceptability? One might fail more when aiming at the center of a target; then again, one is likely to get closer to the bullseye if one aims at the center rather than simply in a general direction. After all, even a brief reading of the Prophets will remind one that God wants mercy rather than sacrifice (Matt 9:13; 12:7). But how does one get at the heart of a concern, whatever it may be, without getting trapped in the mechanisms designed to further it?

Third, notice the power of grace and the transformative promise of divine Presence. Those who have received grace most fully ought to be willing to extend it most liberally; but why is this sometimes not the case? Jesus emphasized treating others as we ourselves might like to be treated and taught us to give lovingly, with no expectation of return. Likewise, persons should be willing to extend the same measure of forgiveness to others as they might hope to receive for themselves; if that doesn't motivate graciousness, few things could! Being anxious for nothing, but seeking first the kingdom of heaven and its righteousness, leads to the meeting of one's true needs—sometimes because in that pursuit, real needs are distinguished from lesser ones. Whatever the case, in the coming of Jesus as the Messiah/Christ, Isaiah's vision of "God with us" is fulfilled. Christ's presence is encountered among his followers as they gather in his name, and Christ promises to accompany his followers in mission unto the ends of the age. That's part of Matthew's good news.

Chapter 3

The Gospel According to Mark

Begin with the text. Read the Gospel of Mark, and note important themes and details that come to mind.

Author: traditionally, John Mark of Alexandria, the former companion of Paul

Audience: believers in Jesus among Greek-speaking audiences

Time: ca. 70 CE, around the time of the destruction of the temple in Jerusalem

Place: possibly Rome or another setting in the Gentile mission

Message: The kingdom of God is at hand; turn around, believe, and follow Jesus.

The Gospel of Mark describes the ministry and message of Jesus with a great sense of urgency. At the outset, Jesus declares: "Now is the time! Here comes God's kingdom! Change your hearts and lives, and trust this good news!" (Mark 1:15). John the Baptist is presented as fulfilling the prophecy of Isaiah as *"a voice shouting in the wilderness: 'Prepare the way for the Lord; make his paths straight'"* (1:3), and when John's ministry comes to an end, that of Jesus is launched (1:14). Jesus's ministry then continues in Galilee and finally makes its way to Jerusalem, where he cleanses the temple and is tried, crucified, and buried. He then appears to his follows after the resurrection. Mark's is the shortest and the roughest of the four canonical Gospels, and the Greek text is punctuated with *kai euthus* ("and immediately") thirty-nine times. As well as conveying the urgency of the message, this device may also reflect the piecing together of disparate units of material—the sort of editorial process involved in gathering traditional material from preachers and others in telling the story of Jesus.

51

I. Crises and Contexts

Assuming that Mark was finalized around the time of the destruction of the temple in Jerusalem, several contextual issues are worth noting at the outset. With the ministry of Jesus being heralded by John the Baptist, considering how Jesus and John would have been perceived by the populace, as well as by Roman and Jewish leaders, is of value. Thinking also about Nero's persecution of Christians in Rome and the Roman siege of Jerusalem, especially if those crises posed something of a backdrop for the delivery and finalization of some of Mark's material, may also be helpful in understanding some of the emphases and nuances of Mark's story of Jesus.

Messianic Pretenders According to Josephus

Parallel to the first-century Jewish messianic leaders mentioned by Luke (Theudas, Judas the Galilean, the Egyptian—Acts 5:36-37; 21:38), Josephus mentions several other first-century messianic figures, which might help the reader understand how the ministry of Jesus was perceived by himself and by others—both similarly and contrastively. First, while not explicitly referred to as a messianic figure, *Simon of Peraea*, a tall and robust slave of Herod the Great, led a revolt in 4 BCE, claiming to be king and putting a diadem crown on his head as soon as Herod died. He burned and ransacked Herod's palace in Jericho and welcomed his followers to help themselves to the spoils (Josephus, *Antiquities* 17.10.6-7; *Wars* 2.4). Coming to his aid were fighters from Peraea to the east, but they were no match for the head of Herod's army, Gratus, who joined forces with Roman troops from Syria. When Simon's fighters were routed, he escaped for a while but was then beheaded after being captured.

Another kingly pretender, *Athronges the shepherd*, launched with his four brothers a series of attacks against the forces of Herod's successor Archelaus and Roman soldiers, but after a couple of years his forces were either killed or disbursed. Gratus again won out. Josephus also mentions *Judas son of Hezekiah*, who, following the death of Herod in 4 CE, raided his palace in Sepphoris and confiscated weapons to use against the Romans. Reportedly, Varus of Syria punished the revolt by crucifying two thousand Jews as a disincentive to rebellion (*Antiquities* 17.10.10; *Wars* 2.5.2). Josephus describes this time period as full of chaos and banditry.

After Herod's son Archelaus was exiled in 6 CE and replaced by the first of fourteen Roman prefects, Quirinius the prefect of Syria was put in charge of gathering Roman taxes in the region. He liquidated the resources of Archelaus in Jerusalem and instituted a census whereby Jewish subjects would be required to pay their taxes in Roman currency. This was problematic for two reasons. First, it was more difficult for farmers and herdsmen to convert their goods into currency; paying in goods was easier for common folk, and this left many susceptible to infractions and thus punishment. Second, because Roman coins displayed the image of the Roman governor, this was seen as idolatrous by righteous Jews. This led to a tax revolt by *Judas the Galilean* (originally from Gamala) and a Pharisee named Zadok (from the school of Shammai). Judas declared that this new system of tribute was the first step toward enslavement, and that God's people needed to be free from Roman rule (Josephus, *Antiquities* 18.4-5). He called for devout loyalty to God and declared that God would reward opposition to Rome, either in this life or the next. According to Josephus, the rebellion of Judas laid the ground for the Zealot movement, which Josephus viewed as the primary reason for economic instability and famine over the next half-century or so. Three decades after the death of Judas, his sons Jacob and Simon were crucified by Tiberius Alexander as insurrectionists (Josephus, *Wars* 2.5.2). This may be why Luke dates the work of Judas after Theudas, differing from the order presented by Josephus.

The next Messianic leader on the scene is described by Josephus as *the Samaritan prophet* (ca. 36 CE), who gathered hundreds of followers at the base of Mount Gerizim, promising to retrieve the hidden relics of Moses. Whether this Samaritan leader was claiming to recover the contents of the lost Ark of the Covenant, which in Hebrew scripture led to being victorious in battle, or whether the leader saw himself as the prophet like Moses predicted in Deuteronomy 18:15-22 (in Samaritan tradition, the *Tahib*, a prophetic Messiah) is unclear. Nonetheless, Pilate intercepted the expedition and blocked their way to the mountain. Many were killed, and of the leaders that were captured, many of them were also put to death. This caused a Samaritan council to appeal to Vitellius, prefect of Syria, and he had Pilate removed to Rome for consultation. In the meantime, Pilate was replaced as prefect of Judea by Marcellus (Josephus, *Antiquities* 18.4).

Less than a decade later, *Theudas* (ca. 45 CE) sought to reenact the conquest of Canaan by gathering an "army of conquest" on the east side of the Jordan River (Josephus, *Antiquities* 20.5). At his command the waters would part and God would deliver the city (and the rest of the promised land) into their hands. The Roman Procurator Fadus, however, refused to play the role of the soon-to-be-conquered Canaanites, and sent a garrison of soldiers in for a surprise attack. The rebellion was quelled, and the head of thwarted Theudas was paraded in Jerusalem on a pole as a disincentive to further reenactments of the biblical conquest narratives.

According to Josephus, an anonymous leader simply described as the *Egyptian prophet* (ca. 55 CE) again gathered a group of insurrectionists numbering around four thousand men on the Mount of Olives, preparing for another conquest like that of ancient Jericho. He declared that at his command the walls of Jerusalem would crash down and God would deliver them into the city. However, the Roman Procurator Felix refused his role in the drama, and Roman soldiers and cavalry once again thwarted the plan (Josephus, *Antiquities* 20.8). Four hundred were killed, and another two hundred were captured, but the Egyptian leader himself escaped, leading to rumors that he might return to Jerusalem at any time for an encore. Note that in Acts 21:38, the Roman officials ask Paul if he might be the returning Egyptian; Paul clarifies that he is not.

Josephus also mentions *John the Baptist* (ca. 26–28 CE), who came proclaiming repentance from sins and a call to righteous living; some historians might thus associate him with other first-century messianic Jewish leaders, interested in overthrowing the Romans. Given his clear association with Jesus, some scholars have guessed that Jesus was thus a failed zealot whose followers spiritualized his mission rather than regarding him as a defeated political revolutionary. Josephus, however, clearly distinguishes John the Baptist from messianic pretenders before and after him, referring to John as a good man who called people to virtue and righteousness (Josephus, *Antiquities* 18.5). Josephus even speculates on the view of many Jews at the time that Herod's defeat at the hand of Aretas, King of Arabia, was a punishment from God because he had beheaded John, an authentic prophet of the Lord.

With these sorts of diverse messianic perspectives in the air, it is easy to understand some of the diverse ways Jesus and his followers would have understood their mission, and how they might have been perceived by others. Luke numbers among the Twelve "Simon the Zealot" (Luke 6:15; Acts 1:13); note that Jesus has to instruct his disciples to put away the sword (Matt 26:52; John 18:11). Consider also that at the feeding of the five thousand in the wilderness, Jesus seats the crowd in groups (companies?) of fifty and a hundred; the number of the crowd includes only the men (potential soldiers? Mark 6:40-44). Given that the Passover (celebrating deliverance from Egypt) was near, might this large gathering have been perceived as a nationalistic march to Jerusalem, joining thousands of others against the Romans as a march to liberation? Is that why the crowd seeks to rush Jesus off to make him a "king," believing he was the messianic prophet Moses had predicted (John 6:1-15)? One can even sense the palpable fear of Roman retaliation among the chief priests and Pharisees after the crowd welcomes Jesus in his triumphal entry into Jerusalem. In their exchange with Caiaphas, he worries that "the Romans will come and take away [as in, *destroy*] both our temple and our people" (John 11:47-50).

Therefore, Jesus is "sacrificed" in Jerusalem in more ways than one—"it is better for you that one man die for the people rather than the whole nation be destroyed" (John 11:50). As rebellion in Jerusalem had broken out during the early reign of Archelaus, one can understand why tensions were high and why Pilate had come to Jerusalem from his seaside palace in Caesarea Maritima. Might the insurrectionist legacy of Judas the Galilean have played a role in Peter's denying his being a follower of Jesus when bystanders in the courtyard asked him if he were a *Galilean* (Mark 14:70-71)? Given that Judas Iscariot is from Kerioth—the only Judean among the Twelve (Mark 14:10)—one wonders how he might have perceived the prophet from Galilee. Most remarkable among these perceptions, however, is the consistent way Jesus asserts that he is *not* a political or military leader; his mission is other. Still, nationalistic expectations and hero-laced associations would have been hard to overcome, which helps us understand what Jesus was up to and what he wasn't. In the light of these many pretenders, the warning of Mark 13:21-30 becomes acutely relevant: "Then if someone says to you, 'Look, here's the Christ,' or 'There he is,' don't believe it. False christs and false prophets will appear, and they will offer signs and wonders in order to deceive, if possible, those whom God has chosen. But you, watch out! I've told you everything ahead of time." In Mark, Jesus takes great pains to distinguish himself from violent revolutionaries and nationalistic leaders.

Nero's Persecution of Christians in Rome

Within a decade or two the Jesus movement reached Rome, and Emperor Claudius became so concerned over debates among Jewish members of society over "*Chrestus*" (Christ) that he expelled a good number of Jews from Rome in 49 CE. Actually, he did not technically expel them all; he simply forbade their worshipping together in their synagogues, causing many to leave. Therefore, many also returned in 54 CE, after his death, as Nero was more tolerant. By 60 CE, thousands of Christians inhabited the Roman capital, but transcending the memory of being responsible for the earlier expulsion of Jews must have been a challenge for Jesus adherents. Upon their return, many would worship with Jewish family and friends in the synagogues on the Sabbath (Saturday), but they would also hold meetings in house churches on the first day of the week (Sunday). Paul's greetings to many households of believers in Romans 16 documents this type of gathering. Because of the egalitarian character of the movement, slaves and masters would worship and share fellowship together—a rare phenomenon that was offensive to Roman aristocratic sensibilities. Further, their worshipping of Jesus as the Christ—a man who was put to death as a common criminal—raised suspicion among those who found the movement puzzling.

In 64 CE a fire broke out in Rome, just happening to coincide with the clearing of an area on which Nero (reigning 54–68 CE) hoped to build his new palace. The fire got out of control and destroyed, by some estimations, two-thirds of the city, burning for six days or more (Dio Cassius, *Roman History* 62.16-18). Of course, Nero was then happy to build his villas and palace on the Palatine Hill, although the new construction came at great cost to those who had lost their homes and livelihoods in the process. As a means of diverting the blame, Nero accused Christians of setting the fire and began persecuting them as scapegoats. According to the Roman historian Tacitus, Nero not only blamed Christians for the incident, but he also began rounding them up and killing them in the Coliseum for entertainment. As followers of Jesus were committed to nonviolence, they offered little resistance, which made their capture and persecution a fairly manageable diversion.

> Covered with the skins of beasts, they were torn by dogs and perished, or were nailed to crosses, or were doomed to the flames and burnt, to serve as a nightly illumination, when daylight had expired. Nero offered his gardens for the spectacle, and was exhibiting a show in the circus, while he mingled with the people in the dress of a charioteer or stood aloft on a car. Hence, even for criminals who deserved extreme and exemplary punishment, there arose a feeling of compassion; for it was not, as it seemed, for the public good, but to glut one man's cruelty, that they were being destroyed. (Tacitus, *Annals* 15.44)

It was during this time that many Christian leaders lost their lives, and according to tradition, this is when Peter and Paul were martyred in Rome. Imagine, though, the preaching of Peter and others on the practical relevance of the way of the cross for believers. It might have been much easier to deny being a follower of Jesus or to try to avoid suffering for one's commitments. Especially in the Gospel of Mark, though, the cost of discipleship is clear, and within Rome and in other parts of the emerging Christian movement, its message would have had considerable existential value.

The Destruction of the Temple in Jerusalem

One of the great devastations in Judean history is the Great War with Rome (66–73 CE) in which Vespasian, Titus, and Domitian (all Roman generals who then became Caesars—the Flavian Dynasty) intended to teach the Jews a lesson, culminating with destroying the temple in Jerusalem in 70 CE. Josephus laments this chapter in Israel's history, blaming the "fourth philosophy" of the Zealots for the events leading up to an unfolding set of cataclysmic disasters (*Antiquities* 18.7-9). The numbers may be inflated, but according to Josephus, 1,100,000 Jews were killed during the siege of Jerusalem, and nearly a hundred thousand other Jews were captured and forced into slavery. He recounts terrible stories of starvation inside the city, even including the story of a starving mother cannibalizing her baby—things were that bad (Josephus, *Wars* 5.3)! Jesus's apocalyptic discourse in Mark 13, about the sun and the moon being blotted out and the warning of pregnant women needing to flee the city must have been pressingly relevant for Mark's audiences. They were likely experiencing the horrors described, and yet they were being called to faithfulness and trust despite the onslaught.

> In those days, after the suffering of that time, the sun will become dark, and the moon won't give its light. The stars will fall from the sky, and the planets and other heavenly bodies will be shaken. Then they will see the Human One [Son of Man] coming in the clouds with great power and splendor. Then he will send the angels and gather together his chosen people from the four corners of the earth, from the end of the earth to the end of heaven. (Mark 13:24-27)

II. Features of Mark

Mark has no birth narrative; it simply begins with announcing "The beginning of the good news about Jesus Christ, God's Son" (Mark 1:1). Good news, of course, is what the word *gospel* means. As a herald would sound a declaration of the emperor, so the first of the Gospel writers declares the good news of what God has done through the life, death, and resurrection of Christ Jesus. This is similar also to Paul's language. Yet Mark does far more than outline the Christ Events; Mark also constructs an engaging story of God's redemptive work in the ministry and work of Jesus as the Christ.

While it is difficult to know what parts of Mark's story of Jesus originate with tradition being used and what is a factor of the narrator's crafting, Mark groups stories in threes,[1] includes both individuated reports and general sum-maries of Jesus's ministry, and tends to group material together in terms of categories (agrarian parables, controversy stories and dialogues, types of mir-acles, judgment sayings, and eschatological discourses). One of Mark's most interesting features is inclusion and intercalation: the posing of one theme, interrupted by another, and then followed by the original theme.[2] This shows a constructive intentionality underlying Mark's narrative approach as an origi-nal gospel narrative.

Sharing the Jewish Jesus with Gentile Audiences

Unlike Matthew and Luke, Mark explains Jewish customs and translates Hebrew and Aramaic terms into Greek for his non-Jewish audiences. The puri-fication customs of Jews regarding the washing of their hands and ritual cleans-ing baths are explained, as well as rules about washing containers and sleeping mats (7:2-4), noting also that Jesus broke those codes (v. 5). All foods are de-clared "clean" by Jesus (7:19). The value of the two copper coins is calculated (worth a penny) to contrast the value of the widow's contribution to that of the wealthy (12:42). The first day of the festival is noted as being when the Pass-over lamb was sacrificed (14:12), the "Day of Preparation" is contextualized as being "just before the Sabbath," and Joseph of Arimathea is introduced as "a prominent council member who also eagerly anticipated the coming of God's kingdom" (15:42-43). In these ways, Mark provides a bridge between oral Jesus tradition in Palestine and Gentile audiences in the diaspora.

Aramaic Terms Translated into Greek

- Jesus calls James and John *Boanērges*—"Sons of Thunder" (3:17)

- Taking her by the hand, Jesus says: *Talitha koum*—"Young woman, get up." (5:41)

---

1. Note the three callings of the disciples (1:16-20; 2:14-17; 3:13-19), the three predic-tions of Jesus's death and resurrection (8:31; 9:31; 10:32-34), Jesus's three interrogations of his sleepy disciples at Gethsemane (14:32-42), and the mentions of the three leading disciples—Peter, James, and John (9:2; 14:33).

2. For instance, see the website of Felix Just, outlining ten examples of inclusion and intercalation in Mark: "The Gospel according to Mark: Literary Features & Thematic Em-phases," last modified June 22, 2012, http://catholic-resources.org/Bible/Mark-Literary.htm.

- Irresponsible adults wrongly diminish their responsibility to care for their parents by claiming their possessions are *corban*—"a gift I'm giving to God" (7:11)

- Jesus heals the man who was deaf, declaring *Ephphatha*—"Open up" (7:34)

- The site of the crucifixion is listed as *Golgotha*—"Skull Place" (15:22)

- At the ninth hour (3:00 p.m.) Jesus cries out in a loud voice: *Eloi, Eloi, lama sabachthani*—"My God, my God, why have you left me?" (15:34)

The Son of Man as the Son of God

While Mark presents Jesus as God's Son, Jesus calls himself the Son of Man.[3] At the outset, the narrator describes the subject of his Gospel as being "Jesus Christ, God's Son" (1:1). At his baptism a voice from heaven declares: "You are my Son, whom I dearly love; in you I find happiness" (1:11), and at the Transfiguration a voice sounds from the cloud: "This is my Son, whom I dearly love. Listen to him!" (9:7). Demoniacs and evil spirits declare Jesus's authority: "I know who you are. You are the holy one from God" (1:24), "You are God's Son!" (3:11), and "What have you to do with me, Jesus, Son of the Most High God?" (5:7). When the centurion sees how Jesus dies on the cross, he exclaims: "This man was certainly God's Son" (15:39). So Jesus is clearly attested to be God's Son by the narrator and the characters within the narrative.

Then again, it is not only third-person references that affirm Jesus's Sonship in Mark. When the high priest asks him if he is "the Christ, the Son of the blessed one," Jesus responds, "I am. And you will see the [Son of Man] sitting on the right side of the Almighty and coming on the heavenly clouds" (14:61-62). Jesus also speaks of God as his Father in intimate terms; in Gethsemane, he prays: "Abba, Father, for you all things are possible. Take this cup of suffering away from me. However—not what I want but what you want" (14:36).[4] And a pivotal parable by Jesus in Mark is that of the owner of the vineyard and the reception of his son:

---

3. The translators of the Common English Bible render the title "the Human One."

4. *Abba* is an intimate and familiar way of referring to a parent (like "daddy" or "papa"); Paul also uses that language when referring to the Spirit of Adoption and the Spirit of God's Son making believers children of God through Christ Jesus (Rom 8:15; Gal 4:6).

A man planted a vineyard, put a fence around it, dug a pit for the winepress, and built a tower. Then he rented it to tenant farmers and took a trip. When it was time, he sent a servant to collect from the tenants his share of the fruit of the vineyard. But they grabbed the servant, beat him, and sent him away empty-handed. Again the landowner sent another servant to them, but they struck him on the head and treated him disgracefully. He sent another one; that one they killed. The landlord sent many other servants, but the tenants beat some and killed others. Now the landowner had one son whom he loved dearly. He sent him last, thinking, They will respect my son. But those tenant farmers said to each other, "This is the heir. Let's kill him, and the inheritance will be ours." They grabbed him, killed him, and threw him out of the vineyard.

So what will the owner of the vineyard do? He will come and destroy those tenants and give the vineyard to others. Haven't you read this scripture, *The stone that the builders rejected has become the cornerstone. The Lord has done this, and it's amazing in our eyes?* (12:1-11)[5]

While "Son of God" and "Son of Man" are often thought of as emphases upon Jesus's divinity and humanity, such a distinction doesn't quite fit the facts of the biblical text. While "Son of God" becomes an increasingly meaningful confession for believers,[6] Jesus's Sonship in Mark is primarily a reference to his agency in doing God's work. And this is precisely what his being the "Son of Man" also conveys. While the use of this term is also expanded in Matthew and Luke, in Mark the Son of Man has the authority to forgive sins (2:10), is Lord of the Sabbath (2:28), must undergo great suffering and be killed by the Jewish leaders and after three days rise again (8:31), will be ashamed of those who are ashamed of him when he comes in glory (8:38), will rise from the dead (9:9), will suffer mistreatment and contempt (9:12), comes not to be served but to give his life as a ransom for many (10:45), will be seen coming in clouds with great power and glory (13:26), is woefully betrayed into the hands of sinners (14:21, 41), and will be seen seated at the right hand of God's power and coming with the clouds of heaven (14:62). In this last reference, the Son of Man is equated with "the Christ, the Son of the Blessed One" in the previous verse. The emphases here are not exactly upon Jesus's humanity.

---

5. The irony of the rejected building block becoming the cornerstone ties in Ps 118:22 with the mission of Jesus. It also is referenced in the preaching of Peter in Acts 4:11 (cf. also Eph 2:20 and 1 Pet 2:6).

6. Over the two or three explicit times it is used in Mark, "Son of God" occurs seven times in Matthew and Luke and eight times in John.

Therefore, both terms are references to Jesus's divine agency, and as Son of Man language never made it into the confessions of the early church or any of the epistles, its origin probably lay with the way Jesus referred to himself, as portrayed in all four Gospels. What, though, did it mean? Daniel 7:13-14 sketches a vision of one like a Son of Man, who on behalf of the Ancient of Days comes on heavenly clouds and is given dominion over all the kingdoms of the earth. Then again, the Son of Man in Ezekiel (mentioned over ninety times!) names the prophet addressed by God and called into humble service, charged with speaking God's truth and judgment to Israel in parables and riddles. Both of these images sound like the way Jesus speaks in the Gospels, different though they be. Scholars debate which meaning might have been closer to Jesus's self-understanding; some wonder if he used the term as a prophetic challenger of the religious leadership of his day, while others wonder if it represents more of an apocalyptic mission overall. Still others wonder if Jesus chose this sort of self-reference precisely because of its ambiguity—making it hard to categorize what Jesus came to do in neat and tidy boxes. Whatever the case, the Sonship of Jesus refers to his divine agency, and in Mark it focuses on the cross.

The Works and Words of Jesus in Mark

While Matthew and Luke present additional miracles and teachings of Jesus, Mark's story of Jesus nonetheless gives a robust sense of Jesus's ministry. While modernists will either dismiss or pose naturalistic explanations for the wonders, Mark presents them as evidence of Jesus's divine agency. Of course, claims to wondrous feats were not unique to the Jesus movement, as purported miracles were a not uncommon subject of rhetoric, but Mark's story of Jesus would certainly have evoked an appealing resonance in the Greco-Roman world in which it was delivered. Note that Jesus's wonders tend to be grouped into three categories, the first of which involved healings of the sick, beginning with the healing of Simon Peter's mother-in-law in Capernaum and a few general references (1:32-34; 3:10; 6:5, 13, 53-56).

Jesus's Healings in Mark

- Simon Peter's mother-in-law (1:29-31)
- The man with a skin disease (1:40-45)
- The paralytic in Capernaum (2:1-12)
- The man with the withered hand (3:1-5)

- The daughter of Jairus and the woman with an issue of blood (5:21-42)
- The deaf man with a speech impairment (7:31-35)
- The blind man at Bethsaida (8:22-25)
- Blind Bartimaeus in Jericho (10:46-52)

Interestingly, most of these healings are performed either on the Sabbath or in conjunction with a synagogue. It is as though Jesus is challenging Sabbath regulations, showing that Sabbath is not simply about what one does not do but about furthering the redemptive work of God. When he and his disciples are challenged by the Pharisees about picking a bit of grain to eat on the Sabbath, Jesus cites the example of David and his men eating the bread of the priest in the temple (2:23-26), then declaring: "The Sabbath was created for humans; humans weren't created for the Sabbath. This is why the [Son of Man] is Lord even over the Sabbath" (2:27-28).

Jesus further demonstrates his divine agency by casting out demons and delivering the mentally and emotionally afflicted from their inward sources of torment. He was not the only exorcist of his day, and many of the exorcisms were performed upon people in neighboring regions—from the "other side" of the sea, pig herders and the like, those among the Hellenistic villages of the Decapolis. Upon being accused of having a demon himself, Jesus reports that he is binding the "strong man" and plundering the household of the adversary in performing these works of spiritual power (3:22-30). Not all of his disciples are comfortable with exorcising work, though, as John the Son of Zebedee asks whether those casting out demons in Jesus's name should be stopped. Jesus is not threatened, however, and he responds that "Whoever isn't against us is for us." Further, "I assure you that whoever gives you a cup of water to drink because you belong to Christ will certainly be rewarded" (9:38-41).

Jesus's Exorcisms in Mark

- The man in the Capernaum synagogue with an unclean spirit (1:23-27)
- The Gerasene demoniac (5:1-20)
- The daughter of the Syrophoenician woman (7:25-30)

- The mute boy with an unclean spirit (9:17-29)
- General references (1:34, 39; 3:11, 22-30; 6:7-13)

In addition to demonstrating power over physical ailments and spiritual affliction, the Markan Jesus also demonstrates his power over nature. Two primary types of miracles are performed here: two feedings of multitudes and two calmings of the sea. Matthew follows Mark's four nature miracles rather closely, but Luke only includes one feeding, and he even moves the confession of Peter to follow the other feeding, that of the five thousand. Interestingly, Luke's work there and in over six dozen other instances happens to coincide with John's account.[7] The impact of these accounts, however, is made explicit in the narrative. As a result of Jesus's calming the storm, his disciples exclaim: "Who then is this? Even the wind and the sea obey him!" (4:41). After both of the feedings the narrator declares that everyone "ate until they were full" (6:42; 8:8).[8]

Jesus's Nature Wonders in Mark

- Calming the wind and the waves (4:35-41)
- The feeding of the five thousand (6:31-44)
- Calming the wind and the waves (6:47-53)
- The Feeding of the four thousand (8:1-9)

Of course, if a feeding and a sea crossing occurred once, they could also occur a second time, although the events in Mark 6 and 8 are quite similar. One difference involves the number of baskets used to pick up the fragments after the feedings: twelve in one case and seven in the other. If the first instance represents the way the story was told affirming the twelve apostles within Jewish Christianity, might the second represent the way the story was told in supporting the seven deacons who were appointed to minister to Hellenistic believers (Acts 6:1-7)? Another insight also follows from noting Mark's account. While Jesus's warning about being wary of the "yeast of the

---

7. For a full analysis of the feeding and sea-crossing narratives among the Gospels, see Paul N. Anderson, *The Christology of the Fourth Gospel: Its Unity and Disunity in the Light of John 6*, 3rd printing (Eugene, OR: Cascade Books, 2010).

8. This same result is recorded in the other three feeding narratives in Matthew and Luke (Matt 14:20; 15:37; Luke 9:17). John's Jesus, however, challenges those who seek him the following day, claiming, "I assure you that you are looking for me not because you saw miraculous signs but because you ate all the food you wanted" (John 6:26).

Pharisees and Sadducees" in Matthew refers to their teaching (Matt 16:1-12), and the "yeast of the Pharisees" in Luke refers to their hypocrisy (Luke 12:1), the warning in Mark 8:11-21 regarding the "yeast of the Pharisees as well as the yeast of Herod" seems to refer to the lust for signs and wonders. Or, as Jesus in John might have put it, "Happy are those who don't see and yet believe" (John 20:29). Therefore, despite the wonder-attestations in Mark, Jesus calls for modesty and non-ostentation; his work is redemptive rather than sensationalistic, and this theme is developed more fully elsewhere.

The teachings of Jesus in Mark are less developed than they are in Matthew and Luke, but they nonetheless make strong points about the ways of God and the character of the kingdom. Something new is in the works, beyond what older structures can contain, and the kingdom is like nature: it cannot be stopped, and it continues to grow with explosive power, even if out of sight or unnoticed. Rather than serving as illustrations of abstract truth, however, the parables in Mark function as vehicles of judgment. They expose the ignorance of outsiders and confirm the knowledge of those who really do get it. After telling the parable of the soils, Jesus says to his followers: "The secret of God's kingdom has been given to you, but to those who are outside everything comes in parables" (4:11). In that sense, the parables in Mark expose incomprehension as much as they illuminate the truth—an emphasis that is softened in Matthew and Luke.

Parables of Jesus in Mark

- The Doctor and the Sick (2:17)
- The Wedding Guests and the Bridegroom (2:19-20)
- Patches and Wineskins (2:21-22)
- Plundering the Divided Household and Binding the Strong Man (3:23-30)
- The Sower and the Soils (and its interpretation, 4:2-20)
- Lamps and Measures (4:21-25)
- The Subtly Growing Seed (4:26-29)
- The Mustard Seed (4:31-32)
- Purity and Food (and its interpretation, 7:14-23)
- Body Parts and Temptations (9:43-48)
- Salt and Saltiness (9:50)

- The Vineyard, the Tenants, and the Son (12:1-12)
- The Fig Tree (13:28-31)
- The Alert Doorkeeper (13:33-37)

At the outset of his ministry, Jesus's teaching in Capernaum is hailed as having new authority—unlike that of the scribes and Pharisees (1:21-28), and Jesus is called "teacher" (4:38; 9:17, 38; 10:17, 20, 35; 12:14, 19, 32; 13:1) and "rabbi" (9:5; 11:21; 14:45) by his disciples and others numerous times in Mark. Nonetheless Mark also features with prominence the confusion and lack of understanding among Jesus's disciples and others (4:11-13). His disciples often fail to understand his teachings (7:17-19; 9:30-32), and at times they do not grasp the meaning of his works (6:51-52; 8:17-21). At other times, they simply do not know how to respond or are afraid to expose their confusion (9:6; 14:40). In Mark 11:30-33 Jesus turns the tables and asks the legal experts a hard question himself: whether John was from heaven or not. To evade the implications of their not having heeded John's message, while the populace sees John as an authentic prophet, they simply claim not to know. In addressing the Sadducees' and Pharisees' squabbles over the resurrection, Jesus puts his finger on the source of their miscomprehension: "Isn't this the reason you are wrong, because you don't know either the scriptures or God's power?" (12:24). And of course, this lack of comprehension is only explicable as a fulfillment of Isaiah's prediction long ago, that people would neither see nor perceive the message of the prophet (Isa 6:9-10).

Did Jesus Predict His Death and Resurrection?

Given that the death and resurrection of Jesus are so central to the preaching of the apostles, one can appreciate that historical scholars question whether Mark's three presentations of Jesus's references to his death and resurrection originate in Jesus's historical self-understanding or in later theological perspectives on his mission (cf. John 2:22). After Peter's confessing of Jesus to be the Christ, Jesus declares: "The [Son of Man] must suffer many things and be rejected by the elders, chief priests, and the legal experts, and be killed, and then, after three days, rise from the dead." At this, Peter rebukes him, but Jesus then rebukes Peter for thinking in human terms instead of understanding God's ways (8:29-33). As they travel through Galilee, Jesus says again: "The [Son of Man] will be delivered into human hands. They will kill him. Three days after he is killed he will rise up." Yet, his disciples not only do not comprehend; they are described as being afraid to know what he was talking about (9:30-32). Jesus's third prediction of his suffering and death comes as he and his disciples travel to Jerusalem. "Look!" he says, "We're going up to Jerusalem. The [Son of Man] will be handed over to the chief priests and the legal experts. They will condemn him to death and hand him over to the Gentiles. They will ridicule him, spit on him, torture him, and kill him. After three days, he will rise up" (10:33-34). Demonstrating the epitome of miscomprehension, James and John then ask to sit at his right and left in glory, whereupon Jesus declares: "You don't know what you're asking! Can you drink the cup I drink or receive the baptism I receive?" (10:35-38). Like Peter, they mistake Jesus's glorification as triumph rather than embracing his anticipated suffering and death.

While the theological meaning of Jesus's suffering and death gets developed later, what if Jesus's words represent political understandings rather than theological ones only? For anyone aware of two thousand Jews having been crucified following the plundering of the Roman armory in Sepphoris three decades earlier, the reality of a Roman cross was anything but a spiritualized abstraction. Given the parable of the vineyard and the killing of the owner's son (12:1-12), Jesus's speaking in blunt terms about his own suffering and death cannot be limited to these three predictions alone; they likely reflect at least some aspect of missional consciousness, despite the reported miscomprehension of his followers. They also receive distinctive corroboration in John, including references to Jesus's being paradoxically "lifted up," implicitly on a Roman cross, as the glorification of the Son of Man (John 3:14-15; 6:51; 8:21-30; 12:23-36; 13:31-33; 18:32). Thus, the theme is attested in multiple ways among the gospel traditions, despite bearing theological associations.

Even more problematic, some historians will argue, is the possibility that Jesus also anticipated his being raised from the dead in three days, and that theme is also reported to have been totally miscomprehended in the Gospels (see especially Mark 9:9-10). In all three of the predictions of his death in Mark, Jesus also references his being raised up in three days (Mark 8:31; 9:31; 10:34), and yet the theme presents itself in several other ways, as well. First, challenging the unbelief of Sadducees, the reality of the resurrection is confirmed on the basis of Moses before the burning bush—the God of Abraham, Isaac, and Jacob is the God of the living, not the dead (Exod 3:15; Mark 12:26-27). Second, after the shepherd is stricken and the sheep scattered, Jesus will go before his disciples into Galilee, where he will reunite with them later (Mark 14:27-28; 16:7). Third, the prophet must perish in Jerusalem, and on the third day Jesus will complete his work (Luke 13:31-33). Fourth, the emphasis upon the third day is alluded to as "the sign of Jonah," who was in the belly of the fish for three days (Matt 12:39-41; 16:4; Luke 11:29-30). Fifth, when the Jewish leaders in John ask by what authority Jesus purges the temple, he replies: "Destroy this temple and in three days I'll raise it up" (John 2:18-21). Interestingly, while that saying is not recorded in the Synoptics, it is alluded to twice in Mark (Mark 14:56-59; 15:29-30). Sixth, Jesus's followers are reminded twice after the event that he and the scriptures had predicted his rising on the third day (Luke 24:1-9, 44-48), and it is on account of Jesus's having predicted such that the Jewish leaders ask for an armed guard and an official seal on the stone of Jesus's tomb (Matt 27:62-66)—an odd thing to do if there had not been previous discussions of after-death developments.

Whether historical memory shaped theology or whether theology shaped historical memory may finally be impossible to determine. The Apostle Paul passes along what he feels was "most important" regarding the death, resurrection, and appearances of Jesus as the Christ in 1 Corinthians 15:3-8, and yet the diverse and corroborative anticipations of Jesus's final days make them seem more than mere projections of an eventual set of beliefs. Whatever the case, the tension between the disciples' miscomprehension and later fuller understanding draws later audiences into the story, inviting them to become members of Mark's insider-community—those who see things from the narrator's perspective.

Messianic Secrecy and Disclosure

One of the most puzzling features of Mark is the Messianic Secret. On one hand, Jesus sends his disciples out by twos, commissioning them to preach the gospel, cast out demons, and heal the sick (Mark 6:7-13). On the other hand, after healing the deaf and speech-impaired man in the Decapolis, Jesus commands witnesses to be silent about it, but they proclaim it all the more (7:36). Messianic secrecy is sharply muted in Matthew and Luke, but why would Mark's Jesus proclaim the kingdom of God, perform wonders and call for a response to the good news, but then command people to secrecy?

The Messianic Secret in Mark

- Jesus silences the demon before his first exorcism (1:25).

- Jesus forbids the demons to speak because they recognize him (1:34).

- After healing the man with a skin disease, Jesus commands him to say nothing to anyone but to show himself to the priest and to offer a sacrifice (1:44).

- Jesus commands the demons not to tell who he is (3:12).

- After raising the daughter of Jairus, Jesus strictly orders that no one should know about it (5:43).

- Jesus enters a house in Tyre but does not want anyone to know he is there (7:24).

- After healing the deaf man with a speech impairment, Jesus commands people to tell no one about it (7:36).

- After healing the blind man in Bethsaida, Jesus says, "Don't go into the village" (8:26).

- After Peter's confessing him to be the Christ, Jesus commands the disciples to tell no one (8:29-30).

- After beholding Moses and Elijah at the Transfiguration, Jesus orders Peter, James, and John not to tell what they have seen until after the resurrection of the Son (9:9).

- Jesus ministers throughout Galilee but does not want anyone to know about it (9:30).

Extensive debates have raged on how to interpret these injunctions to secrecy in Mark. Over a century ago Wilhelm Wrede argued that the Messianic Secret in Mark was not historical, but Mark's invention to explain the distance between the relatively modest impact of Jesus's ministry and later Christian beliefs about Jesus as the Messiah.[9] However, in the light of diverse messianic expectations of the first century CE, a more plausible inference is that the secrecy motif in Mark coheres with Jesus's challenging "the yeast" of the Pharisees, which in Mark refers to the seeking of sensationalistic signs and their popular implications. If Herod and others were interested in signs and wonders, and if people flocked to Jesus when they heard of his deeds of power and teaching with authority, this would have skewed an understanding of his mission toward an uprising against Rome in ways that Jesus himself sought to avert. Perhaps he did not see Rome or Herod as the enemy, but violence and domination; he clearly did not see zealotry as the answer, as he called for

---

9. Wilhelm Wrede, *The Messianic Secret*, trans. J. C. G. Grieg (Cambridge: James Clarke and Co., 1971).

68

forgiveness and reconciliation. If Jesus of Nazareth sought to end the spiral of violence, perhaps he came to bring a different sense of God's dynamic leadership, and his counterviolent, nonnationalistic, antipartisan representation of the kingdom required distancing from conventional revolutionary approaches precisely because of their predictable appeal—a reality that could only be apparent after his death and resurrection (Mark 9:9).

Indeed, the press of the crowds and the challenges of celebrity status are featured more extensively in Mark than in Matthew and Luke. After healings and words of power, crowds gathered from far and near, posing something of a hindrance to Jesus's ministry in Mark (5:21-34). Because the healed leper does not keep quiet, Jesus can no longer go into towns (1:45), and when word gets out that Jesus is once again in Capernaum, so many people pack the house that a paralyzed man has to be lowered through the roof to get to Jesus (2:1-4). Several times Jesus gets into a boat to teach because of the press of the crowds (2:13; 3:7-10; 4:1), and sometimes Jesus boards a boat or goes off into the wilderness to pray—simply to get away from the crowds (4:35-36; 6:32, 45-46). When he enters a house the crowd is so large that he and his disciples cannot get anything to eat (3:20), and sometimes Jesus has to get away from the crowd to minister to people effectively (7:17, 33). Then again, Jesus at times has compassion on the crowd, for they are "like sheep without a shepherd," and he exhorts them to follow him, just as he does his disciples (6:34; 8:2, 34). The power of the crowd is noted in Mark, but so is its fickleness. Religious leaders are said to fear the crowd (11:18, 32; 12:12), and while the crowd is delighted with Jesus to begin with (12:37), they eventually turn on him, calling for the release of Barabbas and the crucifixion of Jesus. Even Pilate is afraid of the crowd (15:8-15), so Mark's secrecy motif points to Jesus's commitment to his mission in the face of competing visions and agendas. Here Mark demonstrates a good deal of political realism, not simply theological concern.

Conversely, Jesus's messianic disclosure is also explicit in Mark. In response to the question of the high priest, "Are you the Christ, the Son of the blessed one?" Jesus says, "I am. And you will see the [Son of Man] sitting on the right side of the Almighty and coming on the heavenly clouds" (14:61-62). He rides into Jerusalem on a donkey's colt, fulfilling the prophecy of Zechariah 9:9 as an unmistakable identification with the Davidic Messiah typology (Mark 11:1-10), and he calls himself the Son of Man. Nonetheless, part of his disclosure appears to relate to the timing of his mission, pivoting upon its culmination in Jerusalem (10:32-34).

III. The Message of Mark

In addition to the urgency of Mark's presentation of Jesus, Mark calls the reader to consider the value and cost of discipleship—what it means to follow Jesus, which will inevitably involve the way of the cross. Rather than revealing the character of God's kingdom, Mark's parables show how its mysteries might be grasped by insiders but are often missed by outsiders. After all, God's ways are fraught with paradox: "Whoever wants to be great among you will be your servant. Whoever wants to be first among you will be the slave of all, for the [Son of Man] didn't come to be served but rather to serve and to give his life to liberate many people" (Mark 10:43-45).

"Follow Me!" Says Mark's Jesus

Discipleship in Mark is emblemized by Jesus's inviting people to follow him. To follow Jesus as a teacher is to become a learner—a disciple—and several callings to follow Jesus are featured in Mark. After being baptized by John and being tested in the wilderness, Jesus comes across two sets of brothers (Simon and Andrew, and James and John, sons of Zebedee); he calls them to become fishers of persons (1:16-20). Jesus later comes across Levi, son of Alphaeus, at a tax booth and issues a similar invitation (2:14). A bit later Jesus ascends a mountain and calls the Twelve as apostles (3:13-19), and after Peter's confession Jesus invites his would-be disciples to deny themselves and take up their crosses in following him (8:34). He pointedly calls the rich man to sell his possessions and give the money to the poor on his way to following him (10:21), and the invitation to follow Jesus is replicated in other gospels, as well.[10]

Note that in the calling of the Twelve in Mark 3:13-19, it is Jesus who calls his followers. It is not a result of their ambition or scheming; it is his initiative and vocation to which they are invited to respond. Second, they are called to be with him, learning from the Master as a first-hand venture. Third, Jesus then sends them out as *apostles*—meaning ones who are sent—with authority to preach and to cast out demons. Later the Twelve are commissioned by Jesus on an apostolic mission (6:7-13), continuing in his teaching (4:10; 9:35) and in his traveling ministry (3:7; 8:10, 27; 10:32; 11:11; 14:17, 20). Jesus commissions two of his disciples on special tasks (11:1; 14:13), and he

---

10. In addition to the four passages in Mark, Matthew and Luke add "Follow me, and let the dead bury their own dead" (Matt 8:22; Luke 9:59-60) and "Those who don't pick up their crosses and follow me aren't worthy of me" (Matt 10:38; Luke 14:27). In John, Jesus calls Philip, saying, "Follow me" (John 1:43), and twice in the last chapter he calls Peter to "Follow me" (John 21:19, 22).

takes Peter, James, and John with him on several special occasions (9:2; 13:3; 14:33). Women also accompany Jesus in some of his ministry;[11] notably, it is they who are present at the crucifixion, while members of the Twelve are not.

The Secret of the Kingdom

While most of Jesus's parables are best interpreted as conveying one primary meaning, the parable of the sower and the soils is different. It is an allegory, with distinctive meanings connected to each of the main elements explained by Jesus. First, the "seed" scattered by the farmer is the *word* of the gospel. The hardened path might pose initial openness, but Satan steals the word away. The rocky ground is like rootless people, who respond quickly but cannot endure distress or abuse; therefore, they fall away easily. Others are like the soil infested with briars; they receive the seed, but it is crowded out by the worries of life: "the false appeal of wealth, and the desire for more things break in and choke the word, and it bears no fruit." The good soil, however, receives the seed and embraces it, yielding ratios of thirty, sixty, and a hundred to one (4:14-20).

This grand opening parable in Mark explains why some respond to the gospel and others do not. Distractions and lesser concerns obstruct the effect of the word, yet when it is received, the harvest is multiplied. The point is to foster faithfulness in broadcasting the seed of the good news and to also trust the results to God. This is where the Markan understanding and misunderstanding motif also connects with Mark's use of scripture. In contrast to Matthew, which cites the Old Testament to demonstrate Jesus's fulfilling Moses and the Prophets as the Messiah/Christ, Mark tends to cite scripture to show how people get it wrong. John the Baptist heralds the prophecy of Isaiah 40:3-4, raising up the valleys and bringing down the mountains (Mark 1:2-3); Isaiah 29:13 is cited to show how hypocritical people are—honoring God with their lips while their hearts are far away (Mark 7:6-7); the Ten Commandments are best followed in the love of God and neighbor (Deut 6:5; Lev 19:18) rather than a legalistic approach (12:29-31); the lack of belief in Jesus is explicable as fulfilling the prophecy of Isaiah 6:9-10—that people will look but not see and hear but not comprehend (Mark 4:12; 8:18).

Mark also shows the fulfilled prophecy of Malachi 4:4-5 in presenting the coming of Moses and Elijah, signaling the Day of the Lord. First, Elijah and Moses (the prophet) are associated with the ministry of John the Baptist, who

---

11. Women feature even more pronouncedly among Jesus's followers in Luke and in John.

prepares the way for Jesus (Mark 6:15-16; 8:28; 9:11-13). His pointing to Jesus (1:2-11) as an authentic prophet (11:27-33) is complemented by Jesus, who continues his work even after John's death. A second way the coming of Elijah and Moses anticipates the coming Day of the Lord occurs at the Transfiguration, when these two prophets of old appear with Jesus, and his garments become radiant (9:2-8). While the report of the Transfiguration is not to be shared until after the resurrection, responses to John the Baptist are measures of people's authentic faith, and Herod and the Jewish leaders fail that test.

The character of the kingdom in Mark is not elaborated as it is in Matthew; rather, Jesus's parables heighten its hiddenness and ironic discernment. Like a quietly growing seed, the kingdom continues to advance, and from small seeds great things happen (4:26-32). Some of the kingdom parables in Mark emphasize entry and the lack thereof. If one's body parts lead to forfeiting the kingdom, one is better off without them—a clearly hyperbolic point (9:47). Children are welcomed by Jesus, for God's kingdom belongs to such as these, and one must become like a child in order to enter (10:14-16). The wealthy will find it hard to enter the kingdom—as difficult as a camel passing through the eye of a needle (10:23-25). And the legal expert who affirms the love of God and neighbor over burnt offerings and sacrifices is not far from the kingdom (12:32-34). In these and other ways, the reality of the kingdom is a paradoxical one, glimpsed by some but exposing the blindness of others.

The Way of the Cross

Mark's Jesus calls people to follow him, but the way is problematic; it will inevitably involve the way of the cross. Whether one's heart has been ransacked by the deceiver (4:4, 15; 8:33-38), whether one's shallow faith cannot withstand the rocky path of trials and persecution (4:5-6, 16-17; 13:9-13), or whether one's reception of the gospel is choked out by the thorny material worries of life (4:7, 18-19; 10:21-25), the choice is clear. To protect one's life is to forfeit it; the only way to attain the gift of life is to risk losing everything in reckless abandon. Says Jesus: "All who want to come after me must say no to themselves, take up their cross, and follow me" (8:34). Therefore, the way of the cross for disciples is charted unmistakably by the Master.

Because Jesus Will . . .

- suffer many things and be rejected by the elders, chief priests, and the legal experts, and be killed (8:31)

- suffer much and be rejected (9:12)
- be delivered into human hands and killed (9:31)
- be handed over to the chief priests and the legal experts, condemned to death, handed over to the Gentiles, ridiculed, spit upon, tortured, and killed (10:33-34)
- have come not to be served but to serve, and to give his life as a ransom for many (10:44)
- be grabbed, killed, and thrown out of the vineyard (12:8)
- be betrayed into the hands of sinners (14:41)

Jesus's Followers . . .

- must say no to themselves, take up their cross, and follow him (8:34)
- must be willing to release their lives for the sake of the good news if they want to save them (8:35)
- will share the martyrological cup and the baptism of Jesus (10:38-39)
- must be willing to be the servant of all (10:43-44)
- will be handed over to councils, beaten in synagogues, and stand before governors because of Jesus (13:9)
- will be betrayed by family members and will be hated because of Jesus's name (13:12-13)

Just as the predictions of what will happen to Jesus come true by the end of the narrative, so will it be regarding the path ahead for his followers. And yet, the way of the cross is a paradoxical one, as undeserved suffering yields redemption, and death finally leads to life. After the cross comes the resurrection, and divine action in the mission of the faithful servant becomes the hope of believers who follow Jesus faithfully toward Golgotha. Those who have left family and friends to follow Jesus will be welcomed into his new family, receiving "one hundred times as much now in this life—houses, brothers, sisters, mothers, children, and farms (with harassment)—and in the coming age, eternal life" (10:30). And, at the time of trial, they need not worry about what to say, for it will be given them by the Holy Spirit, and "whoever stands firm until the end will be saved" (13:11-13).

IV. Engaging Mark

The original ending of Mark shows the disciples being afraid (16:8), and Mark's "second ending" provides a more upbeat conclusion, added some time in the second century (16:9-20). Nonetheless, this post-Markan addition is canonical, and one of the themes that comes through authentically is *hardness of heart* (*sklērokardian* in Greek, like "cardio-sclerosis"). Mark 16:14 refers to the refusal of some disciples to believe that Jesus had risen from the dead (a reference to Thomas in John 20:24-29?) despite the testimony of the faithful. Hardness of heart, however, is also described in two of Mark's earlier passages, which shed light on Jesus's overall ministry. The hardened hearts portrayed in Mark 3:1-6 refer to the theologically conservative, who advocate keeping Sabbath laws at all costs—looking on suspiciously as Jesus heals the man with the withered hand. Those with hardened hearts in Mark 10:1-12 are challenged by Jesus because they stretch the law to accommodate their building a case for divorce, even at the expense of the vulnerable. Therefore, the actions of Jesus in Mark challenge both conservatives and liberals, calling for concern for the needy and the vulnerable as the heart of the Mosaic Law.

As you consider Jesus's prophetic ministry in its original settings as portrayed in Mark, how would Jesus challenge hardness of heart today, as people might be tempted to ignore others' needs out of concerns to be biblically correct or to stretch biblical teachings to accommodate their selfish interests also at the expense of the vulnerable?

Second, how might an understanding of messianic secrecy in Mark illumine the way Jesus saw his mission as a striking contrast to the political and violence-oriented zealotry of contemporary messianic pretenders in first-century Judaism? Further, can God's ways ever be furthered through popularistic or political agendas, or do these set back one's endeavor to be faithful to the dynamic activity of God's leadership? Does the transvaluation of God's kingdom relate to political realities as well as religious ones? If so, what does following Jesus look like in later generations?

Third, what might the way of the cross have implied for Jesus's followers during his ministry (ca. 30 CE), during Nero's persecution of Christians in Rome (ca. 64–67 CE), and during the Roman destruction of Jerusalem (ca. 66–73 CE)? How might believers then have been challenged in seeking to follow the pattern and teachings of the Master, and how might that impact an understanding of authentic discipleship in later generations? If the way of the cross really is a paradoxical venture, how much faith does faithfulness require, and how does the empowerment of grace make a difference?

Chapter 4

The Gospel According to Luke

Begin with the text. Read the Gospel of Luke, and note important themes and details that come to mind.

Author: traditionally, Luke the companion of Paul

Audience: uncertain, audiences in the Greco-Roman world including Jews and Gentiles

Time: after Mark and before Acts, plausibly around 85 CE

Place: uncertain, but showing sensitivity to the larger Mediterranean world

Message: Jesus is the exemplary savior of the world.

The Gospel of Luke is written to "most honorable Theophilus" (lover of God, cf. Acts 1:1), and together with a second volume (Acts of the Apostles) it offers a full history of the ministry of Jesus through the first generation of the early church. Taken as a whole, this two-volume history makes up about a quarter of the entire New Testament. Like Matthew, Luke incorporates most of Mark's material, but in chapters 10–19 Luke includes a fair amount of distinctive material. Between 20 and 25 percent of Luke's material is shared with Matthew, but not found in Mark, leading most scholars to imagine their use of a common unnamed tradition, although if Luke had access to Matthew's material that could also explain some of the overlap. Luke's historical approach shows great affinity with classical historiographies of his day, and his "carefully ordered account" (1:3) would be recognized as a standard historical treatment of Jesus and his followers by Greek-speaking audiences of the late first century. It also includes some of the material found otherwise only in John, which assists a fuller understanding of his own statement of purpose:

> Many people have already applied themselves to the task of compiling an account of the events that have been fulfilled among us. They used what the original eyewitnesses and servants of the word handed down to us. Now,

after having investigated everything carefully from the beginning, I have also decided to write a carefully ordered account for you, most honorable Theophilus. I want you to have confidence in the soundness of the instruction you have received. (Luke 1:1-4)

I. Crises and Contexts

Written with a Gentile audience in mind, the Gospel of Luke addresses some of the larger issues of his day with the story of Jesus's mission and teachings. In that sense, he builds a case for the Jesus movement to be respected among Roman and Jewish officials and any other leaders of society, sketching the story of an exemplary figure who ministered to the poor, embraced Samaritans, and elevated the role of women. This is made possible because of the Holy Spirit being poured out on account of Jesus's mission, and the restoration of the kingdom has indeed come. Readers can better understand Luke's story of Jesus through appreciating several contextual issues of which first-century audiences would have been aware. In the light of Caesar being referred to as the Divine Son, presenting Jesus as Lord and Christ challenges such claims. Given the acute onslaught of famine and economic hardship in the Mediterranean world, concern for the poor by Jesus and his followers would have commanded moral respect. And, given tensions between Jews and Samaritans, Jesus's embracing Samaritans would have challenged dehumanizing prejudice in more ways than one.

Caesar, the Son of God

When modern readers of the New Testament consider such divine titles of Jesus as "Son of God" or "Christ," the tendency is to see these terms as claims of Jesus's uniqueness. Indeed, they are, and certainly within Judaism there is only one God in the heavens, and the call to "love the LORD your God" in the *Shema* ("Hear, Oh Israel . . . ," Deut 6:4-5) has as its primary emphasis the conviction that "The LORD our God, the LORD is one!" (NKJV). In addition, standard Jewish views of the Messiah/Christ did not envision him being divine; they simply considered "the Anointed One" to be a powerful agent of God's world-changing saving and redemptive action. Competing for divine status in the Greco-Roman world were the Roman emperors from Julius Caesar on. Having been murdered in 44 BCE (Beware the Ides of March!), the Roman senate conferred on him the honor of *Divus Iulius* (Divine Julius) two years later, and coins were minted with such acclaim on them. Caesar Augustus (31 BCE–14 CE) also called him *Divi Filius* (Son of God), and during the New Testament era the Roman emperor was referred to as the Son of God, although different Caesars varied in terms of how they expected to be regarded. While the practice continued off and on into the second century CE, it was only Caligula (37–41) and Domitian (81–96) who required emperor worship as a public means of demonstrating loyalty.

This being the case, emphasizing the divinely appointed mission of Jesus as the Christ came to define his being, not just his works. Also, as early Christians worshipped together, hymnic material developed expressing their beliefs in Jesus as God's Son and savior of the world. This is observable in the early christological hymns found in Philippians 2:5-11, Colossians 1:15-20, and Hebrews 1:1-4, and also in the later *Logos* hymn in John 1:1-18. Luke also includes hymnic material in his first two chapters, which probably reflects confessional worship material from which he draws his story of Jesus's birth. While Mark has no birth narrative, Matthew and Luke both include their renditions of the virginal conception of Jesus and his wondrous birth. And the angel declares to the shepherds near Bethlehem that a savior is born, "Christ the Lord" (*Kyrios Christos* in Greek, Luke 2:11). In this and in the use of such christological titles as Son of God and savior of the world, early Christians declared their belief in Jesus as Lord—also a pointed challenge to divinity claims of the imperial cult. To say Jesus is Lord is to claim that Caesar is not, and such a confession would have had political implications as well as religious ones.

Poverty in Judea and the Mediterranean World

Economic stability was always a challenge in the Middle East. Water was scarce, famine descended with little notice, trade was variable, and Roman taxation was onerous. Add to those variables the fact that thievery increased alongside zealotry after the death of Herod the Great, sometimes legitimated by anti-Roman nationalistic goals, and stable economic growth became elusive. Those with land and wealth (about 3-5 percent of the population—often connected with the Sadducees) found ways to manage, but they often did so by squeezing the vulnerable, who had fewer options. If all one possessed was land, to repay a debt by means of forfeiting one's land not only condemned the head of a household to a landless plight, but it also sentenced one's family and posterity to the same dismal existence—the equivalent of indentured slavery. The new tax system instituted by Quirinius of Syria in 6 CE created new levels of crisis, as having to pay in Roman coin was especially hard on people who practiced subsistence living. War and conflict also took their tolls, as preoccupation with safety and protection diverted energies away from farming and production. As is always the case with conflict, occupying forces used economy-devastating tactics to create submission, so famine and tough economic times were also impacted by political turmoil. Attitudes toward the poor in both Judaism and the larger Hellenistic world often hinged upon whether the poor had no choice in the matter—widows, orphans, and the destitute—or whether people were perceived as irresponsible in managing their situations. In either case, however, giving alms to the poor and alleviating their need was respected as honorable and charitable, and such a value is certainly exemplified in Luke-Acts.

In Acts 11:28-30 Luke mentions a prophecy by Agabus that a famine would befall the region during the reign of Claudius, and this eventuality came to pass around 45–46 CE. The apostles gathered funds and resources from the mission churches and sent them to the elders in Jerusalem. Josephus even mentions that Queen Helena of Adiabene (Armenia), who had converted to Judaism, bought great supplies of corn from Alexandria and dried figs from Cyprus to alleviate the hunger in Jerusalem during the Judean famine (*Antiquities* 20.5). In appreciation of her magnanimity, three monuments were erected near Jerusalem in her honor. The effects of the famine continued for some time, and the combination of Zealot uprisings and the uneven—at times dishonest or even capricious—leadership of Roman procurators over Judea during this time added to economic stress. Thus, economic hardship continued in Judea into the next decade, and the Apostle Paul, in addition to spreading the gospel to Jews and Gentiles throughout the Mediterranean world, also solicited funds for the Jerusalem church (1 Cor 16:1-4), and new believers from as far away as Greece responded generously to the request for help, supporting also Paul's mission (2 Cor 8:1-24; Phil 4:15). Therefore, when Luke shows Jesus as preaching against the rich and showing favor to the poor, heads would be nodding among his audiences. Also, in presenting believers as selling their possessions and meeting the needs of others within the community of faith (Acts 2:42-47; 4:32-37), Luke shows them as taking seriously Jesus's concerns for the poor (Luke 4:18; 6:20; 7:22; 14:13; 16:22; 18:22; 19:8; 21:3) as a material means of touching the world.

Samaritans, Judeans, and Galileans

Relations between Samaritans, Judeans, and Galileans were mixed in the first century CE. Samaria is the region between Galilee to the north and Judea to the south, and after the region was defeated by the Assyrians in 720

BCE, as a means of putting down further resistance, leading members of its society were taken off to Mesopotamia, Persia, and elsewhere, and foreigners were resettled there. When Ezra returned to Jerusalem from Babylon in 458 BCE, Jewish people were forbidden to intermarry with Samaritans, as their Jewish status had been compromised, and both groups appealed to Persia for help in constructing their temples, reflecting some competition. The Samaritans had their own Pentateuch, and they felt Ezra and others had added too much to the books of Moses. Rather than a king like David, the Samaritans anticipated the Messiah as a prophet like Moses, and their scriptures identified Mount Gerizim as the authorized place of worship rather than the temple in Jerusalem. Tensions continued during the Hellenistic period, as Samaritans were more willing to welcome Greek influences than the Jews were. A temple to Zeus was also built on Mount Gerizim, and Antiochus Epiphanes claimed to make Zeus manifest by expanding Syrian domination. During his reign (175–163 BCE), Samaritans denied being Jewish, and they were hence disowned by Judeans and Galileans. After John Hyrcanus (134–104 BCE) wrested Judea away from the Syrians, he raided Samaria, destroying the Gerizim temple around 110 BCE. By then, Greeks from Macedonia had also settled in the region, and Hyrcanus exported some of them as slaves to other regions. Over a century later (ca. 9 CE) Josephus reports that Samaritans snuck into the Jerusalem temple the opening night of Passover and scattered human bones on the porticoes, in effect defiling the temple (*Antiquities* 18.29-30). Around 50 CE, as Galileans traveled to a festival in Jerusalem, one of them was killed in Samaria. Galilean leaders appealed to the Roman governor Cumanus to crack down on Samaria, but as he did nothing, leading to retaliations, whereby Jewish forces gathered and launched a raid against Samaria, massacring many in their villages. Cumanus then captured the Jews who had invaded Samaria and had them killed, but after bringing Samaritan offenders to trial in Rome, three of them were sentenced to death (Josephus, *Wars* 2.232-246).

At the time of Luke's writing, the Samaritans would have been a people by whom both Galileans and Judeans felt betrayed. Not only had they intermarried with other ethnic and religious populations (forbidden by scripture), but they had also sold out to the Hellenists when things got tough with Antiochus and the like. Yet Jesus and his followers "had to go through Samaria" on their way between Galilee and Jerusalem (John 4:4; Luke 17:11), and both Luke and John include interactions between Jesus and Samaritans. Luke points out that the one leper among the ten who showed gratitude was a *Samaritan* (an emphatic point, Luke 17:16), and while the Jewish religious leaders find it easy to pass by the wounded man traveling between Jericho and Jerusalem, the one who did the right thing was "one of *them*"—a Samaritan (Luke 10:30-37). In response to the legal expert's question, "Who is my neighbor?" Jesus's parable answers by saying in effect: "No one isn't."

II. Features of Luke

The "carefully ordered account" of Jesus's ministry provided by Luke expands upon Mark, as Matthew does, but it includes a variety of other material and features. Rather than presenting Jesus as the Jewish Messiah, he is featured as the savior of the world (Luke 1:69; 2:11; cf. Acts 5:31; 13:23) and a light to the Gentiles (Luke 2:32; Acts 13:47; 26:23). Before his ascension Jesus declares to his disciples that "a change of heart and life for the forgiveness of sins must be preached in his name to all nations, beginning from Jerusalem" (Luke 24:47), and the basis for that proclamation is laid out in Luke's story of Jesus. As a more universally targeted gospel, Luke omits sections from Matthew's Sermon on the Mount dealing with the Jewish law, and his genealogy goes back to Adam, not just Abraham. Luke's narrative is written in very good classical Greek (especially 1:1-4), and yet it also contains Semitic sections in it (especially 1:5–2:52) reflecting the Jewish worship life of the early church. While Luke follows Mark's story fairly closely between Luke 3–9, things change when Jesus sets his face toward Jerusalem (9:53). In the next ten chapters, Luke charts his own course and orders most of his distinctive material as part of a travel narrative—on the way to Jerusalem. Some special features of his message include concerns for the poor, favorable treatment of Samaritans and women, and emphases upon prayer and the Holy Spirit.

The Birth of the Christ-Child

Like Matthew, Luke begins his story of Jesus based on Mark with a birth narrative and a bit later a genealogy, but Luke's approach to these two introductory themes is completely different. Is that merely a coincidence, or is it knowingly and on purpose? Whatever the case, Luke's genealogy comes after Jesus's baptism instead of at the very beginning. It includes seventy-eight generations instead of forty-two, reverses the order from late to early, and it goes all the way back to Adam, son of God, rather than Abraham, father of Isaac. Also, no women are mentioned in Luke's genealogy, which is odd, given Luke's tendency to favor the roles of women in his narrative. In the presentation of names between Abraham and David, Luke and Matthew are quite similar, but between David and Jesus, Luke traces the lineage through Nathan (one of David's other sons) rather than Solomon.

Also different from Matthew, Luke's birth narrative begins with the wondrous birth of John the Baptist before that of Jesus. Rather than featuring the wonder of a virgin's conception, however, this story is that of an infertile couple struggling to conceive. Like Abraham and Sarah in Genesis and Elkanah and Hannah in 1 Samuel, they are very old. Zachariah and Elizabeth are both from priestly families and thus may have Sadducean connections, and Gabriel's announcement of a son declares a fulfillment of the prophecies of Malachi 4:5-6 and Isaiah 40:3-4 in that John will be like Elijah, returning the hearts of fathers to their children and preparing people to receive the Lord's coming (Luke 1:16-17; 3:4-6). Also as in the story of Hannah and young Samuel, the promised child is to be dedicated to the Lord, and in John's case, he is to be a Nazarite—set apart for the Lord's service, not drinking wine or liquor, and filled with the Holy Spirit even before his birth (Luke 1:15). Luke then makes the connection between John and Jesus, explaining that Mary and Elizabeth are cousins. As in Matthew's account, Mary conceives by the Holy Spirit as a virgin, but in contrast to Matthew's story, the focus is on Mary and her feelings rather than Joseph.

Locating Mary and Joseph in Nazareth, Luke explains their movement to Bethlehem for the birth of Jesus as a factor of the census of Quirinius, creating a chronology problem. If Jesus was born before Herod died in 4 BCE, and if the census of Quirinius is after the dismissal of Herod's successor Archelaus in 6 CE, that represents a nine-year difference. Then again an earlier census may have preceded the tax and its later mechanisms, so Luke is possibly overread on this matter. Whatever the case, Luke employs the occasion of a census to get Mary and Joseph on the move from Nazareth to Bethlehem, allowing Jesus to be born in the city of David as the Lord's Messiah (2:4, 11). Also in contrast to Matthew's royal ambassadors from the east following a star, Luke features angels appearing to lowly shepherds watching their flocks by night—singing hymns of praise to the God of Israel. The shepherds likewise come to see the Christ-child and find him in a manger, along with Mary and Joseph.

According to Jewish custom, Mary and Joseph have Jesus circumcised on the eighth day, and in the temple they meet two elderly saints: Simeon, who has received a promise that he will not die until he has seen the Lord's Christ, and Anna, a prophet, who fasts and prays for the redemption of Jerusalem (2:21-38). Just as Mary and Zechariah broke forth into hymns of praise (along with the angels), here Simeon's prayer offers an earnest hope for God's salvation to be a glory for Israel and a light to the Gentiles:

Now, master, let your servant go in peace according to your word
  because my eyes have seen your salvation.
You prepared this salvation in the presence of all peoples.
It's a light for revelation to the Gentiles
  and a glory for your people Israel. (2:29-32)

Back in Nazareth, Jesus is reported to be growing in wisdom and stature (2:40, 52), and Luke includes the only canonical story of Jesus's childhood.[1] As Jesus and his family visit Jerusalem for the Passover festival, they lose track of him and begin their return trip to Galilee without him. Upon noticing his absence, they return to Jerusalem and find him in the temple engaging the Jewish leaders in discussion. In the exchange that follows, Jesus declares: "Why were you looking for me? Didn't you know that it was necessary for me to be in my Father's house?" (2:49). They do not understand his words at the time, but the implication is that they later find extended meaning in the light of his eventual ministry. For a second time, Luke notes that Mary treasures these things and remembers them (2:19, 51), perhaps implying her being a source of some of this tradition, although such cannot be verified.

The Temptation of Jesus

Luke alone dates the beginning of John's ministry to the fifteenth year of Tiberius's reign (which would have been around 28 CE), and he notes that Jesus began his ministry around the time of his thirtieth year (3:1, 23). After being baptized by John, Jesus returns from the Jordan filled with the Holy Spirit and is led into the wilderness to be tempted. Whereas Mark only describes the testing in a couple of verses, Matthew and Luke add nearly a dozen—many of them with word-for-word similarities (Mark 1:12-13; Matt 4:1-11; Luke 4:1-13). While the first temptation in Matthew and Luke is nearly identical, the second and third are reversed in their order. If they shared a common source (such as hypothetical Q, as most scholars have believed) the question then arises: which might have been the original order, Matthew's or Luke's? Whatever the case, Luke's rendering of Jesus's three temptations shows his mastery of three threats to his authentic mission.

---

1. Interestingly, the *Infancy Gospel of Thomas* fills in the gap between Jesus's infancy and his trip to Jerusalem as a twelve-year-old with several folkloric legends of what the boy Jesus might have said and done.

First, Jesus is tempted by the devil to be *relevant*—to turn stones into bread and meet the needs of human hunger (4:3-4); he overcomes the deceiver by appealing to Deuteronomy 8:3 and God's sustaining word: "It's written, *People won't live only by bread.*" Next, he is tempted to be *powerful*—to have sway over all the kingdoms of the earth if he will but worship the devil (4:5-8); Jesus responds citing Deuteronomy 10:20: "It's written, *You will worship the Lord your God and serve only him.*" The third test in Luke involves the temptation to be *sensational*—to cast himself off the highest pinnacle of the temple to be rescued by angels, lest his foot be dashed against a stone (and here the devil quotes scripture: Ps 91:11-12); Jesus slaps scripture back, citing Deuteronomy 6:16: "*Don't test the Lord your God*" (4:9-12). While the tempting of Jesus to be relevant, powerful, and sensational is sketched in a more realistic setting within John's rendering of the feeding of the five thousand (the only miracle included in all four Gospels—also featuring the bandying of scripture back and forth, John 6:1-66), Matthew's and Luke's accounts address the very issues most central to the secrecy motif in Mark. Jesus's messianic agency is directed toward the furthering of God's redemptive purposes, not aimed at fulfilling popularistic expectations—sometimes instead challenging them directly.

Jesus's Inaugural Declaration and His Mission to the Poor

Luke also adds theological content to Jesus's rejection at his hometown, Nazareth, in Mark 6. Here and elsewhere Luke takes liberties with Mark's order, crafting the narrative to suit his own purposes. Rather than showing Jesus's ministry beginning with the calling of disciples, exorcisms, and the healing of Peter's mother-in-law (cf. Mark 1:16-31), Luke features Jesus preaching in the synagogue and reading from Isaiah 61:1-2, declaring: "Today, this scripture has been fulfilled just as you heard it" (Luke 4:16-21).

The Spirit of the Lord is upon me,
> because the Lord has anointed me.
He has sent me to preach good news to the poor,
> to proclaim release to the prisoners
> and recovery of sight to the blind,
> to liberate the oppressed,
> and to proclaim the year of the Lord's favor. (4:18-19)

In so doing, Luke declares his understanding of Jesus's ministry and what he came to do. Likewise, this is to be the mission of the church, as laid out in Acts: the Spirit of the Lord is upon Jesus the Anointed One (the Messiah/Christ), the gospel is preached to the poor (not just the poor in spirit), humanity is liberated (inwardly and outwardly), the blind receive their sight (spiritually and physically), and the time of Jubilee (when all debts are forgiven) is come.

A special feature of Luke's concern is his understanding of Jesus's mission to the poor. When John the Baptist's disciples report back to him about Jesus, asking if he is the one to come or whether they should look for another, Jesus sends this word back:

> Go, report to John what you have seen and heard. Those who were blind are able to see. Those who were crippled now walk. People with skin diseases are cleansed. Those who were deaf now hear. Those who were dead are raised up. And good news is preached to the poor. Happy is anyone who doesn't stumble along the way because of me. (Luke 7:22-23; cf. also Matt 11:2-6)

Jesus introduces the parable of the great supper in Luke 17:7-14 (cf. Matt 22:1-14; Luke 14:15-24) with a direct teaching on humility, which includes the injunction to invite the poor, those who cannot repay, in addition to the crippled, lame, and blind, to a lunch or a dinner (v. 13). It is precisely the non-transactional aspect of a gracious gift that extends divine love; that is the point. And in Luke's parable of the rich man and Lazarus (16:19-31), those who have much in this life will long for the possession of the righteous in the afterlife, pleading for mercy. Luke includes the parable of the rich man (a "ruler" in Luke 18:18-23) which is also in Mark and Matthew (Mark 10:17-22; he is "young" in Matt 19:16-22), and in all three renderings, upon the command of Jesus to sell all his possessions and give the money to the poor, the man goes away sad because he is very rich. Luke takes this parable seriously and includes other emphases along that line. Luke also includes the story of the poor widow giving two copper coins; giving out of her poverty is more virtuous than the rich giving out of their abundance (Luke 21:1-4; also in Mark 12:41-44).

One of Luke's especially memorable narratives is that of Zacchaeus, a leader among the tax collectors (Luke 19:1-10). Being of short stature, he climbs up a sycamore tree to see Jesus passing by; Jesus shares table fellowship with him in his home, which causes consternation over his being a guest of a "sinner." Table fellowship, of course, was an extension of grace and acceptance of another. Around a meal together, enmity was ended and differences reconciled. The psalmist references a prepared table in the presence of one's enemies as a reconciling event (Ps 23:5), so when Jesus dines with tax collectors and sinners (even before they repent), this offends those seeking to keep Jewish purity codes. In the Zacchaeus story, the tax collector repents, and he is also willing to make restitution. He willingly gives half his possessions to the poor, and if he has cheated anyone, he promises to repay them fourfold. At this Jesus declares: "Today, salvation has come to this household because he too is a son of Abraham. The [Son of Man] came to seek and save the lost" (19:9-10).

The Sermon on the Plain

Luke's concern for the poor shows up clearly in his presentation of the Beatitudes, which are delivered not upon a mount but on a plain (Luke 6:17-49). Of the 107 verses in Matthew 5:3–7:27, Luke includes only 37 in this setting, although he does include about 40 other verses in other chapters (especially Luke 11–16). While the degree to which Luke and Matthew made use of a common source for this material is uncertain, several things are clear about Luke's rendering. First, his presentation is far less Jewish and more universal in its orientation. Rather than focusing on how to interpret Jewish laws, Luke's Jesus discusses how to behave as God's children—emphasizing the Golden Rule (6:27-38) and how to avoid self-deception: get the log out of your own eye first before seeking to remove the speck in the eye of another (6:39-42). Second, only four blessings are mentioned rather than Matthew's nine, although four negative sayings are added (6:20-26). Third, rather than blessing *the poor in spirit*, Luke's Jesus blesses *the poor*. There's a big difference there, especially for the economically poor.

Happy Are You . . .

- who are poor, because God's kingdom is yours.
- who hunger now, because you will be satisfied.
- who weep now, because you will laugh.
- when people hate you, reject you, insult you, and condemn your name as evil because of the [Son of Man]. Rejoice when that happens! Leap for joy because you have a great reward in heaven. Their ancestors did the same things to the prophets.

85

That being the case, the Beatitudes in Luke have far more of a social-concern feeling to them over and against their spiritualized thrust in Matthew. Likewise, rather than levy seven woes against scribes and Pharisees, Luke's Jesus slams the rich and those who have plenty, reminding them that the tables will be turned in due time. To take Luke's Jesus seriously is to embrace material reversals of socioeconomic status, not just attitudinal changes. In that sense, Luke's Jesus is quite radical socially, calling for building on a strong foundation of social action among his authentic followers.

How Terrible for You . . .

- who are rich, because you have already received your comfort.

- who have plenty now, because you will be hungry.

- who laugh now, because you will mourn and weep.

- when all speak well of you. Their ancestors did the same things to the false prophets.

Lord, Teach Us to Pray . . .

While separated from the Beatitudes by several chapters, Luke's Jesus also gives his disciples the Lord's Prayer (11:1-4), although it is again shorter than the version in Matthew and less embellished.[2] Rather than contrast authentic praying with praying as a public show (Matt 6:5-8), the prayer Luke's Jesus offers his followers addresses their request for him to teach them how to pray. Appreciating both motives is valuable, but Luke's presentation offers helpful insight for understanding and practicing transformative spirituality after the pattern of Jesus's instruction. Note the elements of prayer here involved: praise and adoration, dedication and intercession, petition and thanksgiving, forgiveness received and extended, and protection and guidance—central aspects of spiritual formation on any account.

Of course, this is not the only exemplary prayer in Luke; in addition to the prayer of the contrite tax collector (also known as "the Jesus Prayer" in some traditions—a prayer for mercy), the beginning of Luke's Gospel also provides several patterns of exemplary prayer and doxology. While the

---

2. Phrases in Matthew's version of the Lord's Prayer not found in Luke include: "who is in heaven," "so that your will is done on earth as it's done in heaven," and "but rescue us from the evil one." The traditional fuller ending, "For thine is the kingdom, and the power, and the glory, for ever. Amen" (Matt 6:13), is not found in the earliest manuscripts but represents a later addition.

hymnic prayers of the birth narrative reflect the worship life of early Jewish Christianity, they have historically become patterns for Christian worship material in later generations, and rightly so. Prayers of individuals in Luke's narrative and parables also are presented in exemplary ways—some positive and some negative.

Prayers Offered in Luke

- Mary's Magnifying the Lord (the *Magnificat* hymn, 1:46-55)

- Zechariah's Prophecy of Blessing (the *Benedictus* hymn, 1:68-79)

- The Angels' Glory to God in the Highest (the *Gloria in Excelsis* hymn, 2:14)

- Simeon's Prayer of Salvation (the *Nunc Dimittis* hymn, 2:29-32)

- Prayers for Mercy by the Rich Man ("Father Abraham," 16:24, 27-28, 30)

- The Prayer of the Proud Pharisee (self-righteous boasting, 18:11-12)

- The Prayer of the Contrite Tax Collector ("The Jesus Prayer," 18:13)

In addition to these prayers and Jesus's teachings on prayer, Luke also features five prayers offered by Jesus. Other than the Lord's Prayer, these are but one or two sentences each in length. The first prayer, a doxology, introduces the intimacy of the Father-Son relationship, which is also cited in Matthew and developed more extensively in John—speaking of the Father-Son relationship in an intimate way (Luke 10:22; Matt 11:27; John 3:35; 7:29; 10:14-15; 13:3; 17:2, 25). The others reflect expressions of Jesus's desire before the Father. Each of these is worthy of study, and together they present something of Luke's own theological understanding of Jesus and his exemplary role in the prayer life of his followers.

Prayers of Jesus in Luke

- Jesus's Praise and the Father-Son Relationship (10:21; cf. Matt 11:25-26):

- ○ "I praise you, Father, Lord of heaven and earth, because you've hidden these things from the wise and intelligent and shown them to babies. Indeed, Father, this brings you happiness."

- The Lord's Prayer for His Disciples to Follow (the Lord's Prayer, 11:2-4; cf. Matt 6:9-13; John 17:1-26):

  - ○ "Father, uphold the holiness of your name.
    Bring in your kingdom.
    Give us the bread we need for today.
    Forgive us our sins,
        for we also forgive everyone who has wronged us.
    And don't lead us into temptation."

- Jesus's Prayer on the Mount of Olives (22:42; cf. Mark 14:36; Matt 26:39; John 12:27; 18:11):

  - ○ "Father, if it's your will, take this cup of suffering away from me. However, not my will but your will must be done."

- Jesus's First Prayer on the Cross (23:34; cf. Acts 7:60):

  - ○ "Father, forgive them, for they don't know what they're doing."

- Jesus's Second Prayer on the Cross (23:46):

  - ○ "Father, into your hands I entrust my life."

An interesting feature of Jesus's prayers and teachings on prayer in Luke is that elements of the Lord's Prayer in Luke 11:2-4 are all also found in other texts. Praise and adoration are featured centrally in the hymns of the birth narrative and Jesus's outlining the Father-Son relationship (10:21-22); the restoration of the kingdom is actualized within and among Jesus's followers (17:21); the one who asks receives (11:5-10); the one who forgives is thus forgiven (6:37), and Jesus forgives his executioners on the cross (23:34); Jesus prays for his followers and admonishes them to be in prayer about the trials they are about to face (22:40, 46). In that sense, Jesus answers his disciples' request to teach them to pray not simply by telling them how to do it; he shows them how, as well.

. . . and Jesus Set His Face toward Jerusalem . . .

A striking turning point in Luke's narrative comes at 9:51, reporting that Jesus "set his face to go to Jerusalem" (NRSV). As a result, those he meets in Samaria want to have nothing to do with him, and James and John offer to call down fire from heaven to consume them, but Jesus sets them straight (9:53-56; they are called "sons of thunder" in Mark 3:17). Between Jesus's determining to go to Jerusalem in 9:51 and his arrival at Jerusalem in 19:11 we have most of Luke's distinctive teachings and miracles of Jesus—a Jesus who ministers *on the way* to Jerusalem. Luke also adds a comment on the special place of Jerusalem in his response to the Pharisees' warning that Herod is out to kill him (13:31-33), as Jesus declares that it is "impossible for a prophet to be killed outside of Jerusalem." Thus, it is not only in Mark that Jesus is portrayed as predicting his death in Jerusalem and rising on the third day as central to his mission; it also emerges in other gospel traditions, and distinctively so.

Because of the coherence of the material in these ten chapters, scholars such as B. H. Streeter supposed that this unit of material represents a pre-crafted L-Source, which Luke has supposedly incorporated into his storyline. However, this section has a fair number of similarities and overlaps with Mark and Matthew (and even some with John), so it is not exclusively Lukan material. Thus, a stronger inference is that Luke has taken some liberty to construct his own presentation of Jesus's ministry as a travel narrative, arranging familiar and distinctive material according to his own interests. If a gatherer of L-tradition material could have put the content of Luke 10–19 together, so could Luke have done so as a creative narrator. As all but one of the sixteen parables and the four miracle stories distinctive to Luke are found within this travelogue section, Luke's distinctive contribution is here apparent.

Parables Unique to Luke

- The Two Debtors (7:41-43)
- The Good Samaritan (10:30-35)
- The Shameless Neighbor (11:5-8)
- The Rich Fool (12:16-21)
- The Returning Master (12:36-38)
- The Narrow Gate (13:24-30)
- The Best Seats at the Table (14:7-11)

- The Fool at Work (14:28-30)
- The Fool at War (14:31-32)
- The Lost Coin (15:8-10)
- The Prodigal Son (15:11-32)
- The Dishonest Manager (16:1-9)
- The Rich Man and Lazarus (16:19-31)
- The Servant Who Serves without Reward (17:7-10)
- The Unjust Judge and the Persistent Widow (18:1-8)
- The Pharisee and the Tax Collector (18:9-14)

Luke's distinctive presentation of Jesus's miracles is also worth noting. First, Luke adds several miracles that are in neither Mark nor Matthew. One of these involves raising from the dead the son of the widow from Nain (7:11-17)—an event a bit more dramatic than the raising from death's door the daughter of Jairus (8:40-56). Another healing is of a woman who has had an infirmity for eighteen years; it is the Sabbath, but Jesus lays his hands upon her, and she becomes well (13:10-17). After all, if the Sabbath would not be blemished by rescuing an ox from a ditch or a well, why should it be a problem to heal sick humans on the Sabbath (13:15; 14:5)? This motif continues with the next healing miracle—the healing of a man with dropsy, or swelling (14:1-6). Finally, the healing of the ten lepers features the gratitude of one person among the ten, and he is a *Samaritan* (17:11-19).

A second thing to note about Luke's miracles is that some of them are in Matthew but not in Mark. In addition to common sayings materials, this fact suggests to most scholars that Luke and Matthew shared a common source besides Mark, a *Quelle* (the German word for "source") source or a "Q" document, although no actual text of such a source is known to exist. However this material might have come together, here are some of its features: similarities between Luke and Matthew that are not in Mark.

Double Tradition Material (in Matthew and Luke, but Not in Mark)

- The Ministry of John the Baptist (Luke 3:7-9; 7:18-35—Matt 3:7-10; 11:2-19)
- The Temptation of Jesus (Luke 4:1-13—Matt 4:1-11)
- Beatitudes (Luke 6:20-23—Matt 5:3-12)

- Other Sayings (love enemies, judge not, be hearers and doers, the house on the rock; Luke 6:27-49—Matt 5:38-48; 7:1-27)

- The Healing of the Capernaum Servant (Luke 7:1-10—Matt 8:5-13)

- The Cost of Discipleship (Luke 9:57-62; 14:26-27; 17:33—Matt 8:19-22; 10:37-39)

- Jesus Sends His Disciples Out on a Mission (Luke 10:2-16—Matt 9:37-38; 10:9-15; 11:21-23)

- The Father-Son Relationship (Luke 10:21-24—Matt 11:25-27; 13:16-17)

- The Lord's Prayer (Luke 11:2-4—Matt 6:9-13)

- Answers to Prayer (Luke 11:9-13—Matt 7:7-11)

- Beelzebul and the Finger of God (Luke 11:14-26—Matt 12:22-30, 43-45)

- The Sign of Jonah (Luke 11:29-32—Matt 12:38-42)

- The Single Eye (Luke 11:34-36—Matt 6:22-23)

- Woes to Pharisees (Luke 11:39-54—Matt 23:2-36)

- Fearless Confession (Luke 12:2-9—Matt 10:26-33)

- Earthly Anxiety and Heavenly Treasures (Luke 12:22-34—Matt 6:19-21, 25-34)

- Watchfulness, Divisions, the Times, Accusers (Luke 12:35-59—Matt 24:42-51; 10:34-36; 16:2-3; 5:25-26)

- Leaven, the Narrow Gate (Luke 13:20-30—Matt 13:33; 7:13-14, 22-23; 8:11-12)

- Lament over Jerusalem (Luke 13:34-35—Matt 23:37-39)

- The Lost Sheep (Luke 15:1-7—Matt 18:12-14)

- Two Masters, the Law, Forgiveness (Luke 16:13, 16-17; 17:3-4—Matt 5:18; 6:24; 11:12-13; 18:15, 21-22)

- The Day of the Son of Man (Luke 17:22-37—Matt 24:37-42)

- The Talents (Luke 19:11-27—Matt 25:14-30)

Here we have a considerable body of material—nearly a quarter of Luke and Matthew, but material that is not in Mark. Much of it involves word-for-word similarities, so a literary connection of some sort is likely. The material includes primarily sayings and parables, but it also includes some narrative and miracle material. It begins with John the Baptist, emphasizes the cost of discipleship and faithful living, and concludes with the anticipated return of the Son of Man. Notice there is no Passion narrative or resurrection account. As a result, if this material might reflect one of Luke's sources, it could provide a window into the earlier stages of gospel traditions, implying closer proximity to the ministry of Jesus and early preaching about it. Luke also coincides with Matthew in over seven hundred incidents of "minor agreements" (that is, adding or omitting one or two words in comparison to Mark), but those features cannot be explained as effectively by means of inferring a distinctive shared source; they might imply that Luke used some form of Matthew as one of his sources.

Another thing to notice about Luke's material is that at least six dozen times he departs from Mark and coincides with John. While some of the details added by Luke are rather incidental, others are quite significant. Luke adds details, units of material, aspects of Jesus's teachings, associative links, and a miracle found otherwise only in John; he changes the order and presentations of events in ways that cohere with John; he at times seeks to harmonize Mark and John; and, he adds Johannine theological content (especially regarding women, Samaritans, and the Holy Spirit). In my view, this reflects his awareness and use of the Johannine tradition—probably in the oral stages of its development.

As with all Gospel writers, Luke's presentation of Jesus's ministry is ordered first by his own understanding of what happened and why it is significant. Luke also has in mind what his audiences need to know, and his own theological perspectives affect the ways he tells the story. He makes use of diverse sources of historical information (as declared in Luke 1:1-4), some of which is written (at least Mark) and some of which is attributed to "eyewitnesses and servants of the word" (*logos*—1:2). Whether such sources included a shared source with Matthew (a *Quelle*-source) or an earlier form of Matthew, or even the formative Johannine tradition, scholars will debate. Whatever the case, Luke presents his own orderly account of a Jesus worth following as savior of the world. That applies to "most honorable Theophilus" and to lovers of God everywhere.

92

III. The Message of Luke

Like Mark and Matthew, the Gospel of Luke tells the story of Jesus, who ministered in Galilee, healed the sick, liberated the inwardly oppressed, taught about the kingdom of God, and traveled to Jerusalem where he was tried, maltreated, crucified, and buried, whereupon God raised him from the dead on the third day. He appeared to his disciples, and Luke makes special reference also to Jesus's ascending into heaven. As a general way of describing Jesus's teaching and mission, he often concludes or begins a unit with a general statement such as "He welcomed them, spoke to them about God's kingdom, and healed those who were sick" (Luke 9:11), presenting a portrait of Jesus quite similar to those in Mark and Matthew. Luke's characteristic features are also worth noting, as they convey a sense of his particular message along several distinctive lines.

Samaritans and Goodness

Especially when viewed against Jesus's commissioning his disciples in Matthew, saying, "Don't go among the Gentiles or into a Samaritan city" (Matt 10:5), it is striking that Luke's Jesus ministers among them as he travels through the area (9:51-56; 17:11; cf. John 4:4). Of course, some of the Samaritans' appraisals of Jesus are less than positive due to his travel to Jerusalem, and tensions between Samaritans and Jews are noted in the story (cf. John 4:9). Nonetheless, the healed Samaritan leper alone demonstrates exemplary gratitude among the ten (Luke 17:16), and the hospitable Samaritan in the parable (10:30-37) exemplifies what it means to be a good neighbor—both pointed examples intended to disturb the self-righteous and the ethnocentric.

The subsequent mission to Samaria undertaken by Peter, John, and Philip in Acts 8:1-25 furthers the effective mission to Samaria already begun in John 4:39-42, and this also fulfills Jesus's prophecy in Acts 1:8, that his disciples would be his witnesses in all Judea *and* Samaria (cf. Acts 9:31; 15:3). Followers of Jesus are thus called to transcend historic divisions and to be agents of grace and reconciliation across ethnic, religious, and political boundaries at home and abroad. If Samaritans can be receptive to the gospel, becoming good neighbors and grateful recipients of healing, these reminders point the way forward instead of pointing the finger.

The Favoring of Women in Luke

Another emphasis of Luke's distinctive material includes the favoring of women. The birth narratives center on Elizabeth, Mary, and Anna, and each of them plays a pivotal role in God's redeeming of humanity. This builds empathy with the situation of women related to barrenness, pregnancy, childbirth, widowhood—all potential means of glorifying God and furthering the kingdom. Luke adds the gratitude of a "sinful" woman to the anointing of Jesus (7:36-50), the healing of a woman with an eighteen-year infirmity (13:11-13), Jesus's special relationship to Mary and Martha (10:38-42), the plight of grieving women (23:27-31), and the post-resurrection reports of women at the tomb encouraging the apostles (24:22-24). Mary Magdalene, Joanna, and Susanna provide material means of support to Jesus and the Twelve (8:1-3); women are *not* insignificant in Luke.

In addition to narratives featuring women in Luke, women are also mentioned in parables as central characters. In the parable of the woman and her coin, she searches diligently until she finds the coin that is lost—just as the shepherd leaves the ninety-nine and searches for the one lost sheep (15:4-10). If God or Jesus may be associated with the tender of the sheep, should God or Jesus be associated with the woman? If so, this presents God in a female way. And, in the parable of the persistent woman, the woman who continues to ask for justice from the judge will finally receive a hearing—simply because of her resolve (18:1-8). Thus, the widow plays an exemplary role in the narrative, inviting others to follow her resilient example. While Luke includes four times as many references to women as does Mark, citing several that are also in Matthew and John, women are also paired alongside men in Luke.

Pairs of Women and Men in Luke

- The angel Gabriel appears to Zechariah; the angel Gabriel appears to Mary (1:8-23, 26-38)

- Mary sings a hymn of praise; Zechariah sings a hymn of praise (1:46-55, 68-79)

- Simeon sees Jesus as the fulfillment of prophecy in the temple; Anna prophesies about Jesus in the temple (2:25-35, 36-38)

- The widow of Zarephath in Sidon was reached by Elijah; Naaman the Syrian leper was reached by Elisha (4:25-26, 27)

- The Samaritan is a good example; Mary is a good example (10:25-37, 38-42)

- Persistently a neighbor asks for bread; a widow asks for justice (11:5-8; 18:1-8)

- A woman in the crowd shouts: "Happy is the mother who gave birth to you and who nursed you"; a man at dinner declares: "Happy are those who will feast in God's kingdom" (11:27; 14:15)

- Remember Lot; remember Lot's wife (17:28-31, 32-33)[3]

The Gospel Comes to the Lost

During his meeting with Zacchaeus the tax collector (Luke 19:9-10), Jesus declares: "Today, salvation has come to this household because he too is a son of Abraham. The [Son of Man] came to seek and save the lost." Several things emerge in considering this passage. First, note the way that Jesus seeks out the alienated man even before his life has changed. Jesus dines with sinners in Mark and Matthew, but he makes special efforts to do so in Luke. After calling Levi to follow him, Levi throws a party in his home, and there Jesus dines with tax gatherers and others; it is the sick who need a doctor, not the well (5:27-31). Jesus is thus accused of being "a glutton and a drunk, a friend of tax collectors and sinners" (7:34), but then he is invited to dinner at the home of a Pharisee, where a sinful woman anoints his feet and is forgiven of her sins (7:36-50; cf. also 11:37-38). As tax gatherers and sinners cluster around Jesus, the Pharisees and legal experts retort with disgust: "This man welcomes sinners and eats with them" (15:1-2). In all these situations, Jesus humanizes the other and extends God's grace in the sharing of table fellowship. Zacchaeus is thus not simply a despised tax collector; he too is a child of Abraham. Therefore, in dining with and accepting both the outcasts and the insiders, Jesus indeed seeks and saves the lost.

A second thing to note is that what is honorable to God is authentic contriteness and a humbled appraisal of one's condition. The parable of the tax collector and the Pharisee shows the contrast between two attitudes among those praying in the temple. The Pharisee is pleased with his own righteousness, while the tax collector cannot even lift his eyes. Rather, he

---

3. For a fuller list, including Luke's engagement of Mark and Q narratives, see Felix Just, "Story Pairs in Luke's Gospel," Electronic New Testament Educational Resources, last modified December 31, 2012, http://catholic-resources.org/Bible/Luke-Pairs.htm.

strikes his chest, asking God to be merciful to him, a sinner. In Jesus's estimation, the latter went away justified; the former did not (18:9-14). "All who lift themselves up will be brought low, and those who make themselves low will be lifted up." This line repeats the conclusion of the earlier parable of the table honor (14:7-11). There Jesus instructs his followers to take the lowest seat at the table rather than a higher one; it is better to be invited to the head of the table than to be asked to step aside, having overreached one's place. And, at the Last Supper, Jesus instructs his followers to serve one another rather than to argue over who is greatest (22:24-30). Therefore, around table fellowship God's grace is extended and received; humility leads to grace, and grace leads to humility. Further, the extension of grace—undeserved love—is presented as authentically humbling and transformative. Therefore, in witnessing the great catch of fish, even Peter is smitten with conviction: "Leave me, Lord, for I'm a sinner!" (5:8). Yet Jesus calls him and invites him to fish for people.

This leads to a third insight regarding Jesus's mission to seek and save the lost, featured especially clearly in the three parables in Luke 15 regarding the lost sheep, the lost coin, and the lost son. At the conclusion of each of these stories, the final point emphasizes the joy in heaven and on earth over just one sinner who repents (15:4-7, 8-10) or one lost person who is found (15:11-32). In the context of Jesus's having been criticized by the legal experts and Pharisees over his dining with sinners and the undeserving, the central target of the third parable is neither the repentant son nor the gracious father; it is the bewildered older brother, who despite playing by the rules has not felt celebrated by the father. While his faithfulness is not disparaged, the point is that it is especially the responsible and the faithful who should be celebrating the return of the prodigal. After all, the father declares to all the faithful, "You are always with me, and everything I have is yours. But we had to celebrate and be glad because this brother of yours was dead and is alive. He was lost and is found" (15:31-32). Heaven celebrates such redemption, and so should all who are authentically concerned with the ways and workings of God.

God's Kingdom Is *entos humōn*—Among/Within You

One of the puzzling texts of Luke is 17:20-21, where, after Pharisees ask Jesus when God's kingdom is coming, he replies, "God's kingdom isn't coming with signs that are easily noticed. Nor will people say, 'Look, here it is!' or

'There it is!' Don't you see? God's kingdom is already *among you*."[4] Therefore, the question is whether the eschatological establishment of God's reign in the world happens by means of the transformation of the individual, one person at a time, or involves the collective gathering, changed persons who will bring about change in the world as a community of the new age. Then again, both may be true, and arguable, when considering the overall message of Luke.

Affirming the corporate sense, the social concern that Jesus advocates in Luke is seen in terms of eschatology. God's saving-redeeming leadership will be actualized by his faithful followers who care for others the way God cares for all. Followers of Jesus are called to sell their possessions and give the money to the poor (Luke 12:33; 18:22); they are to show mercy to the poor as extensions of God's love in the world, as this embraces the mission of Jesus (4:18; 6:20). Furthering the kingdom happens as people work together in ministry teams, challenging the ways of the world and bringing about a more ordered and just society—in the name of God's love and mercy. This involves embracing Samaritans and whoever might be considered "the other" within a social context; it involves respecting the elderly and children, seeing them as full members of the kingdom; it involves celebrating the leadership and service of women as well as men, as that is the example Jesus set. Furthering God's dynamic reign happens collectively in the changing of society for the better.

However, the individual sense of *entos humōn* is also supported by the overall Gospel of Luke, so the power of personal transformation cannot be ignored. When a Pharisee invites Jesus to dinner, a discussion ensues over purity (11:37-54). Upon noticing that Jesus does not wash his hands in the prescribed way before the meal, the Pharisee is astonished, but Jesus replies (vv. 39-41): "Now, you Pharisees clean the outside of the cup and platter, but your insides are stuffed with greed and wickedness. Foolish people! Didn't the one who made the outside also make the inside? Therefore, give to those in need from the core of who you are and you will be clean all over." After all, a good tree produces good fruit and a bad tree bad fruit—from one's inner self (6:43-45). And the key to being the good soil, receptive to the seed of the gospel, is to have a good heart (8:15). In these ways, the power of the kingdom is inward, contrasted to looking for external deliverance from those claiming to

---

4. "Among you" is the rendering in the CEB, NJB, and NRSV; the KJV, ASV, and older NIV (with a footnote referencing the other reading) translate it *"within you."* Here the Greek can be rendered fittingly in either direction (the ESV and the RSV go with "in the midst of you" and the newer NIV and the NASV "in your midst"); factors include the other occurrence of *entos* in the New Testament being translated "inside of the cup" (Matt 23:26) and this particular "you" being plural in Greek.

be the Messiah/Christ, calling "Lo, here; lo, there" (17:21). Thus, the power of the kingdom in Luke is within you *and* among you; it is in your midst.

The Holy Spirit and Prayer

Luke also features with prominence the work of the Holy Spirit and the power of prayer. It is by the Holy Spirit that most of the events in the birth narrative take place: John the Baptist will be filled with the Holy Spirit (1:15), the Holy Spirit will overshadow Mary as she conceives (1:35), Elizabeth is also filled with the Holy Spirit (1:41), Zechariah is filled with the Holy Spirit before making his prophetic expression of praise (1:67), and the Holy Spirit rests on Simeon, promising he will not taste death before seeing the Lord's Messiah (2:25-26). While John baptizes with water, Jesus will baptize with the Holy Spirit and fire, and while Jesus is praying the Holy Spirit descends in the form of a dove at his baptism (3:16, 21-22).

Luke notes that, filled with the Holy Spirit, Jesus is led into the wilderness for his testing (4:1), and overflowing with the Holy Spirit's joy Jesus declares the Son's mutual knowing of the Father (10:21-22; cf. Matt 11:25-27). Rather than good gifts (Matt 7:11), the persistent petitioner will receive the Holy Spirit (Luke 11:13), and while Luke follows Mark on the unforgivability of blasphemy against the Holy Spirit (Mark 3:28-30; Matt 12:31-32; Luke 12:10-12), he adds a reference to the Holy Spirit as the source of guidance and help during times of trial and persecution: "The Holy Spirit will tell you at that very moment what you must say" (12:12; cf. Mark 13:9-13; Matt 24:9-14; Luke 21:12-19).

Again, Luke's accentuation of the Holy Spirit's empowering work bears impressive similarity to the work of the *paraklētos* as the Holy Spirit sent by the Father and the Son in John (John 14:16-17, 26; 15:26; 16:7, 13; 20:22), and the connection between prayer and the Holy Spirit continues to be expanded in Acts (Luke 3:21-22; Acts 4:31; 8:15-17). Prayer is thus also a central part of Luke's message and presented in several ways. First, people are presented as authentically praying in a variety of contexts: Zechariah and the assembly in the temple (Luke 1:10-13), Anna in the temple (2:37), John's disciples as a regular discipline (5:33), Jesus and his disciples up the mountain (9:28), and Jesus insisting the temple should be a house of prayer, not a den for crooks (Isa 56:7; Mark 11:17; Matt 21:13; Luke 19:46). Jesus is featured many times as praying in Luke: he prays before the heavens open and the Holy Spirit descends (3:21-22); after performing miracles Jesus withdraws to a solitary place to pray (5:15-16; 9:18; 11:1); Jesus prays on a mountain before calling his disciples (6:12-13) and before his transfiguration (9:28-30). On the night of his arrest, Jesus goes out to pray with his disciples on the Mount of Olives, praying earnestly—even sweating great drops of blood—and exhorting also his disciples to be praying instead of sleeping (22:39-46). He also declares that he has been praying for Simon (22:31-32), and he instructs his disciples to pray for those who mistreat them (6:28; Matt 5:44).

The right way to pray, according to Luke, is with authenticity and persistence. Again, the advance of the kingdom does not depend on popularity or the wiles of the crowd; rather, Jesus shows a pattern of seeking communion with God in solitude. In Luke's view, people need to "pray continuously and not . . . be discouraged" (18:1). Those who seek find, and those who ask receive. In conjunction with the seven featured prayers and the five prayers of Jesus in the Gospel of Luke, meaningful elements of prayer may be said to include the following.

Meaningful Elements of Prayer in Luke

- Praise and Adoration
- Thanksgiving and Gratitude
- Humbled Dedication
- Intercession on Behalf of Others
- Petition for One's Own Needs
- Forgiveness Extended and Requested
- Supplication for Strength and Protection
- Guidance and Expectancy

The message of Luke thus features Jesus as Lord and Christ, the exemplary savior of the world, who embraces the poor, regards Samaritans as neighbors, empathizes with women, heals the sick, and sets free the captives. Empowered by the Holy Spirit, the kingdom of God is actualized within and among Jesus's followers, and in following him they become servants of the world and one another. The power of prayer lies in authenticity and persistence, and following the assertions of Jesus in Mark, people's faith has made them well (Mark 5:34; 10:52; Luke 8:48; 17:19; 18:42).

IV. Engaging Luke

In coming to grips with the distinctive presentation of Jesus in each of the Gospels, particular emphases are worth engaging. Consider first how Luke's presentation of Jesus as the universal savior of the world, including a light to the Gentiles, might have been received by audiences in the late-first-century Gentile and Jewish worlds. Are there particular features that might be compelling in your view, and would those same features be compelling for audiences of later generations? If so, how so, and if not, why not?

A second question for engagement involves the social concerns exemplified by Luke's Jesus. What might good news to the poor, to women, to Samaritans, to tax collectors, and to Pharisees have meant to people back then, and why did Jesus share table fellowship with them? That being the case, what would it mean today for followers of Jesus to extend God's healing grace to disenfranchised or oppressed individuals and groups within our contexts? And as Jesus's followers today pray for the needs of those around them, might they also feel moved to become part of the means by which those prayers are answered? How might that relate to the kingdom of God being within them and among them?

Third, what might we learn from considering the presentation of prayer in the Gospel of Luke? Which positive examples seem worth emulating, and which negative examples should be avoided? Might Jesus's teaching and example regarding life-producing elements of prayer find practical application in terms of spirituality for today's readers? If so, how so, and if not, why not? If today's readers were to take one or two minutes (or as long as they need) on a daily basis to focus on each of the elements of meaningful prayer listed above, what difference might that make for present-day enrollees in the school of Christ?

Finally, what do we do with the fact of great numbers of similarities and differences among the Synoptic Gospels? Might word-for-word similarities suggest some sort of contact between literary or non-literary sources? If so, what might those connections look like? And what do we do with the differences—especially those found when we include the Gospel of John? Take a bit of time to look up several sets of passages, noting as many of the similarities and differences as you can. Then, record your impressions and your questions. Some of those may be addressed in the following excursus on plausible relations among the Gospels. Before that, though, look up and reflect upon these passages:

a) Matthew 4:1-11; Mark 1:12-13; Luke 4:1-13; John 6:26-66

b) Matthew 22:34-40; Mark 12:28-34; Luke 10:25-28

c) Matthew 5:1-12; Luke 6:20-23; John 13:17; 20:29

d) Matthew 16:13-20; Mark 8:27-30; Luke 9:18-21; John 6:67-71

e) Matthew 26:6-13; Mark 14:3-9; Luke 7:36-50; John 12:1-8

Now, if you care to, look up several subjects in Bible encyclopedias or dictionaries, either in print or online: "Synoptic Hypothesis," "Griesbach Hypothesis," "Markan Priority," "Q Hypothesis," "Two-Source Theory," "Farrer Hypothesis," and "Bi-Optic Hypothesis" and consider how any of these literary approaches to the Gospels might account for the fact of multiple similarities and differences. And how might any of them contribute to meaningful interpretation of the Gospels for today's readers?

A Bi-Optic Hypothesis—
A Theory of Gospel Relations

Matthew, Mark, and Luke are called "the Synoptic Gospels" for good reasons; they look alike (*syn* = similar; *optic* = eye, or view), but more importantly, they view the ministry of Jesus through a basically similar perspective. If John represents an independent perspective as an individuated Jesus tradition, however, the question is whether or how to include John among the Gospels in terms of its origin and development.[1] Further, if John knew any of the Synoptic traditions, or if they knew of John's tradition, might this account also for ways they converge and diverge? Convergence is a more telling sign of contact, but divergence might also have its own implications. The similarities and differences among the four canonical Gospels have been engaged and addressed from the second century CE until today, and they must be addressed analytically because of the complexity of the facts and the importance of the implications. If the Gospels present historical information about the Jesus of history, however, what do we do with the fact that they also present differences as well as similarities? If the Gospels are primarily the result of theological developments of early believers, what do we do with historical claims?

On these matters, over-simplistic traditional views are inadequate: "the Gospels represent four different perspectives of Jesus's followers—no problem—like seven blind men describing an elephant, the tail seems like a rope; the leg seems like a tree; the side seems like a wall; the ear seems like a fan . . ." Even by traditional accounts, Mark and Luke are not written by followers of Jesus, but by co-laborers with Paul; they never met Jesus. And the naked man fleeing without his clothes is *not* identified as the author of Mark (Mark 14:51-52), so just because that passage is found only in Mark does not imply Markan

---

1. D. Moody Smith's book on the subject provides the most helpful overview: *John Among the Gospels*, 2nd ed. (Columbia: University of South Carolina Press, 2001).

emphasis. If Mark was used by Matthew and Luke, it is an omitted passage, not an added one, suggesting its perceived insignificance by two of the three Gospels. Further, it is unlikely that both Matthew and John were written by eyewitnesses; Matthew does not claim to be, although John does. And the main reason for excluding Matthew from apostolic authorship is that it is too closely tied to Mark and does not display an independent memory of Jesus's ministry. Then again, John is rejected by critical scholars because it is too different from Mark—a striking contradiction among critical methodologies!

Thus, critical scholarship has developed a variety of flawed assumptions, though some of them for good reasons. Working with a "safer" approach to the sources of Gospels as "traditions" rather than apostles tends to diminish the role of eyewitnesses and apostolic preachers, whose contributions likely underlie all four traditions—and more.[2] Put otherwise, gospel traditions were *not* disembodied sets of ideas floating around in abstract form; they were early Christian leaders—some of them apostolic eyewitnesses, though not all of them—teaching and preaching about the Jesus they remembered or had heard about, applying the memory of Jesus's words and works to the needs of later audiences. That's what theology does, but that's also what historical reporting does; there is no such thing as historic irrelevance. Historical significance always implies inferred importance—essentially a subjective reality; otherwise, it would not be worth either remembering or repeating. Therefore, apostolic reporting and preaching certainly was a resource for all four of the canonical Gospels (and perhaps even some of the non-canonical ones—say, parts of Thomas), although other material is included as well. So, the challenge is to find ways forward in understanding how the Gospels came together, enabling meaningful interpretation in later generations.

Early Attempts at Understanding the Four Gospels and Their Relationships

While information is uneven, the history of Gospel usage in the second century displays several features. Mark was probably circulated among the

---

2. Luke states clearly that he is making use of written materials, as well as what he has heard from eyewitness testimony (Luke 1:1-4), and John's narrator claims to be incorporating eyewitness memory (John 19:34-35; 21:23-24) into his account. Two significant works challenging the diminishing of eyewitness memory in the study of gospel traditions are Richard Bauckham, *The Gospels and the Eyewitnesses; The Gospels as Eyewitness Testimony* (Grand Rapids: Eerdmans, 2008); and James D. G. Dunn, *Jesus Remembered; Christianity in the Making*, vol. 1 (Grand Rapids: Eerdmans, 2003).

churches in the final third of the first century, and it was added to by others—including several additional endings (most notably Mark 16:9-20). Although he claims to never have met any of the apostles of the Lord, Papias (active ca. 100–130 CE) sheds valuable light on how the Gospels were written—especially Mark, as perceived from a Johannine perspective. Scholars have failed to note the implications of what Papias has heard from John the Elder ("presbyter" means "elder") regarding Mark's composition and order—a detail that may also account for John's complementarity to (and differences from) Mark.

> "This also the presbyter said: Mark, having become the interpreter of Peter, wrote down accurately, though not in order, whatsoever he remembered of the things said or done by Christ. For he neither heard the Lord nor followed him, but afterward, as I said, he followed Peter, who adapted his teaching to the needs of his hearers, but with no intention of giving a connected account of the Lord's discourses, so that Mark committed no error while he thus wrote some things as he remembered them. For he was careful of one thing, not to omit any of the things which he had heard, and not to state any of them falsely." These things are related by Papias concerning Mark.
>
> But concerning Matthew he writes as follows: "So then Matthew wrote the oracles in the Hebrew language, and every one interpreted them as he was able." And the same writer uses testimonies from the first Epistle of John and from that of Peter likewise. And he relates another story of a woman, who was accused of many sins before the Lord, which is contained in the Gospel according to the Hebrews. These things we have thought it necessary to observe in addition to what has already been stated. (Eusebius, *Ecclesiastical History* 3.39.15-16)

While Eusebius describes Papias as a man of small intelligence (*Ecclesiastical History* 3.39.13), that comment was related to his millenarian apocalyptic views, not his views of gospel traditions, which Eusebius respects and furthers. Interestingly, if Papias's view is correct, Mark is not an eyewitness but a gatherer of apostolic preaching material—including Peter's but not limited to that resource. This would account for rough transitions in Mark's narrative and for its stringing stories and sayings together "like pearls on a string"—not necessarily representing a knowing chronology, but crafting a general progression from the beginning of Jesus's ministry to its climax in Jerusalem. More difficult to understand is his description of how Matthew was composed and used, as well as a reference to the Gospel to the Hebrews; the text of the woman caught in adultery was added to John's text later (John 7:53–8:11), and some ancient manuscripts include it in Luke.

Around the middle of the second century (160–170 CE, based on Justin's work), Tatian compiled a synthesis of the four Gospels, omitting the genealogies of Matthew and Luke and some problematic material. It was called the *Diatesseron* ("according to the four"), and this harmony of the Gospels was used for worship and teaching among the churches.

In response to Marcion's exclusion of some of the Gospels, Irenaeus called for a fourfold set—neither more nor less. As a means of distinguishing the character of the four Gospels, Irenaeus connects the four evangelists with the four living creatures of Revelation, who surround the throne of God and bear witness to the Lamb:

> For the first living creature, it says, was like a lion, signifying his active and princely and royal character; the second was like an ox, showing his sacrificial and priestly order; the third had the face of man, indicating very clearly his coming in human guise; and the fourth was like a flying eagle, making plain the giving of the Spirit who broods over the Church. Now the Gospels, in which Christ is enthroned, are like these.[3]

Therefore, in Christian writings and artwork the four Gospels are represented by these four creatures, leading to speculation as to each of the Gospels' development as a factor of image-associations, of which there were many differing combinations. Irenaeus associates the royal lion with John; Luke is associated with the ox, connected with the priestly sacrifices of Zechariah; Matthew, with the emphasis on its genealogy and humility, is associated with the image of a man; and Mark, with its prophetic thrust, is associated with an eagle. Other patristic writers, however, arrange the associations between the creatures and the Gospels differently—the most characteristic being to connect John with the eagle, soaring above the others with a transcendent perspective. By the end of the second century, Clement of Alexandria continued this John-Synoptic differentiation by regarding John as the "spiritual Gospel" written last, after the other Gospels had presented the "bodily aspects" (*sōmatika*) of Jesus's ministry. The mistranslation of *sōmatika* as "external facts" by A. C. McGiffert (Eusebius, *Ecclesiastical History* 6.14.7) has wrongly influenced modernist scholars to thus imagine the historical reporting of Jesus's ministry to be limited to the Synoptics, to the exclusion of John. As a result, John's mundane features have been largely overlooked by critical scholars, as have Synoptic theological features.

---

3. Irenaeus, *Work Against Heresies*, in *Early Christian Fathers*, trans. and ed. Cyril C. Richardson (London: SCM, 1953), 3.11.8.

In the fifth century, Augustine of Hippo interprets Matthew's placement in the canonical order to indicate that Matthew was written first among the Gospels, inferring that Mark abbreviated Matthew and was followed by Luke and John (*De Consensu Evangelistarum* 1.3-4). This allows also for the two Gospels attributed to apostles (Matthew and John) to enclose the other two, as parents embracing their children. As a result, Augustine departs from Irenaeus on the four creatures of Revelation 4:7. He thus connects Matthew with the royal lion, seeing that Matthew's Jesus is born of the lineage of David; Mark with the man, as it has no wondrous birth narrative; Luke with the sacrificial ox, repeating the Zachariah-priestly connection; whereas John "soars like an eagle above the clouds of human infirmity and gazes upon the light of the unchangeable truth with those keenest and steadiest eyes of the heart" (Augustine, *De Consensu Evangelistarum* 1.6). For over a thousand years the Augustinian view prevailed among interpreters, with Matthew thought to be the first of the Gospels to be written, Mark being seen as an abbreviation of Matthew, and John soaring like an eagle above the rest.

The Synoptic Hypothesis— A Modern Advance

In the late-eighteenth century, Johan Jakob Griesbach constructed a literary theory upon Augustine's approach, arguing *Matthean Priority*. What has come to be known as *the Griesbach Hypothesis* is that Luke built upon Matthew, and Mark summarized them both, explaining its brevity. Problems with this view, however, are many. First, Mark is the roughest among the canonical Gospels, and its language is the most choppy. Later editors tend to refine things stylistically instead of adding syntax problems. Second, several of Mark's theological problems seem to be ironed out by Matthew and Luke; in Mark 6:5 Jesus *could* do no miracles because of the unbelief of the Nazarenes, whereas Jesus simply did no miracles in Matthew 13:58. Luke omits that part altogether. Likewise, Mark's Messianic Secret motif is diminished in Matthew and Luke, whereas Peter's confession in Mark ("You are the Christ," Mark 8:29) is more fully developed in Luke ("the Christ sent from God," Luke 9:20) and Matthew ("You are the Christ, the Son of the living God," Matt 16:16). Third, if Mark knew of Matthew and Luke, why would he omit some of the most memorable sections—the birth of Jesus, the Beatitudes, the Lord's Prayer, appearance narratives, and so many of Jesus's words and works?

It makes far more sense to infer that Matthew and Luke added material to Mark than that Mark omitted such compelling material.

In the mid-nineteenth century, Heinrich Julius Holtzmann and others argued for *Markan Priority*, and this remains the leading view of most scholars since. It makes more sense to see Matthew and Luke as building upon Mark than Mark's being a rougher, more problematic abridgment. The result has been an expanded interest in Mark over the last several decades, whereas it had been neglected for centuries. If Mark was the first Gospel written, then Matthew and Luke were finalized later. With some 230 of their verses showing impressive similarity, while not found in Mark, an unknown source also came to be inferred. This led to the *Two-Source Hypothesis*, which was furthered by the designation of that source as "Q" by Johannes Weiss around the end of the nineteenth century (*Quelle* means "source" in German). Therefore, it was assumed that Matthew and Luke made use of two sources, one known and the other unknown, Mark and Q, and this continues to be the foundational explanation for how the similarities and differences among the Synoptic Gospels came to be.

In 1924, however, B. H. Streeter[4] not only affirmed Matthew's and Luke's uses of Mark and Q, but he also put forward a *Four-Source Hypothesis*, concluding that Matthew and Luke also used two other independent sources, M and L. Noting connections between James and Matthew, Streeter inferred that the M tradition had an earlier origin in Jerusalem, but that it was finalized in the Jewish-Christian center of Antioch, where other Christian tradition was added. Luke's tradition, Streeter argued, had its own development in a place such as Caesarea Maritima, combining with Q along the way, and drawing on other sources, including the Jewish-Christian worship material in the birth narrative. Streeter's four-source theory is more compelling to many than the two-source theory because it seeks also to account for the development of the distinctively Matthean and Lukan traditions. Of course, Luke may well have simply organized his independent material on his own rather than its having had an earlier stage of formalization, which Streeter called "Proto-Luke." Streeter does not do much with the Johannine tradition in relation to the other Gospels, though, other than to acknowledge its independent character and development.

One of the main problems with the *Q Hypothesis*, however, is that it does not account for many *minor agreements* between Matthew and Luke, where they add a word or two to a passage in which they otherwise seem

---

4. B. H. Streeter, *The Four Gospels: A Study of Origins* (London: Macmillan, 1924).

to be following Mark. If Q, by definition, had no overlap with Mark, those features remain unexplained. Also, given the fact that no manuscript evidence for Q exists, it is impossible to know if Q was one source or several, or whether it might have had any overlap with Mark if it did indeed exist. Was it an oral or a written tradition, or both? In 1964, William Farmer argued a *Two-Gospel Hypothesis*: that Matthew was written first, and that Mark built upon two Gospels, Matthew and Luke.[5] This theory still bears the problems of why Mark would leave out so many of the best parts of Matthew and Luke, including their shared double tradition—especially if it assumes that Mark reconciles Matthew and Luke.

In 1955, Austin Farrer wrote an important essay calling for dispensing with Q, and his argument has been taken up by Michael Goulder and Mark Goodacre, proposing that Luke made use of Mark and Matthew.[6] While most scholars still embrace either a two-source or a four-source approach, the *Farrer Hypothesis* has the advantages of affirming Markan priority, while still accounting for the minor agreements between Matthew and Luke as a factor of Luke's using Matthew instead of hypothetical Q. Then again, the places where Luke and Matthew do overlap suffer from multiple differences in sequence, and it might seem more plausible to infer that Matthew's highly teachable material was added to Q than to imagine Luke leaving it out, so this stance also has its limitations.

Most scholars accept some form of a Synoptic Hypothesis, and in my view, the strongest inferences in descending order are as follows.

✳ Key Elements of a Synoptic Hypothesis

- First, Mark was written as the first of the gospel narratives, and Matthew made use of about 90 percent of Mark, often in word-for-word ways.

- Second, Luke also made use of Mark, though not as closely as Matthew, drawing in about 60 percent of Mark into Luke's narrative.

- Third, the use of a common source such as Q by Matthew and Luke is highly plausible (at least an oral tradition with some

---

5. William Farmer, *The Synoptic Problem* (Dillsboro: Western North Carolina Press, 1964).

6. See especially Mark Goodacre, *The Case against Q: Studies in Markan Priority and the Synoptic Problem* (Harrisburg: Trinity Press International, 2002).

written parts in it), although it could be that Luke had access to Matthew or some form of the M tradition.

- Fourth, Matthew and Luke both made use of other traditions (labeled "M" and "L"), although any of the sources used may have been in a different form than we have them now.

A Four-Source Synoptic Hypothesis

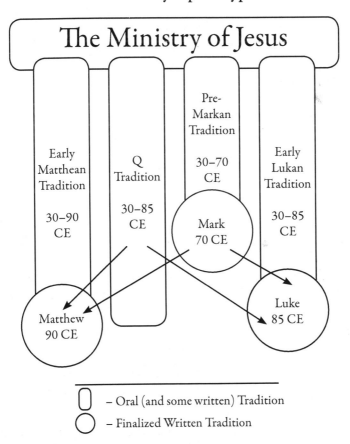

Therefore, most scholars embrace a two-source or a four-source approach, and such is warranted by the evidence. A glaring weakness, though, with all approaches to the Synoptic problem is that none of them does anything with the Gospel of John. If John represents an independent Jesus tradition with different perspectives from the beginning, though theologically developed, might it require consideration alongside the other Gospels? This would call for a new theory; we might call it *a Bi-Optic Hypothesis.*

A Bi-Optic Hypothesis—Bringing John into the Mix

The Gospel of John alone argues that the primary source for its material was an eyewitness, the beloved disciple, who leaned against the breast of Jesus at the Last Supper and whose "testimony is true" (John 21:23-24). The question is whether such is a knowing opinion or simply a rhetorical claim with no basis in knowledge—therefore a false assertion. Of course, John is so different from the Synoptics that it makes it easier for interpreters to ascribe John's story of Jesus to theological factors rather than historical ones, thereby expunging it from canons of historical memory about Jesus and his ministry. And yet, this is a simplistic and facile way out of the problem, as John's final compiler claims the opposite, and John also includes apparent historical tradition that is not in the Synoptics.

The de-historicization of John appeals to some historical-critical scholars, as it is much easier to deal with the Synoptics' literary and historical issues without John in the mix. But is this a robust approach or a timid one? Ascribing John's origin to theology rather than history has also come to be preferred by some traditionalist scholars because if John were judged historically correct where it differed from the other Gospels, this would create new problems for interpreting the canonical Gospels. Therefore, critical and traditional scholars have settled for a more manageable compromise, differing from the early church, claiming that John is not historical but is theological only; three against one, John is the lone Gospel out. However, if Matthew and Luke built upon Mark, it is not a three-to-one majority; it is a factor of John and Mark—two Gospels having individuated perspectives, perhaps from day one—deserving to be analyzed critically as *the Bi-Optic Gospels.*

Several issues have prevented scholars from considering John in relation to the other Gospels, and some are strong, but others are weak. Strong is the view that in some cases one must choose between John and the Synoptics; harmonization works in some cases but not in all. Weak is the view that the judgment must always go in one direction; in some cases the Synoptic presentation may be more historically plausible, but in some cases the Johannine might be. Strong is the view that theological investment might corrupt objective reporting of events. Weak is the view that historic events were never accorded significance or theological weight. In that sense, all the gospel traditions are historical *and* theological; the question is: how so? Strong is the view that Mark set the pattern for writing gospel narrative, followed by Matthew and Luke. Weak is the view that John operated the same way as the Synoptic writers. Unlike Mark, John is not a gatherer of disparate traditions into a narrative whole; John has its own story to tell. And, unlike Matthew and Luke, instead of building *upon* Mark, John appears to have built *around* Mark. Such is the kernel of a *Bi-Optic Hypothesis*. Thus, John indeed is different, but some of that differentiation may have been on purpose—and historically motivated, not just theologically so.

In drawing John into the fray of Gospel-relations studies, a view of John's composition is first required. Among the three dozen riddles of the Fourth Gospel,[7] the most problematic are as follows: the prologue uses different vocabulary than the rest of the Gospel and is in a poetic-strophic form, suggesting an independent history of composition; chapter 5 seems to flow into chapter 7, as Jesus is in Galilee in John 4 and 6 but in Jerusalem in John 5 and 7; John 14:31, where Jesus says, "We're leaving this place"—yet is followed by three chapters of discourse and prayer material—seems to have been followed by the arrival at the garden in 18:1; John 20:31 seems to have been a first ending ("these things are written so that you will believe . . . "), as John 21 seems to have been added after the death of the beloved disciple (21:23); and a final editor (the compiler) acknowledges an eyewitness (John 19:35) and the beloved disciple (21:24) as the source(s) of the tradition he is finalizing, so the compiler presents himself as a different person from the evangelist. Despite multiple approaches to John's composition, the most straightforward approach is to infer (at least) an earlier and a later edition, perhaps by the same hand, or perhaps by an evangelist and a final compiler. In my view, the following inferences deal with John's perplexities in the simplest, most plausible way, building on the strongest views of Rudolf Bultmann, Raymond Brown, and Barnabas Lindars.[8] It builds on the second-century view that two Christian leaders named "John" were buried in Ephesus—one "the disciple"

---

7. Paul N. Anderson, *The Riddles of the Fourth Gospel: An Introduction to John* (Minneapolis: Fortress, 2011), 25–91.

8. Ibid., 125–155.

and the other "the Elder"—the former being associated with the composition of the Gospel, and the latter being associated with the Epistles.[9]

A Two-Edition Theory of John's Composition

- A first edition of the Johannine Gospel by the beloved disciple, although perhaps with the help of an editor (ca. 80–85 CE)

- The writing of the Johannine Epistles by John the Elder (ca. 85–95 CE)

- The compiling of the finalized Gospel of John by the Elder after the death of the beloved disciple (ca. 100 CE), adding at least the following material:

  o The prologue (John 1:1-18)

  o The feeding, sea-crossing, discussion, confession of Peter (John 6)

  o The later discourses and the prayer of Jesus as his last will and testament for the church (John 17)

  o Continuing appearances of the resurrected Lord, the restoration of Peter, and fellowship with the disciples (John 21)

  o References to the eyewitness and "the Beloved Disciple" (John 13:23; 19:26, 35; 20:2)

Approaches to the issue of John's relation to the Synoptics have been complicated by simplistic analyses looking at John and "the Synoptics"—as though they were all gathered together in one place during the last decade or two of the first century CE. Of course, they were not; the earliest gathering of Gospels together came half a century or so later. Therefore, John's developing tradition must be considered in relation to each of the Synoptic traditions (including Q—if there was a Q) in order to make sense of the literary facts. The two poles within scholarship on this issue, of course, maintain that either John was totally dependent upon the Synoptics (after all, John was probably finalized last and tends to expand theologically upon the mundane) or that John was totally independent from the Synoptics as a whole (if John did not

---

9. This theory holds no matter who the Gospel writer and its editor might have been, but textual evidence does support the author of the Epistles being the final compiler of the Gospel—here Bultmann's reasoning is strong.

know of the Synoptics, omissions are less problematic). More likely is a more nuanced view—that when John's tradition is considered in relation to each of the Synoptic traditions independently, new sets of insights develop. This approach contributes to a fuller understanding of how John was written and perhaps also provides a key to gaining new insights into the development and character of the Synoptics themselves. Therefore, John may be the key to understanding the Synoptics instead of an irritant to be disparaged or ignored.

A Two-Edition Theory of Johannine Composition

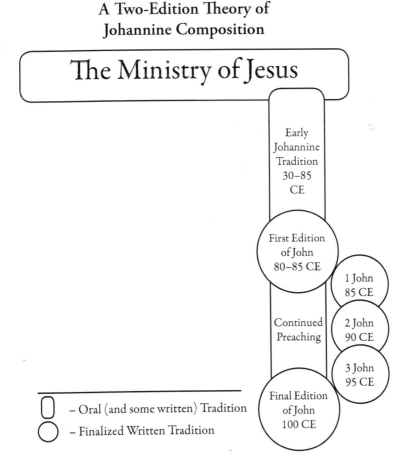

John and Mark

John and Mark should thus be considered first. In looking at the similarities and differences between John and Mark, several similarities present themselves at the outset. First, a variety of non-symbolic, illustrative details common to John and Mark alone can be noted, and this is by definition the sort of material Matthew and Luke exclude from their incorporations of Mark. Therefore, it is unlikely to betray a text-to-text relationship, reflecting either Mark's use of a Johannine text or John's use of a Markan text in a literary way—as Matthew and Luke apparently used a written form of Mark. For instance, the green/much grass (Mark 6:39 ←→John 6:10) is where the people at the feeding sat, and 200 and 300 *denarii* is what the feeding and the anointing spices would cost (Mark 6:37; 14:5 ←→John 6:7; 12:5). While these details are omitted by uses of Mark as a written source (and thus are not likely to be added imitations of reality—what scholars call "mimesis") they more plausibly reflect the sort of buzzwords and associations that stick between preachers and oral purveyors of tradition rather than a literary device that adds detail to create a sense of realism within an otherwise fictive account.

While it cannot be known who might be the sources of the pre-Markan and the early Johannine tradition, the fact that Peter and John are presented as traveling in ministry together through Samaria in Acts 8 suggests the sort of way that some of these early Markan-Johannine contacts might have transpired. If preachers in the apostolic era heard each other preach, or if they preached alongside each other, some cross-influence is likely. However, if contact happened during the oral stages of their traditions, it is impossible to know whether Mark's tradition influenced John's, or vice versa, or both. Therefore, instead of imagining "influence" in one direction only, it might be best to infer "interfluence" between gospel traditions during their oral stages.[10] Further, secondary orality is also a possibility, as speaking about a written source, or writing about an oral source, might also have been the case. Because *none* of the similarities between John and Mark (or between John and any of the other Gospels) is identical, a literary-derivative relationship is unlikely, but early interfluentiality is plausible.

A singular type of relationship between John and Mark might also be the wrong inference, in that the Johannine evangelist may also have heard the Gospel of Mark performed in a meeting for worship as it made its way among the churches—perhaps more than once.[11] Such a phenomenon is suggested by the *Muratorian Fragment*, which describes John the apostle noting the other

---

10. Raymond E. Brown referred to this phenomenon between the early Markan and Johannine traditions as "cross-influence" in his *An Introduction to the Gospel of John*, ed. by Francis Moloney (New Haven: Yale University Press, 2003), 102–4. I call it interfluence.

11. Ian D. Mackay, *John's Relationship with Mark: An Analysis of John 6 in the Light of Mark 6 and 8* (Tübingen: Mohr Siebeck, 2004).

Gospels and being encouraged to set his own perspectives to writing after considering them. Most interesting is that John's narrator seems to be setting the record straight here and there when it comes to Mark's presentation of the Jesus story. Further, if John's first edition was the second gospel narrative to have been produced, its author would not have felt intimidated by a multiple witness, so correcting and augmenting Mark might have seemed a responsible thing to do, especially if the Johannine evangelist had his own story to tell. Everyone improved upon Mark, including Mark's second ending.

Interestingly, the first edition of John (assuming the above theory is plausible) would have had five miracles, not eight, and these are precisely the five signs *not* in Mark or the other Gospels. And if John's first ending contained a reference to Mark, it could be fittingly understood as defending John's non-duplicative augmentation of Mark as intentional: "Jesus did many other miraculous signs in his disciples' presence, signs not recorded in *this* scroll [i.e., "I know Mark's out there, stop bugging me for leaving things out . . ."]. But these things are written so that you will believe . . . " (John 20:30-31). That being the case, note the first edition of John as a plausibly modest correction and augmentation of Mark.

John's First Edition's Relation to Mark

- Interfluence during the oral stages of tradition
    - Such mundane details as two hundred and three hundred denarii and much/green grass at the feeding are likely shared between preachers of the traditions
- A modest correction of Mark:
    - Jesus and John ministered at the same time before John was thrown into prison (John 3:24 vs. Mark 1:14)
    - Jesus was received in Samaria and Galilee despite being rejected at Nazareth as a prophet without honor (John 4:44-45 vs. Mark 6:4-5)
    - Jesus traveled to and from Jerusalem several times during his ministry instead of just one visit and Passover
    - The temple cleansing was early instead of late
    - Singular healings of a lame person and a blind person instead of multiple accounts

- ○ The Last Supper the evening before the Passover instead of a Passover dinner

- ○ Messianic disclosure instead of secrecy; metaphorical images instead of parables

- An augmentation of Mark:

  - ○ Early miracles of Jesus: the *first* sign and the *second* sign (John 2:11; 4:54)—*before* the miracles performed in Mark 1

  - ○ Judean miracles of Jesus in addition to Galilean ones: in Jerusalem and Bethany (John 5; 9; 11)

  - ○ Conflicts with the Jewish leaders in Jerusalem over several visits instead of one final one (John 5; 7–10)

  - ○ Added narratives, dialogues, and teachings of Jesus not included in Mark

The features of the material in John's first edition address very fittingly the Johannine Elder's critique of Mark, as cited by Papias above. First, Mark took down Peter's preaching correctly, but in the wrong order—John sets the record straight and locates the temple cleansing early, along with multiple trips to Jerusalem. What this might suggest is that Mark's chronology is not a knowing one, but rather a general, conjectured construct: Jesus's early and middle ministry in Galilee, followed by his final ministry in Jerusalem. Note that Mark locates all of the controversy teachings and dialogues at the end, after Jesus arrives in Jerusalem. That creates a climactic thrust of the narrative, although it is unlikely that Jesus did little confrontation of religious leaders before his final visit to Jerusalem. Such being the case, it makes perfect conjectural and narrative sense to locate the temple cleansing at the end—a fitting climax to the narrative, explaining also why religious leaders and Romans wanted Jesus gone. It requires no historical knowledge to infer that Jesus's creating a temple disturbance led to his arrest and death, whereas John's rendering, that religious leaders wanted to kill Jesus (and Lazarus) because of his signs, is less likely to have been concocted. Again, the Johannine Elder as cited by Papias may have been wrong about Mark's chronology being a bit off, but a Johannine opinion to that effect might explain John's alternative chronology: it was aimed at setting Mark's itinerary straight as a historical interest rather than a theological one.

The second Johannine critique of Mark (according to Papias) is that it represented not the exact message of historical Jesus, but Peter's preaching about Jesus as a means of addressing the needs of his audiences. Here the Johannine critique appears to have morphed into imitation. If Mark represents preaching crafted to the needs of audiences . . . well, so can (and perhaps, so should) John's rendering of Jesus's words and works. This might explain also the liberty the Fourth Evangelist takes with his presentation of Jesus's teachings. Rather than speaking in parables (apparently some disciples disliked their ambiguity, John 16:29), Jesus speaks plainly about things and ties imagery referenced in the Synoptics to his own mission within John's distinctive I-Am sayings. Whereas scholars are quick to imagine that John's distinctive rendering of Jesus's teachings was a factor of spiritualized theologizing, perhaps John's rendering Jesus's teachings in his own words came as a factor of following Peter's lead, feeling the freedom to paraphrase Jesus's teachings to address the needs of his audiences within the emerging Johannine situation.

A third critique of Mark in Papias's report, that of duplication and redundancy, is reflected in the evangelist's not making use of the miracles or teachings of Jesus found in Mark in John's first edition. This might explain why even the references to the Transfiguration and the calling of the Twelve are omitted from John; they're already in Mark. Even in the later material added to John's first edition, where the compiler harmonizes the Johannine Gospel with the others (by this time, familiarity with Luke and Matthew is likely), only one feeding and one sea-crossing narrative are included instead of two. Despite covering a similar set of events in the Passion narrative, John's account retains its distinctiveness and thus betrays little duplication of Mark. Therefore, John's engagements with Mark are interfluential, corrective, and augmentive; John's account of Jesus's ministry is different on purpose.

John and Luke

John and Luke evidence a different set of relationships. Assuming that Luke used Mark, the Johannine-Lukan connections are best approached as noting that Luke departs from Mark in ways that coincide with John. This could be accidental, but it more likely reflects some sort of inter-traditional contact. Since John is finalized later than Luke, scholars have assumed that John drew from Luke, but Luke's most notable features (birth narratives, memorable parables, emphases on the poor, the Lord's Prayer and Beatitudes) are not found in John. More plausible is that Luke had at least partial access to some of John's formative tradition—enough to add material, change

Mark's order to be closer to John's here and there, and to make several adjustments that happen to coincide with John's presentation of Jesus. Consider these ways in which Luke appears to have employed the Johannine tradition as reflecting what he has received from "eyewitnesses and servants of the word [*Logos*]" (Luke 1:2).

John's Formative Impact upon Luke

- Luke adds Johannine incidents and details to his use of Mark:
  - A great catch of fish is added (arrows here denote John's influence upon Luke: John 21:1-14➻Luke 5:1-11)
  - Mary and Martha are mentioned as sisters (John 11:1-45; 12:1-11➻Luke 10:38-42)
  - Jesus prays for his disciples to endure the time of trial (John 17:15➻Luke 22:31-32)
  - Jesus invites his followers to see and touch his hands (John 20:20, 27➻Luke 24:39-40)
  - Jesus eats fish and bread with the disciples after the resurrection (John 21:9-13➻Luke 24:28-43)
  - Satan enters Judas (John 13:27➻Luke 22:3)
  - the "right" ear of the servant is severed (John 18:10➻Luke 22:50)
  - the tomb is one in which no one has ever been laid (John 19:41➻Luke 23:53)
  - Peter arrives at the tomb and sees the linen cloths lying there (John 20:5➻Luke 24:12)
  - "Siloam" is only mentioned in John and Luke (John 9:7, 11➻Luke 13:4)
- Luke draws from John's tradition in presenting an orderly account:
  - only one sea-crossing and feeding are used instead of Mark's two (John 6:1-21➻Luke 8:22-26; 9:10-17)
  - Luke relocates the confession of Peter after the feeding of the five thousand, *not* the four thousand

- ○ Luke changes Mark's head-anointing of Jesus to a foot-anointing, as it is in John (John 12:1-8➟Luke 7:36-50)

- ○ Luke moves the servanthood discussion and the prediction of Peter's denial to the Last Supper (John 13:1-17, 38➟Luke 22:24-30, 34)

- ○ Jesus's post-resurrection appearances begin in Jerusalem (John 20:19-29➟Luke 24:13-53)

- Luke harmonizes John and Mark, adding some Johannine emphases:

  - ○ Luke harmonizes Mark's and John's versions of Peter's confession ("You are *the Christ*" + "You are the Holy One *of God*" = "You are *the Christ of God*"—Mark 8:29; John 6:68-69➟Luke 9:20)

- Luke adds theological themes most characteristic of John:

  - ○ *The Holy Spirit* (presented distinctively as "wind"—John 3:8➟Acts 2:2) will teach believers what they need to know and say (John 14:26➟Luke 12:12), providing "comfort" (*paraklēsis*—John 14:16, 26; 15:26; 16:7➟Luke 2:25; Acts 9:31)

  - ○ *Women* are featured with prominence: Jesus enters the home of Mary and Martha and is served by Martha (John 12:1-8➟Luke 10:38-42); the mother of Jesus plays leading roles (John 2:1-12; 19:25-27➟Luke 1:26–2:51); women make confessions (John 11:27➟Luke 11:27); and women are reported as having seen two angels/men in radiant clothes at the empty tomb (John 20:12➟Luke 24:4, 23)

  - ○ *Samaria* and *Samaritans* are featured with prominence (John 4:4-42➟Luke 17:11; Acts 1:8; 8:1, 5, 9, 14; 9:31; 15:3), as Jesus and his followers are reported as traveling through Samaria (John 4:8, 27-38➟Luke 9:51-56; Acts 8:1-25; 15:3) and Samaritan persons are presented as favorable examples for later audiences (John 4:39-42➟Luke 10:30-37; 17:11-19)

Given that Luke presents John the apostle speaking in a characteristically Johannine way (Acts 4:19-20; cf.1 John 1:3; John 3:32), Luke is clearly aware of John's contribution and plausibly some of his tradition. While other scholars have argued that Luke made use of John as a written tradition,[12] Luke does not move the temple cleansing early, and he locates the great catch of fish at the first calling of Peter, rather than his re-calling. Another indication that Luke has heard some of John's material is the way he changes the head anointing (in Mark 14:3-9) to a foot anointing (as it is in John 12:1-8; Luke 7:36-50). Such a move is unlikely without a historical or traditional precedent; John's providing such is a likely inference. Note, however, that Luke adds the appearance of Mary Magdalene right afterwards (Luke 8:2); perhaps he has heard the name "Mary" (sister of Lazarus in John 12:1-8) but associated her with another Mary. This might also explain why Luke supposes a woman who is much grateful must have received much forgiveness—a conjectural leap, as Mary Magdalene is never directly associated with being promiscuous in the canonical Gospels; such is a later development. In addition to an elevated presentation of women, Luke adds several of John's theological motifs to his use of Mark, including Jesus's regard for Samaritans and emphases upon the Holy Spirit. In these ways, the impact of John's tradition upon Luke is formative, orderly, and theological.

John and Q

The relation between *Q and the Johannine tradition* poses the most difficult problems for two inevitable reasons: first, the existence of Q is itself a question, and second, the contacts between hypothetical Q and the Gospel of John are minimal. Nonetheless, several contacts between John, Matthew, and Luke (to the exclusion of Mark) are intriguing and suggestive. Note that they not only include sayings; they also include narratives.

Q Tradition and John

- The *bolt out of the Johannine blue*—"My Father has handed all things over to me. No one knows who the Son is except the Father, or who the Father is except the Son and anyone to whom the Son wants to reveal him." (John 3:35; 7:28-29; 10:14-15; 13:3; 17:1-3, 22-25 ⟶ Luke 10:22; Matt 11:27)

---

12. Arguing Luke's dependence on John are F. Lamar Cribbs, "A Study of the Contacts That Exist between St. Luke and St. John," *Society of Biblical Literature: 1973 Seminar Papers,* vol. 2, ed. George MacRae (Cambridge, MA: Society of Biblical Literature, 1973), 1–93; and Mark A. Matson, *In Dialogue with Another Gospel?* (Atlanta: Society of Biblical Literature, 2001).

- The *Paradox of Life: loving life and losing it; releasing life and finding it* (John 12:25→Matt 10:39; Luke 17:33—cf. also Mark 8:35-37; Matt 16:25-26; Luke 9:24-25)

- The *healing at a distance in Capernaum*—the son of the royal official in John (John 4:46-54); the servant of the Centurion in Q (Matt 8:5-13; Luke 7:1-10)

- Claiming to be *children of Abraham* is a touted value disparaged by John the Baptist (Matt 3:9; Luke 3:8) and Jesus (John 8:33-39).

- The *ripe harvest is come* (John 4:35→Matt 9:37-38; Luke 10:2)

Discerning the character of potential contact here is a challenge, but several modest inferences follow. First, these contacts might simply reflect the sharing of a common set of themes going back to early tradition, or even back to Jesus himself. If so, they suggest John's traditional earliness as well as that of Q. Second, it could be that John's tradition has depended on Q, although this is unlikely for several reasons. The healing in Capernaum in Q has already garnered stereotypical features in Q—the Roman is a Centurion; as he commands with authority, so does Jesus. The Johannine rendering, however, is more primitive—the royal official is concerned about a family member; of the two renderings, Q is the more developed. And the disparaging of proud claims to be children of Abraham by John the Baptist in Q is sketched in a more nuanced form in John 8—it results as a misunderstanding of Jesus's speaking of liberation, whereby Jewish leaders assert their freedom (not having been slaves) as children of Abraham. The Johannine rendering is more textured and laced with socio-religious awareness. Likewise, the ripe harvest motif in Q is already aimed at mission (people need to pray to the Lord of the harvest to send forth laborers to assist in Christian mission), whereas in John, it simply conveys the conviction that the harvest is ready—a reference to Jesus's mission in Samaria, not the later mission of his followers. A fourth feature, which is most telling, is that the Father-Son relationship is an intricate Johannine theme, which is tersely cited in Q. Especially in this case, it certainly is a Johannine motif that is displayed in Q. Therefore, these Johannine-Q contacts reflect at the very least Johannine influence upon the Q tradition, suggesting its primitivity and formative impact on other traditions.

John and Matthew

Distinctive contacts between *Matthew and John* are also meager, and it is impossible to know for sure which way the influence might have gone. As these contacts are fairly subtle and indirect, a likely inference is that there may have been some cross-influence during the later stages of their development—perhaps even following the first edition of John, as the beloved disciple continued to preach and write about Jesus's being the Jewish Messiah, about church unity, and about how the risen Lord leads the church in the later decades of the first-century Christian movement. These contacts seem closest to the later material in John, where affirmations of Jesus as the *Logos* and aspects of church unity are emphasized. That being the case, similarities and differences between the Matthean and the Johannine traditions are nonetheless telling.

Matthew and John

- Reinforcing in terms of Jesus's being the Jewish Messiah
  - ○ Both Matthew and John show Jesus to be fulfilling many scripture passages as the Jewish Messiah
  - ○ Jesus fulfills the Law of Moses by getting at the heart of the Law (Exod 20:1-20; Matthew) and fulfilling Moses's prophecy (Deut 18:15-22; John)
- Dialectical in terms of posing alternative views of community and leadership
  - ○ Both Matthew and John advocate a theology of Presence; Christ is present where two or three are gathered in his name (Matt 18:20) and through the Holy Spirit available to all (John 14–16)
  - ○ Images of the church include the foundational rock (Matt 16:18), the Shepherd/gate/sheepfold/sheep (John 10:1-10), and the vine/branches (John 15:1-5)
  - ○ Christian unity is emphasized with the parable of latecomers to the fold (Matt 20:1-16) and Jesus's reaching out to sheep from other folds (John 10:16)

- Corrective in terms of Christ's leadership in the church

  ○ Blessedness comes not from making the correct confession (Matt 16:17) but from obeying Jesus's instructions and believing without having seen (Matt 7:24-27; John 13:17; 20:29)

  ○ Rather than Peter being called "first" among the apostles (Matt 10:2) the beloved disciple arrives at the tomb first, before Peter (John 20:4)

  ○ In contrast to Jesus's entrusting Peter (and his followers) with instrumental keys to the kingdom of heaven (Matt 16:19), Peter is portrayed as affirming Jesus's sole authority to lead (John 6:68-69)

These similarities and differences between the Matthean and Johannine traditions do not evidence direct literary influence in one direction or another, but they do reflect intertraditional engagement—probably in the oral stages of their traditions. As dialogues with local Jewish communities evoked apologetic developments within the Johannine and Matthean sectors of the early Christian movement, mutual reinforcement can be seen in their yoking of scripture-fulfillment connections with words and events in Jesus's ministry, demonstrating him to be the Jewish Messiah. They also betray later stages in the histories of gospel traditions, as approaches to church leadership and community organization become central concerns of the second and third generations of the movement. However, in addition to dialectical engagement between these two traditions, the Johannine presentation of Jesus's post-resurrection leadership is more fluid and Spirit-based than structural and organizational. In that sense, John's presentation of Jesus's leading the church in egalitarian ways, including women alongside apostles and emphasizing relationships, appears to be a corrective to rising institutionalization in the late first-century situation.

Rather than reflecting a direct engagement between Johannine and Matthean traditions, however, we may have a case here of how Matthew's ecclesiology is being represented in the Johannine situation. For one thing, Matthew's approach to leadership, while structure-oriented, is also family-oriented and gracious. While Peter receives instrumental keys in Matthew 16:17-19, he is also asked to be forgiving (seven times seventy!) in Matthew 18:21-35. Therefore, Matthew's approach combines graciousness with structure and hierarchy, which can work well together. However, all it takes is one strident appropriation of structural leadership for a problem to emerge. If "Diotrephes, who likes to put himself first" (3 John 1:9-10) has been disparaging members of John's community and keeping them out of his church, that might have called for an ideological corrective as the Elder finalized the witness of the beloved disciple after his death.

John's Later Material and the Synoptics

- John's prologue (1:1-18) poses an engaging introduction affirming Jesus's divine origin (alongside Matt 1–2, Luke 1–2, and 1 John 1:1-4)

- One feeding and sea-crossing (instead of two), followed by Peter's confession (John 6), harmonize John's account with those of the Synoptics

- The additional discourses of Jesus and his prayer for unity (John 15–17) emphasize the ongoing work of the Holy Spirit with reference to persecution, leadership, and church unity

- The second set of appearance narratives (John 21) rectify and co-opt the memory of Peter, as well as affirm the exemplary leadership of the beloved disciple

- The appeal to the trustworthy eyewitness and contribution of the beloved disciple testify to a suffering Jesus and a legitimation of the Johannine rendering of Jesus's ministry—acknowledging its intentional differences with the Synoptics (19:34-35; 21:24-25)

John's final-edition material appears to play several harmonizing roles in relation to the Synoptics, and by around 100 CE, it is likely that all three Synoptic Gospels are known by the final compiler. First, as a complement to the birth narratives of Matthew and Luke, John's *Logos* hymn is added by the compiler to an otherwise mundane beginning of John's Gospel featuring (like Mark) the witness of John the Baptist. Second, the feeding, sea-crossing, and Peter's confession material of John 6 is added as a means of standardizing John's narration of Jesus's ministry with well-known reports of Jesus's ministry. Third, Jesus's final instructions for his disciples to follow are added to the last discourse, including reminders of the Holy Spirit's sustaining guidance and an expanded version of the Lord's Prayer for his disciples (John 15–17). Fourth, Peter's threefold denial around a charcoal fire is rectified by an opportunity to make a three-fold affirmation (John 18:17-18, 25-27; 21:15-18), and his authority is co-opted and pointed toward the beloved disciple, who shows the way forward as the typological example of discipleship for others to follow. In that sense, while John's first edition augments and corrects Mark, John's final edition harmonizes its narrative (still defending its selectivity, John 21:25) with the Markan Gospels in a bi-optic way.

Therefore, while the Synoptic Hypothesis has made great strides in understanding the relations between the Gospels, a Bi-Optic Hypothesis takes those advances further. Beginning with Mark as the first of the Gospels, while Matthew and Luke built upon Mark, John appears to have built around Mark, augmenting and correcting Mark in its early edition. As such, it may have been the second gospel, although it does not appear to have circulated beyond a localized setting. Luke appears to have incorporated a variety of Johannine units and details in Luke's augmentation of Mark, and perhaps Q did also in some modest ways. If there was no Q tradition, perhaps Matthew had access to the Johannine oral tradition as well as Luke. Some interfluence between John's tradition and those of early Mark and later Matthew seems a likely inference. The value of bringing John into the mix is that it not only clarifies John's place alongside the other Gospels but also sheds light on how they may have come together. Mark is thus a general chronology, but not an exacting one, gathered with some redundancies but setting a foundational pattern for other gospel narratives to follow. Luke drew on Mark and likely Q, but also upon other traditions, plausibly the Johannine. And John and Matthew show emerging approaches to community and church organization while also being in dialogue with each other. Therefore, a bi-optic five-source approach, while more expansive than a two- or a four-source theory, nonetheless addresses issues critically that other approaches have not.

A Bi-Optic Hypothesis—A Theory of Gospel Relations

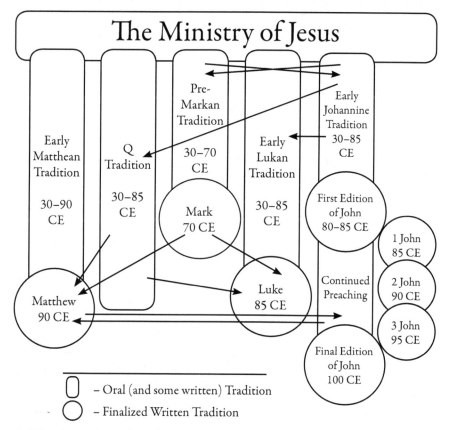

The Ministry of Jesus

Pre-Markan Tradition

Early Johannine Tradition
30–85 CE

Early Matthean Tradition

Q Tradition

30–70 CE

Early Lukan Tradition

Early Matthean Tradition
30–90 CE

30–85 CE

Mark
70 CE

30–85 CE

First Edition of John
80–85 CE

1 John
85 CE

Matthew
90 CE

Luke
85 CE

Continued Preaching

2 John
90 CE

3 John
95 CE

Final Edition of John
100 CE

◊ – Oral (and some written) Tradition

○ – Finalized Written Tradition

Paul N. Anderson. *The Fourth Gospel and the Quest for Jesus: Modern Foundations Reconsidered*, LNTS 321 (London T&T Clark) ©2006. p. 126

Chapter 5

The Gospel According to John

Begin with the text. Read the Gospel of John, and note important themes and details that come to mind.

Author: traditionally identified as John the son of Zebedee, although it may have been finalized by John the Elder

Audience: likely Jewish and Gentile audiences as well as Jesus followers in its later stages

Time: first edition finalized ca. 80–85 CE; later edition finalized ca. 100 CE, after the death of the beloved disciple

Place: traditionally Ephesus in Asia Minor; no better site exists

Message: These things are written that people might believe that Jesus is the Christ, the Son of God, and thus have life in his name (John 20:31).

The Gospel of John is the most distinctive among the four canonical Gospels, and yet it also bears striking similarities with the three Epistles of John. Its story of Jesus begins with a hymn to Christ as the pre-existent *Logos*, the Word of God, and the prologue of the Gospel (John 1:1-18) is very similar in its language and content to the prologue of the first Epistle (1 John 1:1-4). Echoing corporate convictions, the community affirms: "*We* have seen his glory, glory like that of a father's only son, full of grace and truth" (1:14b), and "From his fullness *we* have all received grace upon grace" (1:16). In the epilogue, the final compiler asserts about the author: "This is the disciple who testifies concerning these things and who wrote them down. *We* know that his testimony is true" (21:24). Therefore, in addition to telling the story of Jesus, the Gospel of John also represents the convictions of Johannine Christians and their understanding of Jesus's mission. In that sense, the message is not only pastoral; it is also apologetic. John's first concluding statement declares, "Then Jesus did many other miraculous signs in his disciples' presence, signs that aren't recorded in this scroll. But these things are written so that you will believe that Jesus is the Christ, God's Son, and that believing, you will have life in his name" (John 20:30-31).

I. Crises and Contexts

While John's narrative and the message of the three related epistles clearly reflect the context of at least one Christian community within the Gentile mission, it is a mistake to assume that the same dynamics covered the entire history of Johannine Christianity. Rather, a better way to conceive of its context is to envision a larger *Johannine situation*, including several crises over several decades. During some of that time a community was a primary feature of Johannine Christianity, but a less defined existence seems to have preceded John's community phase, and a multiplicity of Christian communities seems to have followed it. When the Johannine situation is considered in longitudinal perspective (say, from 30–100 CE), at least six or seven crises seem to have been acute, and while they were largely sequential, they were also somewhat overlapping. Indeed, an impending crisis rarely waits to rear its ugly head until after the previous one is resolved! Rather, more acute crises tend to push aside less pressing ones, which still continue to fester until their intensity wanes, though they rarely totally disappear. Therefore, within three overall phases or periods of the Johannine situation, at least two crises appear to have been pressing within each phase in considerably different ways, with a seventh transcending all three periods.

Jesus the Messiah in Galilean Perspective

The first phase in the Johannine situation represents a Galilean period between the death of Jesus and the translocation of the evangelist and others to a new setting within the Gentile mission (ca. 30–70 CE). Within this period John's gospel narrative comes together, and preaching about the works of Jesus is likely accompanied by expansions into his words. The evangelist reaches out to fellow members of Jewish society, but resistance continues among the religious leaders in Jerusalem, and some competition continues among followers of the Baptist. While the second and third periods have the benefit of corroboration from the Johannine Epistles, and even Revelation, the two crises of the first period are suggested merely by the gospel narrative itself.

First, *the problem of Jesus's having come unto his own but having been rejected by them* continues to be a problem for his followers (1:11), as John's memory of Jesus's mission features an extended treatment of tensions between the Galilean prophet and the religious leaders of Jerusalem. They are called *Ioudaioi* in Greek, which can either be translated "Judeans" or "Jews." It is wrong, though, to see here tensions between Judaism and Christianity, as the Gospel of John is written by a Jew, about a Jewish prophet, to Jewish and Gentile audiences, claiming that Jesus was indeed the Jewish Messiah. As in the *War Scroll* of Qumran, the tensions here are within the Jewish family, which is what makes them intense. While individuation from parental Judaism seems to be reflected in the reference to "their Law" in John 15:25 (likewise, "your law"—8:17; 10:34), Jesus declares to the Samaritan woman that "salvation is from the Jews" in John 4:22, and Nicodemus (a leader among the Jews) stands up for Jesus in Jerusalem citing "our law" as a basis for it (7:51). Therefore, John is pro-Jewish, despite its negative presentation of some Jewish leaders who reject Jesus.

Pointedly, however, the embellished presentation of the warm reception of Jesus in Samaria and Galilee (4:5-54) is contrasted to his mixed reception in Jerusalem and Judea. Not all the Judeans fail to believe, however; many do believe on the basis of his words and works (7:31; 8:30-32; 9:38; 10:42; 11:27, 45; 12:42). Conversely, John explains the others' lack of faith as a result of not having known the Father or his love (5:37-42; 7:28; 8:19, 55; 16:3; 17:25); they search the scriptures and cling to Moses, but they fail to note that Moses wrote of Jesus (John 5:46; Deut 18:15-22). In their Jerusalem-centered mindset, Judean religious leaders insist that the Messiah does not come from Galilee; he must come from David's city in Bethlehem (John 7:41-52)—from the central south, not from the peripheral north. Labeled with an ethnic slam, Jesus is marginalized as being "a Samaritan" and having a demon by the Jerusalem leaders (8:48), who are thus presented as loving the praise of humans rather than the glory of God (12:43). While they justify themselves on the basis that Pharisees and other religious leaders have not believed in Jesus (7:45-48), the narrator points out the irony that they were also wrong in that judgment, as even some of the Jewish leaders secretly believed (7:50; 12:42). Therefore, the first crisis in the Johannine situation reflects the struggle of the northern prophet's uneven reception by the religious leaders in Judea, which continues to be a problem among his followers into the next generation. Revelation is always a challenge to religion, and while prophets are rejected at home (Mark 6:4), they also are rejected elsewhere.

A second crisis follows *among the followers of John the Baptist*. Is John the Messiah, or is Jesus? This was their question, and as a means of addressing its nagging continuation, John is presented in this gospel narrative as making several self-effacing claims. First, John declares that he is not the Christ and neither Elijah nor the prophet (1:19-21; 3:28). Rather, he is the bridegroom, whose joy is fulfilled in Jesus's becoming greater and his becoming lesser (3:29-30). Put otherwise, John is not the light, but he came as a witness to Jesus as the light; while Jesus came after him, he was before him (1:6-8, 15, 27, 30), and the whole reason John came baptizing was to point Jesus out (1:31). In preparing the way of the Lord in the wilderness, John declares of Jesus, "Look! The Lamb of God who takes away the sin of the world!" (1:29, 36). Second, the baptisms of John and Jesus are contrasted; John came baptizing with water, but Jesus baptizes with the Holy Spirit (1:33). Interestingly, the baptism of Jesus is not narrated in this Gospel, and John claims not to have recognized Jesus until he witnessed the Holy Spirit descending upon him, whereby he came to see Jesus as the Son of God (1:31-34). Third, John's followers leave him and follow Jesus (1:37-44), and when other disciples of John become worried that Jesus is gaining more followers than John, John is presented as affirming this development (3:22–4:1). In presenting the early ministry of John the Baptist as happening alongside that of Jesus, before John is thrown into prison (3:24, vs. Mark 1:14), competition with the followers of the Baptist is addressed by means of John's pointing to Jesus—the reason for his entire mission.

The Roman Invasion and the Johannine Diaspora

The Roman invasion of Judea and destruction of the temple, ranging from 66–73 CE, brought a huge cataclysm to the Jewish nation and also to the Jesus movement within it. Given that the temple was destroyed, and that most of the priests were killed, the religious center of power within Judaism shifted from the Sadducees to the Pharisees between 70 and 90 CE. From this time forward, never again were sacrifices offered in the Jerusalem temple, and the local synagogue became the gathering place for Jews scattered around the world, as well as in Palestine. As a result, Jewish religion shifted from a faith of the worship cult, with its festivals around the temple in Jerusalem, to a faith of the book, with its regulations and advice about how to live in Jewish ways. The Pharisees thus gained ascendency within the movement, and a special focus on the Law of Moses and faithful adherence to its precepts became the central organizing thrust of Jewish worship and identity. Therefore, councils of Jewish leadership gathered in Jamnia (*Javneh*), west of Jerusalem near the Mediterranean coast, and later in Usha, Shefar'am, Sepphoris, and other centers in Galilee over the next century or so. Within that period and following, continuing standardization of the Hebrew scriptures took place, as the authority of the Sadducees was replaced by that of the Pharisees.

Within this movement in Judaism to a synagogue-centered religion, the synagogue liturgy involving Eighteen Benedictions recited in meetings for worship also underwent a change. The twelfth benediction, the *Birkat ha-Minim*, is actually a curse against the heretics (*minim*), and Gamaliel II urged the adding of a curse against the Nazarenes (*notserim*, or *nosrim*) as a means of disciplining those whose faith and practice might not have been in conformity with Jewish standards of orthodoxy. Something like this may have been at work earlier in Qumran, condemning the Sadducees of Jerusalem as apostates, and it may also have been used as a political statement against zealots, who in association with Judas the Galilean ran the danger of evoking a Roman retaliatory response. By the time that Justin Martyr described his *Dialogue with Trypho the Jew* ca. 150–160 CE, however, references to Jews cursing Christians in their synagogues gives rise to the view that the *Birkat* at least eventually was aimed at disciplining followers of Jesus of Nazareth, seeking to correct their embracing two Gods—Jesus and the Father—which violated the Law of Moses and Jewish monotheism (Deut 6:4). Imagine how followers of Jesus of Nazareth would have felt if expected to recite the following confession in Jewish meetings for worship around this time:

[1] For the apostates, let there be no hope. [2] And let the arrogant government [of Rome] be speedily uprooted in our days. [3] Let the Nazarenes [*nosrim*] and heretics [*minim*] be destroyed in a moment. [4] And let them be blotted out of the Book of Life and not be inscribed together with the righteous. [5] Blessed are you, O Lord, who humble the arrogant.[1]

Scholars debate the degree to which the *Birkat* was aimed at Jesus adherents, or whether it was simply experienced by them as a challenge to their belief in Jesus as the Son of God, but one thing is clear. When Johannine leaders moved to a diaspora setting, where fellowship with the local Jewish community was of central importance to the life of the Johannine community, a new set of tensions arose. According to Eusebius, during the Roman invasion of Jerusalem the apostles scattered to various parts of the world, and John the apostle went to Ephesus in Asia Minor, the heart of Gentile mission. Other settings have been suggested for the Johannine community to have taken root, such as Alexandria in Egypt or Antioch in Syria, but neither of these offers an improvement over the traditional view. As Ephesus and its environs were the central gateway to the west (Greece, Rome, Alexandria, and beyond), commerce and travel through the Lycus Valley would have given the area a cosmopolitan feel. Jewish communities in the area had been established for hundreds of years, which is why Paul's mission included that region to

1. Quoted in Aaron Milavec, *Salvation Is from the Jews (John 4:22): Saving Grace in Judaism and Messianic Hope in Christianity* (Collegeville, MN: Liturgical Press, 2007), 96.

begin with. Therefore, in the second phase of the Johannine situation (70–85 CE), a new set of crises developed in its new diaspora setting.

As a third crisis, *engagements with local synagogues* following the Johannine translocation would have met with several issues. First, Johannine leaders would have found fellowship with Jesus adherents meeting in local synagogues for Sabbath worship, but they might also have enjoyed first-day meetings for worship in the homes of Gentile believers. Second, enjoying fellowship with local Jewish communities and leaders would have had major significance. Connections between members of local synagogues and Galilean religious communities would have insured a warm welcome among the Jewish leaders in this new setting, and these relationships would have been highly valued. Third, however, as Johannine leaders shared their conviction that Jesus was indeed the Jewish Messiah, this would have evoked a set of mixed reactions within the new setting. Some Jews likely received the news and came to see Jesus as the fulfillment of the Jewish calling to be a light to the nations and a blessing to the world. Others, however, would have felt consternation over talk of Jesus's divine Sonship, as it must have seemed a challenge to Jewish monotheism, and one can imagine the *Birkat ha-Minim* serving to discipline creeping ditheism—belief in two Gods instead of one.

That being the case, three texts in the Gospel of John, when read against this backdrop, provide potential insight into the third crisis of the Johannine situation. In 1968 J. Louis Martyn[2] argued that the three times the narrator or Jesus mentions people who were put out of the synagogue (*aposynagōgos*) for confessing Christ openly (9:22; 12:42; 16:2) are explicit references to the effect of the *Birkat ha-Minim*, associated with the leadership of Gamaliel II, as Jewish councils gathered in a number of settings following the destruction of Jerusalem. As is noted in the case of the blind man and his family in John 9:22, "the Jewish authorities had already decided that whoever confessed Jesus to be the Christ would be expelled from the synagogue." The point is that reporting synagogue expulsion for Christ-confessors "back then" implies that the threat was also an acute reality for John's audience at the time of its delivery in the 80s. Therefore, the presentation of Jewish leaders rejecting Jesus and his followers five decades or so earlier must have taken on fresh rhetorical relevance, as Jewish family and friends in this new setting were also unevenly responsive to the gospel message that Jesus was the Messiah/Christ. In the light of Pharisaic emphases upon being disciples of Moses (9:28) and Jewish pride in being children of Abraham (8:33, 39), the emphasis upon the

---

2. J. Louis Martyn, *History and Theology in the Fourth Gospel,* 3rd ed. (Louisville: Westminster John Knox, 2003).

healing of the blind man points out that those who claim "we see" are actually exposed as being blind (9:39-41).

While several scholars have argued that because close relations were shared between Jews and Christians during this time it is unlikely that the *Birkat* was aimed at Jesus followers, this view is problematic.[3] Granted, inferences of widespread synagogue expulsions are overdrawn, but it is precisely the closeness of relationship that would insure tensions with local Jewish leaders in a diaspora setting, especially over claims that Jesus was the Son of God. Put otherwise, reciting the Johannine prologue in most Jewish synagogues during this time period would probably have caused at least some consternation. To imagine otherwise is naïve. Another thesis is that the *Birkat* against the "Nazarenes" was aimed against zealot messianic enthusiasts, inspired by Judas the Galilean and his followers, and that the objection to confessing Jesus as "the Christ" in Jerusalem around 30 CE was motivated by the threat of a Roman onslaught.[4] The fear of Roman retaliation against Jewish messianic uprisings is certainly palpable in the exchange between the Jewish council and Caiaphas in John 11:47-50, so the *Birkat* against followers of the Nazarene may have had more than one chapter of relevance for Johannine believers in Jesus.

Emperor Worship under Domitian

With the ascendancy of Domitian as emperor (81–96 CE), a new crisis emerges: public emperor worship becomes a standard expression of loyalty to Rome throughout the empire. The Judean crisis had been an especially intense concern of General Vespasian and his two sons, Titus and Domitian, all of whom participated in the Judean campaign and later became emperors as part of the Flavian Dynasty. While Vespasian and Titus had been rather generous to their adversaries, Domitian reintroduced the practice of emperor worship, requiring subjects to regard him as "Lord and God" (*dominus et deus* in Latin). Over a million Jews were killed in the Judean war, and Vespasian's

---

3. Steven T. Katz, "Issues in the Separation of Judaism and Christianity after 70 C.E.: A Reconsideration," *Journal of Biblical Literature* 103 (1984): 43–76; Reuven Kimelman, "*Birkat Ha-Minim* and the Lack of Evidence for an Anti-Christian Prayer in Late Antiquity," *Jewish and Christian Self-Definition*, vol. 2, *Aspects of Judaism in the Greco-Roman World*, ed. by E. P. Sanders et al (Philadelphia: Fortress Press, 1981), 226–44; Adele Reinhartz, *Befriending the Beloved Disciple: A Jewish Reading of the Gospel of John* (New York/London: Continuum, 2001).

4. Jonathan Bernier, *Aposynagōgos and the Historical Jesus in John: Rethinking the Historicity of the Johannine Expulsion Passages*, Biblical Interpretation Series 122 (Leiden: E. J. Brill, 2013).

targeted strategy of killing all members of the household of David, so as to stamp out Jewish royal and messianic aspirations, was taken further by Domitian, who also brought to trial the sons of Jude, as extended members of Jesus's family. The Roman presence in Asia Minor during this time reflects competition for imperial favors between the great cities of the region. In particular, Ephesus and Pergamum vied against each other for the status of *neokoros*—"keeper of the temple"—leading to civic insistence on pleasing Rome, lest the flow of imperial favors and subsidized building projects diminish.[5]

This led to a fourth crisis in the Johannine situation, coinciding with the third: *negotiating the demands of the imperial cult under Domitian.* Going back to the reign of Vespasian, following the destruction of the Jewish temple in 70 CE, a global tax was placed upon the Jewish people (*fiscus Iudaicus*), transferring their support of the Jewish temple in Jerusalem to the temple of Jupiter in Rome (the Roman equivalent of the Greek god Zeus). The amount to be paid, now by all Jews across the Roman Empire—not just adult males but including females, children, and the elderly—was two drachmas, the equivalent of the annual temple tax previously paid to support the temple in Jerusalem. This amount was no accident! During Domitian's reign, while Jews were not required to worship Caesar publicly, they were expected to tithe annually to Rome, and Domitian raised the bar to include not only those who were of Jewish origin but also those who practiced Jewish ways. Suetonius describes witnessing a man, ninety years of age, who was examined publicly to see if he was circumcised, and thus required to pay the tax. Domitian increased the rigor of the requirement, as some Jews and converts to Judaism had denied being Jewish in order to get around the taxation. The fact that Emperor Nerva (96–98 CE) relaxed the standard reflects the perception of a needed adjustment after Domitian's reign.

The impact upon Jesus followers, however, would have been pressing. On one hand, it might have seemed convenient to distance oneself from the local synagogue, so as not to be required to pay the extra Jewish tax. On the other hand, with the requirement of public emperor worship for the rest of the populace, this would have challenged Jewish and Christian monotheists alike, forcing them to confess Caesar as Lord and/or offer incense to his name or to suffer the consequences of being labeled an "atheist" and a traitor to the state. While evidence of how the local Roman presence in Asia Minor would have enforced such policies is lacking, celebrating the emperor's birthday with the opening of the Olympic-type games in Ephesus probably coincided with the

---

5. Stephen J. Friesen, *Twice Neokoros: Ephesus, Asia, and the Cult of the Imperial Flavian Family*, RGRW 116 (Leiden: E. J. Brill, 1993).

opening of Domitian's temple in October 89 CE, and such occasions would have called for public support of the emperor. As Jewish believers in Jesus were in the process of separation from the synagogue (and perhaps declared separate by synagogue leaders) this would have posed a challenge: they could no longer claim a Jewish dispensation, allowing liberty on the worshipping of Caesar. For Gentile believers in Jesus, the consequences were the same—perhaps leading to suffering or even death if they refused. The reverencing of magistrates was a longstanding practice in the Mediterranean world, so Gentile believers might not have seen emperor worship as that serious a matter. Whatever the case, the presentation of Pilate as not comprehending truth in John 18:38 and the featuring of Thomas confessing Jesus as, "My Lord and my God!" (20.28) would have had anti-Domitian overtones. The implications of costly discipleship for Jesus followers thus opened a new chapter in the history of the Johannine situation.

Dialogues with Other Christians

The third phase of the Johannine situation (85–100 CE) saw the expansion from a primary community to developing engagements with other Christian individuals and communities in Asia Minor and beyond as a second Asia-Minor period. Dialogues with Jewish communities continued, as did issues related to the imperial cult and pressures toward assimilation into Gentile ways of living at the expense of Jewish ones, but new crises also emerged.

The fifth crisis involved *Gentile-Christian docetizing tendencies toward assimilation* in terms of faith and practice, which the Johannine Jewish leaders sought to counter. As with the crises in the second Johannine period, those within the third are also reflected in the Johannine Epistles and Apocalypse, but even in the Gospel of John a pointed attack on tendencies to minimize the suffering of Jesus is clear. Jesus suffered and died, and the eyewitness testifies that "water and blood" came out of his pierced side (John 19:34-35). John's prologue emphasizes that the Word became *flesh* (1:14), and as the bread Jesus offers is his *flesh*, given on the cross for the life of the world, his disciples must be willing to ingest his flesh and blood if they expect to be raised with him on the last day (6:51-58).

While scholars have long interpreted denials of Jesus's humanity in the Johannine writings as a reflection of emerging Gnosticism, that movement develops several decades later, and is probably not a factor in the Johannine situation just yet. For now, the target is Docetism—the denial of Jesus's flesh-and-blood humanity (*dokeō* means "seem" or "appear"—Jesus just seemed

135

to suffer and die; he really didn't). While most Gnostics were Docetists, not all Docetists were Gnostics. Docetizing tendencies were products, however, of several things. First, Gentile believers, in their Hellenic worldviews, were likely open to Jesus's divinity; after all, if Caesar was the son of God, and if persons of exceptional talent and accomplishment were attributed divine status, including Jesus as the anointed Christ in that pantheon of gifted beings was no problem; the problem was imagining the Son of God to be fully human. The divine cannot be reduced to fleshly mortality, so assumed the Hellenistic mindset. More attractive, however, were the implications of Docetism in terms of discipleship. If willingness to follow Christ faithfully in the presence of the rising pressures to worship the emperor might have been exhorted on the basis of Jesus's having suffered, the docetic denial of his human suffering and death became especially attractive. If Jesus did not suffer or die, neither need those who follow him. Therefore, the attraction of Docetism among Gentile believers was the appropriation of cheap grace and the avoidance of costly discipleship. Note also that nearly all the emphases upon Jesus's incarnated humanity are found within John's later material. And the addressing of the "antichrists" who claimed that Jesus did not come in the flesh (1 John 4:1-3; 2 John 1:7) is especially clear in the material the Elder has added to the earlier witness of the beloved disciple. The driving issue behind Docetism was thus its existential implications over the attractiveness of its content: a non-suffering Jesus makes worldly assimilation an easier prospect.

The sixth crisis in the Johannine situation *reflects a corrective dialogue with rising institutionalization* in the late-first-century church. In the letters of Ignatius of Antioch, written in Smyrna on his way to his execution in Rome a decade or so later than the finalization of the Gospel of John, all four of these crises in the second and third phases of the Johannine situation are described. First, in these letters, Ignatius warns of Judaizers seeking to garner adherence to the way of Moses (*Magn.* 8, 10; *Phld.* 6), as to return to Jewish religion is to deny the grace of Christ. Second, he calls for the willingness to suffer and die, even at the hands of the Romans—as he himself is destined to do (*Magn.* 5; *Rom.* 4, 6, 8; *Smyrn.* 2, 5, 7; *Trall.* 10). Third, he warns against denying the flesh of Jesus (*Phld.* 4-5; *Rom.* 7; *Smyrn.* 1–2, 4–5, 7, 12; *Trall.* 6, 8, 10–11) as the schismatics do. Finally, he calls for unity under one bishop as unity under Christ, thereby avoiding schism and division (*Eph.* 4–6, 20; *Magn.* 1–6; *Phld.* 1–4, 7–8, 10; *Smyrn.* 8–9, 12; *Trall.* 1–3, 7, 12–13). It is thus no coincidence that in the later material of the Gospel of John we find most of the appeals to abide in Christ and his community (e.g., John 6:56; 15:1-9) and that in John 17 Jesus prays that his followers will be one. The Johannine approach to church unity is to call for believers to love one another and to abide in Jesus's love (John 13:34-35; 15:10, 12, 17). That is how to deal with the world's hatred, and it is accompanied by the injunction to love not the world and by Jesus's prayer that they will be protected while in the world (15:19; 17:14-17). Apparently, though, from the report of 1 John 2:19, some Johannine Christians have broken off from the community, so divisions are now a problem.

It also appears that Johannine Christians were suffering their own set of rejections from other Christians, as Diotrephes "the primacy-lover" (3 John 1:9-10) not only rejects Johannine traveling ministers but also expels members of his own church willing to take them in. Whatever the reasoning of Diotrephes, the Johannine Elder has written to "the church," whence Diotrephes apparently derives his authority (might that be Antioch, where Ignatius presides?) and promises to come for a personal visit—somewhat following the church discipline outline of Matthew 18:15-17. Therefore, it appears that this final crisis in the Johannine situation brings forth a corrective response to rising institutionalism in the late-first-century church, calling to mind a more egalitarian, familial, and Spirit-based approach to Christian leadership and church unity. Therefore, after the death of the beloved disciple, John the Elder gathers the fruit of his continuing ministry and adds it to the Gospel, which he then circulates around 100 CE. Pointedly, this later material shows Peter affirming Jesus's sole authority (6:68-69), the risen Christ leading his followers faithfully by means of the Holy Spirit (John 15–16), Jesus's prayer for unity within the church and the protection of his own in the world (John 17), and a renewed emphasis upon loving and nurturing the flock of Christ for all Christian leaders—Petrine or otherwise (21:15-17). This may also explain why parallel contrasts to each of the points in Matthew 16:17-19 can be found in John, as we may see here a dialogue over how Peter's receiving the keys to the kingdom is being interpreted and appropriated within the later Johannine situation.

This intertraditional dialogue points to a seventh crisis within the Johannine situation, *a running dialogue with other gospel traditions*, which likely spanned the other six—from the beginning of the Johannine tradition until its finalization in written form. In addition to some of the dialogical points mentioned above in relation to the Markan Gospels, John also features several other contrasting presentations of Jesus and his ministry: (a) The crowd's having eaten and been satisfied is declared to be the wrong valuation of the feeding according to John's Jesus (John 6:26—versus Mark 6:42; 8:8; Matt 14:20; 15:37; Luke 9:17); (b) Mark's messianic secrecy is counterbalanced by John's messianic disclosure; (c) the institution of a meal of remembrance at the Last Supper is absent from John, and so is the narration of Jesus being baptized by John; (d) women are presented as making confessions as well as men in John (John 11:27); (e) the Judean ministry of Jesus is featured in John in addition to his Galilean ministry in the Synoptics; (f) it is clarified (versus Mark 9:1; Matt 16:28; Luke 9:27) that Jesus never said he would return before the last of the eyewitnesses had perished (such a rumor was a product of Peter's misunderstanding of Jesus to begin with; John 21:22-23). As described in the previous excursus, interfluential dialogues between the Johannine tradition and the early Markan and later Matthean traditions are likely, which may account for some Johannine-Synoptic similarities as well as some differences. In the light of these events, a likely historical outline of the Johannine situation can be presented, involving the following crises and features.[6]

A Historical Outline of the Johannine Situation

Period I: The Palestinian Period, the Developing of an Autonomous Johannine Jesus Tradition (ca. 30–70 CE)

Crisis A—Dealing with North/South Tensions (Galileans/Judeans)

Crisis B—Reaching Followers of John the Baptist
(The oral Johannine tradition develops.)

Period II: The First Asia Minor Phase, the Forging of a Johannine Community (ca. 70–85 CE)

Crisis A—Engaging Local Jewish Family and Friends

Crisis B—Dealing with the Local Roman Presence
(The first edition of the Johannine Gospel is prepared.)

Period III: The Second Asia Minor Phase, Dialogues between Christian Communities (ca. 85–100 CE)

Crisis A—Engaging Docetizing Gentile Christians and their Teachings

Crisis B—Engaging Christian Institutionalizing Tendencies (Diotrephes and his kin)

---

6. Of course, not all of these dialogues are full-fledged crises, but they did involve tensions and contextual concerns to be addressed. For a fuller treatment, see Paul N. Anderson, *The Riddles of the Fourth Gospel: An Introduction to John* (Minneapolis: Fortress Press, 2010), 134–41.

Crisis C—Engaging Dialectically Other Christians' Presentations of Jesus and His Ministry (actually reflecting a running dialogue over *all three* periods)

(The Evangelist continues to teach and perhaps write; the Epistles are written by the Johannine Elder, who then finalizes and circulates the testimony of the beloved disciple after his death.)

II. Features of John

Even a cursory glance at the Gospel of John makes it clear that its text is full of riddles theological, historical, and literary. Only a few of these can be engaged within an introductory chapter on John, but they are fascinating nonetheless.[7] For instance, most of John's theological themes are filled with tension. John's Jesus is the most human and the most divine anywhere in the New Testament; the Son is equal to the Father but can do nothing except what the Father commands; the Holy Spirit is sent by the Father and the Son; Jesus's miracles are embellished but also existentialized; eschatology is present as well as future; many of the Judeans reject Jesus, yet salvation is of the Jews; salvation comes only through Jesus, yet Jesus as the Light enlightens all; divine sovereignty is clear, yet so is free will; sacramental themes abound in John, yet rites are not instituted; the Gospel is written that all might come to faith and believe, yet believing is associated with remaining in faith—abiding with Jesus and his community faithfully.

Historically, John is similar to the Synoptics, yet also very different. Instead of only one Passover, Jesus's ministry in John spans three; instead of the temple cleansing at the culmination of Jesus's ministry, John places it at the beginning; instead of visiting Jerusalem only once, Jesus visits at least four times in John; instead of a Passover meal, the Last Supper is on the day before the Passover in John. As John claims to be written by an eyewitness, how could its differences from the Synoptics be so extensive? Further, a good deal of characteristic Synoptic content is missing from John: Jesus's speaking in parables about the kingdom of God, the temptation of Jesus, demon exorcisms, birth narratives, the Beatitudes, the calling of the Twelve, the Transfiguration scenario, the baptism of Jesus, and the institution of a meal of remembrance. And several Johannine features are missing from the Synoptics:

---

7. Of course, not all of these dialogues are full-fledged crises, but they did involve tensions and contextual concerns to be addressed. For a fuller analysis of three dozen Johannine riddles—their character, origin, and interpretation—see ibid., 25–91.

such miracles as turning water into wine and the raising of Lazarus, the I-Am sayings of Jesus, the mention of particular characters such as Nathanael, Nicodemus, and the woman at the well, and extensive debates with Jewish leaders in Jerusalem. John also has a great deal of mundane archaeological details, so John is extensively earth-bound as well as theologically developed.

Literarily, John's riddles include several intriguing features. The prologue is set in poetic form, and some of its vocabulary is not found in the rest of the Gospel; the narrator declares his reason for writing at the end of chapter 20, but then another chapter continues the story; the story of the woman caught in adultery (7:53–8:11) is not found in the earliest manuscripts but was added in the second century; references are made to both past and future events in the narrative; repetitions and variations abound, as similar themes are repeated in slightly different ways; discourses develop theologically what has happened and will happen in Jesus's signs and other events; John's dialogues are constructed so as to show comprehension and miscomprehension rhetorically; contacts are apparent between other Gospels and John, but none of the passages are the same, verbatim; rough transitions abound between Galilee and Jerusalem in John 4–7, and while Jesus says "We're leaving this place" in John 14:31, they do not arrive at the garden until three chapters later in John 18:1; and the final editor refers to the beloved disciple as the author of the narrative, while also accounting for his apparent death. Strange literary features, indeed!

Scholars seek to address these and other riddles in a variety of ways, sometimes posing complex theories of composition to do so, but they largely are the result of several dialogical factors. First, the evangelist was a dialectical thinker, who reflected on themes in both-and ways instead of either-or dichotomies. Second, John's central motif is a Prophet-like-Moses agency Christology rooted in Deuteronomy 18:15-22, where the Revealer communicates God's liberating truth to the world; and yet, the response is uneven. Third, we have a dialectical situation in which John's material is delivered over several decades, addressing several crises and contexts. Thus, high christological emphases seek to convince audiences that Jesus is the Messiah/Christ and Son of God, and incarnational emphases assert that Jesus also really suffered and died. Fourth, a variety of literary techniques are used by the narrator as means of drawing the reader into an imaginary dialogue with Jesus—including the crafting of misunderstanding dialogues and great discourses of Jesus. Fifth, assuming the evangelist was at least aware of Mark, John's narrative provides an alternative presentation of Jesus's ministry; John is different on purpose. Sixth, in addition to intertraditional engagement, we also see signs of intratraditional development—earlier impressions reflected upon

140

later, acknowledging new insights and emerging perspectives. These aspects of John's character and composition account for most of its riddles as components of an autonomous tradition that is dialogically developed. I call it John's *dialogical autonomy.*

The outline of John's Gospel, like those of the Synoptics, begins with the ministry of John the Baptist, launching Jesus's ministry in Galilee. It expands into other miracles and teachings of Jesus, including intense engagements with religious leaders in Jerusalem, culminating in final discourses of Jesus, followed by his arrest, trials, death, burial, and appearance narratives. Hemmed in by a prologue and an epilogue, the first half of John has been called the "Book of Signs," while the second half is called "the Book of Glory." They were never, of course, separate books, but they do constitute two major parts of John's Gospel narrative, which appear to have been supplemented by an added beginning and ending.

A Basic Outline of the Gospel of John

- The Prologue (1:1-18)
- The Book of Signs (1:19–12:50)
- The Book of Glory (13:1–20:31)
- The Epilogue (21:1-25)

Parenthetical Asides

An interesting feature of the Gospel of John is that it contains a number of different types of parenthetical asides. While these could reflect the additions of a later editor, they may just as easily represent the clarifying work of the narrator. Whatever the case, they explain things in ways that help the reader make sense of the story—at times clarifying the meaning of the text, and at other times connecting the ministry of Jesus of Nazareth with non-Jewish, Gentile audiences. Like Mark, John's narrative includes a number of translations of Hebrew and Aramaic terms into Greek as well as explanations of Jewish customs in a cross-cultural way.

Translating Jewish Terms for Non-Jewish Audiences

- John's disciples call Jesus "*Rabbi*" (which is translated "teacher" —1:38)

- Andrew declares to Peter, "We have found the *Messias*" (which is translated "Christ"—1:41)

- Jesus calls Peter "*Cēphas*" (which is translated "rock"—1:42)

- The Samaritan woman says, "I know that *Messias* is coming" (who is called Christ—4:25)

- Jesus instructs the blind man, "Go, wash in the pool of *Siloam*" (this word means "sent"—9:7)

- Mary turns and says to Jesus in Hebrew, "*Rabbouni!*" (which means "teacher"—20:16)

In addition to translating Hebrew and Aramaic terms into Greek, the narrator also explains Jewish customs and provides background information for the benefit of Hellenistic audiences who might not understand the development of the plot otherwise. At times, it simply provides the actual Jewish name of a person or place (*Thomas, Gabbatha, Golgotha*), which is named otherwise with a Greek name. At other times, background information is provided as a help to audiences at a distance. The dialogue between Jesus and the Samaritan woman was exceptional for several reasons—especially given historic conflicts between Jews and Samaritans. And, it was highly ironic that the crowd should prefer Barabbas over Jesus, because the former was a thief. These explanations heighten the tension of the narrative for audiences distant from Palestine.

Explanations of Jewish Customs and Background Information

- "Jews and Samaritans didn't associate with each other" (4:9)

- "After this Jesus went across the Galilee Sea (that is, the Tiberias Sea)" (6:1)

- "Thomas (the one called *Didymus* [the twin])" (11:16; 20:24)

- "The servant's name was *Malchus*" (18:10)

- "They shouted, 'Not this man! Give us Barabbas!' (Barabbas was an outlaw.)" (18:40)

- Pilate's judgment seat is on the Stone Pavement (in Hebrew, *Gabbatha*—19:13)

- Jesus is crucified at the Skull Place (in Hebrew, *Golgotha* —19:17)

Translations of Aramaic and Hebrew terms function in similar ways in both Mark and John, and in that sense, they likely represent contact between early apostolic preaching and later, written stages of gospel traditions. If John's narrator, though, was familiar with Mark—perhaps having heard it read or performed in one or more meetings for worship—one might infer possible engagements of Mark, both augmenting Mark and apparently setting some things straight. The early ministry of John the Baptist covers the time period *before* John was thrown into prison (arrows here denote John's targeted corrections of Mark: John 3:24 ⟶ Mark 1:14); despite Jesus's declaring (in Mark 6:4) that a prophet is only without honor in his home town, not all northerners rejected him—including Samaritans and Galileans (John 4:44-45); the value of the feeding is not physical but spiritual (John 6:26 ⟶ Mark 6:42; 8:8); the deceptive role of Judas and the subversion of virtue is interjected into the challenging of the anointing (the real interest was not saving the money for the poor but skimming money from the collective purse; John 12:6 ⟶ Mark 14:4-5); and Jesus never really promised to return before the last of the apostles died—that was Peter's misunderstanding from day one (John 21:23 ⟶ Mark 9:1).

John's parenthetical asides also explain and clarify meanings covered earlier in the Johannine text. Sometimes this device simply expands on what has just previously been mentioned (the servants at the wedding knew where the water had come from, but the steward did not—2:9 ⟶ 2:5-8; the other disciple's being known to the high priest makes other things possible—18:16 ⟶ 18:15). At other times a connection is made between a figure who played a role earlier in the narrative ("Caiaphas was the one who had advised the Jewish leaders that it was better for one person to die for the people"—18:14 ⟶ 11:49-53; the beloved disciple is the one who had leaned against the breast of Jesus—21:20 ⟶ 13:23) reminding the reader of the person's earlier role. Yet another function is to clarify what was not necessarily meant by earlier statements: while Jesus and his disciples were baptizing, it was not Jesus who baptized, but his disciples who did so (4:2 ⟶ 3:22; 4:1). This is not necessarily a difference of opinion; it simply clarifies what was meant earlier, as well as what was not.

In addition to clarifying references earlier in the text, John also includes clarifications of details that emerges later in the text, but this is really puzzling! Do we have a prediction of the future, or might this suggest a disrupted history of the text within a complex composition process? If the prologue was added later, some of its message might refer to what John the Baptist had earlier said, though it follows later in the narrative (1:15 ⟶ 1:30). Further,

Mary is introduced as having anointed Jesus's feet in John 11, but that does not happen until John 12 (11:2➡12:1-8); so John's clarifying the future, as though it is presently known, is an odd narrative feature indeed. And some anticipation of what will come later regarding the feeding (6:6➡6:11), Judas's betrayal of Jesus (6:64, 71; 13:11➡18:2-5), and the outpouring of the Holy Spirit (7:39➡20:22) is also forecasted as a means of preparing the reader for what will follow.

Other asides clarifying historical events in Jesus's ministry are also added. The disciples were not present at the well-scene, as they had gone into the city to buy food (4:8); Moses gave commandment about circumcision, "although it wasn't Moses but the patriarchs" (7:22➡Gen. 17:11); "Judas (not Judas Iscariot) asked, 'Lord, why are you about to reveal yourself to us and not to the world?'" (14:22); the one who saw the water and the blood offers a true testimony, and he knows what he says is true (19:35); and, regarding the beloved disciple who wrote these things, "We know his testimony is true!" affirms the Johannine community (21:24).

Some of these asides appear to be added by the final compiler, but many of them also could just as easily represent the work of the evangelist—clarifying the narrative for later audiences.

The Works of Jesus in John

The works of Jesus in John are both similar to and different from his works in the Synoptics. Like the Synoptics, John's Jesus performs miracles, called "signs" (*sēmeia*), which also heal the lame and the blind, produce a healing from afar, bring people forth from the dead, feed the multitude, present a sea-crossing deliverance, and lead to a great catch of fish. Unlike the Synoptics, John's signs include turning water into wine, and most of John's miracles are not found in the Synoptics. Nonetheless, like the Synoptics, healings are performed on the Sabbath, and they provoke interest in Jesus as well as threatening religious leaders. Distinctive in John are the ways that the signs of Jesus lead into expansions upon the spiritual meaning of Jesus's works, and in that sense, dialogues with and discourses by Jesus often follow the signs. For instance, Jesus not only provides bread for the multitude; he himself is the Bread of Life. He not only restores the sight of the blind man; his signs expose the blindness of those who claim to see. Jesus not only raises Lazarus from the tomb; he is the resurrection and the life. Therefore, it is the spiritual *sign*-ificance of the signs that is even more pronounced than their selection in John.

144

The Signs of Jesus in John (* also in other Gospels)

- The first sign in Galilee: The water into wine (2:1-11)
- The second sign in Galilee: The healing of the royal official's son (4:46-54)
- The healing of the invalid by the pool (5:1-15)
- *The feeding of the five thousand (6:5-15; also in Matt 14:14-21; Mark 6:34-44; Luke 9:12-17)
- *The sea crossing (6:16-21; also in Matt 14:22-33; Mark 6:45-53)
- The healing of the man born blind (9:1-41)
- The raising of Lazarus (11:1-45)
- *The great catch of fish (21:1-11; also in Luke 5:1-11)

Another thing to note is the tension between the high and embellished character of John's signs and their diminished valuation—Jesus says to Thomas, "Do you believe because you see me? Happy are those who don't see and yet believe" (20:29). And despite John's first seven signs beginning with a party miracle and concluding with the resurrection of Lazarus, Jesus is presented as chiding people for their signs-faith (4:48), declaring after the feeding, "I assure you that you are looking for me not because you saw miraculous signs but because you ate all the food you wanted. Don't work for the food that doesn't last but for the food that endures for eternal life, which the [Son of Man] will give you. God the Father has confirmed him as his agent to give life" (6:26-27). Here Jesus is presented as challenging the view that signs are required for people to believe. Rather, it is their revelatory meaning that is important. Therefore, the works of Jesus function in John to help people see the truth they convey in ways beyond what the sheer observable will substantiate.

In addition to posing a different perspective on the meaning of Jesus's miracles, John also offers an alternative understanding to the Synoptic explanation as to why miracles might not happen. In the Petrine tradition underlying Mark, and also carried further in Matthew and Luke, the relative dearth of miracles is not seen as a function of God's failure; it is the human lack of faith that is at fault. It is peoples' faith that has healed them (Mark 5:34; 10:52; Matt 8:13; 9:22, 29; 15:28), so if people would simply believe, with faith as solid as that of a mustard seed, great things would indeed happen (Matt 17:20; Luke 17:6). In John, however, tragedy and the relative dearth of wonders is explained not as a factor of human fault or lack of faith but rather as an occasion for God to be glorified. This is especially the case regarding the man born blind and the death of Lazarus (9:1-5; 11:4). In Mark, anything asked for in faith will be received (Mark 11:24; Matt 21:22); in John, what is asked in the name of Jesus will be granted as a means of glorifying God and furthering God's work in the world (John 11:22; 14:13; 15:7, 16). Therefore, we see in John on this issue two levels of dialogue—one as a dialectical reflection on the relative dearth of miracles within the ministry and perspective of the evangelist, and a second as a factor of intertraditional engagement with a key Synoptic perspective. Such dialogues have continued among readers of the Gospels ever since, and they probably originated among purveyors of gospel traditions.

Travels of Jesus in John

Another feature of Jesus's ministry in John involves his visits to Jerusalem. In contrast to the single visit in the Markan Gospels, John's Jesus goes back and forth between Galilee and Jerusalem a multiplicity of times. The first visit to Jerusalem in John shows Jesus clearing the temple at the first Passover of his ministry, an inaugural prophetic sign. Jesus's second visit to Jerusalem involves a healing of an invalid at the Pool of Bethsaida, and he meets with growing resistance, to the extent that religious leaders make plans to kill him. Jesus's third visit to Jerusalem in John 7 interestingly continues the discussion of the healing on the Sabbath in John 5, yet it leads into a long series of debates with Jewish leaders regarding Jesus's authority. After the healing of the blind man in Jerusalem and continued debates with the Jewish leaders, the narrator abruptly announces that it is winter, and that the festival now being celebrated is Hanukkah (10:22). Without a mention of his departure, the narrator describes Jesus discussing whether to return to Judea, given Lazarus's illness in Bethany (11:7), and his triumphal entry to Jerusalem happens in the next chapter. Therefore, four or five visits by Jesus to Jerusalem are described in John, and unlike the single year of ministry in the Synoptics, they cover two or three years at least.

When compared with Mark's rendering of Jesus's single visit to Jerusalem, John's presentation seems more realistic from a historical and chronological standpoint. It probably took more than one year for Jesus's ministry to get going (although Mark's feeding narrative does reference springtime—green grass, Mark 6:39—which would have been a year before Mark's final Passover), and observant Jews would have traveled to Jerusalem at least three times a year to celebrate the pilgrimage festivals of *Passover* (springtime), *Weeks* (late spring/early summer—seven weeks after Passover), and *Booths* (harvest time). Therefore, Jesus's referring to having taught in the temple day after day (Mark 14:49) and the fact that Jewish leaders came from Jerusalem and other regions to witness the ministries of John and Jesus (Mark 1:5; 3:8, 22; 7:1) long before entering Judea in Mark 10:1, make it highly unlikely that he was unknown in Jerusalem before his final visit. Otherwise, the Roman soldiers might have been more willing to arrest him, given his riding into the city on a donkey's colt (fulfilling Zechariah 9:9) and the crowd's shouting out, "Hosanna! *Blessings on the one who comes in the name of the Lord!* Blessings on the king of Israel!" (Matt 21:9; Mark 11:9-10; John 12:13, citing Ps 118:25-26).

In addition to providing occasions for Jesus to visit Jerusalem, the named festivals have some features that coincide with presentations of Jesus's ministry in John. Related to the *Passover* motif, John the Baptist declares Jesus to be the Lamb of God (1:29, 36); Jesus is "sacrificed" politically on the day before the Passover; and just as the bones of the Paschal lamb should not be broken, the legs of the other victims were broken but not Jesus's (Exod 12:46 ➠John 19:31-36). In addition, many people from Galilee are said to have visited Jerusalem on the Passover (4:45; cf. 2:23) to purify themselves (11:55), and Jewish leaders are presented as wanting to keep legal restrictions against sharing fellowship with the uncircumcised or touching any dead thing (Exod 12:43-49; Num 9:6-10➠John 18:28; 19:31) thus forbidding them from entering Pilate's headquarters and hurrying the death of the crucifixion victims. A blood-daubing hyssop branch, ironically, is used to lift the sponge of vinegar to Jesus's lips (Exod 12:22➠John 19:29), heightening the sense of religious realism.

A good deal of political realism also is palpable around the Passover motif. Given that the Romans were especially anxious around Passover gatherings, Pilate has left his seaside palace at Caesarea Maritima and traveled to Jerusalem for the occasion: a judicious precaution, given previous Passover revolts in Jerusalem. Pilate keeps the custom of releasing a prisoner at Passover (18:39-40), a means of appeasing restless crowds, but the crowds demand Barabbas—a bandit. It was also at the first Passover in John that Jesus predicted the destruction of the temple forty years hence (2:19), the multitude of five thousand was ready to coronate Jesus as a kingly leader at John's second Passover (6:4, 14-15), and Caiaphas worries about a Roman backlash against the multitudes following Jesus at John's third Passover (11:49-55). This explains why the tensions are high during Jesus's final Passover visit to Jerusalem. Therefore, the narrator's noting that "the Passover was near" three times in John conveys not primarily a theological point; it heightens the sense of political tension felt during Roman occupation and the fear of a retaliatory response during Israel's leading national festival.

While the feast in John 5 is unnamed, it shows Jesus engaging with religious leaders in the temple area who are offended at his having healed the invalid on the Sabbath. This leads to debates over scripture and Moses (bearing similarities with the Festival of Weeks—celebrating God's giving the Law to Moses), and the debate over the healing on the Sabbath continues in John 7. There, however, the festival is that of Booths (or Tabernacles), where the Jews celebrated the fall harvest by spending a week in tents and remembering the forty years Israel spent camping in the wilderness on the way to the promised land (Lev 23:33-43). Two central themes of this festival are replicated in John. First, *light* is central to this festival, as Yahweh led the Israelites in the wilderness by a pillar of cloud by day and of fire by night (Exod 13:21); Jesus claims to be the light of the world in John (8:12; 9:5; 11:9). Another theme associated with Booths is *water*. At the end of the harvest, participating in the Festival of Booths insures a supply of rainfall for the following year's crops (Neh 8:14-18), and in the middle of the festival the priest would gather water from the Pool of Siloam, just outside the temple, and would pour out the water in the sacrificial area as a joyous celebration of bounty received and anticipated. It is fitting that at the culmination of the festival Jesus stands and declares a promise of living water, flowing from one's innermost being (Jer 2:13; 17:13➝John 7:37-38). The theme of light also fits the Festival of *Dedication* (10:22-23), and given that it was winter, gathering near the Porticoes of Solomon would have provided some shelter from the wind. Therefore, in addition to conveying religious significance, the presentation of the festivals in the Gospel of John also echoes religious realism as would have been experienced by observant Jews in Jerusalem before it was destroyed in 70 CE.

Jewish Festivals in John

- The first Passover festival, in Jerusalem (*Pesach*, 2:13, 23; 4:45)
- The unnamed feast, in Jerusalem (5:1)
- The second Passover festival, in Galilee (*Pesach*, 6:4)
- The festival of Booths/Tabernacles, in Jerusalem (*Sukkot*, 7:2, 37)
- The festival of Dedication, in Jerusalem (*Hanukkah*, 10:22)
- The third Passover, in Jerusalem (*Pesach*, 11:55-56; 12:1, 12, 20; 13:1, 29; 18:28, 39)

Mundane Details in John

A fair number of mundane details corroborated by archaeology and to-pography also accompany John's narrative. Bethabara across the Jordan (ap-parently changed to the more familiar "Bethany" by an early copyist, 1:28) shows signs of an early baptismal site; Bethsaida, home of Philip, Andrew, and Peter, shows signs of being a fisherman's village (1:44; 12:21); large lathed stone jars, used for purification purposes, have been discovered in the region (2:6); Jesus and others go "down to Capernaum" (2:12) and "up to Jerusa-lem" (2:13; 5:1; 11:55), showing awareness of elevation differences; Aenon near Salim has ample waters for baptizing (3:23); Samaritan worship sites are found on Mt. Gerizim, and Jacob's well is nearby (4:6, 20); the five porticoes around the Pool of Beth-zatha reflect four rows of columns surrounding two pools, with a fifth row in the middle (5:2); the middle of the Sea of Galilee is indeed three or four miles from shore (25 or 30 *stadia*, 6:19); a second Pool of Siloam, a *mikveh* pool of purification used for cleansing by those entering the temple area (9:7) was discovered in 2004; Bethany is indeed less than two miles from Jerusalem (15 *stadia*, 11:18); the Kidron Valley is crossed on the way to the garden (18:1); the *Praetorium* of Pilate is described (18:28, 33), and the stone pavement supporting Pilate's judgment seat is called in Hebrew (or possibly Aramaic) *Gabbatha* (meaning "ridge of the house," 19:13); *Golgotha* (the Hebrew word for "place of the skull," 19:17) is located "near the city" and thus outside the city wall (19:20; cf. Heb 13:12); a spike through the anklebone of a crucified victim (likely with the leg broken) was recently discovered in Jerusalem, confirming John's presentation of the crucifixion scene (John 19:31-33; 20:25). These and other details could have been added to make the story more graphic, but they certainly correspond with known realities in Palestine before it was destroyed by the Romans from 66–73 CE.[8]

The Words of Jesus in John

The language of Jesus in John is somewhat similar to that of the Synoptic Jesus, but in many ways it is different. Missing or diminished are such themes as forgiveness, the kingdom, and giving to the poor; distinctive emphases include such themes as believing, loving, and eternal life. Further, the Johan-nine Jesus speaks in the language of the evangelist, so it seems we have some-thing closer to his own rendering of Jesus's teachings than the actual language

---

8. For dozens of archaeological and topographical features in John see Paul N. Anderson, "Aspects of Historicity in John: Implications for Archaeological and Jesus Studies," in *Jesus and Archaeology*, ed. by James H. Charlesworth (Grand Rapids: Eerdmans, 2006), 587–618.

of Jesus. Then again, putting an understanding in one's own words repre-sents the truest form of learning, so despite John's interpretive presentation, a distinctive memory of Jesus's ministry nonetheless still comes through. For instance, even though the literary form of the metaphorical I-Am sayings in John is not found in the Synoptics, each of the nine images is, so one cannot say on the basis of the Synoptics that John's presentation of Jesus's teachings has no connection with the Jesus of history. Further, the Jesus of the Synop-tics also makes absolute I-Am statements (Mark 6:50; 14:62), including a reference to God's word to Moses before the burning bush in Exodus 3 (Mark 12:26). So, while such a theme is more fully developed in John, it cannot be said that it is absent from the Markan Gospels.

The I-Am sayings of Jesus in John (in Greek, *egō eimi*) function in engag-ing ways. The *absolute* use of the term can have several meanings, functioning as something of a *double entendre*. On one hand, *egō eimi* without an associ-ated image can simply mean "I am so and so . . ."—a personal introduction. It can also be a form of identification—"It is not someone else; it is I." It can also refer to location, "Where I am," or association, "I am the one I claim to be." And yet, the term can also be used with reference to God's sustaining help in Isaiah, where God consoles Israel by saying "I am the LORD who . . . " protects, delivers, and provides for her redemption (Isa 42:6, 8; 43:3, 10-11, 15; 44:6, 24; 45:5-6, 18). Then again, Jesus's declaration "I assure you, before Abraham was, I Am" (John 8:58) sounds much like Yahweh's theophanic (ap-pearance of God) declaration to Moses before the burning bush in the wilder-ness in Exodus 3:14: "I Am Who I Am. So say to the Israelites, 'I Am has sent me to you.'" In response to Jesus's statement in John 8, the Jewish leaders pick up stones to kill him—the penalty for blasphemy (Lev 24:16). While most of the other absolute I-Am statements of Jesus in John are not theophanic in their association, the words of Jesus at the sea-crossing (John 6:20) appear to have had an association with Exodus 3:14 in the Johannine tradition; con-versely, in Mark 6:50 the words appear to have been interpreted as an iden-tification: "Be encouraged! It's me [i.e., not a ghost]. Don't be afraid." Such differences of impression from the earliest stages of traditional memory may account for at least some aspects of the different presentations of Jesus's min-istry within the Johannine and Markan Gospels—two bi-optic perspectives from day one. In the Johannine tradition, an early association along these lines may even have contributed to the evangelist's perception and memory of Jesus's significance and his representations of Jesus and his ministry in his own preaching and teaching.

Absolute I-Am Sayings of Jesus in John

- "*I Am*—the one who speaks with you [that is, the Messiah]" (4:26)

- "*I Am*. Don't be afraid" (during the sea crossing, 6:20)

- " . . . where *I am* you can't come" (7:34, 36; 8:21)

- "If you don't believe that *I Am* [that is, he that is from above], you will die in your sins" (8:24)

- "When the [Son of Man] is lifted up, then you will know that *I Am* [that is, the one declaring to the world what I have seen and heard from the Father who sent me]" (8:28)

- "I assure you, . . . before Abraham was, *I Am*" (8:58)

- "I'm telling you this now, before it happens, so that when it does happen you will believe that *I Am* [that is, your teacher and lord]" (13:19)

- "Father, I want those you gave me to be with me where *I am*" (17:24)

- "*I Am*" (in response to the guards' asking if he is Jesus of Nazareth; 18:5, 6, 8)

Also distinctive are John's presentations of Jesus-sayings linking *egō eimi* with a metaphor or an image that renames the subject. While all of these terms or notions are also found in the Synoptics, their form is distinctively Johannine. Each of the images and terms (bread, light, shepherd, gate, resurrection, life, way, truth, vine) represents both historic typologies of Israel and its promise for the world, while also addressing the existential condition of all humanity. These themes would captivate the interest of Jewish and Gentile audiences alike within a Greco-Roman setting. What humans need in terms of nourishment, guidance, liberation—that is what Jesus offers and is. Because John's I-Am metaphors connect God's blessings promised to Israel to the rest of the world by means of Jesus's mission as the Christ, key themes from the teachings of Jesus have been woven into the teaching and preaching of the evangelist, conveying the blessings of Israel to the world.

John's I-Am Sayings with the Predicate Nominative

- "I am *the bread of life*" (6:35, 41, 48, 51)

- "I am *the light of the world*" (8:12; 9:5)

- "I am *the gate of the sheep*" (10:7, 9)
- "I am *the good shepherd*" (10:11, 14)
- "I am *the resurrection and the life*" (11:25)
- "I am *the way, the truth, and the life*" (14:6)
- "I am *the true vine*" (15:1, 5)

In addition to Jesus's discourses and teachings, the Gospel of John features over three dozen dialogues with Jesus, many of them extended ones. While the discourses of Jesus describe God's saving-revealing work as the divine initiative, inviting a human response of faith, many of the dialogues begin with the discussant taking the initiative, either asking a question or making an overly confident statement. Invariably, when an individual or group takes the lead, they are exposed as miscomprehending, and misunderstanding in narrative is always rhetorical. It exposes flawed views that the narrator seeks to correct, and often those views can be inferred in the audiences of the evolving Johannine tradition. Dialogues with Nicodemus and religious authorities in Jerusalem challenge Jewish audiences; the dialogue with Pilate challenges Roman authorities; dialogues with disciples challenge docetizing Christians; dialogues with Peter challenge Diotrephes and his kin (3 John). When discussants get it right, however, either from the beginning or eventually, such presentations pose positive examples for audiences to embrace. Here John's contextual, literary, and theological features of the narrative converge.

Dialogues between Jesus and . . .

- his disciples (1:35-51; 4:27, 31-38; 9:1-7; 11:1-16; 14:1-31; 16:17-33)
- Nicodemus (a leader among the Judeans, 3:1-21)
- the Samaritan woman (4:4-42)
- the religious leaders in Jerusalem (5:16-47; 7:14–8:59)
- the crowd, the Jewish leaders, the disciples, and Peter (6:25-70)
- the seeing blind man (9:35-41)
- the sisters of Lazarus (11:17-45)
- the Greeks and the Jerusalem crowd (12:20-36)

- Peter (13:1-20; 21:15-23)
- the high priest and the guard (18:19-24)
- Pilate (18:28–19:16)
- Mary Magdalene (20:11-18)
- Thomas (20:24-29)

Of special interest among the characters in John's narrative are particular women, some of whom play momentous roles in its plot. The mother of Jesus (not mentioned by name) is present at the beginning and end of Jesus's ministry, and the woman at the well becomes an apostle to the Samaritans. Mary and Martha play important roles around the raising of Lazarus, and their gratitude follows as Mary anoints the feet of Jesus with costly ointment. In addition to the disciple Jesus loved (13:23; 19:26; 20:2; 21:7, 20), it is also said that Jesus loved Mary, Martha, and Lazarus (11:5), although this does not mean that the beloved disciple was a member of the Lazarus family. At the cross women are present, and Jesus entrusts his mother to the beloved disciple. Finally, Mary Magdalene is the first one to behold the risen Lord, and she becomes the apostle to the apostles. Women play no small role in John's story of Jesus, and that fact has considerable implications for future readers.

Women in John

- The mother of Jesus—present at his first sign (2:1-11) and at the cross (19:25-27)
- The woman at the well—an apostle to the Samaritans (4:4-44)
- Mary and Martha—sisters of Lazarus, confessor of Jesus (Martha), and anointer of Jesus (Mary) (11:1-45; 12:1-11)
- A woman in labor—an image of eschatological travail (16:21-22)
- A woman in the courtyard—exposing Peter (18:15-17)
- Women at the cross (including Mary, wife of Clopas, 19:25)
- Mary Magdalene—the apostle to the apostles (also present at the cross, 19:25; 20:1-18)

The effect of John's narrative is to draw the hearer/reader into a believing relationship with Jesus as the Christ. Those characters in the story who get it right serve as positive examples to follow; those who get it wrong serve as negative examples to avoid. If indeed John's prologue reflects a worship hymn (see "Excursus IV") that has been added as a new beginning to the final edition of the Gospel, later readers are prepared experientially for what they will then read or hear. Also, if the first edition actually began with the passages referring to the witness of John the Baptist in John 1:6-8, 15, and 19-37, with the three verses of the *Logos* hymn crafted around it, the original beginning of John's Gospel looks a good deal like the beginning of Mark.

III. The Message of John

The message of the Gospel of John is expressed clearly in both the prologue and its statement of purpose. The Light that enlightens everyone was coming into the world, empowering all who believe in Christ to become children of God (1:9-13). And John's story of Jesus is written that people might believe and have life in his name (20:31). Indeed, the signs of Jesus show that he is sent from God (3:2; 9:16), and if people cannot fully believe in Jesus as the Christ, they are exhorted to at least believe in his works as a means to that end (10:38). John's witnesses testify that Jesus is the Messiah/Christ, and in addition to persons, witnesses also include Jesus's words and works. Finally, the fulfilled words of Caiaphas, of Jesus, and the scriptures show Jesus to be the one of whom Moses wrote (5:46), and like the Gospel of Matthew, John adds several types of scripture-fulfillment claims and associations. Some are left on the implicit level, while others are declared more explicitly. John's purpose, therefore, is highly apologetic, but coming to faith in Jesus as the Christ is only the beginning; several implications continue.

The Purpose(s) of John

In addition to facilitating belief in Jesus, John also has several other purposes in the light of its two editions. First, the five signs of Jesus in John's first edition function as an augmentation of Mark, as these are distinctive to John. Jesus's first two signs in Galilee thus fill out the early ministry of Jesus before the events narrated in Mark 1, and the other three signs fill out the Judean ministry of Jesus augmenting Mark's lone southern miracle in Jericho. Interestingly, Matthew corroborates John's moves, here. Matthew places the Capernaum healing from afar (though slightly different in John) just before the healing of Peter's mother-in-law (Matt 8:5-17), and he notes the miracles that Jesus had performed on the lame and the blind in the temple area (Matt 21:14) found otherwise only in John (5:1-15; 9:1-7). This purpose of augmenting Mark is alluded to in John 20:30, where the narrator acknowledges that "Jesus did many other miraculous signs in his disciples' presence, signs that aren't recorded in *this* scroll" (emphasis mine).

A second feature of John's purpose is that it presents the five signs of Jesus as playing a role similar to the five books of Moses, thus bolstering its presentation of Jesus as the Jewish Messiah. In contrast to his association with Elijah and the prophet Moses in the Synoptics (Mark 9:11-13), in this Gospel the Baptist is presented as denying that he is either of these figures (John 1:19-25) because Jesus thus fulfills the typologies of both Moses and Elijah associated with the messianic promise in Malachi 4:4-5. This may also explain why the Transfiguration is missing from John, in addition to not wanting to duplicate Mark. The associations with Moses and Elijah are even more pronounced in the feeding and sea-crossing narratives of John 6, so the emphasis continues in John's later material, as well. The debates with Jewish leaders are most intense in John 5 and 7–10, though, and they appear to have cooled some by the time the Jewish leaders are portrayed in John 6.

A third purpose of John can be seen in the character of its later additions, in that some of this material appears to be harmonizing John with the Synoptics. Again, the feeding, sea-crossing, discussion of the loaves, and Peter's confession pull John's narrative into line a bit more closely with the other Gospels (John 6). And the final teachings and prayer of Jesus complement their parallels in the Synoptics (John 15–17), and the promise that Jesus would meet his disciples in Galilee (Mark 16:7; Matt 28:7, 10, 16) is fulfilled in John 21, where Peter's pastoral role is also restored and somewhat co-opted. The final ending of John (21:25) echoes the first ending (20:30-31) in defending John's autonomy ("Jesus did many other things as well. If all of them were recorded, I imagine the world itself wouldn't have enough room for the scrolls that would be written"), although in adding John 6 and 21, the final compiler appears to have rectified John's distinctiveness a bit.

A fourth purpose of John is also exposed in its later material, in that the invitation to believe is associated with abiding in Jesus and his community. Therefore, while the first edition appears to have been crafted to reach external audiences, the later material seems especially relevant to internal audiences. Given the secessions and tensions reflected in the Johannine Epistles (e.g., 1 John 2:19), it is understandable that Jesus would pray that his followers would be one (17:11, 21-23). As Jesus's followers experience tribulation in the world (16:33), his disciples are called to embrace the cross, and those who ingest Jesus's flesh and blood abide in him and he in them (6:51, 56). Given that docetizing ministers deny the suffering and death of Jesus (1 John 4:1-3), the eyewitness testifies to his human suffering (John 19:34-35). Therefore, continuing in faith implies the call for Jesus's followers to remain in him and he in them, abiding in his love (15:1-10).

A fifth purpose of John is to show the way forward in terms of how the risen Lord seeks to lead the church. In the light of Diotrephes who loves primacy in 3 John 1:9-10, the juxtaposition of Peter and the beloved disciple in John takes on ecclesial meanings. Note also the similarities and differences between the keys-to-the-kingdom passage in Matthew 16:17-19 and the presentation of Peter's confession in John 6. Here it is *Jesus* whose sole authority Peter affirms, and in John 14–16 Jesus promises to lead his followers by the ever-accessible work of the Holy Spirit, available to all. Therefore, it is a plurality of apostolic leadership that Jesus commissions in John 20:21-23, and the priesthood of all believers is established by the Johannine Jesus. While Peter's leadership is affirmed in John 21:15-17, it is also chastened toward loving and caring for the flock, and the beloved disciple provides a link between Peter and the Lord (13:23-25; 21:7), emphasizing the centrality of relational connectedness with Jesus for all believers. With this in view, after the death of the beloved disciple (21:23), the Johannine Elder compiles the Fourth Gospel around the turn of the first century CE and circulates it as the last will and testament of Jesus for the church, featuring the witness of the beloved disciple, claiming on behalf of his community that "we know that his testimony is true" (21:24).

Therefore, John's Gospel has several purposes beyond leading audiences to believe in Jesus as the Messiah/Christ. Coming to faith is the beginning, but continuing in faith is also a palpable concern—especially in the later material. There the emphasis is to abide in Jesus and his community, even if it may involve suffering and a high cost of discipleship. Yet, it is in the fleshly suffering of Jesus that his followers are invited to embrace the way of the cross (1:14; 6:51-53; 19:34). Therefore, the overall thrust of John's message still functions to facilitate belief in Jesus as the Christ, the Son of God, in order that by believing, humanity might experience life in his name (20:30-31).

John's Christology—The Heart of the Story

Among John's various riddles, its theological tensions are among the most provocative. In John Jesus is presented as the most human and the most divine anywhere in the New Testament. Also, the Son is equal to the Father, yet he also declares himself to be subservient to the Father; but where did these tensions come from, and how are they to be interpreted? Was the author senile, demented, or contradictory, or might we have a multiplicity of literary sources involved, each with its own distinctive presentation of Jesus as the Christ to convey? The latter view is that of Rudolf Bultmann, who located different christological strains within what he thought were sources underlying John, assuming that dissonant content was also added later. When all of his stylistic and contextual criteria for inferring multiple sources of John's Christology are considered, however, the evidence is less than compelling, and the final editor seems more conservative rather than intrusive.[9] Therefore, these tensions are part and parcel of the evangelist's understanding of Jesus, which reflects a dialectical thinker, presenting his material within a dialectical situation, crafting the narrative to engage readers within an imaginary dialogue with Jesus.

The Gospel of John actually has two beginnings, and before the prologue was added, John 1:19-51 provides a compelling introduction to Jesus as the Christ, featuring a host of christological titles at the outset. Jesus is described by John the Baptist as one "whom you don't recognize" (1:26), "the Lamb of God who takes away the sin of the world" (1:29, 36), "the one who baptizes in the Holy Spirit" (1:33), and "the Son of God" (1:34; also by Nathanael, v. 49). When John's disciples abandon him and follow Jesus, they and Nathanael refer to him as *rabbi*, which means "teacher" (1:38, 49). He is also called the *Messias*, which means "Christ" (Andrew, 1:41); "the one Moses wrote about in the Law and the Prophets" and "Jesus, Joseph's son, from Nazareth" (Philip, 1:45); "the king of Israel" (Nathanael, 1:49); and finally, the Son of Man (Jesus, 1:51). These titles emphasize Jesus's original role as a teacher of his followers, while also reflecting a developed understanding of his mission as the Messiah/Christ from the evangelist's perspective.

John's prologue also conveys its own set of convictions, set in the form of a worship piece. The in-the-beginning Word (1:1, 14), God (1:1), the Light that overcomes darkness (1:5), the true Light that enlightens all people (1:9), the flesh-becoming Word (1:14), the Father's only begotten Son (1:14; v. 18 in later manuscripts), and the only-begotten God who is at the Father's side (1:1; v. 18 in earlier manuscripts) articulate a set of worship confessions within Johannine Christianity regarding Jesus as the Christ and God's Son. These references express a full range of Christian beliefs regarding the saving-revealing mission of Jesus as the Christ.

Note, however, John's emphases upon Jesus's full humanity, as well. The incarnational "flesh" of Jesus is insisted upon in John (1:14a; 6:51, 53-56),

---

9. An in-depth analysis of these issues is available in Paul N. Anderson, *The Christology of the Fourth Gospel*, 3rd printing (Eugene, OR: Cascade, 2010), as well as my foreword to Bultmann's *The Gospel of John: A Commentary*, The Johannine Monograph Series, vol. 1 (Eugene, OR: Wipf & Stock, 2014).

and his humanity is acknowledged by others (1:45; 10:33; 18:5-7). References to his human family are clear (1:45; 2:1-12; 6:42; 19:25-27), and not even his brothers believed in him (7:5). Out of his side flow physical blood and water (19:34), and Thomas is allowed to touch Jesus's flesh wounds with his finger and hand (20:27). Further, Jesus is presented as displaying human pathos and emotion: he weeps over Lazarus's death (11:35); his heart is deeply troubled (11:33; 12:27; 13:21); he groans (11:33, 38); on the cross he thirsts (19:28); he loves his own (11:3, 5, 36; 13:1, 23, 34; 14:21; 15:9, 10, 12; 19:26). Therefore, John's Jesus is presented as both human and divine, and these themes are both early and late. From an early perspective, people are represented as having something of a spiritual encounter in the presence of Jesus, and the narrator also comments upon mundane features in the narrative. From a later perspective, Jesus is worshipped as the Christ, but emphases are also made upon his fleshly humanity and his having died on the cross. Therefore, high and low christological content in John is both early and late.

When considering these tensions in John's Christology, it is important to consider central passages that convey John's understanding of Jesus as the Christ. When such passages as John 1:1-18; 3:31-36; and 12:44-50 are considered alongside 20:30-31, several features surface reflecting the central thrust of John's Christology involving the Son's relation to the Father. First, the One who comes from above testifies to what he has seen and heard from the Father; he does not speak his own words, only God's, yet the world does not receive his testimony. Second, Jesus comes as a light into the world so that everyone who believes in him should not remain in darkness but should receive the light of life. Third, whoever believes in him believes not only in him but in the One who sent him, for he speaks the words of God authentically; his authenticity is also confirmed by his words coming true. Fourth, whoever accepts his testimony certifies that God is true; that one receives eternal life, but to reject him is to receive judgment on the last day, and that one must endure God's wrath. Fifth, the One whom God has sent gives the Spirit without measure, and the Father loves the Son and has placed all things into his hands; the Father's commandment and loving gift is eternal life.

While Bultmann argued that this agency theme reflected a gnostic perspective on God's dialogue with humanity by means of angels and intermediary beings, there is nothing in this overall structure that would not fit entirely well with Jesus's fulfilling the Prophet-like-Moses agency motif of Deuteronomy 18:15-22. Therefore, rather than reflecting two different Christologies—one high and one low—John's presentation of the Son's relation with the Father, both equal to and subordinate to the Father, represents flip sides of the same coin: central features of the Jewish agency motif, confirmed by his word coming true (13:18-19; 14:28-29; 16:2-4; 18:8-9, 31-32). Ironically, Jesus is accused by Jewish leaders as being the presumptuous prophet who should be put to death (Deut 18:20), yet they do not perceive what the narrator shares with his audiences, that Jesus really does fulfill the typology of the authentic prophet predicted by Moses long ago.[10]

Jesus as the Prophet Like Moses (Deut 18:15-22)

- The Lord God will raise up a prophet like Moses from fellow Israelites; he's the one people must listen to (Deut 18:15).

  ○ *Jesus* is anticipated as (John 1:17; 3:14; 6:32; 7:19, 22), is written about by (1:45; 5:46), and is identified as being *a prophet like Moses* (John 6:14-15).

  ○ The Son witnesses to what he has *seen and heard* from the Father (3:32; 5:19, 30; 6:46; 8:26, 38, 40; 14:24; 15:15); *hearing* the Son implies *believing* in him (3:36; 5:24; 6:45; 8:51) and *knowing* his voice (10:3-4, 16; 18:37).

  ○ *Rejecting* the Son implies having neither heard nor seen the Father (5:37-38; 8:47), and the one not embracing Jesus's words receives judgment (12:46-48).

- God will put God's words in his mouth, and he will tell them everything commanded him (Deut 18:18).

  ○ The words of the Father are spoken by Jesus (John 3:11, 34; 6:63, 68; 7:16-18, 28; 8:28, 38, 55; 12:44-50; 14:24, 31), and those who receive the agent receive the sender (1:12; 3:36; 5:24; 12:44; 13:20; 14:21-24; 15:10).

  ○ Jesus not only speaks the word of God; he *is the Word* of God (1:1, 14).

  ○ The Son's word is to be *equated* with that of the Father precisely because he says nothing on his own, but only what he hears and sees from the Father (5:19; 10:28-29, 32, 38; 12:49-50; 17:21), conveying identically the divine command (10:18; 12:49-50; 14:31; 15:10).

---

10. Cf. Paul N. Anderson, "The Having-Sent-Me-Father—Aspects of Agency, Encounter, and Irony in the Johannine Father-Son Relationship," *Semeia* 85, ed. Adele Reinhartz (1999): 33–57.

○ Jesus comes *in the name of* the Father (5:43), whom he seeks to glorify (12:28), keeping his followers in the name of the Father in unity (17:11-12).

• God will hold accountable anyone who doesn't listen to his words, which that prophet will speak in God's name (Deut 18:19).

○ Those not receiving the Son *have already been judged* (John 3:16-18; 12:47); the Father entrusts all judgment to the Son (5:22, 27), as the truthful words of the Son produce their own judgment if rejected (12:48).

○ The *judgment of the world* involves the casting out of the ruler of the world and the lifting up of the Son of Man (12:31-36; 16:11); the *Paraklētos* will be sent as a further agent of revelation and judgment (16:8-11).

• Any prophet who arrogantly speaks a word in God's name that God hasn't commanded him to speak, or who speaks in the name of other gods, must die (Deut 18:20).

○ Ironically, Jesus is accused of speaking and acting presumptuously in John ("breaking" the Sabbath, 5:16, 18; 7:22-23; 9:16; "deceiving" the crowd, 7:12, 47; and witnessing about himself, 8:13, 53)—and, considered as blasphemy are his calling God his *father* ("making himself equal with God," 5:18) and accusations of making himself out to be God (10:33) and the Son of God (19:7).

○ Thus, the Jewish leaders seek to kill Jesus (5:16, 18; 7:1, 19, 25; 8:37, 40, 59; 10:31; 11:8), or at least to arrest him (7:30, 32, 44; 8:20; 10:39; 11:57); they accuse him of having a demon (7:20; 8:48, 52; 10:20)—and of being a Samaritan (8:48)—and begin to orchestrate his being put to death (11:53; 18:12; 19:7).

○ They also agree to "expel from the Synagogue" anyone who *openly* acknowledges Jesus to be the Christ (9:22; 12:42; 16:2).

• If a prophet speaks in the Lord's name but the thing doesn't happen, then the Lord hasn't spoken that word. That prophet spoke arrogantly and is not to be feared (Deut 18:22).

- ○ *Moses's writings, the Law, and the scriptures* are fulfilled in the ministry of Jesus (John 1:45; 2:17, 22; 5:39, 46; 6:45; 7:38; 10:34-36; 12:14-16; 13:18; 15:25; 17:12; 19:24, 28, 36-37; 20:9), confirming the authenticity of his mission.

- ○ *The word of Caiaphas* regarding Jesus's sacrificial death is ironically fulfilled (even unknowingly, 11:49-52); even Pilate declares (perhaps unwittingly) Jesus to be "the king of the Jews" (19:14-22).

- ○ *Predictions* and earlier words of Jesus are fulfilled in John, especially about his own departure and glorification (2:19-22; 3:14; 4:50-53; 6:51, 64-65; 7:33-34, 38-39; 8:21, 28; 10:11, 15-18; 11:4, 23; 12:24, 32-33; 13:33, 38; 14:2-3, 18-20, 23; 15:13; 16:16, 20, 28, 32; 18:9, 32).

- ○ To remove all doubt, Jesus *declares ahead of time what is to take place* so that it will be acknowledged that he is sent from God (13:18-19; 14:28-29; 16:2-4; 18:8-9, 31-32); thus, he is clearly *sent from God* (3:16-17, 34; 4:34; 5:23-24, 30, 36-38; 6:29, 37-40, 44, 57; 7:16-18, 28-29, 33; 8:16-18, 28-29; 9:4; 10:36; 11:42; 12:44-45, 49; 13:20; 14:24; 15:21; 16:5; 17:3, 8, 18, 21-25; 20:21) and is to be heeded as though heeding the One who sent him.

Furthering the irony, not only do the religious leaders fail to acknowledge the many ways in which Jesus fulfills the identity of the authentic prophet predicted by Moses, after charging Jesus with blasphemy (10:33), they themselves also commit blasphemy before Pilate and the crowd, hailing Caesar as their sole king (19:15). Like the "Son of Man" title, the motif of the Prophet like Moses likely originated in the ministry of Jesus of Nazareth, claiming to be speaking and acting not on his own behalf, but on behalf of the One who sent him. This Jewish agency motif, however, was translated in the Johannine *Logos* hymn into language that Gentile audiences could appreciate, and while some of the terms are different, the overall features of the Son being sent from the Father to the world—as an expression of God's love and calling forth a response of faith to the divine initiative—came to serve as a potent cross-cultural introduction to the finalized Gospel. In the invitation to receive the Father's representative Son, Gentile and Jewish audiences alike are welcomed into the divine family for all who receive him and believe (1:12).

John's View of the Church

While the word for church (*ekklēsia*) is found only in Matthew among the Gospels, John nonetheless presents the community of believers in fluid and dynamic terms. Jesus's followers are described as his flock and his sheep, of which he is the authentic shepherd (10:1-16; 21:15-17), and the vine-and-branches allegory describes the absolute need for the branches to remain connected to the vine (15:1-10). Central to both of these images for church community life is love. While the Jesus of the Synoptics reduces the commandments of Moses to two, loving God and loving neighbor, John's Jesus reduces the key to community life to a single, "new commandment" (13:34)—loving one another as he has loved them. While historical-Jesus scholars might see the injunction to love one another as morally inferior to the command to love one's enemies and one's neighbors—both domestic and alien—the opposite is also true. How can one claim to love God and neighbor if one is not living in loving fellowship with members of one's own community (cf. 1 John 4:7-8)? Therefore, Jesus issues a new commandment to his followers: that they love one another and be willing to lay down their lives for one another, just as he has done for them.

Love and the Commandments of Jesus in John

- Jesus's new commandment is that believers should love one another as he has loved them (13:34; 15:12).

- By believers' love for one another will the world know that they are his disciples (13:35).

- To love Jesus is to keep his commandments and word (14:15, 21, 23).

- Those who do not love Jesus do not keep his word (14:24).

- Those who love Jesus will be loved by the Father and the Son (14:21, 23).

- Jesus's following the Father's commandments reflects his love for the Father (14:31).

- Believers are invited to abide in Jesus's love (15:9).

- To keep Jesus's commandments is to abide in his love (15:10).

- No greater love is possible than laying down one's life for one's friends (15:13).

- Jesus's commandments are given so that his followers might love one another (15:17).

- Jesus has made the name of the Father known to his followers in order that the Father's love might be in them (17:26).

- To love Jesus is to feed and nurture his sheep (21:15-17).

Peter and the beloved disciple are linked together in John, as partners in leadership and ministry, but they are also contrasted in terms of presentation. The beloved disciple always gets it right, thus posing a positive example for audiences to follow; Peter, however, miscomprehends leadership and servant-hood, thus posing a somewhat flawed example to avoid. At the Last Supper, the beloved disciple leans against the breast of Jesus, showing an intimate rela-tionship with the Lord; Peter has to ask him if he is meant when Jesus speaks of his betrayal (13:21-25). Jesus entrusts his mother to the beloved disciple at the crucifixion; Peter is nowhere to be found (19:25-27). The beloved disciple arrives at the tomb of Jesus before Peter but steps aside and allows Peter to enter first; the beloved disciple believes (20:1-10). While they are fishing, the beloved disciple points out the Lord to Peter, who throws his clothes on and hastens to Jesus (21:1-14). After Jesus predicts Peter's death, Peter questions Jesus about the beloved disciple's fate; Jesus rebukes Peter and instructs him: "follow me" (21:18-24).

Presented on his own, Peter also comes up short while being presented as the chief of the apostles. Following his confession, hailing Jesus as "God's holy one" (6:68-69; likewise the exclamation of the demoniac in Mark 1:24), Jesus's response is abrupt, similar to that which follows Peter's objection to the suffering Son of Man in Mark 8. At the Last Supper, Peter fails to understand Jesus's washing his feet, and he also misunderstands the call to servant leader-ship (13:1-17); the apostle is not greater than the one who has sent him (v. 16). And following the resurrection, Peter is hurt because Jesus asks him three times if he loves him (21:15-17). While the two Greek verbs for love (*agapaō* and *phileō*) are often synonyms in John, here Jesus asks Peter twice if he loves him with *agapē* love, implying sacrificial love, yet Peter replies that he loves him with *philos* love, implying friendly love.

Peter is still presented as leader among the apostles in John, but he only partially understands the character of apostolic leadership. While some scholars have thus placed the Johannine evangelist outside of the apostolic circle, the opposite inference may be stronger. Given that Diotrephes, who loves primacy, has excluded Johannine Christians from his church (3 John 1:9-10), the Elder quite possibly feels that Petrine authority has been hijacked by hierarchical leaders and seeks to restore a more primitive and egalitarian model of apostolic leadership precisely because of John's proximity to the charismatic and Spirit-based leadership of Jesus. Therefore, note the ways that the Gospel of John poses contrastive parallels to nearly all the elements of the keys-to-the-kingdom passage added in Matthew to Peter's confession (Matt 16:17-19). Whereas Jesus entrusts Peter and his followers with authority in Matthew, in John Peter affirms Jesus's authority, and apostolic leadership is envisioned in egalitarian, plural, and familial ways. Therefore, models of Christian leadership in Matthew and John can be seen to be in dialogue in the late first-century situation, and each has its own set of strengths and weaknesses.

Models of Christian Leadership in Matthew and John

Apostolic Authority in Matthew

1) Peter makes an embellished confession: "You are the Christ, the Son of the living God" (16:16).
2) Peter's authentic confession is blessed, and getting the content right becomes a basis for apostolic belief (16:17).
3) Peter, called first among the Twelve (10:2), is featured in pivotal narratives (14:28-33; 18:21).
4) "Flesh and blood" have not revealed Jesus as the Christ; the heavenly Father has done so (16:17 NRSV).
5) The image of the church is "petrified"—the church of Christ is founded upon a rock (16:18).
6) Jesus entrusts Peter with the *keys* of the kingdom—an instrumental image of leadership (16:19).
7) An episcopal system of leadership develops in Peter's memory, giving his successors authority to bind and loose (16:19; 18:18).
8) Jesus entrusts Peter and those who follow in his wake with institutional authority (16:17-19).

Apostolic Parallels in John

1) Confessions are made by Nathanael (1:49) and Martha (11:27)—who are not members of the Twelve.
2) Blessedness is equated with serving others (13:17) and believing without having seen (20:29).
3) Apostolic work includes women: the Samaritan woman (4:7-42); Mary Magdalene (20:17-18).
4) Jesus's disciples must be willing to ingest his "flesh and blood"—a reference to the way of the cross (6:51-58).
5) Images for the church are more fluid and dynamic—shepherd and flock (10:1-15); vine and branches (15:1-10).
6) Jesus entrusts the beloved disciple with his *mother*—a familial image of leadership (19:26-27).
7) Apostolic authority to loose and bind is given to a plurality of followers of Jesus, including priestly responsibility to forgive sins (20:23).
8) Peter returns authority (the keys of the kingdom?) to Jesus, as he alone has the words of eternal life (6:68-69).

Lest it be inferred, though, that John's presentation of church leadership is set against Matthew's model as a gracious and familial alternative, it should be noted that Matthew's model itself is imbued with graciousness and nuance, as Peter is asked to forgive seven times seventy (or seventy-seven) times in Matthew 18:22. And in Matthew 20:1-16 believers are asked to be gracious to latecomers to the harvest. All it takes, though, is one strident implementation of structural hierarchy for ideological objections to be raised. The same would be true for problematic excesses of charismatic leadership. The main Johannine concern, however, is to put forward a Spirit-based vision of how the risen Lord continues to lead the church—through the *Paraklētos* (one called alongside as an advocate and helper), the Holy Spirit, who brings to remembrance the teachings of Jesus as needed and who also leads his followers into truth. The Spirit is accessible to all, and effective Christian leadership in John's view hinges upon individual and corporate submission to the dynamic leadership of the risen Lord. Therefore, the task of human leaders is to gather the community into a fellowship wherein walking in the light is enabled by means of discerning and abiding in the truth in unity and love.

The Promise of the *Paraklētos*—the Holy Spirit—in John

- Jesus promises to ask the Father for another *Paraklētos*, who will be with and in his followers forever (14:16; cf. 1 John 2:1).

- The *Paraklētos* "is the Spirit of Truth, whom the world can't receive because it neither sees him nor recognizes him"; but believers know him, because he abides with them and will be in them (14:17).

- The *Paraklētos*, the Holy Spirit, whom the Father will send in Jesus's name, will teach believers everything and remind them of all that Jesus has said to them (14:26).

- When the *Paraklētos*, the Spirit of Truth who comes from the Father and whom Jesus will send from the Father, comes, he will testify on Jesus's behalf (15:26).

- Jesus must depart; otherwise the *Paraklētos* will not come; but if Jesus goes, he will send the *Paraklētos* to believers (16:7).

- When the Spirit of Truth comes, he will guide believers into all the truth; for he will not speak on his own, but will speak

whatever he hears and will declare the things that are to come
(16:13).

The message of John thus calls persons to faith in Jesus as the Christ, and
yet initial faith is only the beginning. Belief's implications extend in a variety
of directions within the history of the Johannine situation, and in that sense
John's purposes are multiple. John's first edition calls people to believe in Jesus
as the Messiah/Christ, and John's later material calls people to abide in Jesus
and his community of faith. Therefore, John's purposes are both evangelistic
and pastoral. As the Son is sent from the Father and the Spirit continues to
instruct believers, Jesus's followers are called to be his partners in ministry—
his friends—conveying his love and presence in the world as his witnesses.
If that happens faithfully, the world might yet believe on the basis of their
witness and their unity.

IV. Engaging John

In engaging the Gospel of John, there are many levels on which the text
can be explored. Spiritually and personally, the hearer/reader is invited into
the community of believers across the bounds of time and space, welcomed
to encounter the love and presence of God. This is what is heralded in the
prologue, and John's community of faith attests to their embracing of the
gospel message while also extending the invitation to others to do the same.
Therefore, as a first question, you might ask how John's prologue both reflects
an interpretation of the gospel's message, followed then by considering how
John's worship hymn functions to draw later members of John's audience into
a transformative encounter with the narrative's subject. How did John 1:1-18
function in its original context, and how does it function for later readers and
audiences?

Second, consider various issues in the Johannine situation and reflect on
how the contents of John's narrative address the various issues likely faced
by John's emerging audiences. For instance, how did John's message engage
original Judean leaders (30–70 CE), and how would John's presentation of
Jesus as the Messiah/Christ have engaged followers of John the Baptist along
the way? Then, following a move to a set of churches in the Gentile mission
(70–100 CE), how might John's presentation of Jesus as fulfilling the writings
of Moses have challenged synagogue leaders regarding the Son's representative
mission from the Father? And in the light of emerging emperor worship under

Domitian, how does John challenge the political power of Rome, calling also for believers to be willing to embrace a suffering Jesus—including costly discipleship—if suffering is required by the truth? Finally, how does John's presentation of Christ's leading his followers by means of the Holy Spirit—accessible to all believers—function as a vision of God's dynamic leadership at the heart of Jesus's ministry? And, in any or all of these cases, what difference might John's story of Jesus make for today's audiences, as well?

Third, how might the Gospel of John pose a complement to, and to some degree a dialectical engagement of, Mark and the other Gospels? While some of John's distinctive presentation has its roots in theological conviction, might some of it also derive from historical knowledge or opinion? John's is the only Gospel explicitly claiming to be written by an eyewitness; of course, that could be a false claim. However, if there might be some truth to the final compiler's assertion that the beloved disciple was responsible for at least some of the narrative's origin and development, how can John be reconciled with the other Gospels; and, despite John's having been expunged from historical-Jesus studies over the last century and a half, is such a view compelling for the future?

The Historical Quest
for Jesus

Given the fact that the four canonical Gospels were written by believers, how do we know their presentations are objective and historical rather than subjective and motivated by theological investments? An outsider to Christianity might ask these sorts of questions, but they also are inescapable for modern Christians.[1] After all, Jesus is presented in very different ways between the Gospels—especially when comparing John and the Synoptics. Does this mean that the Synoptics are motivated by historical interests and that John's differences are accounted for on the basis of John's being a spiritual gospel? Clement of Alexandria described things that way around the turn of the second century CE, but he was simply describing their differences, not commenting on their origins. In perhaps the most pivotal New Testament work of the twentieth century, Albert Schweitzer wrote:

> When, at some future day, our period of civilization shall lie, closed and completed, before the eyes of later generations, German theology will stand out as a great, a unique phenomenon in the mental and spiritual life of our time. For nowhere save in the German temperament can there be found in the same perfection the living complex of conditions and factors—of philosophic thought, critical acumen, historical insight, and religious feeling—without which no deep theology is possible. And the greatest achievement of German theology is the critical investigation of the life of Jesus.[2]

---

1. Likely the best overview of the subject is by Mark Allan Powell, *Jesus as a Figure in History: How Modern Historians View the Man from Galilee* (Louisville: Westminster John Knox Press, 1998).

2. Albert Schweitzer, *The Quest of the Historical Jesus: A Critical Study of Its Progress from Reimarus to Wrede*, ed. W. Montgomery (1906; trans. 1910; New York: Macmillan, 1968), 1.

A. The Early Quest: "Lives" of Jesus

The modern historical quest for Jesus had several beginnings, but it was really Gotthold Lessing's publishing fragments of the writings of Hermann Samuel Reimarus (in 1774) that got the public discussion going. Locked in a desk, and only discovered after his death, Reimarus had written provocatively on whether presentations in the Gospels were ordered by history or by theology. After all, any time someone appeals to the miraculous as an explanation of the course of events, such presentations deserve to be challenged by rational thinkers, so Reimarus claimed. With regards to Jesus and his ministry, Reimarus envisioned Jesus's goal as the political liberation of Israel from Rome—similar to other first-century Jewish prophets—a hope that clearly went unrealized. In response to their dejected state, Jesus's followers stole his body and concocted the story of the resurrection, embellishing his ministry with signs and wonders. "History" was seen by Reimarus in naturalistic terms, so any appeal to supernaturalism was unscientific and uncritical—vulnerable to subjective error rather than objective historiography.

Not surprisingly, debates quickly ensued, with traditional scholars on one side and critical scholars on the other. This led, of course, to charges that liberal scholars were overturning biblical authority, and the fundamentalist reaction against modernism over the next century or more sought to address these and other challenges to Christian orthodoxy. In addressing the differences between John and the Synoptics, Friedrich Schleiermacher (d. 1834) argued that John's Gospel was closest to the historical Jesus because of its intimate connection with its subject.[3] In 1864, however, David F. Strauss countered Schleiermacher, leveraging two dichotomies:[4] first, that theology needed to be divorced from history, and second, that the Synoptics should be privileged historically over John. Jesus studies thus continued with a multitude of studies on folkloric stories and traditions, seeing gospels as forms of ancient biographical narratives ("lives" of Jesus) with their own stories to tell.[5]

---

3. Friedrich Schleiermacher, *The Life of Jesus*, trans. S. M. Gilmour (Minneapolis: Fortress, 1975).

4. D. F. Strauss, *The Christ of Faith and the Jesus of History: A Critique of Schleiermacher's Life of Christ*, trans. L. E. Keck (Minneapolis: Fortress, 1977).

5. D. F. Strauss, *The Life of Jesus Critically Examined*, trans. George Eliot (1835/36, 1860; Minneapolis: Fortress Press, 1977).

B. The Reaction of Neo-Orthodoxy (the "No Quest")

With the publication of Schweitzer's book in 1906, however, a century or more of historical Jesus research came to something of a screeching halt.[6] The last major work Schweitzer engaged was the work of Wilhelm Wrede on the Messianic Secret in Mark, arguing that this feature was not rooted in history but in Mark's own rhetorical interests. If Mark, the Gospel on which Matthew and Luke had built their narratives, was rooted in rhetoric rather than history, scholars wondered what hope there was for conducting any meaningful historical research into Jesus's life and teachings based on the canonical Gospels. As a result, the vigor of Jesus research was replaced by the view that very little can be known historically about Jesus of Nazareth, so scholarship moved in other directions: Neo-Orthodoxy and tradition analysis.

First, as a result of the Neo-Orthodox reaction against liberal theology, reflecting on the terrible slaughter of Christians by other Christians in World War I (as many as sixty million, by some counts), Karl Barth and others became disillusioned with the moral bankruptcy of modern liberal theology. In the light of human inhumanity to humans, the optimistic myth of progress lost its luster. Rather than focus on the Jesus of history, the Christ of faith came to be embraced as the gospel message of the first Christians and the true hope for the world. Thus, the new orthodoxy advocated by Barth, Brunner, and others challenged critical liberalism with biblical truth that preaches—that is its main value, and Barth's nine thousand pages of his thirteen-volume *Church Dogmatics* testify to that conviction.

Investigating the formation of gospel traditions, Rudolf Bultmann forged new directions in terms of New Testament studies with his contributions. Asserting that we are not saved by history, but by faith, Bultmann argued that very little can be known of the Jesus of history; thus, given the impossibility of the task, it should not even be pursued as a venture.[7] Therefore, Bultmann sought to illumine the literary and contemporary-religions backgrounds of the traditions and sources underlying the Gospels,

---

6. Cf. Henry J. Cadbury, *The Eclipse of the Historical Jesus* (Wallingford, PA: Pendle Hill Pamphlets, 1964).

7. Rudolf Bultmann, *Jesus and the Word*, trans. Louise P. Smith and Erminie Huntress (New York: Scribners, 1934).

clarifying also the theological contributions made by the evangelists and their editors.[8] In Bultmann's view, the New Testament needed to be demythologized in order to appreciate its essential and theological meanings. As an example of researching the history of understandings about Jesus, C. H. Dodd sought to identify essential elements in the preaching (*kerygma* in Greek) of the apostles.[9] It would be a mistake, however, to assume that no historical research was being done on Jesus during this period; it was simply more reserved and cautious.[10]

C. The "New Quest"[11]

Indeed, many advances were made the first half of the twentieth century in garnering a fuller understanding of gospel traditions and their relations, but finally, the issue of Jesus of Nazareth—his character, identity, and ministry—could no longer be ignored. Following the anti-Semitism in Europe leading up to World War II and the Holocaust, the Jewishness of Jesus required a new look. Ernst Käsemann, one of Bultmann's students who made a career of disagreeing with his mentor, challenged the eclipse of the historical Jesus in 1951.[12] Despite the religious character of the Gospels, a good deal of information about Jesus can still be ascertained using criteria for determining historicity. If the apologetic interests of the writers can be set aside, some of these criteria include the following.

---

8. See especially, Rudolf Bultmann, *The History of the Synoptic Tradition*, trans. John Marsh (1921; New York: Harper and Row, 1963) and *The Gospel of John: A Commentary*, trans. G. R. Beasley-Murray, R. W. N. Hoare, and John K. Riches, Johannine Monograph Series 1 (1941, E. T. 1971; Eugene, OR: Wipf & Stock, 2014) alongside his *Theology of the New Testament Theology; Complete in One Volume*, trans. Kendrick Grobel (1948–53, E. T. 1970; Waco, TX: Baylor University Press, 2007).

9. C. H. Dodd, *The Apostolic Preaching and Its Developments* (London: Hodder & Stoughton Ltd, 1936).

10. Note, for instance, the works by Henry J. Cadbury, *The Peril of Modernizing Jesus* (1937; repr., Eugene, OR: Wipf & Stock, 2007) and *Jesus, What Manner of Man* (1947; repr., Eugene, OR: Wipf & Stock, 2008).

11. James M. Robinson's book by that title declared the opening of this new chapter: *The New Quest of the Historical Jesus*, Studies in Biblical Theology 25 (London: SCM, 1959).

12. This was his 1951 Göttingen inaugural lecture, delivered in 1953 to a gathering of Bultmann's students: Ernst Käsemann, "The Problem of the Historical Jesus," in *Essays on New Testament Themes* (London: SCM Press, 1964), 15–47.

Criteria for Determining Historicity in the New Quest for Jesus

- Multiple attestation (something occurring in more than one instance or Gospel is privileged)

- Dissimilarity (something unlikely to be invented is privileged because it goes against standard Jewish or Christian views of the day)

- Embarrassment (if something would have been an embarrassment to the early Christian movement, it is unlikely to have been invented)

- Naturalism (more supernatural reports are ascribed to theology rather than history)

- Coherence (features cohering with an overall likely portraiture of Jesus are privileged; others are discarded)

The second half of the twentieth century saw many more treatments of historical Jesus than the first half, and *Jesus of Nazareth* by Gunther Bornkamm set the stage for a host of treatments on Jesus in the decades that followed.[13] Within the New Quest, the approach taken was positivism of verification: unless something is positively verified as being historical, it is set aside. Norman Perrin's dictum was: "If in doubt, leave it out." A noted weakness of this approach, however, is that it fails to put into play the other side of positivism, falsification: unless an incident is proven to be false, it cannot be entirely ruled out. As a result, alternatives to the highly skeptical quest for Jesus have emerged alongside the New Quest.

D. The "Third Quest" for Jesus

In the 1970s and 1980s a variety of new methodologies came to be applied to the quest for Jesus, including the use of social-sciences criticism, religious anthropology, psychological biblical criticism, and new historicism. In 1982, N. T. Wright saw these approaches as constituting a "Third Quest" for Jesus, and much of this work has sought to recover the Jewishness of Jesus,[14] or at least to see him as a historical figure within first-century

---

13. Gunther Bornkamm, *Jesus of Nazareth* (New York: Harper & Row, 1959).

14. See especially Geza Vermes, *Jesus the Jew: A Historian's Reading of the Gospels* (London: Collins, 1973); John K. Riches, *Jesus and the Transformation of Judaism* (London:

Judaism. Therefore, social-sciences methodologies have been helpful along these lines, as have been studies that seek to understand the Jesus movement in the light of Roman occupation.[15] Gerd Theissen's analysis of presentations of Jesus in the narrative form of the Gospels, within their sociological settings, has contributed a greater sense of historical plausibility in the quest for Jesus.[16] Perhaps the most extensive treatment of the subject is the work by John P. Meier (in as many as six volumes) on Jesus as a marginal Jew of his day.[17] Exhaustive in explaining and implementing its approaches to the issues, Meier's work seeks to establish compelling bases for making critical judgments, tending to confirm much of the presentation of Jesus in the Gospels, even if the results are not entirely novel. Another set of advances along these lines has involved the use of archaeology for understanding Jesus of Nazareth and his first-century environs.[18]

E. The Renewed Quest, the Jesus Seminar, and Other Projects

Continuing the New Quest is what the Weststar Institute has called "the Renewed Quest" for Jesus, featured most prominently in the work of the Jesus Seminar, founded by Robert Funk and others in 1985. Building squarely on the contributions of Reimarus and Strauss, the Jesus Seminar systematically worked through every saying and deed attributed to Jesus in the New Testament (including the *Gospel of Thomas* and other early Christian works), seeking to demarcate the historical reliability of all material

---

Darton, Longman & Todd, 1980); Ed P. Sanders, *Jesus and Judaism* (Minneapolis: Fortress Press, 1985); cf. also E. P. Sanders, *The Historical Figure of Jesus* (London/New York: Penguin, 1993).

15. Cf. Bruce J. Malina and Richard L. Rohrbaugh, *Social Science Commentary on the Synoptic Gospels*, 2nd ed. (Minneapolis: Augsburg/Fortress, 2002); Richard Horsley, *Jesus and Empire: The Kingdom of God and the New World Disorder* (Minneapolis: Fortress Press, 2002).

16. Cf. Gerd Theissen, *The Shadow of the Galilean; The Quest for Jesus in Narrative Form* (Minneapolis: Fortress Press, 1987); Annette Mertz, *The Historical Jesus: A Comprehensive Guide* (Minneapolis: Augsburg/Fortress, 1989).

17. John P. Meier, *A Marginal Jew, Rethinking the Historical Jesus*, vol. 1, *The Roots of the Problem and the Person* (New Haven, CT: Yale University Press, 1991), vol. 2, *Mentor, Message, and Miracles* (1994), vol. 3, *Companions and Competitors* (2001), vol. 4, *Law and Love* (2009), vol. 5, (forthcoming on the sayings of Jesus).

18. See especially, James H. Charlesworth, *Jesus Within Judaism: New Light from Exciting Archaeological Discoveries* (New York: Doubleday, 1988); and James H. Charlesworth, ed., *Jesus and Archaeology* (Grand Rapids: Eerdmans, 2006).

pertaining to Jesus of Nazareth. Identifying "seven pillars of scholarly wisdom" (especially building on Mark and Q to the exclusion of John), texts were analyzed at their meetings and voted on with colored beads denoting varying degrees of historicity: black—not historical, grey—unlikely, pink—possibly, red—probably.[19] The beads were then tabulated, and the results were shared with the media, declaring the judgments of critical scholars as to what the Jesus of history did and didn't say and do. The results were meager—only 18 percent of the words going back to Jesus, far more in the *Gospel of Thomas* than in the Gospel of Mark, and almost nothing red or pink was in the Gospel of John (except the relation of Annas to Caiaphas and the fact that Jesus died). Of course, these results are not entirely surprising, as they reflect also the bases for the discussions and the voting, rejecting anything not positively confirmed and disparaging John overall.

Reactions to the Jesus Seminar's work have been strong, with some challenging their methodology and others challenging their dissemination of the results.[20] Nonetheless, in addition to Funk's works on the subject, the contributions of John Dominic Crossan and Marcus Borg, as leading voices of the Seminar, have made their own contributions on understanding Jesus.[21] In reflecting on the various models of Jesus put forward, Borg has also noted various portraitures of Jesus based on various scholars' views, including seeing him as a wisdom-oriented sage, an institution-challenging cynic, a noneschatological prophet, and a holy man.[22] To that list other scholars would add an apocalyptic and eschatological prophet.[23]

Despite the varying methodologies and approaches, the one thing common about the first three quests for Jesus over the last two centuries is that they

19. Robert W. Funk et al., *The Five Gospels: The Search for the Authentic Words of Jesus* (San Francisco: HarperOne, 1996); *The Acts of Jesus: The Search for the Authentic Deeds of Jesus* (San Francisco: HarperOne, 1998).

20. See especially Luke Timothy Johnson, *The Real Jesus: The Misguided Quest for the Historical Jesus and the Truth of the Traditional Gospels* (New York: HarperOne, 1997); and Craig A. Evans, *Fabricating Jesus: How Modern Scholars Distort the Gospels* (Grand Rapids: IVP Books, 2008). N. T. Wright moves beyond critique to extend his own programmatic understanding of Jesus and his mission in *Jesus and the Victory of God* (Minneapolis: Fortress Press, 1996).

21. John Dominic Crossan, *The Historical Jesus: The Life of a Mediterranean Peasant* (New York: HarperOne, 1991); Marcus Borg, *Jesus: A New Vision: Spirit, Culture, and the Life of Discipleship* (New York: Harper & Row, 1987).

22. Marcus Borg, *Jesus in Contemporary Scholarship* (Valley Forge, PA: Trinity Press International, 1994).

23. Cf. Dale C. Allison, *Jesus of Nazareth: Millenarian Prophet* (Minneapolis: Augsburg/Fortress, 1991); Bart Ehrman, *Jesus: Apocalyptic Prophet of the New Millennium* (Oxford: Oxford University Press, 2001).

have all programmatically—not accidentally—excluded the Gospel of John from their quests. This is understandable, given John's riddles; the question is whether or not it is adequate. If we did not have the Gospel of John, and if something like it were to be discovered in a cave somewhere, that would make huge waves in scholarship and the media. The question would be, then, how to approach this "maverick gospel" (to use Robert Kysar's term), given its distinctive accounts and unique claims to first-hand memory of Jesus. Launched in 2001, the John, Jesus, and History Project at the Society of Biblical Literature meetings has sought to hammer hard on all aspects of the issue, including the critical viability of the "dehistoricization of John" and the "de-Johannification of Jesus." Given that these have been the two leading critical platforms of modern scholarship on the Fourth Gospel and Jesus, the question is how sturdy the planks are, and whether both platforms continue to hold.[24] Within this project critical views have been reappraised, leading to the discerning of aspects of historicity in John, followed by glimpses of Jesus through the Johannine lens.

If indeed, the new millennium is bringing in a renewed look at the Gospel of John and calling for the use of John in the quest for Jesus, that might call for a paradigm shift in our quests for Jesus—ones that include John in the mix. The question is how to conduct such a quest critically, and how to deal with John's differences with the Synoptics, as well as its similarities. Perhaps a *fourth quest* will need to sort these things out, as Jesus remembered in the Johannine tradition and within the Johannine situation requires a new look at the Jesus of history as well as the Gospel of John.[25] In addition to a theory of gospel relations that includes the Gospel of John instead of leaving it out, a new set of criteria for discerning the Jesus of history might also call for a new approach—a fourth quest.

New Criteria for Conducting Historical-Jesus Research with John in the Mix

- Corroborative reinforcement (versus multiple attestation; sometimes similar accounts that are not identical are close enough to be suggestive of something historical)

---

24. Cf. Paul N. Anderson, Felix Just, and Tom Thatcher, eds., *John, Jesus, and History*, vol. 1, *Critical Appraisals of Critical Views* (Atlanta: SBL Press, 2007), vol. 2, *Aspects of Historicity in the Fourth Gospel* (2009).

25. This is the judgment of James H. Charlesworth, "The Historical Jesus in the Fourth Gospel: A Paradigm Shift?" *Journal for the Study of the Historical Jesus* 8 (2010): 3–46, as well as Mark Allan Powell, "Things that Matter: Historical Jesus Studies in the New Millennium," *World & World* 29 (2009): 121–35. See also Paul N. Anderson, *The Fourth Gospel and the Quest for Jesus: Modern Foundations Reconsidered* (London: T & T Clark, 2006).

- Primitivity (versus dissimilarity and embarrassment; an early tradition may also be similar to contemporary Judaism and yet might have been embraced faithfully by Jesus's followers)

- Historical realism (versus naturalism; sometimes amazing things happen, and historical realism provides a more nuanced measure of material otherwise rejected)

- Coherence (similar to Synoptic-based coherence but willing to make use of all ancient resources, including the Gospel of John)

- Gradations of plausibility (balancing positivism of verification with positivism of falsification; with few items absolutely ruled in or out, the middle ground is larger and more negotiable)

Within the modern quests for the Jesus of history, the final issue comes down to personal experience. Whatever understanding people might come to, the question is how that relates to their understanding and existence. In that sense, the only relevance of the remembered past is the difference it makes regarding one's engagement with life in the present and the future. That will be the true measure of one's searching, as well as one's finding. With these words Albert Schweitzer closes his book, reminding us of the relation between history, engagement, and experience:

> He comes to us as One unknown, without a name, as of old, by the lake-side, He came to those men who knew Him not. He speaks to us the same word: 'Follow thou me!' and sets us to the tasks which He has to fulfill for our time. He commands. And to those who obey Him, whether they be wise or simple, He will reveal Himself in the toils, the conflicts, the sufferings which they shall pass through in His fellowship, and as an ineffable mystery, they shall learn in their own experience Who He is.[26]

---

26. Schweitzer, *The Quest of the Historical Jesus*, 403.

PART II

THE ACTS OF THE APOSTLES AND THE LETTERS OF PAUL

The Acts of the Apostles continues the story of the Jesus movement into the life of the church over the next three decades, and the letters of Paul document particular engagements with communities and individuals along the way. While the Gospels constitute 47 percent of the New Testament, if we include Mark and Luke-Acts within the Pauline mission, those books number 16 of the twenty-seven books in the New Testament and 59 percent of its content. Luke-Acts alone represents over 27 percent of the New Testament's content. Significant in the presentation of Paul's mission in Acts and his letters is the expansion of the Jesus movement beyond Palestine into Syria, Asia Minor, Greece, and the rest of the Mediterranean world. By extension, Jesus's calling of twelve disciples, symbolizing the restoration of the scattered tribes of Israel in the diaspora, now carries the promise of Abraham's blessing to all who will receive God's gift of grace. That leads to a world-changing impact, and its effects have continued to be felt ever since.

The Acts of the Apostles

Acts is Luke's second volume (also written to Theophilus, Acts 1:1), and one can see Luke's theology as presented distinctively in his Gospel being fulfilled in the life of the early church. Acts covers the growth of the church, and Jesus's prophecy in Acts 1:8 indeed comes true by the end of the book: "you will receive power when the Holy Spirit has come upon you, and you will be my witnesses in Jerusalem, in all Judea and Samaria, and to the end of the earth." Thus, the Holy Spirit is poured out upon women and men and young and old, the mission expands through Samaria and beyond, and the ministry of Jesus is carried forward through the ministries of the apostles and others to the remotest parts of the earth—even unto Rome. Therefore, Luke's two volumes reinforce each other, and Jesus's ascension into heaven at the end of the Gospel of Luke becomes also the point of departure at the beginning of the Acts of the Apostles.

The central figures in Acts are Peter and Paul, and while Peter plays a prominent role in the first half, Paul's mission to the Gentiles features prominently in the second. Giving Paul the last word may reflect Luke's sense of the importance of Paul's mission, but Peter's ministry is by no means slighted; he also ministers to Jewish and Gentile audiences alike, delivers compelling speeches, and performs wondrous signs. Luke uses the first-person plural, "we" or "us," in narrating Paul's later travels (16:10-17; 20:5-15; 20:1-18; 27:1–28:16), making it seem that he accompanied Paul on several of his journeys. This would explain also Paul's expressed appreciation for Luke, whom he calls a beloved physician and coworker, and who is with him in prison (Col 4:14; 2 Tim 4:11; Phlm 1:24). The pivotal scene in the book is the Jerusalem Council in Acts 15, where James the brother of Jesus presides over the gathering of Christian leaders and claims to discern the Spirit's leading that one need not become outwardly Jewish (marked by circumcision) to be a faithful follower of Jesus. Had it not been for this church-council decision, the Jesus movement might have remained a Jewish sect instead of becoming the world's largest religion.

While 90 CE is a reasonable guess regarding its dating, the end of Acts poses a problem. Chapter 28 closes with Paul under house arrest in Rome, yet his death under Nero (ca. 65 CE) is not narrated. Does this mean that Acts was finalized around 61 or 62 CE? If so, that would push Luke's Gospel and its primary source, Mark, into the 50s. As a result, the assumption that Mark was written around 70 CE could be flawed (was there more than one edition of Mark?), and the Gospels may have been written a decade or two earlier than most scholars have thought. Then again, how do we know that Luke wasn't working on a third volume or that his concluding with Paul under house arrest in Rome was ordered by chronology interests rather than theological concerns? Whatever the case, Luke gives the impression of a growing Jesus movement, which he calls "the Way," and the rise and progress of the movement is furthered powerfully by Luke's account. The locations of Luke's writing and audience are impossible to know, but such settings as Rome, Antioch, and Caesarea Maritima are worthy of consideration.

The Letters of Paul

Letters attributed to Paul in the New Testament number 13, and while most are written to groups, some are written to individuals (1 and 2 Timothy, Titus, Philemon). Their canonical ordering has less to do with their chronological sequence and more to do with other factors. Romans is placed first because it is Paul's longest letter, and it is the most theologically programmatic. In Romans Paul declares his understanding of the gospel—that the righteousness of God is received by grace through faith—arguing that the need for God's saving grace extends to Gentiles and Jews alike. Next follow the Corinthian letters, moving from Paul's most expansive manifesto to his most contextual engagements. Paul's shorter letters then follow (from Galatians to 2 Thessalonians), and these are followed by the Pastoral Epistles and Philemon.

In writing to his audiences, Paul follows standard forms of letter writing during his day, and he often receives help from a scribe. Overall, the following outline is characteristic of many of his letters.

The General Form of Paul's Letters

- A greeting (usually in the first verse or two)
- A blessing: "Grace and peace" (appealing to Greek and Jewish values)
- A thanksgiving for his audience ("I thank my God concerning you . . . ")
- Particular contents (the main body of the letter)
- Personal greetings to individuals and groups (and sometimes a reference to scribal details)

Debates around Paul's writings have tended to revolve around three concerns: authorship, dating, and content. On authorship, six letters attributed to Paul are problematic enough to have earned the label "deutero-Pauline" among critical scholars (still within the Pauline mission, but perhaps written by one of his colleagues or scribes), but it cannot be said that they are "non-Pauline" because all thirteen letters cohere closely overall in terms of vocabulary, style, and content. Therefore, it is more critically adequate to call them "questioned" letters, in my judgment, and they are questioned for different reasons.

179

Questioned Letters of Paul

- *2 Thessalonians* is questioned on the basis that it is less intense in its anticipation of the Lord's return, and warnings about "the person who is lawless" (2 Thess 2:7-12) are taken to represent a different eschatology. However, there is no piece of writing in ancient literature more like 2 Thessalonians than 1 Thessalonians, and those questioning Paul's authorship are forced to infer that the author of 2 Thessalonians "imitated" the style and content of 1 Thessalonians. Better to say that Paul's emphasis shifted a bit between his first and second letters to Thessalonica. I also see the shift in eschatological thrust as a minor development, reflecting movement from anticipating acutely the Lord's return to addressing conventional concerns given its delay—an understandable adjustment.

- *Ephesians* and *Colossians* are questioned because they employ distinctive language and references to the "mystery" or "secret plan" that is in Christ, using more cosmic language to describe the gospel. Righteousness in Ephesians is somewhat connected to moral character, causing some to infer works rather than grace as the emphasis, and Ephesians does not mention personal greetings, despite Paul's having lived there. This, however, is a poor argument, as 2 Corinthians also lacks such greetings, and Ephesians is likely written to a region rather than an individual community. Nonetheless, these books are filled with Pauline themes and language, and they fit very well contextually the interreligious situation in the Lycus Valley of Asia Minor. Marcion calls Ephesians Paul's letter to the Laodiceans, so if it was a circular, sent to churches around Colossae and Hierapolis—calling for Christian unity—that would make perfect sense.

- *The Pastoral Epistles—1 and 2 Timothy and Titus* are the most distant from Paul's other writings, and yet their being written from prison in Rome to individual pastoral leaders at a later time in Paul's life would of course involve some differences in language and concern; anything else would be a surprise. Nonetheless, such distinctive phrases as "this saying is reliable and deserves full acceptance" (1 Tim 1:15; 4:9) or simply "this saying is reliable" (1 Tim 3:1; 2 Tim 2:11; Titus 3:8) are striking in these letters, as are lists of qualifications for elders, pastors, and overseers. However, if these letters are written to individual leaders such as Timothy and Titus, of course they'll be different from other letters written by Paul. In particular, the personal appeals to bring the writer's coat, parchments, and scrolls and to come before winter (2 Tim 4:13, 21) seem imbued with realism; these are details unlikely to have been fabricated.

Given that the questioned letters of Paul are not conclusively non-Pauline (unlike Hebrews, which stylistically is clearly not written by Paul), they do not deserve to be distanced from the rest of Paul's letters. Further, to do so may distort an overall sense of Paul's work. In the light of second criticality, "not necessarily" does not imply "necessarily not." As early as the middle of the second century CE, the Muratorian Fragment attributes all of Paul's letters to Paul's hand, and so does Marcion except for the Pastoral Epistles. Because reasonable explanations account for most of the differences, their even more pervasive continuities with the rest of Paul's writings pose a stronger case for regarding them as questioned letters rather than secondary ones. Put otherwise, if any of these six letters had no name attached to it, Paul would be the first figure to be associated with their composition on the basis of style and content alone. Second Thessalonians follows naturally after 1 Thessalonians. Ephesians as a circular seems to be an expansion of the letter to Colossians, which bears connections with Philemon and shows socio-religious sensitivity to Asia Minor churches, just as Philippians reflects awareness of Macedonian believers. And if the Pastorals were written toward the end of Paul's life, the transition from charismatic leadership to institutional leadership is perfectly understandable; the absence of such is what would be unlikely.

If Paul's letters were organized in terms of their dating, however, either 1 Thessalonians or Galatians might be regarded as the first of his letters. If 1 Thessalonians (followed shortly by 2 Thessalonians) was written after Paul's visit on his second missionary journey, a date of 51 CE is a safe guess. However, if Galatians was written after Paul's first missionary journey, the conflict over which Paul confronted Peter to his face (Gal 2) may have been what precipitated the Jerusalem Council in Acts 15 around 48–49 CE. So if Galatians was written to churches in southern and eastern Asia Minor, Galatians could be the first of Paul's writings—followed later by a more extensive treatment of the gospel message in Paul's Epistle to the Romans around 57 CE or so. The

Corinthian letters were written also around that time (say, between 55 and 58 CE), and such letters as Colossians, Philemon, Ephesians, and Philippians appear to have been written from prison, which could have involved Paul's imprisonment in Caesarea or Ephesus as well as Rome. The letters to Timothy and Titus appear, then, to have been written from Rome, and they are the latest of the Pauline letters, whether authored by Paul or not.

A chronology of the early Christian movement thus looks something like this:

30 CE—Pentecost; believers receive the Spirit

34/35 CE—The martyrdom of Stephen and the calling of Saul

40 CE—Emperor Gaius Caligula attempts to set up an image of himself in the Jerusalem temple

44 CE—The death of James the son of Zebedee

46–48 CE—Paul's first missionary journey

48/49 CE—The Jerusalem Council

49 CE—Emperor Claudius bans Jewish worship in Rome due to controversies over "*Chrestus*"

50–52 CE—Paul's second missionary journey

53–57 CE—Paul's third missionary journey

59 CE—The shipwreck on Paul's voyage to Rome

59–61/62 CE—Paul's Roman imprisonment and house arrest

62 CE—The death of James, the brother of Jesus and head of the Jerusalem church

64–68 CE—Emperor Nero persecutes Christians in Rome

64/65 CE (or slightly later)—Paul's and Peter's deaths in Rome under Nero

Chapter 6

The Acts of the Apostles

Begin with the text. Read the Acts of the Apostles, and note important themes and details that come to mind.

Author: Luke, companion of Paul

Audience: "most excellent" Theophilus

Time: 85–90 CE

Place: unknown—perhaps Antioch or Caesarea Maritima

Message: The followers of "the Way" were faithful and successful—witnessing to Christ with spiritual empowerment in Jerusalem, Judea, Samaria, and the remotest parts of the earth.

Luke's second volume, the Acts of the Apostles, presents the fullest history of the early Christian movement. In so doing, it furthers several purposes. First, it sketches the rise and progress of the Jesus movement, extending the gospel to Jewish and Gentile audiences alike. Second, it features the ministries of two leading figures: Peter and Paul. As leaders among the twelve apostles, Peter and John play important roles in connecting the ministry of Jesus with the larger mission to the Gentiles, which Paul and his associates carry further in the second half of the story. James, Stephen, Philip, Barnabas, Silas, and others also feature prominently in furthering the mission. Third, Luke's presentation shows how the movement advances despite hardships, obstacles, and persecution. It therefore reflects the work of God and the power of the Spirit as part of a larger story—a cosmic one. Fourth, Luke's story of the movement provides inspiration and guidance for how later believers might also deal with challenges and adversity. In that sense, the Acts of the Apostles not only informs later generations as to what happened; it also offers an instructive set of patterns for how the church might continue to prosper in the future.

I. Crises and Contexts

Whereas Luke's first volume covers the birth, childhood (briefly), and ministry of Jesus, his second volume covers the time period from the ascension of Jesus to the imprisonment of Paul (ca. 30–61 CE). Within this time period, we see the Jesus movement growing from a few disciples to thousands, despite persecution and hardship, extending the message of Jesus as the Christ to known parts of the Mediterranean world. The rise and progress of the movement, however, also encounters several crises. Luke thus narrates that story in ways that actually become his message—showing the way that early believers met those challenges with buoyant effectiveness, empowered by the Holy Spirit and with divine assistance. It would be a mistake, though, to view Luke's second volume as simply narrating the advance of the Jesus movement. It also sketches a larger and more cosmic story—the restoration of the kingdom to Israel and the extension of Israel's divine blessing to the rest of the world (Acts 1:1-8).

The Outpouring of the Spirit and the Witness of the Apostles

From the outset, a number of crises and responses to them are narrated by Luke: what will Jesus's followers do after he ascends into heaven? Two men appear and instruct them to await his like return, so they gather in Jerusalem for worship and prayer (Acts 1:1-14). What will the eleven remaining disciples do after Judas's betrayal and suicide? Peter calls for the appointing of another to take his place, and Matthias is chosen—allowing God to make the choice by the drawing of straws (1:15-26). As believers are gathered for worship on Pentecost, fifty days after the Passover, the Holy Spirit is poured out, described as "a sound from heaven like the howling of a fierce wind" and accompanied by "individual flames of fire alighting on each one of them." Then "they were all filled with the Holy Spirit and began to speak in other languages as the Spirit enabled them to speak" (2:1-4). Amazed, Jews from many diverse nations hear the Galileans speaking in their own languages, so the gift of discernment is also noted (2:5-11).

Interpreting the outpouring of the Holy Spirit to be a fulfillment of Joel 2:28-32, Peter then rises to address the crowd. These persons are not drunk; rather, old and young, male and female have received the Spirit—the Day of the Lord has indeed arrived! Further, the words of David are fulfilled, that the Lord's presence assures victory over the grave (Ps 16:7-11), and God's enemies are made into a footstool for the Lord's feet (Ps 110:1). With piercing conviction, Peter declares: "Therefore, let all Israel know beyond question that God has made this Jesus, whom you crucified, both Lord and Christ." In response to the appeal to change their hearts and their lives, Luke reports, three thousand were saved that day, and this momentous event at Pentecost signals the birth of the early church. Note, however, that the crisis is presented as a result of a spiritual manifestation. The outpouring of the Spirit is a gift—a blessing of divine origin and design, calling forth a response to what God is doing. In that sense, the growth of the Jesus movement is not simply presented as acts of the apostles; it reflects the acts of God.

Peter and John then continue their witness about Jesus as the Christ. Peter performs a healing on the lame man outside the temple (Acts 3:1-10), which amazes the crowd and becomes an occasion for Peter to testify to his understanding of Jesus as the prophet predicted by Moses in Deuteronomy 18:15-22 (Acts 3:11-26). Peter continues his testimony before the Jewish Council the next day, which leads to the astonishment of the Jewish leaders, who marvel at the theological sophistication of Peter and John, despite their not having received formal theological training (4:13; cf. similar accusations about Jesus in John 7:15). As Peter and the apostles continue to hold religious leaders accountable for the death of Jesus, the Jewish Council becomes more and more threatened by the Jesus movement. However, the great leader among the Pharisees, Gamaliel, reasons with the others, comparing followers of Jesus with those of Theudas and Judas the Galilean, who fell away after their deaths: "If their plan or activity is of human origin, it will end in ruin. If it originates with God, you won't be able to stop them. Instead, you would actually find yourselves fighting God!" (Acts 5:38-39). In showing the opposite trend among the followers of Jesus, Luke sketches an explicit contrast between followers of messianic pretenders in Galilee and followers of Jesus of Nazareth.

The Persecution of Believers and the Transformation of Saul

Following Pentecost, Peter and John set out in ministry, continuing the healing and proclamational work of Jesus. Their challenging of religious leaders, however, evokes opposition, and several attempts to put down the movement follow. First, Luke reports that leaders of the Jewish Council in Jerusalem seek to kill the apostles (5:33); Gamaliel's calming counsel, though, prevails. Second, upon hearing the powerful preaching of Stephen, members of the so-called "Synagogue of Former Slaves"—converts to Judaism from various parts of the Mediterranean world—accuse him of speaking against the temple, Moses, and God (6:8-15). He is brought before the Jewish Council and delivers a powerful testimony to the history of God's redemption in Israel, culminating in God's redemptive work through Jesus as the Christ (7:2-53). In addition to promoting Stephen's compelling witness, Luke also presents him as a mirror image of Jesus before his executioners—his face radiant with the Spirit, looking to heaven, and asking that this sin not be held against those who are stoning him. A zealous young man named Saul is presented as an approving witness to the martyrdom of Stephen, even one who holds the coats of those stoning Stephen to death (7:54-60).

A second wave of persecution is reported as following directly, leading to believers scattering throughout Samaria and Judea. Saul's role is also reported by Luke as wreaking havoc upon the church and throwing men and women believers alike into prison (8:1-3). Saul even procures letters from the high priest in Jerusalem to deliver to synagogues in Syria, commissioning him to bring followers of "the Way" to Jerusalem as prisoners (9:1-2). On his way to Damascus, however, Saul is driven to the ground by a blinding light, whereupon the risen Christ appears to him and declares, "Saul, Saul, why are you harassing me?" Those with him hear the voice, but they see nothing (9:3-7). Saul is then taken to Ananias, whom the Lord uses to restore Saul's sight and to instruct him in the ways of Jesus. As a result of his conversion, Jewish authorities in Damascus and Jerusalem then seek to put Saul to death, although he escapes their designs and relocates safely to the coastal town of Caesarea. Later, Luke informs the reader that his name is also "Paul" (13:9), and in two of his later speeches he also describes, in somewhat different terms, his transformative Damascus-road experience (22:6-11; 26:12-18). Thus, in the rest of Acts, Paul the zealous persecutor of the Way becomes its greatest advocate.

The movement continues to expand, despite other persecutions and hardships: the apostles are persecuted by Herod (James the son of Zebedee is killed by the sword, and Peter is imprisoned, 12:1-11); as Paul and Barnabas minister in Antioch, Iconium, Lystra, and Derbe, Jewish leaders stir up crowds against them and stone Paul in Lystra, leaving him for dead (14:19); when Paul and Silas arrive at Philippi, Paul exorcises a fortune-telling slave woman, but her owners are upset and have Paul and Silas thrown into prison (16:11-40); while Jewish leaders from Beroea are receptive to the gospel, those of Thessalonica oppose the work of the apostles, and seeking to persecute Paul, they attack the household of Jason and bring hardship to the mission (17:1-15); after Paul's witness is effective in Corinth, Jewish leaders complain to Gallio, the proconsul of Achaia, that Paul is preaching against the Law, and they beat up Sosthenes as a means of intimidation (18:12-17); after pagan-worship artisans convert to the gospel in Ephesus, burning their valuable trinkets and instruments, a riot ensues, with a great crowd gathering in the amphitheater yelling for two hours, "Great is Artemis of the Ephesians!" (19:18-20, 23-41); after Paul arrives back in Jerusalem, Jews from Syria seize him in the temple area and seek to kill him, claiming he has brought Gentiles into the temple area (this was forbidden on pain of death; 21:27-36); after Paul's defense before the Jewish Council, forty Jewish leaders make a vow to neither eat nor drink until they have killed Paul (23:12-15); Paul is taken by a Roman garrison to Caesarea Maritima and stands trial before the chief priests, who accuse him falsely of causing a disturbance in the temple—Felix does not find him guilty but leaves him in prison for two years as a favor to the Jewish leaders (23:23–24:27); when Felix is succeeded by Festus, Festus is lobbied to return Paul to Jerusalem (the Jewish leaders intend to kill him during the transfer), but Paul appeals to Caesar as a Roman citizen, whereupon Paul also declares his case to Agrippa (25:1–26:32); after arriving in Rome, Paul is placed under house arrest, and there Jewish leaders are responsive to his message, and Paul continues to minister in Rome largely unimpeded (28:16-31).

Therefore, despite repeated instances of persecution and opposition, the mission of the church continues to thrive, and God provides a way forward at every turn.

The Mission to the Gentiles and the Jerusalem Council

Following Paul's first missionary journey, a good deal of consternation arises over his taking the gospel of Jesus as the Jewish Messiah/Christ to the Gentiles. Especially at Antioch and Iconium, as Paul and Barnabas preach that the prophecy of Isaiah has been fulfilled and that a light has been extended to the Gentiles, many of them believe, causing Jewish leaders to be threatened. In response to Gentile believers' joining the movement, leaders from Judea assert: "Unless you are circumcised according to the custom we've received from Moses, you can't be saved" (15:1). As Paul and Barnabas oppose this teaching, they are sent from the church at Antioch (where believers are first called "Christians," 11:26) to Jerusalem, seeking to find a way forward in unity. What results is the most important decision in the first Christian generation—one need not become outwardly Jewish to become inwardly an authentic follower of Jesus. Several features of the way Luke relates the response to the controversy are significant.

The Jerusalem Council as a Pivotal Event (15:6-35)

- Around a difficult issue, Christian leaders come together, in one place, at one time; it is a meeting for worship in which business is conducted.

- Input is gathered from all sides of the issue—Peter, Paul, Barnabas, and others share their perspectives so that they can be considered together in a common setting.

- Having heard the input, the issues are sorted and weighed prayerfully in silence, allowing discernment to emerge.

- James, the brother of Jesus, then makes a pivotal contribution, distinguishing the substantive issues from the symbolic ones—the real issues involve staying away from "the pollution associated with idols, sexual immorality, eating meat from strangled animals, and consuming blood" (15:20)—these are the central concerns, of which circumcision is a sign.

- Agreement is thus achieved, welcoming repentant Gentiles into the community of faith, while not requiring them to become outwardly Jewish.

- A letter is then sent to the churches, sharing the process and the corporate decision made, calling for adherence to the consensus of the apostolic council, distinguishing the substance of faith in Jesus as the Jewish Messiah from outward signifiers.

This pivotal event in the history of the early church allowed for the followers of the Way to extend God's promise of blessing to the children of Abraham beyond a particular religious expression to include all people of the world as adopted members into Abraham's family. This, of course, created new problems for the Jewish movement, as the admission of Gentile believers led to the individuation of Jesus adherents away from Judaism. Acts 15 also provides a remarkable case study for corporate decision making within the emerging history of the church. As mature believers come together to attend, discern, and mind the leadership of the risen Christ, leading into unity through the Holy Spirit, it is believed that the Lord's Prayer is answered— that God's will might be done on earth as it is in heaven. Such is the form and character of effective Christian leadership in every generation.

Miscellaneous Threats to the Way

In addition to the trials mentioned above, a variety of miscellaneous crises pose threats along the way in Acts, only to be surmounted by divine intervention and the workings of the apostles. For instance, while the apostles and others enjoy the blessedness of selling their possessions and contributing the funds to the welfare of the community, Ananias and Sapphira conspire to sell a piece of property but deceive the apostles in their contribution, keeping some of the money back for themselves (5:1-11). Peter thus confronts them with prophetic knowledge, and they fall down dead. Others also misuse or misunderstand spiritual power: in Samaria, Simon the sorcerer seeks to procure the spiritual power of the apostles, but he is rebuked by Peter (8:9-24); on Cyprus, Elymas the sorcerer seeks to turn the governor against Paul and Barnabas, but Paul rebukes him, and he is smitten with blindness (13:4-12); after Paul heals a lame man in Lystra, the priest of Zeus wants to make garlands for Paul and Barnabas and to offer sacrifices to them, but they reject the offer and point to the one true God as the source of all (14:8-18). In contrast to these threats, the empowerment of the apostles is presented as authentic and effective.

Another problem is that some believers in Jesus receive the water baptism of John (by Philip and Apollos) but do not receive the Holy Spirit until they receive the laying on of hands by Peter and John (8:4-17) and by Paul (18:24–19:7). One can understand why Paul reports partisan divisions between those who claimed to be "of Paul," "of Cephas," "of Apollos," and "of Christ" (1 Cor 1:12). Threatening also the mission of the apostles is the discouragement of John Mark, who decides to return to Jerusalem instead of continuing on with Paul and Barnabas in Pamphylia (Acts 13:13). Thus, when Barnabas wants to take John Mark with them on their second missionary journey, Paul refuses because of his earlier abandonment of the mission. Therefore, Barnabas parts company with Paul and goes on to Cyprus with John Mark, while Paul continues on through Syria and Asia Minor with Silas (15:36-41).

In addition to personal crises, several natural challenges also threaten the rise and progress of the movement. When a famine is predicted by Agabus, believers feel led to make contributions to the brothers and sisters in Judea, carried to them by Paul and Barnabas (11:28-30). Agabus later comes down to Caesarea from Jerusalem, prophesying that if Paul goes up to Jerusalem he will be bound and turned over to the Gentiles. Undaunted, Paul sets out for Jerusalem nonetheless (21:10-15). Later, on the way to Rome a storm and an ensuing shipwreck nearly bring the story to an end, but God provides, and none are lost (27:1-44). Paul's ministry also continues on the island of

Malta, where despite being bitten by a poisonous snake, he suffers no ill effects (28:1-6). Therefore, in spite of a good number of crises, the Jesus movement makes steady headway from beginning to end in Acts, as reporting the rise and progress of the Way receives an inspiring narration by Luke.

II. Features of Acts

While the book of Acts presents the history of the early Christian movement in ways that are in keeping with standard Greco-Roman historical narrative, like all historical presentations, it also has its own rhetorical points to make along the way. Some of these include showing that despite obstacles and setbacks, the Jesus movement continues to prosper—by divine assistance and the courage of the apostles. Another feature involves the speeches given by the apostles—especially Peter and Paul. Luke crafts a concise understanding of their contextual message in each case, but that also becomes a means of furthering his own message. Additionally, presentations of their ministries also show their continuity with the spiritually empowered ministry of Jesus; his healings, exorcisms, and raising the dead did not cease with the termination of his earthly ministry. Rather, Jesus's service continues on in the ministries of the apostles and the life of the church.

The Rise and Progress of the Way

The rise and progress of the Jesus movement, "the Way" according to Luke, is largely a fulfillment of Jesus's prophecy in Acts 1:8: "you will receive power when the Holy Spirit has come upon you, and you will be my witnesses in Jerusalem, in all Judea and Samaria, and to the end of the earth." This forward advance is also documented by Luke's inclusion of progress reports along the way. As the movement makes headway geographically and chronologically, moving from Jerusalem to surrounding regions (i.e., Judea and Samaria, followed by missions in Syria, Asia Minor, Greece, and the Mediterranean world) and finally to Rome, it becomes clear to the reader that the prophecy of Jesus has indeed come true. Note, therefore, six or seven progress reports that divide the narrative into episodes—like stained glass windows in a cathedral. Over a century ago, Oxford historian C. H. Turner described these as "six panels" on the walls of a church;[1] I might note seven episodes, where progress reports punctuate the narrative.

---

1. C. H. Turner, "Chronology of the New Testament," *Hastings Dictionary of the Bible*, vol. 1, ed. James Hastings (New York: Scribner, 1898), 421.

Seven Episodes of the Rise and Progress of the Way

- Episode 1: The Birth of the Church in Jerusalem (1:1–2:47)

  - *Advances:* the appointing of a twelfth apostle, Peter's sermon in Jerusalem, and the outpouring of the Spirit at Pentecost

  - *Progress report:* "They praised God and demonstrated God's goodness to everyone. The Lord added daily to the community those who were being saved." (2:47)

- Episode 2: The Growth of the Church in Jerusalem (3:1–6:7)

  - *Advances:* the ministries of Peter and John and the appointing of seven deacons to care for the Greek believers

  - *Progress report:* "God's word continued to grow. The number of disciples in Jerusalem increased significantly. Even a large group of priests embraced the faith." (6:7)

- Episode 3: The Expansion of the Mission into Samaria and Syria (6:8–9:31)

  - *Advances:* the martyrdom of Stephen, the ministries of Philip, Peter, and John in Samaria, and the conversion of Saul

  - *Progress report:* "Then the church throughout Judea, Galilee, and Samaria enjoyed a time of peace. God strengthened the church, and its life was marked by reverence for the Lord. Encouraged by the Holy Spirit, the church continued to grow in numbers." (9:31)

- Episode 4: The Spirit's Coming to the Gentiles and the Extension of the Church to the Coast and to Antioch (9:32–12:24)

  - *Advances:* Peter's vision at Joppa, Cornelius and his household receiving the Spirit at Caesarea, and the growth of the church at Antioch

  - *Progress report:* "God's word continued to grow and increase." (12:24)

- Episode 5: The Expansion of the Way into Asia Minor (12:25–16:5)

- ○ *Advances:* Paul's first missionary journey, mixed responses, and the Jerusalem Council

- ○ *Progress report:* "So the churches were strengthened in the faith and every day their numbers flourished." (16:5)

- Episode 6: The Expansion of the Way into Greece and Europe (16:6–19:20)

  - ○ *Advances:* Paul's second and third missionary journeys and the success of the Way

  - ○ *Progress report:* "In this way the Lord's word grew abundantly and strengthened powerfully." (19:20)

- Episode 7: The Return to Jerusalem and the Expansion of the Church to Rome (19:21–28:31)

  - ○ *Advances:* Paul's escape from plots to kill him, his testimonies before magistrates, and his journey to Rome

  - ○ *Progress report:* "Unhindered and with complete confidence, he [Paul] continued to preach God's kingdom and to teach about the Lord Jesus Christ." (28:31)

Speeches in Acts and the Preaching of the Apostles

Just as the teachings of Jesus are featured in the Gospels, the speeches of the apostles are featured in Acts with special prominence. Not only do they show the effect of compelling witness (many believe on the basis of their witness), but the speeches also further Luke's understanding of the gospel message. While these sometimes hours-long speeches are obviously presented in digest form, they reflect distinctive features, showing Luke's understanding of the particular emphases that would have been made by various leaders. They also cast valuable light upon the message of the apostles, as their preaching and emphases form a pattern for later preachers to follow. Key speeches by Peter, Stephen, Paul, and James are as follows:

Speeches of Peter in Acts

- 1:15-22 (among the family of 120 believers)—Let us appoint a twelfth apostle!

- 2:14-40 (to the gathering at Pentecost)—God's Spirit is poured out on all people!

- 3:12-26 (to the crowd outside the temple)—You are heirs of the prophets and God's covenant with Abraham!

- 4:8-12 (before the Jewish Council)—Jesus whom *you* crucified *God* has raised up!

- 5:29-32 (before the Jewish Council)—We must obey God rather than humans!

- 8:20-23 (to Simon the sorcerer)—Change your life; repent from your wickedness!

- 10:34-43 (with Cornelius and Gentiles)—God is no respecter of persons or groups!

- 11:5-17 (to the believers in Jerusalem)—I received a vision making unclean foods clean!

- 15:7-11 (at the Jerusalem Council of believers)—The Gentiles too have received the Holy Spirit!

The Witness of Stephen in Acts

- 7:2-53 (before the Jewish Council and his accusers in Jerusalem)—Israel's promise and covenant are fulfilled in Christ Jesus.

Speeches of Paul in Acts

- 13:16-41 (at the synagogue in Pisidian Antioch)—We proclaim to you the good news that God promised our ancestors!

- 17:22-31 (at the Areopagus in Athens—Mars Hill)—I worship the unseen God, in whom we live, move, and exist!

- 20:18-35 (his farewell to the Ephesian elders)—Watch yourselves and the whole flock; stay alert lest you be deceived!

- 22:1-21; 23:3-6 (his defense in Jerusalem)—The Lord appeared to me and called me to preach to the Gentiles.

- 24:10-21 (his trial before Felix)—I am a follower of the Way!

- 25:10-11 (before Festus)—I am guilty of nothing; I appeal to Caesar!

- 26:2-27 (his defense before King Agrippa)—I was transformed by a heavenly vision and am faithful to it.

- 27:21-26 (to the shipmates during the storm)—An angel appeared and said all will be well; fear not!

- 28:17-28 (to the Jewish leaders in Rome)—I was falsely accused in Jerusalem; Isaiah's prophecy is true: Israel's blessing extends also to the Gentiles.

The Discerning Judgment of James

- 15:13-21 (to the Jerusalem Council of believers)—We should not overburden those Gentiles who are truly turning to God; they should simply abstain from food offered to idols, sexual immorality, and the blood of strangled animals.

In addition to these speeches, two letters are also included: the letter of James and the Jerusalem Council regarding rescinding the requirement of circumcision while affirming moral standards (15:23-29) and the letter from the Roman commander Claudius Lysias to Governor Felix asserting Paul's innocence (23:26-30).

In considering the leading speeches in Acts, the following reflections emerge. First, the role of Peter as an advocate and spokesman for the twelve apostles is clear. His insistence on appointing a replacement for Judas affirms the role of many eyewitnesses beyond the apostolic band, and it also insures the larger vision of Jesus's mission—involving the restoration of the twelve scattered tribes of Israel, which takes place in the mission to the diaspora.

A second point is that central to each of Peter's speeches is the featuring of some mighty act of God. The outpouring of the Holy Spirit, with rushing winds and tongues of fire, fulfills the prophecy of Joel! This Jesus whom *you* crucified, God has now raised up! It is not *our* power that performs the healing, but God's! It is not *my* idea to declare unclean foods acceptable; it was revealed in a vision! The Gentiles too have received the Holy Spirit; in Christ Jesus, the blessings of Israel are offered to all! Further, we must obey *God* rather than humans! If such *dunamis* (power-oriented) rhetoric was part of Peter's own preaching, it would be no surprise that this was the sort of material Mark sought to preserve in his gathering of Jesus tradition before the deaths of Peter and other apostles.

A third thing to note is that Stephen's witness preserves the voice of the seven deacons (servant-leaders) chosen by the twelve to attend to the needs of the Greek-speaking believers in Jerusalem. All of them have Greek names (including Philip, who is differentiated from Philip the apostle by modern scholars, but not by Luke), and Stephen's witness gives them voice. Stephen's narrating the history of God's redemption in Israel also affirms convictions within some of diaspora Judaism regarding the spiritual value of the temple over its physical and geographical place. The dwelling place of God is larger than that, and through the prophet predicted by Moses (Deut 18:15-22) and the agency of the Son of Man (Dan 7:13), God's everlasting covenant is extended to the entire world for those who believe.

A fourth feature to note involves the contextually sensitive character of the speeches of Paul. Like Peter's first speech and like Stephen's witness, Paul's first speech rehearses the history of Israel and shows that God's salvation history has now culminated in his Son Jesus Christ, who has become a light to the nations and the inaugurator of a new covenant. Paul also shows remarkable cultural sensitivity to the philosophers and citizens of Athens on Mars Hill, quoting their poets with the proclamation of the gospel. In his farewell to the Ephesian elders, Paul shows particular pastoral sensitivity, and as he offers his defense before his trials in Jerusalem and before Roman officials, he shows that Jesus is the end-goal of the Law of Moses and the basis for saving faith. As a consequence of having encountered the risen Lord on the Damascus road and having been sent by him to the nations, Paul is presented as a rightful apostle alongside the Twelve, and he is given the last word in the story.

A fifth feature involves the wisdom and discernment of James. As the brother of Jesus, James (nicknamed "James the Righteous") is presented as the first head of the church in Jerusalem—operating in a family-oriented model of organization (a caliphate—or headship). In Jerusalem Luke affirms that both Sadducees and Pharisees have become followers of Jesus, and the combination of God-fearers from diaspora settings, as well as members of diverse sectors of society (economically, culturally, and religiously) must have involved an extremely diverse group of people gathered into community as part of the Jesus movement with no small degree or amount of tension. James thus is portrayed as upholding the more conservative side of the movement in Jerusalem, while Peter, Paul, and Stephen play bolder roles in taking the gospel to the Gentiles. Therefore, James's role in distinguishing the central concerns from their signifying markers shows the wisdom of a discerning leader, and his religiously conservative role among the apostolic leaders serves to maintain an essential place at the table among the Jewish leaders in Jerusalem.

In addition to programmatic speeches by Peter, Stephen, Paul, and James, Luke also includes several other testimonies as well as incidental comments in the dialogue. In so doing, he brings the narrative to life with testimonies both for and against the protagonists. These include:

(a) additional testimonies by apostles and other believers: Peter and John (4:19-20), the Twelve (6:2-4), Philip (8:30), Paul and Barnabas (13:46-47; 14:15-17, 22), Agabus (21:11);

(b) testimonies from newcomers to faith: the Ethiopian eunuch (8:31, 34, 36), Cornelius (10:30-33), Lydia (16:15), the jailer (16:30, 36), followers of Apollos (19:2-3), the Malta islanders (28:4);

(c) negative claims by opponents of the Way: the Jewish Council and the high priest (4:16-17; 5:28), false witnesses (6:11, 14), Simon the sorcerer (8:19, 24), the owners of the slave woman (16:20-21), Jewish leaders in Thessalonica (17:6-7), Jewish leaders in Corinth (18:13), Demetrius of Ephesus (19:25-27), the crowd at Ephesus (19:28, 34), Asian Jews in Jerusalem (21:28), the crowd in Jerusalem (21:36; 22:22; 23:4), chief priests and elders (23:14-15), Tertullus (24:2-8);

(d) encouraging words from neutral supporters of the Way: Gamaliel (5:35-39), Antioch synagogue leaders (13:15), Gallio (18:14-15), the city manager of Ephesus (19:35-40), Pharisees in Jerusalem (23:9), Paul's nephew (23:20-21), the Jews in Rome (28:21-22);

(e) words from divine sources: Jesus, the Spirit, the Lord (1:4-5, 7-8; 8:29; 13:2; 18:9-10; 23:11), two men, an angel, a voice (1:11; 5:20; 8:26; 10:3-6, 13, 15; 12:7-8), the vision of a man from Macedonia (16:9);

(f) words from ambiguous or incidental figures: the fortune-telling woman (16:17), Epicurian and Stoic philosophers (17:18-20, 32), the seven sons of Sceva (19:13), the Roman commander (21:37-38; 22:27-28; 23:19, 22-24), a centurion (22:26; 23:18), Felix (23:35; 24:22, 25), Festus (25:5, 9, 12, 14-22, 24-27; 26:24), Agrippa (25:22; 26:1, 28, 31-32).

In presenting the speeches of the major leaders of the early Christian movement, Luke covers the spectrum of conservatism to liberalism in relation to Jewish concerns. From the most rigorous interests in keeping the Law of Moses to more open understandings of what God requires, the speeches and testimonies of Acts cover the territory. While adversaries also state their cases, and while the roles of others are ambiguous, newcomers to faith attest to their transformative experiences, and believers are reported to be beneficiaries of divine guidance and empowerment. Smaller characters also play important roles in the development of the narrative, and the prospering of the Way is readily apparent.

The Ministries of Peter and Paul

In addition to speeches, the ministries of Peter and Paul shape the thrust of the Jesus movement's advance in Acts. Just as their speeches are similar in number and effect, so also their personal ministries reflect a set of parallel impacts, thus demonstrating their dual effectiveness.

The Ministries of Peter and Paul—Empowered Parallels in Terms of . . .

- *Divine Encounters:*
  - an angel of the Lord appears to Peter in prison (12:7)
  - the Lord appears to Saul on the road to Damascus (9:3-6)
- *Healings:*
  - Peter heals a lame man in the temple (3:2-10); Peter heals the paralyzed Aeneas (9:32-35)
  - Paul heals a lame man at Lystra (14:8-10); Paul heals a woman possessed by an evil spirit (16:18)
- *Acts of Power:*
  - At Peter's confrontations of their dishonesty, Ananias and Sapphira are slain (5:3-10)
  - Paul's words blind Elymas the magician (13:9-11); Paul is not affected by the viper bite on Malta (28:3-6)
- *Deliverances from Prison:*
  - The prison doors in Jerusalem are opened by an angel (5:19); a prison gate is miraculously opened (12:6-10)
  - The earthquake loosens the chains and doors of the Philippian prison (16:26)

- *Raising People from the Dead:*
  - ○ Peter raises Dorcas from the dead in Joppa (9:39-42)
  - ○ Paul raises Eutychus from the dead in Troas (20:8-12)
- *Laying on of Hands:*
  - ○ Peter and John lay hands on Samaritan believers, who then receive the Holy Spirit (8:17)
  - ○ Paul lays hands on followers of Apollos in Ephesus, and they are filled with the Holy Spirit (19:6)
- *Receiving a Vision:*
  - ○ Peter receives a rooftop vision of unclean food now being clean (10:9-16)
  - ○ Paul receives a vision of a man from Macedonia inviting a visit (16:9)
- *General References to Miracles:*
  - ○ Peter heals many from various cities (5:12-16)
  - ○ Paul performs miracles in Iconium (14:3); Paul performs other miracles in Ephesus (19:11-12); Paul heals the diseased on Malta (28:8-9)

While a few others also perform wonders in Acts (the apostles, 5:12; Stephen, 6:8; Philip, 8:6-7, 13; Ananias, 9:17-18), the parallel presentation of Peter and Paul is undoubtedly intentional. In giving Peter the first word, the ministry of Jesus and the Twelve are portrayed with a clear continuity in the first fifteen chapters of Acts. Jesus's healing and teaching ministries continue into the life of the church, and the empowerment of the Spirit is clearly effective. With the calling of Paul and his ministry in the final twenty chapters of Acts (note the overlap of chapters 9–15), the impact of the Jesus movement extends beyond his original followers to hearers of the gospel and to those who also experience first-hand encounters with the Spirit of the risen Lord. This poses an expanded understanding of apostolicity. Apostolic leadership not only includes those who walked and talked with Jesus of Nazareth; it also includes those who encounter his spiritual reality and who are sent by him with a representative commission. Paul exemplifies the expansion of the Jesus movement to include a Christ movement, becoming his apostolic witnesses even unto the remotest parts of the world.

III. The Message of Acts

This is what you heard from me: John baptized with water, but in only a few days you will be baptized with the Holy Spirit. . . . It isn't for you to know the times or seasons that the Father has set by his own authority. Rather, you will receive power when the Holy Spirit has come upon you, and you will be my witnesses in Jerusalem, in all Judea and Samaria, and to the end of the earth. (Acts 1:4b-5, 7-8)

With these words the risen Lord commissions his followers to be his witnesses both near and afar after they are filled with the Holy Spirit. John baptized with water, but Jesus's followers will be immersed in the Spirit—an empowering and transformative reality. Unlike the Great Commission in Matthew 28:18-20, where Jesus's followers are instructed to go to the remotest parts of the world, the Lukan version of the Great Commission calls for Jesus's followers to wait, to tarry, until they are filled with the Spirit (Luke 24:49; Acts 1:4, 8); only then will believers be clothed with power and become compelling witnesses at home and abroad. And, the story of how that happens in Acts also becomes the narrative's message.

The Power of the Spirit and Its Transformative Effects

Continuing one of the central thrusts of his first volume, Luke presents the power of the Spirit and its transformative effects as one of the leading features of the apostolic era. As believers are filled with the Holy Spirit at Pentecost (2:4), the confusion of Babel (Gen 11) is reversed. No longer do languages or cultural differences separate people—cross-cultural understanding and multilingual fellowship are now possible because of the Spirit's reconciling work. At Pentecost, not only are people given the capacity to speak in other languages, but they are also enabled to understand other languages—to discern the meanings whence words come. Young and old, male and female, simple and wise are empowered by the Spirit to minister, and in the birth of the church the Day of the Lord as prophesied by Joel is actualized. The outpouring of the Holy Spirit is also experienced by the centurion Cornelius and his God-fearing household as Peter preaches about Jesus, fulfilling the vision received on the rooftop of Simon the tanner (10:1-48; 11:15). The new age of the Spirit now also includes the Gentiles, thus fulfilling Isaiah 60:1-4.

By the power of the Spirit, believers are also enabled to witness effectively. The witnesses of Peter, Stephen, and Paul are empowered by being Spirit filled (4:8; 7:55; 13:9), and in being filled with the Spirit, believers are bonded together in boldness and joy (4:31; 13:52). Even newcomers to faith receive the Holy Spirit, although it does not always accompany water baptism (8:17; 19:2-6); sometimes it also precedes it (9:17-18; 10:47). Ananias is sent to minister to Saul in order that he might regain his sight and be filled with the Holy Spirit (9:17). Just as the prophets of old had been led by the Holy Spirit in their writings (1:16; 4:25; 28:25), so also the Spirit is at work in the advance of the Way.

With that conviction in mind, Luke narrates the story of how the Spirit also guides believers in timely and fortuitous ways. Philip is led by the Spirit to minister to the Ethiopian eunuch (8:29) and then carried by the Spirit to the coastal regions of Azotus and Caesarea (8:39-40); Peter is led by the Spirit to engage the entourage of Cornelius (10:19-20); the famine in the region is predicted by Agabus through the Holy Spirit's leading (11:28, connected by Luke to the later timeframe of Caesar Claudius—41–54 CE); the Holy Spirit instructs the setting aside of Paul and Barnabas, sending them off on Paul's first missionary journey (13:2-4); the Holy Spirit guides the Jerusalem Council's discernment and decision (15:28); on Paul's second missionary journey he and Silas are forbidden by the Holy Spirit to proclaim the word in central Asia Minor (16:6-7); while Paul resolves in the Spirit to go through Macedonia and on to Jerusalem (19:21), through the Holy Spirit Paul is warned by others not to go to Jerusalem (21:4, 11); yet Paul also explains that he is captive to the Holy Spirit, who testifies in every city that he will suffer (20:22-23).

Therefore, the Holy Spirit is presented by Luke as a prime actor in the unfolding story of the Acts of the Apostles, and readers are thereby invited thus to set their sails to the wind of the Spirit if they want to be incorporated within the apostolic movement. The Spirit transforms, empowers, and guides believers, and such is the dynamism of the Way.

Koinonia and Christian Community

Another central theme in Acts is *koinōnia*—fellowship, which flowers as believers come together in Christian community. Two paragraphs in particular document Luke's impression of the communal ideal. Following the outpouring of the Spirit at Pentecost, Luke describes the early believers as sharing table fellowship together, taking seriously Jesus's commands to sell possessions and to give to those in need, sharing also their possessions in common with one another—the sort of selfless and loving community that everyone might like to join:

> The believers devoted themselves to the apostles' teaching, to the community, to their shared meals, and to their prayers. A sense of awe came over everyone. God performed many wonders and signs through the apostles. All the believers were united and shared everything. They would sell pieces of property and possessions and distribute the proceeds to everyone who needed them. Every day, they met together in the temple and ate in their homes. They shared food with gladness and simplicity. They praised God and demonstrated God's goodness to everyone. The Lord added daily to the community those who were being saved. (2:42-47)

And following the powerful witness of Peter and John in Jerusalem, Luke describes the fellowship of believers as being of one heart and mind, generous with one another, and distributing to all according to their need. If everyone lived this way, the needs of all could surely be met, and this utopian ideal has also become the basis for much of Western economic and social theory, influenced by Luke's convictions about the Way.

> The community of believers was one in heart and mind. None of them would say, "This is mine!" about any of their possessions, but held everything in common. The apostles continued to bear powerful witness to the resurrection of the Lord Jesus, and an abundance of grace was at work among them all. There were no needy persons among them. Those who owned properties or houses would sell them, bring the proceeds from the sales, and place them in the care and under the authority of the apostles. Then it was distributed to anyone who was in need. (4:32-35)

While some interpreters have imagined Luke's descriptions of table fellowship as a eucharistic rite, such inferences go beyond what the text suggests. Rather, it is around the common table that the divine presence is authentically experienced. It was at such common-meal events that believers in Corinth gathered, eating and drinking too much in 1 Corinthians 11, whereupon Paul instructs them to eat at home, going on to institute a symbolic meal of remembrance. Such a symbolic rite may call to mind the Christ Events for the life of the believer, but here Luke connects the table-fellowship practices of Jesus during his ministry with the continuing movement of believers, who gather in his name. Therefore, like the Gospel of John, Luke's presentations of sacramental realities are more incarnational rather than formalistic.

Note also several other themes that emerge from these two reports. First, early gatherings of believers attended the teaching and preaching of the apostles; such is the source of faithful and effective proclamation in later generations. Second, early believers were gathered in unity and were of one mind, not thinking of their own needs but given to addressing first the needs of others; such developments actualize the teachings of Jesus in the Gospel of Luke. Third, the devout and socially concerned example of early believers became a morally compelling factor in the explosive growth of the early church; Luke implies that such will be the case in later generations if future believers follow in their apostolic wake.

The Proclamation of the Apostles and the Power of the Gospel

Given the withering of the nineteenth-century quest for the Jesus of history, largely due to Albert Schweitzer's critique, an interest in the historical message of the apostles came into full bloom. Among scholars in Continental Europe, analyses of the literary forms of materials used by Mark and the other Gospel writers became an interest of study, but so did the history and character of the material underlying the Acts of the Apostles. For instance, given that Luke has crafted his story of the rise and progress of the early church in ways that serve his convictions and theological interests, might there be ways of getting at the historical character and origin of the material he incorporates—especially the speeches in Acts? If such knowledge were accessible, it would not only inform us about the material Luke employed; more importantly, it might shed light upon the historical message of the apostles—bearing highly important implications for later interpreters.

As a means of getting at the proclamation (*kerygma* in Greek) of the apostles, C. H. Dodd sought to infer outlines of early Christian preaching as represented in Acts and also the epistles of the New Testament.[2] Within this analysis, Dodd identifies several elements of the apostolic message apparently shared by Paul, Peter, and others, while also noting various distinctive elements along a number of lines. Dodd's examination of the *kerygma* of the apostles thus points not primarily to the activity of their preaching but to the content of their apostolic message, bearing several key elements.

---

2. C. H. Dodd, *The Apostolic Preaching and Its Developments* (London: Hodder and Stoughton, 1936).

The Kerygma of the Apostles (Especially Paul and Peter)

- The prophecies are fulfilled, and the New Age is inaugurated by the coming of Christ.

- He was born of the seed of David.

- He died, according to the scriptures, to deliver us from the present evil age.

- He was buried.

- He rose on the third day according to the scriptures.

- He is exalted at the right hand of God as Son of God and Lord of the living and the dead.

- He will come again as judge and savior of humanity.

In addition to the speeches of Peter and Paul in Acts, these elements are represented especially clearly in Paul's letters (Rom 1:1-6; 10:6-15; 16:25-27; 1 Cor 1:17-25; 15:3-8; 2 Cor 4:3-7; Gal 1:11-12; 3:13-14; 1 Tim 6:13; 2 Tim 1:8-14; 2:8; 4:1-2) and Peter's letters (1 Pet 1:20; 2:4-12, 21-25; 3:18-22; 4:1-6; 2 Pet 1:16-19). Therefore, this cluster of common elements of the preaching of Peter and Paul may be considered representative of what the apostles claimed about Jesus as the Christ. Note that very little is said within these passages about the teachings of Jesus or the particulars of his ministry. Interests in those elements develop later, as gospel narratives are preserved by Mark and the other evangelists. The apostles simply proclaimed *that* God has acted in history—in the ministry, death, and resurrection of Jesus as the Christ—calling for a response of faith to the divine initiative. And that is the heart of gospel preaching in every generation, calling preachers and hearers alike to consider what the message of the apostles means in later settings and generations.

Not all elements of apostolic preaching are uniform, however; one can also note distinctive elements in the Johannine tradition and the Epistle to the Hebrews, for instance. Even in Acts, the proclamation of Peter, with some echoes in James, exhibits several Jewish traits. These features might not simply represent Peter's ministry; perhaps they convey an impression of how Jesus was proclaimed by and among audiences in Jerusalem as part of a distinctively Jewish crafting of the gospel message.

Additional Features of a Jerusalem (and Petrine) Kerygma

- Jesus is referred to as "Lord and Christ" rather than "Son of God" (Acts 2:36; 1 Pet 3:15)

- Jesus was a servant "faithful unto death" rather than one who "died for our sins" (Acts 3:13, 26; 4:27, 30; cf. Isa 53)

- Believers receive forgiveness "in his name" rather than Christ's interceding for us as the exalted one (Acts 5:31; 10:43)

However the association developed, Luke does present Peter as making the sort of points about Jesus that are also found in 1 Peter, as the cross is referred to as a "tree" (1 Pet 2:24; Acts 5:30; 10:39 ➡Deut 21:22-23), and the building block rejected by the builders has become the cornerstone (1 Pet 2:7; Acts 4:11➡Ps 118:22; cf. also Mark 12:10). Even more distinctive, however, is the witness of Stephen, who recites the salvation history of Israel as a means of pointing to what God is now doing through Christ Jesus. Furthermore, he makes the only reference in the New Testament (outside of self-references in the Gospels) to Jesus's being the Son of Man (Dan 7:13), and he also presents him as the Prophet like Moses (Deut 18:15-22). As these references are not developed in later theological passages or Christian worship material, they may reflect Stephen's contact with more primitive memories of the historical Jesus. In addition, we see a provocative challenge to the temple cult in Jerusalem, emphasizing that the dwelling place of the Most High has never been in temples made by human hands but is in the hearts of the faithful (Deut 4:28; cf. John 2:19; Heb 9:24). In these ways, Stephen's presentation of Jesus as the Christ is radically different from the preaching material of Peter and Paul (although see Acts 3:22).

The Witness of Stephen (Acts 7:2-60)

- Jesus is the Son of Man (7:56)

- Jesus is the Prophet like Moses (7:37)

- The dwelling place of the Most High is not in shrines made by human hands (7:48-50)

Therefore, in the preaching material of Acts, we catch a glimpse of the message and messages of the apostles about Jesus as the Messiah/Christ. While there is a good deal of diversity within that unity, there is also a good deal of unity within that diversity—with extensive implications for later generations.

The Leading of the Spirit and the Advance of the Way

As with most historical narratives, what is selected as worth remembering is also worth imitating. Therefore, in recounting the deeds of the apostles, their advances *are* Luke's message. Luke's second volume therefore conveys strong messages to audiences internal to the Jesus movement as well as those external to it.

For believers, the trustworthy work of the Holy Spirit to empower and to guide is available to individuals and groups alike. Individually, the Spirit can be trusted to guide, even when the way forward is unseen. For communities, followers of the Lord can indeed come together for meetings for worship in which business is conducted, experiencing corporate guidance on pressing matters of direction, faith, and practice. As shown in Acts 10, visions of what God desires can be granted to the praying faithful; what God has made clean is no longer profane. As modeled in Acts 15, input from all sides and perspectives is to be welcomed in the gathered meeting, and central concerns are to be distinguished from symbolizing ones; aspects of preference are worthily distinguished from matters of conscience. Waiting before the Lord together in community, seeking to be led in unity, may take a bit more time, but when a common sense of a way forward is discerned, the group is energized to move forward with understanding and a sense of ownership. When that happens, that's good leadership, by any measure.

For Luke's external audiences, several concerns also become apparent. In addition to telling the story of the movement, Luke also seeks to convince hearers and readers of the truth of the gospel. Acts is not simply a narrative that tells about the advance of the gospel; it also seeks to advance the gospel—inviting a response of faith to the message of what God is doing through the Jesus movement. Luke also takes careful pains to show that the followers of the Way of Jesus are worthy of respect by Roman officials and civic leaders. Not to be confused with the "fourth philosophy" of the Galilean Zealots, who resorted to force and banditry in their opposition to Roman occupation, and despite the fact that Jesus was crucified as a common criminal, the movement embracing his name is neither violent nor a threat. It advocates charity and generous caring for the poor—healing for the sick and inward liberation for the oppressed. In spreading the light of Israel to the nations, the blessing promised to Abraham is made available to all, thus fulfilling the redemptive vocation of Israel among all the families of the earth. In sharing the Way of

Jesus among the Gentiles, wisdom, charity, and virtue are made accessible in ways that are morally compelling. Thus, the Acts of the Apostles not only reports the spreading of the believers' witness to Jerusalem, Judea, Samaria, and the remotest parts of the earth; it also creates that which it reports.

IV. Engaging Acts

In engaging Luke's story of the advance of the Jesus movement, the reader should feel free to focus upon any of the features that seem of greatest interest; there's a lot from which to select! For instance, any of the above features and lists could be explored in particular detail and reflected upon in the interest of recovering the spiritual vitality of the early Christian movement in later situations. Note, for instance, the many obstacles faced by the first Christians. Things might not be easy for believers in later generations, but they certainly were not easy for the apostles and their companions back then, either. Also notice, however, the ways God provided. That will be a source of inspiration for later readers too, as divine assistance most usually comes in unexpected ways. For particular study, though, consider these three features.

First, note the ways that early believers came together for fellowship and worship. They shared common food together and listened attentively to the teaching and preaching of the apostles. They were willing to offer what they had received from God back to God, to be distributed and used among those who were in need. That vision of community is a powerful one, indeed! What would it be like for modern readers of Acts to see their possessions as divine entrustments, not for ourselves, but to be offered back to God for the healing of the world? Such liberality could indeed make a difference in the world, perhaps even in new ways hitherto unimagined.

Second, take a brief inventory of the speeches in Acts, and reflect upon general commonalities, as well as particularities, among the messages of the apostles. What is the diversity within the unity, and what is the unity within the diversity, of the apostles' preaching about Jesus as the Christ? Reflect on those matters, and think about how to put the gospel message in your own terms, crafted for today's audiences; how would you articulate the message of the gospel today? One way to focus this exercise is to compare and contrast the first speeches of Peter and Paul with the witness of Stephen. This would also make an excellent small-group discussion.

Compare and Contrast

- Peter's first sermon (Acts 2:14-41)
- Paul's first sermon (Acts 13:16-41)
- Stephen's witness (Acts 7:2-53)

Third, considering the Jerusalem Council in Acts 15, think about how to apply the wisdom of James to issues in today's societies. After all, the Jerusalem Council forms the basis for the seven Ecumenical Councils of the Christian movement over its first millennium, and it also offers solid wisdom for effective leadership in later contexts. Are there means, though, of experiencing the reality of that to which James testified: "It has seemed good to the Holy Spirit and to us" (15:28 NRSV), or is such a discovery simply an echo of times past? Whatever the case, you might reflect upon how effective Christian leadership might contribute meaningfully in your situation to distinguishing substantive issues from symbolizing ones, offering a way forward in discerning unity. Again, the following elements of effective corporate leadership and discernment may serve as a helpful reminder.

Elements of Effective Corporate Leadership and Discernment

- The meeting for business is a meeting for worship; approach it accordingly.

- Routine matters can be managed in smaller groups; only those matters requiring the discernment of the entire community deserve the consideration of all.

- Input should be invited from all sides; it is only in sorting through differences of perspective in community that common ways forward can be discerned.

- Where differences are identified, core issues deserve to be distinguished from symbolizing ones; matters of conscience deserve priority over aspects of preference.

- When a unitive way forward is discerned, it can be embraced with full energy and ownership; that is how a sense of corporate mission is achieved and effectively advanced.

Paul's Background and Contemporary Religions and Philosophies

Understanding the Acts of the Apostles and the writings of Paul requires a consideration first of Paul's own background and experience, followed by an inventory of contemporary religions and philosophies. In Acts Paul presents himself as being trained under Gamaliel's instruction "in the strict interpretation of our ancestral Law" (Acts 22:3), and he affirms that Jewish leaders in Jerusalem "could testify that I followed the way of life set out by the most exacting group of our religion. I am a Pharisee" (Acts 26:4-5). He is also presented on Mars Hill in Athens as addressing his Greek audience in ways that reflect his understanding of Greek philosophy and poetry, articulating his understanding of the gospel in ways that show familiarity with contemporary non-Jewish views. There he declares:

> God, who made the world and everything in it, is Lord of heaven and earth. He doesn't live in temples made with human hands. Nor is God served by human hands, as though he needed something, since he is the one who gives life, breath, and everything else. From one person God created every human nation to live on the whole earth, having determined their appointed times and the boundaries of their lands. God made the nations so they would seek him, perhaps even reach out to him and find him. In fact, God isn't far away from any of us. In God we live, move, and exist. As some of your own poets said, "We are his offspring." (Acts 17:24-28)

So, how did Paul's religious understandings of faith and culture develop, and how did that affect his understandings of the gospel and its implications?

Paul's Jewish Background

As a member of a Jewish family born in Tarsus, the capital of the Roman province of Cilicia in southeast Asia Minor, Paul refers to his hometown as an important city (Acts 21:39). This was no modest town, and having been schooled under Gamaliel, the grandson of Rabbi Hillel, Paul was probably no modest student, either. The school of Hillel was more liberal than its leading competitor, the school of Shammai, and Gamaliel is certainly shown to demonstrate wisdom and restraint, as he calls for patience with the Jesus movement in Acts 5:34-39. If the movement is like those of Theudas and the Samaritan, it will die out on its own. However, declares Paul's mentor, "If it originates with God, you won't be able to stop them. Instead, you would actually find yourselves fighting God!" (v. 39). Paul also shows affinities with the school of Shammai, especially in his rigorous approach to the Law.

Paul describes his own zeal as having been "passionately loyal to God" to the extent that he was willing to track down followers of Jesus (Acts 22:3-5), punishing and imprisoning them, bearing letters from the high priest authorizing their being brought from other cities to Jerusalem for trial, at times even leading to their death (Acts 8:3; 9:1-2; 26:9-10). And yet, Paul's encounter with the risen Christ on the road to Damascus produces a remarkable transformation. As a result of that event, a most zealous opponent of the Jesus movement becomes its most zealous advocate. After this life-changing experience, Paul comes to see Jesus Christ as the fulfillment and goal of the Jewish Law (Rom 10:4), including its vision of God, God's people, and the future. Countering the work of the Judaizers that followed his ministry, Paul lists his Jewish credentials with some confidence (Phil 3:5-6):

> I was circumcised on the eighth day.
> I am from the people of Israel and the tribe of Benjamin.
> I am a Hebrew of the Hebrews.
> With respect to observing the Law, I'm a Pharisee.
> With respect to devotion to the faith, I harassed the church.
> With respect to righteousness under the Law, I'm blameless.

Paul's less than modest claim, though, is also backed up by his performance. In Galatians, he shows his versatility with the creative and bold interpretation of Jewish scripture, and in challenging his opponents he demonstrates his genius as one of the finest thinkers of his day. He also shows great sensitivity to non-Jewish concerns, in that in challenging the multiple religious shrines on Mars Hill in Athens, he cites the *Cretica* by Epimenides, affirming that in

God "we live and move and have our being" (Acts 17:28 NRSV). Another line from this same passage is also cited by Paul in Titus 1:12, where Cretans are referred to as "always liars, vicious brutes, lazy gluttons" (NRSV)—ironically, composed by Epimenides, a Cretan poet. The second poet quoted in Acts 17:28 is Aratus, as Paul yokes human indebtedness to Zeus in *Phaenomena* 1-5 to the God of Israel: "For we too are his offspring" (NRSV). Indeed Paul illustrates here what he claims in 1 Corinthians 9:22: "I have become all things to all people, so I could save some by all possible means."

Contemporary Religions and Philosophies

In addition to being strongly convinced of the gospel within his personal Jewish mindset, Paul's understanding of it is informed by his contextual worldview.[1] As a first-century Jew, Paul would also have been familiar with contemporary religions and philosophies, and this would also be true of his audiences within the Greco-Roman world—Jewish and Gentile, alike. Therefore, considering some of these leading movements is helpful for appreciating the context from and into which Paul articulates his understanding of God's plan for the blessing of the world.

Rooted in the contributions of Socrates (d. 399 BCE) and Plato (d. 347 BCE), *Platonism* furthered a worldview that became the dominant perspective in the Hellenistic world. This worldview was dualistic; it saw the material world as corruptible and finite, whereas God, or the Ideal Good, is eternal and transcendent. In Plato's theory of forms, what we can see, hear, and touch with our senses is not ultimate reality; these things are physical manifestations of transcendent forms, which are contingent upon timeless ideas, which in turn derive from ideal truth. In crafting the dialogues of Socrates, Plato shows that the way to discern truth is through reason, and dialectic (the soul's dialogue with itself) is the process by which thinking divides truth from error (2 Tim 2:15). The Platonism of Paul's day was eclectic, drawing ideas from a variety of sources, including Judaism. Therefore, Paul's description of the struggle between the spirit and the flesh (Rom 7:13-25) and claiming to be "landing punches on my own body and subduing it like a slave" (1 Cor 9:27) would be well appreciated among those influenced by Platonism of his day.

---

1. N. T. Wright develops this important distinction between Paul's mindset (how he views the world) and his worldview (how he and those around him view things) in *Paul and the Faithfulness of God* (Minneapolis: Fortress Press, 2013).

One of the leading philosophic movements during Paul's day was *Stoicism*, founded by Zeno (d. 263 BCE). Stoicism understood happiness and suffering as the results of how one viewed things. If God could be at work in and through all things, the prime determiner of one's emotive state had to do with how one perceived what was happening and what could be done about it. Because universal reason (the *Logos* of God) is available to all, disciplining one's passions with reason and choosing virtue over the sensual is the way of wisdom over folly. Therefore, it is not the days of one's life that matters, but the life of one's days that counts (with Seneca). Paul's dwelling on the fine things in others, as well as his capacity to be joyful whether he has much or little, would have been well received among those favoring Stoicism in his day (Phil 4:4-12).

In contrast to Platonism, which assumed that the physical and material world was contingent upon the spiritual and ideal world, *Epicurianism* was materialistic in its view of the world and its values. Founded by Epicurus (d. 270 BCE), this philosophy rejected superstitions and myths about divine interventions, emboldening human initiative in dealing with life's givens. Challenging also the value of virtue, as embraced by the Stoics, Epicurianism held that pleasure over pain was the prime goal to be aimed at—a form of hedonism that at times leads to excesses, but not necessarily. Therefore, because there is no transcendent reality or meaning to life, the main value is pleasure in the here and now. Paul cites an Epicurian slogan when he says, "Food is for the stomach and the stomach is for food," and he then reminds his audience that in the end, God will "do away with both" (1 Cor 6:13). Likewise, he seems to be addressing this approach when he says, "Their lives end with destruction. Their god is their stomach, and they take pride in their disgrace because their thoughts focus on earthly things" (Phil 3:19).

Finding their way into the Mediterranean world from Egypt and elsewhere, a number of *mystery religions* would also have been known among Paul's audiences. One of their main attractions involved dispensing the life of the gods by means of sacred meals in which food and drink were consumed as a means of ingesting divine reality—what Ignatius of Antioch described as "the medicine of immortality" (*Letter to the Ephesians* 20.2). In addressing the problems related to people eating too much and getting drunk at fellowship meals in Corinth, Paul moves their full-meal practice to a symbolic meal (1 Cor 11:20-34). In doing so, Paul is actually contrasting the fellowship meal, commemorating the sacrifice of Christ, with pagan religious meals involving food offered to idols and associated licentious behaviors (1 Cor 8:1–10:31). Paul also reminds Timothy that "the mystery of godliness is great: he was revealed as a human, declared righteous by the Spirit, seen by angels, preached throughout the nations, believed in around the world, and taken up in glory" (1 Tim 3:16).

Roman and regional religions were also realities that Jews in the larger Mediterranean world had to deal with, and the importance of circumcision and other outward signs of Jewish faithfulness is that they provided a clear way for Jews to distance themselves from both idolatry and associated questionable moral practices. Without these religious means of bolstering support of Jewish values and resistance to pagan ones, however, Paul's mission to the Gentiles was forced to rely upon theological conviction and exemplary moral action. This is why Paul worked so hard to articulate a reasoned understanding of the gospel, and why he also admonished his audiences to live in irreproachable ways within society at large. While Emperor Domitian later yoked local worship practices to support for Rome, one can still see Paul challenging the pantheistic culture of his day, pointing to the unseen god as the one true god among the many, made visible in Christ Jesus (Acts 17:22-23): "People of Athens, I see that you are very religious in every way. As I was walking through town and carefully observing your objects of worship, I even found an altar with this inscription: 'To an unknown God.' What you worship as unknown, I now proclaim to you."

While *Gnosticism* became a major threat to the Christian movement in the middle-to-late second century CE, it is a mistake to assume that all references to pagan religious practices, as well as claims of enlightened wisdom received through participation in Christ, reflect gnostic influences during Paul's day. More likely is the view that Paul's and John's writings influenced expressions of Gentile Christianity that were labeled as "gnostic" by Irenaeus and others who perceived Marcion, Valentinus, and others as threats, whether or not they would have referenced themselves with the same terms. Likewise, refusing to believe Jesus suffered and died is known as *Docetism*, and while most Gnostics were Docetists, not all Docetists were Gnostics. Nonetheless, rooting in eastern Zoroastrianism, Gnosticism addressed the dualistic divide between a perfect God and an imperfect creation by introducing a number of intermediary gods, who performed works of creation and redemption, dispensing saving knowledge and divine wisdom. Humans, being empty vessels of clay and dust, could experience "fullness" (*plēroma* in Greek) by receiving saving knowledge from above, and later gnostic teachers came to see Jesus as one of these divine intermediary agencies. This is not what Paul means, however, when he prays that believers will be "filled entirely with the fullness of God" (Eph 3:19). That comes from participating fully in Christ by faith (3:21), which is God's ultimate plan for the redemption of the world.

In conclusion, Paul's worldview included religious and philosophical components of both Jewish and Hellenistic populations in the first-century Mediterranean world, and these perspectives also overlapped each other. Therefore, just because a theme bears echoes within Stoicism or Platonism, this does not mean it is not also a Jewish view, and vice versa. What is compelling is the fact that Paul operates as an innovative multicultural interpreter of God's saving-revealing action in history through the ministry and work of Christ Jesus, and this is the message Paul conveys to multiple audiences in ways they can understand. However it happened, "God was reconciling the world to himself through Christ, by not counting people's sins against them. He has trusted us with this message of reconciliation" (2 Cor 5:19). And yet, while the gospel is indeed a timeless treasure, its articulation is always time-bound—limited by our capacities to convey God's ultimate truth. Therefore, "we have this treasure in clay pots so that the awesome power belongs to God and doesn't come from us" (2 Cor 4:7).

Chapter 7

Paul's Letter to the Romans

Begin with the text. Read Romans, and note important themes and details that come to mind.

Author: Paul

Audience: to the church in Rome

Time: ca. 57 CE

Place: from Corinth

Message: Jews and Gentiles alike are in need of grace; those who are righteous by faith shall live.

Paul's letter to the Romans may be one of the most important documents in the history of western civilization. Not only are the theologies of Augustine and Aquinas steeped in the wisdom from this book, but Martin Luther's understanding of the gospel was transformed as he read that the righteous shall live by faith (Rom 1:16-17), to which he added the word *allein* (alone) in his German translation of Romans 3:28: one is justified by *faith alone* apart from works of the Law. That insight posed the key to his understanding of the Christian gospel, and in his challenging of the church of his day, which granted indulgences according to the works and contributions of the faithful, the Protestant Reformation began. Two centuries later, as John Wesley heard the preface to Luther's *Commentary on Romans* read in a Moravian worship meeting on Aldersgate Street, his life was changed:

> In the evening I went very unwillingly to a society in Aldersgate Street, where one was reading Luther's preface to the Epistle to the Romans. About a quarter before nine, while he was describing the change which God works in the heart through faith in Christ, I felt my heart strangely warmed. I felt I did trust in Christ, Christ alone, for salvation; and an assurance was given

me that He had taken away my sins, even mine, and saved me from the law of sin and death.[1]

Likewise, Karl Barth, in writing his *Epistle to the Romans* (1918), was completely changed in his theology. In contrast to the liberal view of the previous generation that the Christian faith is about the fatherhood of God, the brotherhood of man, and the eternal worth of the human soul, Barth saw that Paul was right. There is no one righteous, no, not one; all are sinners, in need of God's redeeming grace. As the greatest theologian of the twentieth century, Barth saw that the only theology worth engaging is that which preaches and that which calls for a response of faith to the word of God. He became a leader in the recovery of Neo-Orthodoxy in the modern era, and this was a factor of his having gotten Romans right. Another impact of Paul's letter to the Romans is that Romans 13:1-7 has been the primary basis for British and European political doctrines of the divine right of kings, but that might not involve reading Romans right. Therefore, a contextual reading of Romans is essential for understanding what it says, and just as importantly, what it doesn't.

I. Crises and Contexts

Despite being placed first among his writings, Paul's letter to the Romans falls within the middle of his letter-writing work, representing an expanded and fuller treatment of many of the themes developed earlier in his letter to the Galatians. As such, it is the most comprehensive and magisterial of all of Paul's writings, and it therefore makes good sense for the organizers of the New Testament canon to introduce the rest of his writings with this letter. While the last chapter is filled with personal greetings, Paul had not yet visited Rome. That being the case, though, why did he write such an expansive letter? He probably wrote for several reasons. First, Rome, the capital city of the Empire, was a site of first importance in the Mediterranean world, and its Jewish population was well established and robust. As some of its members had come to believe in Jesus as the Christ, along with some Gentiles, good relations between these groups would have been a pressing concern. Second, as Rome was also a gateway to the rest of the known world, getting things right in Rome would be of paramount importance to the Jesus movement

---

1. *The Journal of John Wesley*, May 24, 1738, in *The Bicentennial Edition of the Works of John Wesley*, vol. 18, ed. W. Reginald Ward and Richard P. Heitzenrater (Nashville: Abingdon Press, 1988), 249–50.

long term. This might account for the care Paul gives this communication, and its impact continues to this day.

Given that Paul is writing from Corinth on his third missionary journey, he sends greetings from Erastus, the treasurer of Corinth (Acts 19:22; Rom 16:23; 2 Tim 4:20), and passes his letter along via Phoebe, a deaconess at the church of Cenchreae (Rom 16:1). Cenchreae is a port-town on the eastern side of the Isthmus of Corinth, reflecting the existence of several Christian communities in that region of Greece. Interestingly, while Paul shows concerns about some women's leadership roles in Corinth, he exhibits no hesitation in affirming Phoebe's leadership and entrusting her with the delivery of this most important letter. While Paul's letter to the Romans is comprehensive in its thrust, however, several contextual crises can still be inferred.

The Expulsion of Jews from Rome

One of the crises in Rome that had arisen less than a decade earlier involved the expulsion of Jews from Rome by Caesar Claudius (ca. 49 CE). According to Suetonius, this was because they "constantly made disturbances at the instigation of *Chrestus*" (Suetonius, *Life of Claudius* 25.4). The number of Jews in Rome would have been as many as fifty thousand at that time, and while they were not actually expelled from the city, Claudius simply forbade their meeting for worship (Dio Cassius, *Roman History* 60.6.6), thus forcing them out of the city if they desired to be observant. Paul runs into Priscilla and Aquila in Corinth, fellow tentmakers, noting that they had come to Corinth because Claudius had ordered the Jews to leave Rome (Acts 18:2). Acts refers to Aquila as a Jew from Pontus, and yet he and his wife Priscilla were apparently partners in ministry with Paul (Acts 18:18, 26; Rom 16:3; 1 Cor 16:19; 2 Tim 4:19). The point here is that tensions had apparently grown so intense within the Jewish sector in Rome over the subject of Christ (*Chrestus* = *Christos*) that the emperor had to interevene. While it cannot be known what percentage of Jews departed from Rome, when they were welcomed back upon Nero's becoming emperor in 54 CE, many likely returned.

Another reported incident, Paul's trial in Corinth by Gallio, also helps the dating of these matters. Given that the Delphi Inscription of Gallio dates his service around 51–52 CE at the latest, it is plausible to date the events in Acts 18 as happening around that time. These markers thus help to date the second missionary journey of Paul as reported in Acts, and this is why his correspondence with believers at Thessalonica is dated around 50–51 CE and why the Jerusalem Council is dated around 49 CE. Regarding the crisis in Rome between believers in Jesus and Jewish members of society, however, Paul shows special concern to help things work out between Jewish and Gentile believers in Jesus. In Romans 16, Paul mentions some two dozen believers, despite his not yet having visited Rome. Quite possibly this reflects his meeting Jews on his missionary travels or in Judea who had fled Rome to other parts of the Mediterranean world. As some of them were settling back into Roman society, Paul wants to make sure they are feeling supported and embraced within the Jewish community of faith and especially affirmed as believers in Jesus as the Messiah/Christ.

Paul among the Jews and the Gentiles

Another factor, however, in Paul's writing to Gentiles and Jews in Rome alike is that he wants to make sure they are getting along with each other. He hopes to help each group appreciate its own place, as well as those of others, within the emerging Jesus movement. Here Paul seeks to insure that Gentile newcomers to faith in Jesus as the Jewish Messiah are not made to feel like second-class citizens among those who know the ways of Moses and Jewish faith and practice as hereditary Jews. Therefore, Paul asserts that all have fallen short of God's righteous standard, Jews and Gentiles alike, and that all are in need of grace—offered to all and received alone through faith. In what he describes as "my gospel" (Rom 2:16; 16:25-27), while judgment comes to all, the mystery of God's reconciling all peoples together is what is revealed in the work of Christ Jesus. Therefore, God is not only the God of the Jews but also the God of the Gentiles (3:29; 9:24), and bringing the hope of salvation to the Gentiles is the reason Paul has been called (1:5, 13; 11:13; 15:8-21).

Alongside that calling, however, an insurmountable puzzlement remained. How could it be that God's chosen people, the Jews, had not universally received their own Messiah and redemption? In addressing this problem, Paul speculates along a number of lines. Paul would even be willing to be cursed if it would help his fellow people receive their blessing (9:3). Of course, simply being a descendent of Abraham does not ensure blessing; consider the cases of Jacob and Esau (9:6-13). Then again, God's people were at one time not God's people; they are simply chosen by God's grace, not as a result of human merit (9:24-26). Paradoxically, the Gentiles stumbled into God's righteousness by faith, while Israel's effort to be justified encountered a stumbling block (9:30-33). Yes, they had zeal, but it was misdirected zeal (10:2). And yet, God is not finished with his chosen people; this is where paradox leads to irony. Perhaps God has granted the blessing to the Gentiles in order to make God's own people mindful of the gift to be most rightfully claimed by them. And in the end, affirms Paul, Israel too will be reached (11:25-36).

The Power of the Spirit and
the Problem of Suffering

In addition to corporate struggles, Paul also presents a personal struggle in Romans 7. In describing the struggle between not being able to do what he aspires to do, and not being able to keep from doing what he tries not to do, Paul cries out in anguish in 7:18-24:

> The desire to do good is inside of me, but I can't do it. I don't do the good that I want to do, but I do the evil that I don't want to do. But if I do the very thing that I don't want to do, then I'm not the one doing it anymore. Instead, it is sin that lives in me that is doing it. So I find that, as a rule, when I want to do what is good, evil is right there with me. I gladly agree with the Law on the inside, but I see a different law at work in my body. It wages a war against the law of my mind and takes me prisoner with the law of sin that is in my body. I'm a miserable human being. Who will deliver me from this dead corpse?

In seeking to understand the basis for Paul's concern, here, interpreters have headed in several directions. One approach sees Paul's ordeal as describing his pre-conversion experience; no wonder he found aspiring to adhere to the Law frustrating, as human effort can never suffice in dealing with human depravity. The problem, though, is that Paul seems to be speaking in the present tense—a palpable struggle even as a mature Christian leader. Another approach sees Paul's work as a figurative instance; he is using first-person language to address the condition of others, not his own. Might the first-person and present-tense diction simply be rhetorical, piquing the imagination of his audience? The third approach takes seriously the fact that even mature Christians struggle, and yet struggle is not the end. After all, Romans 8 follows Romans 7, and there Paul describes the empowerment of the Spirit, which transforms and renews the believer even in one's most profound struggles with coming up short and frustrations on multiple levels. That seems the best way to understand what Paul is saying, and especially if the gospel addresses not only the consequences of sin but also its grip, that is good news, indeed!

II. Features of Romans

As Paul's fullest articulation of the gospel message, his letter to the Romans progresses in compelling ways. The first eight chapters deal with the conviction that all have sinned—Jews and Gentiles alike—and are in need of God's grace. In this section, Paul develops several ways in which grace is received by faith rather than deservedness. The next three chapters address the problem that God's chosen people, Israel, have not entirely received their own Messiah, and yet God intends for all Israel to be saved. The four chapters after that address a variety of concerns regarding Christian praxis, and in some ways, these chapters have been overlooked as the central focus of the book and its concern about righteousness. After all, "God's kingdom isn't about eating food and drinking but about righteousness, peace, and joy in the Holy Spirit" (14:17). The last chapter, then, brings a host of personal greetings, as well as a "shout out" from Paul's scribe, Tertius, who also extends greetings from other associates of Paul (16:22-23). Thus, the outline of Romans is largely as follows.

An Outline of Romans

- Romans 1–8—the reality of sin and God's righteous gift

- Romans 9–11—God's chosen people and their rightful place

- Romans 12–15—practical matters of Christian living and discipleship

- Romans 16—an introduction for Phoebe and final personal greetings

As well as appreciating the general structure of Paul's argument, the reader may observe that each of his topics is developed in sequential-progressive ways. Sometimes subjects discussed earlier are brought into play during a later discussion, but overall, the progression of Paul's thought is compelling, and it is worth noting in its development unit by unit.

The Righteous Will Live by Faith

The first half of Paul's letter develops the theme of God's righteousness, showing that it is received by grace through faith, and not by works of the Law. In his introductory paragraph (1:1-6), he lays out a basic outline of his *kerygma*-proclamation and the gospel, developing the content through the larger argument of the rest of his letter. Here he connects his own calling as "an apostle and set apart for God's good news" with the calling of the beloved saints of God in Rome, "who are called by Jesus Christ [and] are also included among these Gentiles," joined to God in faithfulness and obedience. As he does with the rest of his letters, Paul embraces Gentiles and Jews alike by extending "grace and peace" to his audience. At the beginning and end of his letter, he expresses his desire to come and see them (1:11; 15:24), hoping also to travel on to Spain. While his visit eventually materializes three or four years later, it involves house arrest in Rome, where his ministry continues nonetheless, according to Acts.

Paul's Greeting to the Romans

- From Paul, called to be an apostle of God's gospel, to you who are called to belong to Jesus Christ (1:1-6)

- To the beloved of God in Rome, called to be saints, grace to you and peace (1:7)

- I thank God for your faithfulness, and I hope to come and visit you (1:8-14)

Paul then declares the universal need for grace among Gentiles and Jews alike (1:15–3:31). He is not ashamed of the gospel, for it is the power of God for all who believe, revealed from faith to faith. Both Jews and Gentiles are without excuse, though, as God has revealed his righteous ways, of which all fall short. The Gentiles have been given a natural law, within themselves, showing that they know God's standards but also transgress them. As familiar illustrations, Paul describes idolatry, lust, and even the perversion of lust as the sorts of things that document human depravity; his audiences would likely have agreed. Even the apparent lack of conviction among those who practice shameful deeds shows, according to Paul, that God has given them over to their wantonness, explaining also their apparent lack of shame. Therefore, the Gentiles are full of greed, hate, violence, deception, and mercilessness; and yet, those who judge them, Paul reminds them, are also subject to judgment.

Paul then moves on to claim that the Jews also are without excuse, because neither are they sinless, nor are they successful in seeking to keep the Law they have received through Moses. Therefore, while the Mosaic Law is indeed a gift, it also is an added obligation, as those who live under the Law will be judged by it. Further, to value circumcision as a sign of legal

220

adherence, when one is not keeping the Law inwardly (2:25-29), is to add an additional sin: duplicity, adding further condemnation. At least the uncircumcised Gentiles don't claim to be keeping the standards of Jewish laws, although they are still accountable to a natural law, within. Of course, it is still better to be under the yoke of Jewish faith and practice, because such is the source of understanding God's ways. Revealed in the Law and the Prophets, therefore, is that while all have sinned and come short of the glory of God, humanity is saved by the righteousness of God, atoned for in the faithfulness of Christ Jesus. Therefore, the faithfulness of God is revealed in the display of Christ's sacrifice, inviting humanity to receive that gift as an undeserved grace, to be embraced in faith and to be expressed in faithfulness. This is the way that both Jews and Gentiles are regarded as righteous—receiving God's gift by faith—a believing response to the divine initiative, proclaimed in scripture and actualized in the victory of Christ on the cross.[2] That is how the one who is righteous by faith shall live (Rom 1:16-17, citing Hab 2:4).

The Universal Need for Grace—Among Gentiles and Jews Alike

- The power of the gospel—from faith to faith (1:15-17)

- The Gentiles are without excuse; they have a law unto themselves (1:18-32)

- The Jews are without excuse; the Law is both a gift and a source of judgment (2:1-29)

- God's righteous judgment and the faithfulness of Christ (3:1-31)

For those claiming to limit the blessings of Abraham to those accepting circumcision as the sign of the conditional covenant in Genesis 17, however, Paul harkens back to the unconditional covenants promised to Abraham by God in Genesis 12 and 15. These promises were given because of Abraham's faith, before he was circumcised, not afterwards as a recompense for his religious works. Likewise with David—Paul cites Psalm 32:1-2 to describe the blessedness of being forgiven—itself a gift of grace rather than deservedness. However, lest it be assumed that God's promise of blessing was given simply to bless Abraham and his offspring, the blessing is not for the Jewish nation itself, but for the world's healing. Therefore, the numbering of the stars in the

---

2. For fuller treatments of Paul's theology, see J. D. G. Dunn, *The Theology of the Apostle Paul* (Grand Rapids: Eerdmans, 2006); and N. T. Wright, *Paul and the Faithfulness of God* (Minneapolis: Fortress, 2013).

heavens refers not to the extent of a patriarch's posterity, but to the expanse of the nations that are blessed by his faithfulness. It is Abraham's believing in God that was credited to him as righteousness, and so it is with all who follow in his wake.

Abraham's Faith: Credited as Righteousness

- The heredity of Abraham: not genealogy, but faith (4:1-5)

- The blessing of David: a gift of undeserved grace for the forgiven (4:6-8)

- Circumcision: not a means to Abraham's righteousness, but a sign of his faithfulness (4:9-12)

- The global promise of Abraham is rooted in and received through faith (4:13-25)

In addition to God's unconditional covenant with Abraham, Paul also connects the gift of grace through Christ with two other biblical typologies: Adam and marriage. Just as through the first Adam's faithlessness all humanity received the curse of death, so it is that through the second Adam's faithfulness unto death all humanity now can receive the blessing of eternal life. While sin and death have ruled because of one person's failure, now righteousness and life are made available through one person's obedience. Therefore, in Christ, death no longer rules, but speaking of death and bondage, Paul shifts typologies to address the death of sin and the bondage of the Law. As long as spouses are alive, they remain bound to each other's marriage vows. If one dies, however, the other partner is liberated from the contract and enabled to marry another. While the shift of metaphors is a bit jarring, Paul goes on to say that while the Law is not sinful, it has the effect of binding people to the sin it forbids. Therefore, the death of the Law also liberates people from its obligations, allowing a second relationship—one rooted in faith and faithfulness—with Christ and the Holy Spirit.

Reconciled to God through Christ—The Second Adam and the Second Spouse

- Our weakness bolsters our dependence upon God's unmerited favor in Christ Jesus (5:1-11)

- Through the first Adam came death; through the second Adam (Christ) came life (5:12-21)
- In Christ we are freed from the law of sin and death (6:1-14)
- We are not slaves to lawlessness, now, but servants of God's righteousness (6:16-23)
- When a husband dies, the spouse is set free; with the death of the Law and the believer's dying to it, a new union with Christ and life in the Spirit are possible (7:1-6)

The conflict between aspiration and the flesh continues into the next unit, as the paradoxical effect of the Law creates intrigue with that which it forbids, perhaps because we become like the object of our focus. One of the most controversial questions among Paul's writings, though, is whether he was talking about himself in the frustration between a righteous intent and experiential shortcomings, and if so, whether he was describing the pre-conversion Saul or the post-conversion Paul. Of course, self-talk is a means of communicating to others—Paul's primary concern here—but the question of experience is still an important one. Some have argued that because Paul seems sure of himself and impervious to feelings of inferiority (a Hebrew among Hebrews, and a Pharisee and son of Pharisees, Phil 3:5; Acts 23:6) he could not have been referring to his post-conversion experience; it must have been the pre-conversion Saul being discussed here. That view, however, has several problems to it. First, Paul is literally using himself as the subject here, and he speaks in the present tense. Second, Paul's "conversion" was not from "sin" (he was consumed with self-righteousness and religious zeal) but from religious certainty. In that sense, it was more like a "calling" (like Isaiah in the temple, Isa 6) than a conversion—at least, not a conversion from debauchery. Third, Paul describes in multiple ways his experiential anguish and heartache, let alone his "thorn in the flesh," so the problem may lie with an idealized view of Paul, the mature follower of Christ—assuming naively that Paul had no existential struggles.

If Paul was speaking authentically and experientially in Romans 7, though, what is said of the Lord in Hebrews 4:15 might also be said of the great apostle: he struggled in all ways as we struggle, perhaps even more so. Building on the consequences of the Law as a perfect standard, the very problem with ideals is that they are very seldom fully actualized. Therefore, due to the reality of the fall, that which even committed believers aspire to do and avoid becomes an experiential challenge. Within this existential dialectic, Paul cries out in anguish, being a slave to God's Law in his mind, while also a slave to sin in his flesh: "I'm

223

a miserable human being. Who will deliver me from this dead corpse?" (7:24). The answer to his dilemma, though, Paul also declares experientially: "Thank God through Jesus Christ our Lord! . . . So now there isn't any condemnation for those who are in Christ Jesus. The law of the Spirit of life in Christ Jesus has set you free from the law of sin and death" (7:25–8:2).

Therefore, in Paul's conviction and also in his experience, the power of the gospel is not simply that it sets believers free from the consequences of sin; it also sets them free from its power and grip. Through the Holy Spirit's empowerment, the law of sin and death is itself dealt a death blow. Indeed, the very power that raised Jesus Christ from the dead is at work in the life of the believer, transforming one's life from a self-centered, fleshly existence into the new being, which is in Christ Jesus. Here the righteousness of God is received as an empowering gift, also of grace, enabling the believer to experience the righteous character God as a new reality because of a new, transformative relationship. Believers are given the Holy Spirit as the Spirit of adoption by which they cry out to God, *"Abba,* Father"—a newly created relationship of love—having been welcomed into the family of God by grace. For the revelation of God's saints, creation itself has been groaning, and because believers are now God's children, they are also God's heirs—receiving the same inheritance as Christ. And as joint-heirs with God's Son, those who suffer with him in his death will also share with him in his glory (8:15-25).

Likewise in prayer, we are not abandoned or left alone; the Spirit intercedes for us with groanings that cannot be expressed in words. And the Spirit is also at work in our prayers, even when we do not know how to pray, availing sense and meaning too profound for words. And for those who love God, God is invisibly active, working all things for good—to those called to further God's purpose (8:26-28). Therefore, as with the Son, those God selected are also called, made righteous, and glorified, even against worldly challenges. Because God's sweeping victory is ours through the One who loved us, Paul declares: "I'm convinced that nothing can separate us from God's love in Christ Jesus our Lord: not death or life, not angels or rulers, not present things or future things, not powers or height or depth, or any other thing that is created" (8:38-39). In Christ Jesus, the victory of God is complete!

The Bondage of the Flesh and the Liberation of the Spirit

- Paradoxical effect of the Law (7:7-12)
- The experiential frustration of God's law in one's mind and sin's law in one's flesh (7:13-25)

- The empowerment of the Holy Spirit and deliverance from the grip of the law of sin and death (8:1-8)
- Receiving the Spirit of adoption, by which we cry out, "*Abba, Father!*" (8:9-17)
- The groaning of creation and the revealing of the children of God (8:18-25)
- The empowerment of the Spirit, helping us in our prayers and effecting our victory (8:26-39)

The first half of Romans thus sets forth Paul's understanding of the gospel: all have sinned and come short of the glory of God—Gentile and Jew alike—but in the fullness of time, God has acted in love for the benefit of all humanity in the Christ Events, making the blessing promised to Abraham and his children available to all who believe. God's covenant with Abraham, though, is not given as a reward for Abraham's works; rather, it is promised as a consequence of his faith, and his faith is what was credited as righteousness to him and to those who follow after him. Therefore, the righteousness of God, as revealed in the Law and the Prophets, is extended from faith to faith. As with Adam all share in the condition of human sinfulness, without choice; with Christ as the new Adam all can share in the gift of eternal life, a choice involving the exercise of faith. Within the New Covenant, humanity is set free from the law of sin and death, but the Holy Spirit is also given as a means of empowerment, effecting inward transformation—also as a gift of grace to be received by faith. We thereby become adopted children of God and joint-heirs with Christ, and nothing can separate us from that victorious power and love within the family of God. *That* is good news for the entire world!

The Salvation of Israel and the Hidden Wisdom of God

Despite Paul's affirming God's plan of salvation through Israel, Paul is faced with a challenge: the question of the salvation of Israel and whether she will receive her own Messiah. Of course, even within the family of Abraham, not all received a blessing. As with Esau and Jacob, one receives a blessing; another does not. Thus, being an heir of Abraham's blessing comes not by family lineage but from responsive trust in God and by God's choosing. If God hardened Pharaoh's heart, perhaps he has also hardened the hearts of his people—as a mystery and part of the hidden wisdom of God. However, it is the potter who molds the clay, and not the clay that has a right to question the master craftsman. After all, just as God called the people of Israel before they were a people, God can also call those who are not yet his people as a means of stimulating the chosen ones to faith. God's actions are a stumbling block and an offense to those regarding the Law as a call to works rather than faith, but those who trust in God will never be put to shame.

The Problem of Israel's Rejecting Her Own Inheritance

- I would be willing to be accursed, if it would promote Israel's blessing (9:1-5)
- Heredity does not imply inheritance (9:6-18)
- The potter and the clay (9:19-24)
- Israel's Gentile origin and divine election—the stumbling block of Zion (9:25-33)

Nonetheless, Paul yearns for Israel's salvation. They are zealous, but theirs is a misdirected zeal. Yet within God's saving plan, Christ is the end of the Law—on two counts (10:4). On one hand, God's righteousness—a grace received by faith—is that endpoint to which the scriptures point. On the other hand, receiving God's righteousness comes not as an achievement—deserved by human works—but simply by inward faith. This faith is expressed outwardly by a confession of Jesus as Lord, reflecting one's inward response of faith to God's saving-revealing work. Thus, the Law's role is fulfilled. All who call upon the name of the Lord will thus be saved, yet how will they do so unless someone tells them, and how will someone tell them unless one is sent? Therefore, as Isaiah has said, *"How beautiful are the feet of those who announce the good news"* (10:15, quoting Isa 52:7). This is why Paul has been called as an apostle, to preach the gospel to any and all who might receive it.

The Hope of Israel's Salvation

- Christ the end and goal of the Law (10:1-4)
- Righteousness by the Law, by faith, and by confession (10:5-13)
- The calling of the evangelist and the unevenness of the response (10:14-21)

Despite Israel's varied reception of her birthright, however, God has not abandoned God's people. Just as a remnant remained in the days of Elijah, so some believe now, though others are afflicted with dimness of vision. And yet, through what has happened, God's plan continues to be furthered. In the gospel's having been rejected by God's own, it has been extended to others, who were not God's people. As the Gentiles are brought into God's family, God's own are made mindful of the gift that they could and should be receiving. Therefore, while a branch may be cut off of a tree stump, allowing further growth, branches are also grafted back in—even those that were once cut off. While such practices might not be the best recommendation of horticulture experts, Paul builds on such a metaphor his hope and conviction that in the end, all Israel will be saved. God's ways are a mystery, and God's wisdom is hidden from human sight. And yet, "All things are from him and through him and for him. May the glory be to him forever. Amen" (11:36).

Israel and the Faithfulness of God

- God's faithfulness to Israel and the dimness of human vision (11:1-11)
- The blessing to the Gentiles as a provocation of Israel's jealousy (11:12-15)
- The olive tree: its stump, its pruning, its grafting (11:16-24)
- The hope that all Israel will eventually be saved (11:25-36)

Therefore, Paul's concern is for the reaching of the Jews as well as the reaching of the Gentiles. Despite the fact of their uneven reception of God's righteousness as a gift, offered through Christ, God's work is not yet finished. This is why a preacher is called and sent, that Israel, in its love for the Law, might respond to its goal—effected in Christ Jesus. God might even be stimulating Israel to faith by extending Abraham's promise to the Gentiles, and yet the taking of the gospel to the Gentiles has also been a factor of Israel's uneven response. Therein lies one of God's great mysteries and the hiddenness of divine wisdom.

Not External Conformity, but Inward Transformity by Spiritual Renewal

Because of the theological importance of Paul's treatment of salvation, righteousness, the Law, and faith, however, Romans 12–15 has been somewhat undervalued by interpreters. As in each of his other letters, one of Paul's central concerns is his admonition to stay true to practical aspects of righteous living, exhorting his audiences to be true to the way of Christ, rejecting the ways of the world. Here Paul calls for believers to present their bodies to God as living sacrifices—dedicated alone to God's glory and service, rejecting the attractions of the world as a reflection of their faithfulness. Rather than fighting worldly conformity with a legalistic approach, however, he invites: "Don't be conformed to the patterns of this world, but be transformed by the renewing of your minds so that you can figure out what God's will is—what is good and pleasing and mature" (12:2). Therefore, the means of overcoming worldly influence is the transformation of one's understanding, rooted in an inward desire to embrace what is pleasing to God. God's love for us thus evokes a reciprocal response of love to God.

As a means of furthering unity within the church, Paul then develops metaphors that he also uses together in his letters to Corinthians and Ephesians. As parts of the body need one another and should work together in coordinated ways, so believers should honor one another and cooperate—under the headship and direction of Christ, the head of the church. In addition, as spiritual gifts are given for the edification of the whole body of Christ, they should not be exercised for one's personal benefit but should serve the needs of others, in loving service to the community. Likewise, hospitality should be shown to strangers, and the needs of all should be met. This is the sort of community Jesus's followers should develop as an alternative to the selfish and destructive ways of the world.

Be Not Conformed to the World but Transformed by the Renewing of Your Understanding

- Present your bodies as living sacrifices (12:1-2)

- Regard your value according to your faith (12:3)

- Many parts, one body, Christ is the head (12:4-5)

- Many gifts, but they are products of grace intended for service (12:6-8)

- Love and honor one another, hate what is evil, and extend hospitality to those in need (12:9-13)

More pointedly, following the way of Jesus affects how we respond to those who harass and mistreat us. Do not repay evil with evil, but overcome evil by doing good. Leave judgment up to God, and by loving your enemies their consciences may be piqued—with burning coals of fire heaped upon their heads—but this is only possible if believers reject violence and submit to authorities and conventional laws. After all, God has placed governors over society for human benefit, so believers should be good citizens, pay their taxes, and win their neighbors over with love. Love not only fulfills the Law of God; it also fulfills the laws of society. In all things, though, Jesus's followers should live as children of the day rather than the night, behaving "appropriately as people who live in the day, not in partying and getting drunk, not in sleeping around and obscene behavior, not in fighting and obsession" (13:13). Thus the garb of Christ is donned, and the ways of the flesh are rejected.

Be at Peace with All; Overcome Evil with Good; Love Fulfills the Law

- Bless those who harass you (12:14-17)
- Exact no revenge, but treat your enemy with love (12:18-21)
- Submit to authorities and honor the law (13:1-7)
- Love your neighbor, as love fulfills the law (13:8-10)
- Put off the ways of the flesh and put on the dressing of the Lord Jesus Christ (13:11-14)

In exercising judgment against what is worldly, however, Paul warns believers to resist judging one another. They must be patient with those whose standards are different, whether such implies weakness, pride, or simply a difference of understanding. Further, believers should not allow their personal liberty to become a stumbling block to others. This is especially the case when it comes to matters of food and drink. If Gentile and Jewish believers disagree with each other on such matters, one should not disrespect the other for their convictions. Rather, others should be respected for seeking to be true to their consciences and embraced within the loving community. As a minister of Christ to the Gentiles, Paul reminds his audience that he does not lace his ministry with his own achievements; rather, it is what God has done through Christ Jesus that is of upmost importance. He then expresses his desire to visit believers in Rome before closing his letter.

Giving an Account of Ourselves before God

- Judge not the weaker brother or sister; we are all accountable to God (14:1-12)

- Do not allow your liberty with food to become a stumbling block to others (14:13-23)
- Be patient with the weak; Christ is the servant of all (15:1-13)
- I write you as a minister of Jesus Christ to the Gentiles (15:14-21)
- I hope to come visit you in Rome (15:22-33)

Therefore, in this culminative section, Paul exhorts believers to embody the righteousness he has been describing, including the clothing of the way of Christ—not as a factor of legal conformity, but as a product of spiritual transformity. This is the very goal and evidence of the Holy Spirit's working within the hearts and minds of believers, leading to new lives and a new community of faith. Believers should be patient with one another, sorting through particular matters of conscience, but in this too they will be guided if immersed in Christ's love.

Personal Greetings All Around!

Paul's final chapter in Romans issues personal greetings all around. On one hand, it seems odd that Paul mentions over two dozen people to greet if he has never been to Rome. On the other hand, if he has met some of them in other settings, such as Priscilla and Aquila in Corinth—expelled from Rome by Claudius in 49 CE and perhaps returning since the change of administrations in 54 CE—this may account for this feature. Further, Paul is likely motivated by the concern that further divisions and divisiveness should be avoided as believers and others get resettled in Rome. It could be, for instance, that hard feelings have carried over from factors preceeding and following the expulsion and that Paul wants to diminish the likelihood that they should continue to be a problem among and between Jews and Gentiles in Rome.

Note several other things in his final chapter. First, Paul commends Phoebe, a woman leader from a commercial city in Greece; she is helpful to his ministry and a partner in it. The fact that he sends her as his emissary, and that he ministers alongside Prisca and Aquila, should qualify his disparaging of particular women teaching in Corinth and elsewhere; perhaps the issues there had less to do with capacities of gender and more to do with particular persons and their religious preparedness to teach. Second, note that believers are gathering in house churches (16:5), which was apparently the context in which many believers were gathering for worship (1 Cor 16:19; Col 4:15;

Phlm 1:2). In these settings, women, as heads of the domestic sphere, would have acted as hosts and leaders in Christian worship, as Paul mentions women as well as men in these instances. Third, note the many associations with particular people and their households; Paul is certainly familiar with many in his audience, even if he has not yet visited the city. Note also that Tertius (16:22) inserts his own voice as Paul's scribe, so we also are given hints of how some of Paul's writings were produced, with the help of assistants.

I Send Greetings to the Beloved in Rome

- Commendations of Phoebe, a deaconess from Cenchreae (16:1 2)
- Greet Prisca and Aquila and the church that meets in their house (16:3-5)
- Greet twenty-five other leaders, as well as their households (16:6-16)
- Avoid divisions, and beware of the divisive (16:17-20)
- Greetings from Paul's coworkers, including Tertius, the scribe (16:21-23)

Paul concludes his letter as he began it, with a prayer for his audience, reminding them of his *kerygma*—the message of his proclamation, that the secret mystery of God through the ages has now been manifested in the work of Christ Jesus. As this good news is revealed now to the Gentiles, calling forth their faithful response to God's saving work and commandment, the only response to such a work is an expression of praise to God—a final prayer and a doxology. And on that fitting note of worship, he closes his letter to the Romans.

A Final Prayer and Doxology

- May God strengthen you with my gospel and the *kerygma* of Christ Jesus—the secret mystery hidden for the ages (16:25)
- That secret is now revealed to the Gentiles, through the commandment of God (16:26)
- Glory to God the wise, through Jesus Christ forever; Amen! (16:27)

III. The Message of Romans

Much of the message of Romans is already covered in the survey of its features; its themes are its message. And yet, some of its subjects deserve to be taken a bit further. For instance, in considering the righteousness of God, received by grace through faith rather than earned by works, what did Paul mean in his treatment of the theme as central to the gospel message? How is the gospel the power of God for Jews and Gentiles alike, and what does it mean to testify to the gospel with our lives? These are questions that emerge in taking seriously Paul's lead verses at the beginning of Romans: "I'm not ashamed of the gospel: it is God's own power for salvation to all who have faith in God, to the Jew first and also to the Greek. God's righteousness is being revealed in the gospel, from faithfulness for faith, as it is written, *The righteous person will live by faith*" (Rom 1:16-17).

Receiving the Righteousness of God—A Subjective Gift or an Objective Reality?

Given that humans are fallen and sinful, and that all come short of God's glory, there is no hope for humans to live up to God's righteous standards. This is why all are in need of grace, and why there is no hope for receiving God's favor except by faith. This was true for Abraham, and yet it is also true for those wishing to share in God's promise to bless the world through Abraham and his families. If it was Abraham's faith in God that was credited to him as righteousness (Gen 15:6), then trust becomes the substantive basis for receiving the blessings promised to the world through him. Therefore, in the faithfulness of Abraham, and later in the saving-revealing work of Christ Jesus, God's righteousness is revealed. Grace—God's undeserved favor—is extended as a gift to the world, and the sacrificial death of Jesus on the cross covers the sin of the world for all who believe and receive his reconciling gift through faith. God's righteousness is thus revealed from faithfulness to faith—the only basis for God's gift of eternal life to the world to be received.

Therefore, "Now there isn't any condemnation for those who are in Christ Jesus," as "the law of the Spirit of life in Christ Jesus" sets us free "from the law of sin and death" (8:1-2). The good news is that "no condemnation" refers to release from judgment—both divine and human. After all, the righteous judgment of God is not a matter of disdain or hatred for humanity; it is an extension of God's truth and love. Grace is undeserved love; justice is deserved love. In living by human norms and God's Law (itself a gift of grace), humans submit themselves to deservedness—judgment. Therefore, it is impossible for humans not to live by deservedness because conventional values of fairness, competence, industry, and success inevitably involve rewards according to merit. Nevertheless, humans are also imperfect, and no one is able to live fully into any standard of ideal perfection. This is why God had to step in, availing undeserved love—grace—because of human incapacity to attain any righteous standard, whether the Law of Moses or nature's law within. Further, it is precisely because humans cannot imagine God's undeserved love that the revelation of grace is required—not by God, but by humanity. God's saving grace is so counter-conventional that it is a stumbling block to the Jews and foolishness to the Greeks. It cannot be imagined; it therefore must be revealed. In receiving the righteousness of God, by faith, humanity is thus invited to receive God's gift of unmerited favor, inconceivable though it be. Such is a humbling reality, indeed, to Jews and Gentiles alike!

And yet, a further question follows. Is the receiving of God's imputed righteousness simply a subjective covering of light, while our lives remain in darkness, or does it also empower believers to live in ways pleasing to God as a result? If the latter is the case, receiving the righteousness of God by faith offers believers the very righteous character of God—a transformative reality effected by the sanctifying work of the Holy Spirit. Therefore, the gospel message not only alleviates the death-producing consequences of sin; it also delivers liberation from the death-originating power of sin in the believer's life—transformingly through the empowerment of the Holy Spirit. Believers are thus freed from the law of sin and death by means of adoption into the family of God, given the Spirit of adoption by which children cry out, "*Abba,* Father!" Despite struggles with one's carnal nature, there is no challenge so deep that it cannot be uprooted by the power of the Spirit, who prays within and through believers in accomplishing the purposes of God in the world. God's righteousness is thus conveyed from faith to faithfulness—the only means by which God's sanctifying power can be objectively experienced.

Jews and Gentiles in Rome—Ethnic Rivals or Extended Families?

If Paul's main concern in writing to Jews and Gentiles in Rome was to calm their struggles and to help them achieve greater unity within the community of faith, how does that affect our understanding of his message? For one thing, while explaining access to eternal life was clearly one of Paul's ultimate interests, the acute occasion for his letter likely had to do with more mundane factors concerning individuals and groups getting along better with one another. From our distanced perspective, it might be hard to appreciate the gravity of concern among these groups of people. If Caesar himself had to step in to address Jewish-Christian tensions in Rome, things must have been pretty intense!

Further, a bit of speculation might here be in order. If these disturbances were the result of conflicts over "*Chrestus*" (Christ) around 49 CE, that date follows closely upon the accords of the Jerusalem Council. Might it be that as the results of that decision—that one need not become a Jew outwardly (by circumcision and other religious measures) but need simply abstain from sexual immorality, idolatry, and the eating and drinking of meat and blood offered to idols—was *not* appreciated by others, especially committed Jews? Therefore, Paul and his cohort of Jewish believers in Jesus were probably labeled as "liberals" by Jewish leaders, and Gentiles who hoped to receive the blessings promised to Abraham as a result of believing in Jesus as the Jewish Messiah were probably regarded as second-class citizens by Jewish leaders in Rome, and perhaps even more so by converts to Judaism who had paid the price of circumcision and other measures. Put in ethnic terms, Jews believing in Jesus probably felt they had more in common with fellow Jewish family and friends than with pagan-origin Gentile believers in Jesus, even if some of them might have been monotheistic God-fearers. This is why Paul addressed so forcefully the conviction that *all* have fallen short of God's glory—Jews and Gentiles alike—and that all are in need of God's grace.

Again, the consequences of these issues must have been huge for members of Paul's audience. If Jewish believers in Jesus were to think of their families' futures, would they want their children to be intermarrying with children of Gentile (pagan) parents, whose fellowship orthodox Jews had been instructed to avoid for centuries? And if they were running the risk of being alienated from local synagogues as followers of Jesus and having associated with non-Jews, would that price really be worth it? Further, they might have been impatient with newcomers to faith, wondering if they could ever assimilate into the ways of Moses or even basic features of Jewish faith and practice.

And, how would Gentile believers in Jesus, convinced of Paul's preaching and of a more open understanding of Jewish faith and practice, have regarded pressures of conservative Jews, calling for familiar outward signs of adherence to Jewish ways? On one hand, they might have rejected such pressures as simply legalistic and backward thinking—of no avail to those sharing in the New Covenant established through Christ Jesus. Then again, they might have also felt religiously inferior, even if they were more cultured in other ways. In meetings for worship, as Jewish believers in Jesus recited scripture or quoted wisdom from Jewish teachers or traditions, they might have felt intimidated by the religious groundedness of seasoned and established Jews. This would have been even more pronounced if they came from lower classes or were servants or even former slaves who came to be followers of Christ.

These and other factors help to contextualize some of the reasons Paul emphasizes so strongly that all are in need of God's saving grace and that Abraham's blessing is available to all. At stake also were issues of particular moral judgment, including what to eat or drink, and likewise what not to. On these matters, Paul calls for patience with others, and he emphasizes using one's gifts and resources for the edification of others, while still calling for the abandonment of carnal desires and conformity to the world. Such is what being transformed by the renewing of one's mind involves, and each person should consider one's value according to the faith one has received (12:2-3). Therefore, receiving the righteousness of God by grace through faith is not simply about the afterlife in Paul's message; it also addresses acute concerns in the interest of Christian unity and love.

Obeying Authorities—The Divine Right of Kings or the Power of Christian Witness?

It goes without saying that Romans 13:1-7 is by far the most significant text in the formation of political systems and theory in Western civilization, though challenged eventually by the Magna Carta and the Bill of Rights. In it Paul declares that "Every person should place themselves under the authority of the government. There isn't any authority unless it comes from God, and the authorities that are there have been put in place by God. So anyone who opposes the authority is standing against what God has established" (vv. 1-2). Overall, three interpretations have largely been furthered, and each deserves critical analysis.

Interpreting Romans 13:1-7

- *Interpretation A:* God has instituted the divine right of kings; if the ruler is wrong, he/she will be held accountable; the job of the Christian is to obey orders unquestioningly.

- *Interpretation B:* Unquestioning obedience seems contrary to the Lordship of Christ in Paul's writings; was Rom 13:1-7 added later by a redactor?

- *Interpretation C:* Look at the passage exegetically, in its larger historical and literary context; is the point unquestioning obedience, or does it call for being a compelling witness in love for the other—even one's "enemies"?

On the first interpretation, terrible atrocities have been committed by well-meaning people (Christian and otherwise), feeling they were carrying out God's ways in obeying authorities unquestioningly. This is one reason Christians have been loyal and effective supporters of empires and systems of governance, even if they might have struggled with particular orders. One line of thought has even seen God as working through institutions and hierarchies to the degree that in carrying out orders from one's organizational superiors, if the command is sinful, the responsibility is not upon the head of the instrument; it is on the head of the leader—the one giving the order. Is this really what Paul was saying, though? Would he have advocated believers' worshipping Caesar as Lord (as subjects were required to do a quarter century later under Domitian), or would he advocate doing harm to others if commanded by authorities? Probably not. Therefore, seeing this passage as instituting the divine right of kings is a flawed approach to the text; it calls for obeying authorities for other reasons, but not unthinking obedience.

The second interpretation is likewise flawed. There is no evidence that this text was added by an editor, and it must be interpreted within the larger context under which it falls. In terms of historical context, since the reign of Caesar Augustus, appeals to the "divine Caesar" drew connections between worldly rulers and God's reign. Therefore, Paul is here appealing to conventional expectations, calling people to act respectfully and in obedience to the laws of Rome. This would also have averted another expulsion from the city, if such were an issue, conforming with conventional Roman law. More pointedly, it would have distinguished Christians from Jewish zealots in Galilee and Judea, who had begun a terrorist campaign of stabbing Roman collaborators (called *sicarii*—daggermen), harkening back to Judas the Galilean. One can appreciate how followers of Jesus of Nazareth, who was crucified as a common criminal a quarter century earlier, might have been suspect as this uprising in Judea developed. Paul's point is targeted directly against such associations, calling people to pay their taxes and to honor the governors who served them.

The third interpretation carries these points further and finds support when Romans 13:1-7 is considered in its larger literary context with the paragraphs before and after it. Notice the following themes, which actually call for nonviolence as a Christian witness.

Nonviolence and Reconciliation as a Christlike Witness
(Rom 12:14–13:10)

- "Bless people who harass you—bless and don't curse them." (12:14)

- "Don't pay back anyone for their evil actions with evil actions, but show respect for what everyone else believes is good." (12:17)

- "If possible, to the best of your ability, live at peace with all people." (12:18)

- "Don't try to get revenge for yourselves, my dear friends, but leave room for God's wrath." (12:19)

- "Don't be defeated by evil, but defeat evil with good." (12:21)

- Submit to authorities and respect and honor those you should. (13:1-7)

- "Don't be in debt to anyone, except for the obligation to love each other." (13:8)

- "Love doesn't do anything wrong to a neighbor; therefore love is what fulfills the Law." (13:10)

Therefore, when viewed in its historical and literary contexts, Romans 13:1-7 should not serve as a text to bolster the divine right of kings, nor should Christians be excused for violating conscience in the name of civil obedience. Rather, civil obedience and harmonious civic participation provide a witness even to one's enemies—returning good for evil and love for harsh treatment. The call is for followers of Jesus to love their enemies and not to be overcome by evil and its means but to overcome them with good, loving, and peaceable living. This counter-violent action heaps "burning coals of fire" on the heads of others, and it serves as a powerful witness to the way of Christ, even at the heart of the Roman Empire. In stating this message, Paul challenges the zealotry of Jewish nationalism, but he also retains the willingness to challenge the Roman Empire, as he later gives his life in so doing. At the end of his life, according to tradition, Paul was killed by Nero in Rome; although particulars are unknown, Paul willingly paid the ultimate price for his witness to Christ and his nonconforming way.

237

IV. Engaging Romans

In engaging Paul's letter to the Romans, we find ourselves dealing with one of the most important writings in western history, thus forcing a consideration of earlier engagements but also inviting a reading with new eyes. Flawed are interpretations that see Paul as writing in anguish over his own sin, and therefore projecting the need for relief from his own sense of guilt. Paul was not delivered from an introspective conscience; his Damascus-Road experience was a Christophany—an encounter with the risen Lord—in a way that changed his life and became a calling rather than a conversion. Or, if it was a conversion, as Krister Stendahl reminds us,[3] it was a conversion away from religiosity rather than to it.

Nor in his wrestling with God's choosing of Israel, followed by her uneven response to the Jewish Messiah, did he put forth a paradigm of divine election or predestination. He believed that all could and should respond in faith to the gospel, which is why he was sent as an apostle. Nor did Paul argue a supersessionist view, that the Jewish nation has been displaced by the Christian church as the new Israel. He hoped that all of Israel would be saved, and he saw the grafting of the Gentile shoot into the Jewish stock as a means of bringing God's blessing through Abraham to the whole world—Jews and Gentiles alike—thereby fulfilling the calling of the Jewish nation. Nor does he argue the divine right of kings at the expense of Jesus's clear teachings in the Gospels regarding the love of enemies and the way of nonviolence. If anything, Paul supports the nonviolent way of Jesus, suggesting he has learned about it from the apostles of the Lord. Other themes are also worth engaging.

First, why is the gift of God's righteousness received only as a gift of grace through faith? Is this simply an element of God's new "law," or is it a factor of human incapacity to imagine and receive God's undeserved love? We live by justice and deservedness. In conventional terms, people usually get what they deserve, and justice involves judgment. Whether or not God judges humanity, humans judge themselves; even being confronted by the truth involves the crisis of judgment. Therefore, as there is no possibility for humans to merit God's unconditional positive regard and undeserved love—grace—is it even possible for humans to conceive of such? Maybe this is why Christ had to die—not to absolve the wrath of God or to pay a ransom to a creditor (although see 1 Tim 2:6), but because humanity could not conceive of God's grace in any other way. God's saving grace and its reception by faith was

---

3. Krister Stendahl, *Paul Among the Jews and the Gentiles, and Other Essays* (Philadelphia: Fortress Press, 1976).

revealed in the Law and the Prophets, but it was not until it was declared and revealed in the Christ Events that God's saving action in history made a time-changing difference. So, in God's "reconciling the world to himself through Christ" (2 Cor 5:19), what difference does it make for people's lives today?

A second point worth considering involves the question not only of how believers receive the gospel as a gift of grace through faith, but also of how they receive the empowerment of the Spirit to live in ways that are pleasing to God, furthering God's redemptive work in the world. In Paul's view, the gift of the Spirit's empowerment also comes as a grace, received through faith, and believers are thus adopted into God's family as joint-heirs with Jesus. This leads to the renewing of one's mind—a matter of transformed understanding rather than conformity to an outward standard. The empowerment of the Holy Spirit is possible only as one continues to be given to and set apart for God, as the believer is immersed in a new relationship with God and participates in the new being made available in Christ. As a good tree produces good fruit, faith in Christ leads to works of righteousness and in that sense is evidenced by them. So, how does that happen for today's readers of Paul?

A third issue to reflect upon involves how to be effective witnesses in the world. Where polarizing tensions between groups and their aspirations sometimes leads to labeling and alienation, notice how Paul works with Jews and Gentiles alike, calling them to unity in their central values and challenging each group as they most need. He also calls followers of Jesus to embody his nonviolent and loving way in the world, witnessing to the power of forgiveness and reconciliation, even among one's enemies. The love of enemies, however, cannot be regarded as a mere strategy to manipulate an outcome; it must be rooted in loving concern for the other. In that sense, Paul sees "the enemy" (whoever that may be) as also a recipient of the gospel, and he calls for believers to embody the gospel message by their carriage and being, as well as their words and actions. As 1 John 5:4 would say, "And this is the victory that has defeated the world: our faith."

Chapter 8

The Corinthian Correspondence

Begin with the text. Read 1 and 2 Corinthians, and note important themes and details that come to mind.

Author: Paul

Audience: believers in Corinth

Time: ca. 53–56 CE

Place: from Ephesus (1 Corinthians) and from Macedonia (2 Corinthians)

Message: "So then, if anyone is in Christ, that person is part of the new creation. The old things have gone away, and look, new things have arrived!" (2 Cor 5:17)

While Paul's other letters to churches represent single exchanges (except for 1 and 2 Thessalonians), Paul's letters to the Corinthians should be considered parts of a larger history of correspondence involving visits, reports, letters received, letters sent, and editorial processes along the way. This correspondence reflects exchanges between Paul and individuals and groups at Corinth following his second and third missionary journeys, and they are also built upon Paul's having lived for eighteen months in Corinth, which became one of his primary mission bases for his western ministry. He wrote his letter to the Romans from Corinth and visited at least three times.

The city of Corinth is located on an isthmus between the Saronic and Corinthian Gulfs, where travelers between the Aegean and Mediterranean Seas would sometimes travel by land across the four-mile stretch of road (a canal was later built) rather than take the 200-mile perilous journey around the Peloponnese Peninsula. As home of the Isthmian Games (second only to the Olympic Games), Corinth was a bustling, major city in the Roman Empire during Paul's day. The Acrocorinth, rising over 1,800 feet above the city, boasted a major temple to Aphrodite, and the ruins of more than two dozen other Corinthian temples and worship sites dedicated to a host of pagan deities have been found by archaeologists within the last century or more.

240

At the center of the city was the *agora*—the marketplace—and another temple to Aphrodite was also near the agora. According to Strabo (Strabo, *Geography* 8.6.20; 12.4.36), there were as many as a thousand temple prostitutes at work in Corinth, serving that one cult alone, and the city grew rich because of its many visitors and patrons. Even in Greek literature, to "Corinthianize" (*korinthiazesthai*) was associated with engaging in sexual promiscuity, and such issues are clearly addressed in Paul's writings. City leaders apparently had come to believe in Jesus, and Paul worked alongside Erastus, the city treasurer (Acts 19:22; Rom 16:23; 2 Tim 4:20). Two first-century marble plaques have been discovered in Corinth, each claiming that a civic project had been paid for and dedicated by someone named Erastus—possibly the same person, but unconfirmed. There was also a Jewish synagogue and presence in the city, and Paul worked closely with Prisca (called Priscilla in Acts) and Aquila, fellow tentmakers and Jews expelled from Rome by Claudius, during his stay there. Paul's correspondence with the Corinthians may have included at least four letters, three of which can be identified within what is now known as 2 Corinthians.

I. Crises and Contexts

In contrast to Romans, Paul's letters to the Corinthians are the most contextually driven among his writings. They reflect Paul's explicit responses to concerns in letters and reports he has received, and in addressing those crises in pastoral ways, he lays out larger theological bases for how the community should approach these issues and what it means to become a follower of Jesus within a pagan and interreligious setting. Referring to questions asked, Paul says, "Now, concerning the issues about which you wrote . . . " or simply "Now concerning . . ." (in Greek, *peri de*—1 Cor 7:1, 25; 8:1; 12:1; 16:1, 12) before expanding into his counsel on the issue. Paul also addresses a variety of other problems in the church aside from such references, and these contextual crises are also clearly portrayed in Paul's letters to the Corinthians.

Partisan Divisions in the Church

After a greeting and blessing, Paul raises, at the outset, his concern over partisan divisions in Corinth. Members of Chloe's household have informed him of groups claiming: "I belong to Paul," "I belong to Apollos," "I belong to Cephas," "I belong to Christ," (1 Cor 1:12) to which Paul responds: "Has Christ been divided? Was Paul crucified for you, or were you baptized in

Paul's name?" (1:13). Apparently, the issue revolves around whose ministry (and perhaps baptism) is more effective. If, as narrated in Acts 18–19, some followers of Apollos were not baptized in the Spirit (just in water, after John's baptism) but received the baptism of the Spirit following Paul's praying for them and laying on of hands, they may have felt their spiritual experience was superior to that of others. Or, if Apollos was an outstanding preacher and teacher (especially among Jewish audiences) or if some had personally witnessed Peter's preaching (*Cephas* is his Aramaic name) or even someone connected to John's (Is being "of Christ" a Johannine-sounding reference?) and had been baptized by another leading figure, these claims to notoriety or dynamism might have led some individuals or groups to feel their spiritual or social status was higher than that of others.

To counter such associations, Paul de-emphasizes the baptisms he had performed and points instead to Christ: "Christ didn't send me to baptize but to preach the good news. And Christ didn't send me to preach the good news with clever words so that Christ's cross won't be emptied of its meaning" (1 Cor 1:17). He goes on to insist that one sows, another harvests, but it is God who gives the increase (1 Cor 3:7). Therefore, various ministers and their followers should value the gospel labors of others; the furtherance of the Christian mission takes precedence over the particularity of its instruments.

Immorality in the Church

Another acute and serious problem is that a man in the Corinthian fellowship of believers is involved sexually with his mother—likely his stepmother, if his father married a younger woman as a second wife. Says Paul: "Everyone has heard that there is sexual immorality among you. This is a type of immorality that isn't even heard of among the Gentiles—a man is having sex with his father's wife!" (1 Cor 5:1). To counter this, Paul declares that he will be "present in spirit with the power of our Lord Jesus" when they meet together (5:4), standing against this affront to Jewish and Christian values. After all, "a tiny grain of yeast" affects the whole batch of dough, so the sacrifice of Christ, the new Passover lamb, should be celebrated with "the unleavened bread of honesty and truth, not with old yeast or with the yeast of evil and wickedness" (5:6-8). While the judging of outsiders is another matter, those who claim to be a "brother" or a "sister" in the community of faith, if not repentant from their egregious sins, must be expelled (5:9-13). Otherwise, their sinful values become the new standard, which God will judge.

Court Cases against Believers

Another problem is that believers are taking each other to court instead of working things out peaceably between themselves. Paul finds this problematic for several reasons. First, it seems ironic for followers of Jesus to submit themselves to judgments of the world, when God's people will be judging the world, and even angels, at the end of the age. That being so, can't they manage trivial matters in the here and now (1 Cor 6:1-4)? Second, taking one another to court is a bad witness. It says to the world that believers are incapable of working things out according to what is true, righteous, and just—asking to be judged by the world. Thus, resorting to secular courts of law becomes an admission of personal incapacity to be wise and discerning (6:5-8). Third, as the unjust will not inherit God's kingdom, Paul lists an unsurprising set of vices and reminds people that the Corinthian believers used to be numbered among those who practiced such deeds. However, since believers have been washed clean and made holy unto God by the work of Christ and the Spirit, they ought to be able to discern and repent of wrongdoing of their own volition, rather than waiting until their transgressions are announced in public (6:9-11). For those whose minds and bodies are given to Christ, dedicated to his glory and service, right living and justice ought to be self-initiated and uncontested.

The Question of Marriage

Apparently, believers in Corinth had written Paul with explicit questions about marriage. In 1 Corinthians 7:1 Paul shares, "Now, about what you wrote: 'It's good for a man not to have sex with a woman.'" He then goes on in verse 2 to say: "Each man should have his own wife, and each woman should have her own husband because of sexual immorality." Here it is important to see the first sentence as the statement that Corinthian believers are making, as it helps to contextualize the other things Paul says on marriage. No, he is not against marriage overall, although he cites his own gift of celibacy (and choice to be single) as an opportunity for spreading the gospel, agreeing with their overall point. Their letter, though, seems to be addressing the problem of temple prostitution, among others, and more generally, people having sex with those to whom they are not married.

In response to those problems, Paul gives the following counsel. First, sex should be confined to marriage—a committed relationship between a husband and a wife. Within that sacred relationship, their bodies belong not solely to themselves, but also to each other; they should thus take care to meet the needs of the other within the sacredness of the marriage bond. Second, while it is best to remain single and celibate if one can, marriage is the right choice for couples who feel passionate toward each other. If a man is in a relationship with a single woman, and their love is intense, they should get married, despite the advantages of singleness. Third, even if married couples face religious differences, and if one partner in marriage has become circumcised or a follower of Jesus, they should not get a divorce, as the believer could be a blessing to the other. And, if one is divorced or widowed, one should not try to get remarried, although doing so is not forbidden, although doing so if not forbidden; the advantages of singleness for the sake of the gospel should be appreciated (1 Cor 7:3-40). As Paul also has the return of Christ in view as an earnest hope, this might affect his valuing of Christian mission over family life.

Food Sacrificed to Idols

Another question about which people asked Paul's counsel involved the eating of food offered to idols. While the Jerusalem Council (Acts 15) had not required circumcision but had forbidden sexual immorality, the eating of food offered to idols, the drinking of strangled animals' blood, and idolatry, here Paul somewhat breaks with one of those prohibitions. He says there's nothing wrong with eating meat offered to idols, as long as one does not worship the idol or get involved with the sexual activities associated with such practices, but then he argues that it should not be done. The question is, why? Further, Paul seems inconsistent in his counsel: if it is known by another that the believer knows that food has been offered to an idol, then one ought not to eat it. However, if it is known that a believer or others do not know the source of the food, then eating it is permissible. Contexts in which such issues might have been faced would have included eating areas in the marketplace (the *agora*, which was directly adjacent to temples honoring Aphrodite and other deities), the home of a friend, or even one's own home.

The key to the issue, though, is how the believer's practice might affect those who have a weaker conscience. Some claim to have "knowledge," implying they know the gods are not real because of having a Jewish background or being monotheistic "God-fearers." However, for Gentile Christians who were once involved with pagan worship belief, rites, and associated practices held to be questionable by Jews, pulling away from both beliefs and practices is essential for their growing into a Christ-honoring community of faith. Given that political events and civic festivals would have yoked pagan worship and associated practices to their interests, the pressures to remain involved in pagan cultic festivals would have been strong for citizens of Corinth, especially respected leaders of society. Therefore, in one's example as a believer, first consideration has to be given to how one's liberty in the gospel might affect new believers and their vulnerabilities. If one's freedom might become a stumbling block to another, Paul's advice is to forego it. Abstinence out of concern for another is thus rooted in loving social concern rather than religious legalism (1 Cor 8:1–10:32).

Disorderly Worship

Another feature of the Corinthian situation is that when believers gather together for worship and table fellowship, some of them eat more than their share, leaving others hungry; others eat on their own, without consideration of others; still others get drunk. Paul rebukes them for not showing respect for other members of the community and advises them from then on to eat at home. Paul then moves toward a symbolic meal of remembrance and shares a tradition he has received related to the Last Supper. Here he describes the Lord's body broken for them, as well as the cup of the covenant. They are to remember the Lord's sacrifice, given for them, as often as they eat or drink. This will also be health producing, in Paul's view, but to desecrate the memory of the Lord's sacrifice by one's inconsiderate actions is to bring judgment upon oneself (1 Cor 11:17-34).

Spiritual Gifts

One of the more acute problems in Corinth is that the use of spiritual gifts has created dissension. While Paul does not describe the specific problems faced along these lines, several rise to the surface. First, some of the more demonstrative gifts (healings, miracles, tongues) are held to be more valuable than other gifts. To combat this view, Paul emphasizes the pursuing of "greater gifts"—ones that edify others rather than oneself. Second, some are apparently feeling inferior to others if their gifts do not measure up to more demonstrative ones. To challenge that perception, Paul emphasizes that there is one giver of gifts, the Holy Spirit, who gives gifts according to the needs of the church. Therefore, just as parts of the body complement the other parts and value their roles, believers should value their own giftedness while appreciating also the giftedness of others. Finally, if one has the gift of tongues, it should be exercised in private rather than in public, unless an interpreter is present. In all things, loving concern for the other becomes the basis upon which to use one's gifts within the gathered meeting (1 Cor 12:1–14:40).

The Collection for Jerusalem

Concerned with the famine in Judea during the reign of Claudius (predicted by Agabus, Acts 11:28), Paul seeks to raise money from the Gentile churches to support the needs of the faithful in Jerusalem. Paul reminds his Corinthian audience of what he had taught in Galatia: "On the first day of the week, each of you should set aside whatever you can afford from what you earn so that the collection won't be delayed until I come" (1 Cor 16:2). He then promises to write letters of commendation for any they approve to deliver the gift to Jerusalem, even offering to travel with them if desired. Paul's visit to Macedonia has also brought forth a generous response (1 Cor 16:5; 2 Cor 8:1-6), and his concern to help the mother church in Jerusalem during her time of need engenders a mature sense of mission and mutuality. However, raising funds either for charity or the support of mission becomes controversial. In Corinth, Paul's work raises doubts among some, when compared to "super-apostles," because he does not ask for money to support his own mission; his support has already been raised in Macedonia (2 Cor 11:1-9). Therefore, he faces criticism no matter what he does. If he asks for money, this raises questions; if he does not ask for money, this also raises suspicion among those who question whether he might be skimming the funds he has raised. Thus, he apologizes a bit sarcastically for not having been a burden to them (2 Cor 12:11-19); his labor has been out of love.

The Problem of Suffering

Paul also deals with the question of suffering in personal ways, especially in 2 Corinthians 12:7-10:

> I was given a thorn in my body because of the outstanding revelations I've received so that I wouldn't be conceited. It's a messenger from Satan sent to torment me so that I wouldn't be conceited. I pleaded with the Lord three times for it to leave me alone. He said to me, "My grace is enough for you, because power is made perfect in weakness." So I'll gladly spend my time bragging about my weaknesses so that Christ's power can rest on me. Therefore, I'm all right with weaknesses, insults, disasters, harassments, and stressful situations for the sake of Christ, because when I'm weak, then I'm strong.

While no one knows what Paul's "thorn" might have been, it is clear that he earnestly prayed for relief, but those prayers were not answered as he had hoped. Rather, another answer was given, proffering the sufficiency of grace and reminding him that God's power is magnified by human weakness. Put otherwise, as bad as suffering can be, God can also use it for the good. As God has comforted us in our suffering, God can also use those experiences to be a source of comfort for others (2 Cor 1:3-7). Therefore, believers might be troubled but not crushed, confused but not depressed, harassed but not abandoned, knocked down but not knocked out. While our bodies are under duress, believers are inwardly renewed daily because of the Lord's resurrection power—receiving an eternal weight of glory (2 Cor 4:8-17). As daunting as human suffering can be, it is no match for God's resurrection power, transforming believers from within.

II. Features of 1 and 2 Corinthians

Given that Paul is addressing particular issues and questions aroused by his contextual engagement with Corinthian individuals and groups, much of the content of his letters is organized around the concerns of which he is aware. These exchanges are also revealed in the correspondence between Paul and individuals, and this can be seen in the literary features of the text as they inform a plausible theory of composition and correspondence.

Visits and Letters—A Plausible History of Correspondence

One of the most distinctive features of 1 and 2 Corinthians is the fact that it reflects a multiplicity of exchanges involving visits, emissaries, letters, and editings, better seen as "the Corinthian Correspondence." In 2 Corinthians 2:1-9 Paul describes a painful visit and also an earlier letter written out of the anguish of his heart. That may be taken as 1 Corinthians. And yet, in 1 Corinthians 5:9 Paul says, "I wrote to you in my earlier letter not to associate with sexually immoral people." So it seems that 1 Corinthians is not Paul's first letter, but his second, whereupon 2 Corinthians would then be a third. Then again, how do we know that 2 Corinthians represents only one letter? Given that Paul elaborates on suffering being experienced in 2 Corinthians 10–13 and that he reflects on suffering in chs. 1–9, some scholars infer that Paul's last four chapters may have preceded the other nine, and that they have been arranged as they are by a later editor. So, where is Paul's first letter? Has it been lost, or, if 2 Corinthians is an amalgam, might Paul's first letter, calling for disassociation with immoral people, be incorporated into the collection called 2 Corinthians? While there is no evidence of textual addition or disruption in the ancient manuscripts, an educated guess leads to a plausible inference that 2 Corinthians 6:14–7:1 may have been Paul's first letter.

Three sets of clues point in this direction, although finally, it can only be considered a good guess. First, notice the content: believers are called not to be unequally yoked with unbelievers. The issue here is not a forbidding of marrying an unbeliever, although it has sometimes been interpreted that way. Rather, if connected to 1 Corinthians 5:9-11, the emphasis is upon disciplining members of the church who are unwilling to adhere to its standards of faith and practice. Second, if the two verses before and after 2 Corinthians 6:14–7:1 are read together, a break is impossible to notice. Second Corinthians 6:13 ("But as a fair trade—I'm talking to you like you are children—open your hearts wide too") seems to flow directly into 2 Corinthians 7:2 ("Make room in your hearts for us"), and if that section were omitted, its absence would be indiscernible. Third, the content of 2 Corinthians 6:14–7:1 forms its own coherent unit, thus seeming to match the description of such a letter. This unit of material thus describes in general terms what Paul lays out more specifically in 1 Corinthians 5:9-11.

A Possible Lost Letter?

> Don't be tied up as equal partners with people who don't believe. What does righteousness share with that which is outside the Law? What relationship does light have with darkness? What harmony does Christ have with Satan? What does a believer have in common with someone who doesn't believe? What agreement can there be between God's temple and idols? Because we are the temple of the living God. Just as God said, *I live with them, and I will move among them. I will be their God, and they will be my people.* Therefore, *come out from among them and be separated, says the Lord. Don't touch what is unclean. Then I will welcome you. I will be a father to you, and you will be my sons and daughters, says the Lord Almighty.* My dear friends, since we have these promises, let's cleanse ourselves from anything that contaminates our body or spirit so that we make our holiness complete in the fear of God. (2 Cor 6:14–7:1)

If this is the letter referred to in 1 Corinthians 5:9, several other features are also accounted for. Some of the reports Paul has heard relate to sexual immorality on several fronts: a member of the Corinthian fellowship is openly involved sexually with his mother, pagan worship practices may have involved temple prostitution, and immodesty of clothing and dress (including hair styles) might be giving the wrong message, to say the least. This is what is at stake also regarding the eating of meat offered to idols. Aside from idolatry, moral associations with licentious practices appear also to be in the foreground of Paul's thought. Such concerns are made explicit elsewhere, where John confronts believers in Pergamum and Thyatira three decades later regarding the need to stay away from eating meat offered to idols, as fornication is associated with the practice (Rev 2:14, 20). This was clearly one of the concerns expressed to Paul by personal visits and letters to him from Corinth, and the above unit seems to address it directly, though put in general terms.

A Possible Scenario of the Corinthian Correspondence

- Paul evangelizes in Corinth and cultivates a Christian community over a year and a half (Acts 18; ca. 49–51 CE).

- Paul moves on to Ephesus and meets followers of Apollos, now in Corinth (Acts 19:1-10).

- Paul (at Ephesus) receives bad news from Corinth about immorality there and writes a corrective letter (alluded to in 1 Cor 5:9-11➞2 Cor 6:14–7:1?).

- Members of Chloe's household (Stephanas, Fortunatus, Achaicus—1 Cor 16:17; 1:11) inform Paul of divisions and rivalries; Paul writes 1 Corinthians (a pastoral letter—1 Cor 7:1).

- Paul sends Timothy to try to settle the rivalries (1 Cor 4:17-19) but to little avail.

- Paul visits Corinth and disciplines the church (1 Cor 4:21 "with a big stick"—2 Cor 2:1, "while I was upset").

- Paul writes another letter (2 Cor 10–13?) defending his authority (2 Cor 2:4—"with a very troubled and anxious heart").

- While in Macedonia (Acts 20:1), Paul receives good news from Corinth through Titus and is invited back to Corinth (2 Cor 7:5-16).

- Paul writes the rest of what becomes 2 Corinthians (perhaps—1:1–6:13; 7:2–9:15).

- Is there a third visit (2 Cor 12:14; 13:1)?

Paul's Use of Traditional Material I
(Tradition, Jesus-Sayings, Proclamation)

As in some of his other letters, Paul here makes use of traditional material in several ways. First, he makes references to the "traditions" (1 Cor 11:2; 2 Thess 2:15—*paradosis* in Greek) that have been "handed down" (1 Cor 11:2, 23; 15:3—*paredidōmi* in Greek) to him as being of first importance. This suggests Paul's access to teachings about Jesus from such pillars of the faith as Peter, James, and John (Gal 2:9). Second, Paul references what he has received from the Lord and passes along this content as not of his own making but from the Lord. Therefore, it is unsurprising that many of Paul's sayings bear echoes of the teachings of Jesus as found in the Gospels. Third, Paul includes a unit of material that is of first importance—preaching material (*kerygma*) about Jesus as the Christ as a means of addressing the issue of the resurrection (1 Cor 15:3-8). In that sense, he is not making things up; he is passing along faithfully what he has received and is exhorting believers alongside the apostolic ministries of others.

Tradition Handed Down from the Lord

- The wife should not separate from her husband, even if he is an unbeliever (1 Cor 7:10-14 ←Matt 5:31-32; 19:9; Mark 10:11-12; Luke 16:18)

- Those involved in gospel ministry should be supported (1 Cor 9:14 ←Luke 10:7)

- On the night he was betrayed, the Lord gave thanks and distributed the bread and the cup to be received in remembering his sacrifice (1 Cor 11:23-33 ←Luke 22:17-20)

- Observe love in the exercising of your spiritual gifts (1 Cor 14:1, 37 ←John 13:34; 15:12)

- Authority is given for building one another up, not tearing one another down (2 Cor 10:8; 13:10 ←Mark 9:34-35; John 13:13-17)

Notice here that the explicit references to Jesus's instructions are employed so as to address practical issues of Christian community and to advocate harmonious cooperation with one another. That is understandable, and yet the application seems a bit different from the itinerant ministry of the Galilean prophet. In addition to explicit instructions of Jesus, Paul also repeats many echoes of teachings. While he does not cite some of these directly, and while the Gospels were not yet circulating in finalized forms, these similarities with Jesus's teachings are unmistakable.

Jesus-Sayings in Paul's Writings

- When insulted, bless; when harassed, endure (Rom 12:14; 1 Cor 4:12 ←Matt 5:11, 44)

- Do not return evil for evil, but do good to those who hate you (Rom 12:17 ←Luke 6:27)

- Do not avenge yourselves (Rom 12:19 ←Matt 5:39)

- Judge not (Rom 14:13 ←Matt 7:1; Luke 6:37)

- Food in itself does not make one unclean (Rom 14:14 ←Mark 7:15)

- Pay taxes when due (Rom 13:6-7 ←Mark 12:14-17)

- Love your neighbor as yourself (Rom 13:8-9 ←Mark 12:31)

- Faith can move mountains (1 Cor 13:2 ←Matt 17:20; 21:21)

- A seed does not come to life until it dies (1 Cor 15:36 ←John 12:24)

- Be at peace with one another (2 Cor 13:11 ←Mark 9:50)

- Some will not die until the Son of Man returns (1 Thess 4:13-18 ←Mark 9:1)

- The Lord will return like a thief in the night (1 Thess 5:2 ←Matt 24:42-43)

Again, Paul's use of Jesus tradition is here unmistakable, even though he never met Jesus in the flesh. Sometimes he uses this material directly to make a point; at other times he seems to be engaging themes with which others might have been familiar, reflecting his audience's existing familiarity with such teachings. Again, note the ways the outline of this material coheres with the message proclaimed about Jesus in the Acts of the Apostles, the letters of Peter, and other parts of the New Testament. It reflects the *kerygma* of the apostles, and Paul recites it strategically as a means of affirming his belief in the gospel and hope in the resurrection.

Paul's Preaching of the Message He Had Received

I passed on to you as most important what I also received: Christ died for our sins in line with the scriptures, he was buried, and he rose on the third day in line with the scriptures. He appeared to Cephas, then to the Twelve, and then he appeared to more than five hundred brothers and sisters at once—most of them are still alive to this day, though some have died. Then he appeared to James, then to all the apostles, and last of all he appeared to me, as if I were born at the wrong time. (1 Cor 15:3-8)

Parts of the Body and Gifts of the Spirit

One of the most noted passages in Paul's writings is his treatment of spiritual gifts in 1 Corinthians 12–14. Where some believers are made to feel inferior if they do not possess more demonstrative gifts, Paul affirms the gifts of all, and he reminds his audience of the true source of the gifts, the Holy Spirit, who gives gifts as needed for the edification of the larger body of Christ. Interestingly, in the four places that Paul lists gifts of the Spirit in his writings, he also references parts of the body with Christ as its head. This is not accidental, as Paul employs both images as a means of emphasizing mutuality, coordination, appreciation, and harmony. Another fact goes without saying: 1 Corinthians 13 is between chapters 12 and 14. Love is thus central to the use of spiritual gifts; in fact, it is the greatest of gifts. Nonetheless, note the way Paul makes several lists of spiritual gifts, and note also the way that ordering of the gifts in 1 Corinthians 12:28 prioritizes the effect upon the larger group rather than the individual. Paul also turns things on their heads, calling the more sensational demonstrations the "lesser" gifts. These lists are not exhaustive, though, and Paul's listing of gifts functions to expand awareness of the multiplicity of ways the graces of the Spirit are given to believers rather than to narrow the options.

Gifts of the Spirit According to Paul

- Prophecy, service, teaching, encouragement, giving, leadership, showing mercy (Rom 12:6-8)
- A word of wisdom, a word of knowledge, faith, gifts of healing, performance of miracles, prophecy, the ability to tell spirits apart, different kinds of tongues, the interpretation of the tongues to another—the one Spirit is the giver of the gifts for the edification of the whole (1 Cor 12:8-11)

- "First apostles, second prophets, third teachers, then miracles, then gifts of healing, the ability to help others, leadership skills, different kinds of tongues" (1 Cor 12:28)
- "Some apostles, some prophets, some evangelists, and some pastors and teachers" (Eph 4:11)

Supporting Paul's emphasis on unity, individuality, and mutuality, he also employs the metaphor of the church as the body of Christ, complementing his teachings on the gifts of the Spirit in reinforcing ways. As with spiritual gifts, each body part has its own function that is distinctive and to be valued by the others; likewise, that part should value other parts as well. Playing one's role is central to each part of the body doing its job, and yet, this should be coordinated with others for the greater good of its harmonious functioning. With Christ as the head, all parts of the body take direction from him, just as giftedness stems from the Holy Spirit, and not from the gifted. Likewise turning the valuation of gifts upside down, Paul emphasizes that the less honorable and weaker parts of the body are actually honored and valued the most. Therefore, connectedness to the head and coordination with one another are essential for the proper functioning of the body, which also includes doing one's share fully for the sake of the larger mission.

Parts of the Body According to Paul

- Many parts but different functions; many members but one body (Rom 12:4-6)
- The body of Christ has many parts—Jew and Greek, slave and free—but one Spirit to drink; the foot needs the hand, the ear needs the eye, and the head needs the feet (1 Cor 12:12-21)
- The parts of the body that are the weakest and the least honorable are the greatest and the most honorable; when one part suffers so do the others—they are all members of one another (1 Cor 12:22-27)
- The church is Christ's body, and he is its head; Jews and Gentiles alike share in the same gift of the Spirit—involving one faith, one Lord, one baptism—therefore, build up one another in unity and love, without quarreling or strife (Eph. 1:22-23; 2:14-16; 3:6; 4:1-32; 5:23)

Women in Corinth

In addition to dealing with issues of marriage and remarriage in chapter 7, Paul also addresses issues related to women and worship in 1 Corinthians. In 1 Corinthians 11, proper dress in worship is Paul's concern, and here he emphasizes the importance of women keeping their heads covered when attending meetings for worship. As married women would customarily have covered their heads in public, Paul's injunction that a woman prophesying should do so with her head covered functions as an appeal for modesty within the societal norms of the time (1 Cor 11:4-5). Female believers in Christ who speak in worship should not be confused with women serving in pagan temples, whether prostitutes or not, and the dress/appearance of behaviorally modest believers should not convey signals of sexual availability. This would especially have been the case if converts to Christianity had been former members or even leaders of religious institutions competing with Judaism. Paul also advises wives not to speak in church but to ask their husbands at home if they have questions about things (1 Cor 14:34-35). This seems puzzling, because Paul ministers alongside Priscilla and Chloe and other women, and he earlier references women prophesying in the meeting for worship. Perhaps the issue here is the need for newcomers to faith to become more fully grounded in Jewish-Christian understanding, which appears to include some (not all) women in Corinth, rather than lodging a prohibition against a gender's equal capacity and call to serve alongside their male counterparts in Christian ministry (cf. also Gal 3:28).

III. The Message of 1 and 2 Corinthians

Paul's message in his letters to the Corinthians comes out clearly within the multiple levels of dialogue and exchange as described above. Be that as it may, consolidating some of his points into general themes helps one appreciate his overall message, which then continues to speak to later audiences as well. Within his message, Paul lays out clearly his conviction as to what God has done in Christ Jesus—making of believers a new creation, reconciling the world to Godself, resulting in the calling of believers as his ambassadors—giving them the ministry of reconciliation (2 Cor 5:17-19). Therefore, despite its many contextual asides, the gospel and its implications nonetheless come through clearly in the Corinthian correspondence.

We Preach Christ Crucified—A Scandal to the Jews and Foolishness to the Greeks

Paul's message is not one of religious rhetoric, showing that Christ is worthy of acclaim because of miraculous signs or exceptional zeal. No; Christ died on a cross, showing weakness and human frailty—scandalizing the messianic hopes of Jewish understandings of how God would restore the kingdom to Israel and bless the world through the children of Abraham. In the political "failure" of Jesus, an alternative view of God's saving work is revealed. Nor is Paul's message one of fine-sounding wisdom, out-sophisticating the Greek philosophers of the day and imparting enlightening, saving knowledge from on high. The gospel bears a simple word—that God has acted in the Christ Events, bringing about life paradoxically in the death and resurrection of God's Son, Jesus Christ. For those who are perishing, this news is foolishness—counter-conventional. Things don't work that way in the "real" world, Paul acknowledges. However, to those who are being saved, this is the power of God unto salvation for those who believe, despite being a stumbling block to the Jews and foolishness to the Greeks (1 Cor 1:18-25).

And yet, how does one talk about the gospel in ways that do make sense to those who are veiled in their understanding? Or, how do ministers of the New Covenant convey their understandings in ways that are compelling? After all, the letter kills, but the Spirit gives life (2 Cor 3:6). And though human understanding is obstructed by a veil, when people believe in Christ, the veil is lifted; where the Spirit of the Lord is, there is freedom (2 Cor 3:7-17). Indeed, it seems that the god of the present age has blinded the hearts of those rejecting the gospel that reveals Christ's glory. And yet, it is in the face of Christ that the glory of God is revealed—as light shining forth in the darkness. Therefore, the gospel is a treasure, but it is a treasure housed in earthen vessels to show that the transcendent power belongs to God and not to us (2 Cor 4:1-7). At this Paul declares, "I'm in trouble if I don't preach the gospel" (1 Cor 9:16).

The Power of the Resurrection

In response to the claims of some, that there is no resurrection of the dead, Paul challenges that materialistic view in several ways in 1 Corinthians 15. First, he emphasizes that Christ rose from the dead and appeared to more than five hundred believers, including James, Cephas, the other apostles, and finally, Paul himself. If Christ be not raised, his preaching is useless and believers' faith is worthless. Second, because Christ is the new Adam, he is the first yield of a new harvest. Why else would people perform baptisms for the dead (a practice apparently performed in Corinth out of concern for their eternal destiny)? Third, in thinking about personhood in the afterlife, Paul argues that people will exchange their physical bodies for spiritual bodies— not born of dust but born of heaven. Fourth, Paul describes a mystery—that death is swallowed up in victory, and that believers will not languish in decay, but they shall be changed. Therefore, the gospel brings hope that death is not the end, but rather the beginning of a new existence, whereby believers share in the resurrection of Christ and in the final victory over death.

The Completion of Holiness

A response of faith to the gospel also implies a willingness to live in ways pleasing to God, especially for Gentile believers embracing the faith and practice of Jews. After all, declares Paul, "God caused the one who didn't know sin to be sin for our sake so that through him we could become the righteousness of God" (2 Cor 5:21). As the community of faith then clarifies its moral standards and calls for adherence among its members, Paul affirms this faithfulness as embodying the righteousness of God. This is why willful and public departures from the community's values cannot be tolerated if those values are to be maintained. And, it cannot be otherwise; if leaders in the community do not uphold the community's standards, those standards cannot be maintained. Therefore, Paul calls for repentance among those who are not living in ways pleasing to God, and he declares, "let's cleanse ourselves from anything that contaminates our body or spirit so that we make our holiness complete in the fear of God" (2 Cor 7:1). This relates to aspects of honesty, sexual expression, rejecting idolatry, communal harmony, and loving consideration of others, and Paul exhorts his audience to embrace such values as the completion of holiness within the body of Christ.

The Greatest Gift Is Love

The center of Paul's exhortation is characterized by love—love for God and love for one another. In rejecting the idolatry of pagan worship, Paul calls for the love of God to reign supreme in the hearts and lives of believers. In helping the weaker brother or sister stay true to the community's values, Paul calls for loving those with tender consciences and thereby foregoing personal liberties out of concern for the vulnerable. This is why Paul declares there is nothing wrong with eating meat offered to idols, in and of itself, while then exhorting people not to do so. If it might lead another into destructive practices and beliefs, the conscientious believer should be willing to restrain himself or herself out of love for others.

Another example of loving consideration involves the exercise of spiritual gifts. While demonstrative gifts might edify the individual, the greatest gifts within the community of faith are those that edify others rather than oneself. Therefore, unless an interpreter can make a message known to the larger group, Paul prefers words of content over expressions of ecstasy. The goal is the edification of the corporate body of Christ rather than the individual, and as many parts make up the body, so many forms of giftedness contribute to the edification of the group if exercised in love.

IV. Engaging 1 and 2 Corinthians

Paul's letters to the Corinthians offer multiple possibilities for engagement, and the best way to apply the contextual wisdom involved is to consider the ways he addresses needs within the Corinthian situation, then applying that counsel to today's contexts. Sometimes this will involve identifying parallels between earlier communications and today's needs. Contemporary readers might not face such issues as eating meat offered to idols, but being considerate of the needs of others who might be vulnerable should lead the believer to limit some freedoms out of consideration for others. Therefore, discerning Christian ethics are ordered not by legalism, but by loving concern. That being the case, several features of Paul's correspondence with the Corinthians deserve special focus in their engagement.

First, Paul's counsel dealing with rivalries between individuals and groups is worth considering in later generations. The ministries of others should be appreciated and supported, and one should also do one's part in furthering the overall mission of the church. There is a multiplicity of gifts but one giver of gifts—the Holy Spirit, lest any should be unduly proud. And as Christ is the head of the church, his direction should be embraced and heeded; helping others also in their faithfulness edifies the entire group. After all, one plants, another waters, and still another harvests, but it is the Lord that gives forth the increase. So consider how present-day tensions and rivalries among Christian leaders might be transcended by following Paul's counsel along these lines.

Second, consider the impact of Christian freedoms upon the vulnerable within your community; are there lifestyle liberties that might be a source of harm to others? If so, what would love dictate in terms of foregoing some liberties as a means of living an exemplary life, beyond reproach? One can understand how the use of illicit drugs and the abuse of alcohol have been prime considerations for such restraints, especially if one is not aware who might be affected by one's example. Then again, irresponsible and damaging practices should not be tolerated within the community of faith, even if following the lead of others, so self-defeating behaviors deserve to be challenged whatever their basis for legitimation. And yet, loving concern for the vulnerable might lead to taking up new causes rooted in social concern, so in that sense, meaningful applications of Paul's counsel here will involve creativity and discernment.

Third, Paul's response to suffering bears remembrance on several levels. When suffering continues without abating, despite unanswered prayer and other forms of treatment, the sufficiency of God's grace poses a way forward. As undesirable as suffering may be, there is no pain so deep or affliction so intense that God's presence and power cannot make a difference. Sometimes that difference, however, is perceptual. One is given a new way of perceiving one's struggles, and one might even glimpse a bit of what God might be doing—not only despite the suffering, but sometimes, even through it. Further, God comforts us in our suffering in order that we might be a source of comfort to others. And that is good news, indeed!

Chapter 9

Paul's Shorter Epistles to Churches: Galatians–2 Thessalonians

Begin with the text. Read Galatians, Ephesians, Philippians, Colossians, and 1 and 2 Thessalonians, and note important themes and details that come to mind.

Author: Paul (although some question Paul's authorship of 2 Thessalonians, Colossians, and Ephesians)

Audience: believers in southern and central Asia Minor (Galatians, Colossians, Ephesians) and in northern Greece (1 and 2 Thessalonians and Philippians)

Time: as early as 48–49 CE (Galatians); 50–51 CE (1 and 2 Thessalonians); 58–60 CE (Colossians, Ephesians, Philippians)

Place: Paul wrote Galatians (possibly) from Antioch; 1 and 2 Thessalonians (possibly) were written from Corinth; Philippians, Colossians, and Ephesians (possibly) were written from Rome while Paul was under house arrest.

Message: In Christ there are no differences (Galatians); we celebrate one faith, one Lord, one baptism (Ephesians); rejoice in the Lord always (Philippians); the mystery of Christ transcends all (Colossians); anticipate and be prepared for the coming Day of the Lord (1 and 2 Thessalonians).

Paul's six shorter letters to churches continue the addressing of contextual issues faced by early Christian communities. The eventual separation from local synagogues has probably not yet taken effect, as many followers of Jesus in the Mediterranean world around this time would gather for worship in the local synagogue on the Sabbath, but on the first day of the week, in memory of the appearances of the resurrected Lord and the outpouring of the Spirit, they would meet in people's homes. Therefore, house churches would gather in the main room of the home of a leading family, sharing the reading of

259

Jewish scripture and sometimes a letter or other written material, singing hymns of praise to God and Christ, speaking words of instruction and encouragement, and sharing a common meal together.

Because men would exercise leadership in the civic realm, and the woman of a household would command responsibility over the domestic situation, women likely shared leadership in worship within this familial pattern of organization. In Paul's letters to these five churches, he shows special sensitivity to their situations, and he writes letters for encouragement and instruction— intending some to be read in particular churches' meetings for worship and others to be circulated among the churches to be read in multiple settings. The letter to the Laodiceans (Ephesians) represents the latter.

I. Crises and Contexts

In writing to adherents of Jesus in particular cities, however, it would be wrong to infer that Paul has in mind only one house church. Rather, as several house churches would have met for worship in a given city, and even more would have developed in the region as the movement grew; even letters to particular churches would have been shared with others. Paul's letters were probably not gathered together as a complete collection until a generation or two later, but it would not take much to imagine believers gathering his letters and copying them for greater accessibility and use. By the time 2 Peter is written, Paul's letters are referenced as being misunderstood by those who also distort the other scriptures, so some of that process may have developed rather early, especially regionally (2 Pet 3:16). Nonetheless, a central crisis or two can be discerned within each of Paul's shorter letters, and getting a sense of these helps one also appreciate the thrust of his message.

Paul Opposes Peter to His Face, Because He Was in the Wrong!

Whereas Peter had dined with new believers in Antioch previously, when men came from James, concerned about the orthodoxy of the Pauline mission to the Gentiles, Peter refused to eat with the Gentile believers so as not to come across as endorsing Paul's controversial ministry. In Jewish custom, to break bread together was to declare essential unity with the other. Around table fellowship, there is no enmity, as all is reconciled in the sacramental presence of the divine. This would have been fine if Gentile believers in Jesus had become circumcised—declaring their unity with Jewish faith and practice. However, as some had come to believe in Jesus as the Jewish Messiah without donning outward signs of Judaism, this raised consternation among conservative Jews—even those who had come to believe in Jesus as the Christ. Therefore, proselytizing individuals and groups were willing to embrace those coming into the blessedness of Jewish fellowship but wanted them to declare outwardly their adherence to the Law of Moses in turning away from idolatry, sexual immorality, and other counter-Jewish practices (non-kosher foods, for example). In particular, circumcision is what made a strong statement to that effect.

Paul's confrontation of Peter, however, was no mere conflict of personalities. In Paul's view, Peter's behavior denied the very core of the gospel (Gal 2:14). From a conservative Jewish standpoint, God's covenant with Abraham in Genesis 17 included circumcision as a sign of commitment to God's covenant. From Paul's perspective, the question is whether salvation by grace through faith is enough, or whether it also requires outward, religious symbolization to be effective. As a means of addressing this issue, Paul hearkens back to God's unconditional covenant with Abraham in Genesis 12, referring to God's covenant with Abraham as being a covenant of promise, pointing to Christ rather than Abraham's descendants (Gal 3:6-29). Here Paul resorts to rough-and-tumble argumentation: those clinging to the covenant of Sinai are actually children of the slave woman, Hagar, whereas those embracing the covenant of promise and grace are the children of Sarah (4:21–5:1). And, if people are really all that zealous for circumcision, why not go all the way and castrate themselves (5:12)? Wow! If Paul's letter to the Galatians was written after his first missionary journey, it is conceivable that this confrontation with Peter, as pressured by the Judaizers, may have precipitated the need to convene the Council in Jerusalem, as narrated in Acts 15. Now that was a crisis!

The Death of Believers and the Delay of the *Parousia*—Christ's Appearance in Glory

One element of early Christian preaching promised that Christ would return before eyewitnesses died and that he would reward the faithful in the afterlife (Mark 9:1). This teaching seems especially prevalent in the messages of Peter and Paul, although John 21:18-23 questions what Jesus actually said on the matter. In Paul's mission to Thessalonica, however, the hope that the faithful would be rewarded is threatened by the fact that some of them have already died before the return of Christ, and their loved ones worry that they will therefore forfeit their heavenly reward. Paul thus assures them that the departed will indeed receive their reward; when that final trumpet sounds, the dead in Christ will rise first, and their loved ones will meet them in the air. This is meant to comfort grieving ones, while still providing hope in the Lord's return (1 Thess 4:13-18).

A second problem follows the first, as Paul encourages believers not to give up hope but to continue anticipating the imminent return of Christ. Apparently, in response to the injunction to wait for the Lord's return, some might not have planned effectively for the future. Therefore, Paul is forced in 2 Thessalonians 3:6-15 to exhort people to be responsible: "If anyone doesn't want to work, they shouldn't eat" (3:10). Paul's speculation about the Day of the Lord references "the person who is lawless" setting himself up in God's temple (2 Thess 2:1-12), which seems to allude to Emperor Caligula (37–41 CE), who insisted on divine honors and sought to introduce a statue of himself in Jerusalem's temple in 40 CE (Philo, *Embassy to Gaius* 30.199-203). This sort of action brought about Jewish protests in Egypt and elsewhere, seen by Paul as a blasphemous throwback to Antiochus IV, who had introduced a statue of Zeus to the Jewish temple two centuries earlier. Followed by the expulsion of Jews from Rome less than a decade later, these alarms provoke Paul's anticipation of the Lord's return, followed also by the problem of how to hold onto hope despite the delay of the *Parousia*.

Imprisoned, Yet Not Confined

Paul suffers imprisonment several times during his ministry; sometimes it is a factor of being persecuted, but at other times it is ironically for his protection (Acts 16:20-39; 21:33–28:31; Eph 3:1; 4:1; 6:20; Col 4:3, 18; 2 Tim 1:8; 2:9; Phlm 1:1, 9). In dealing with his imprisonments, however, Paul views them as opportunities for continuing the work to which he is called. In Acts, most of Paul's speeches occur after he has been taken into custody in Jerusalem, and being in Roman custody allows him finally to bring his gospel witness to Rome. While in prison, however, Paul ministers to other prisoners, devotes his energies to prayer, and writes many of his letters. Were it not for Paul's imprisonments we might have fewer than half of Paul's thirteen letters, as only his letters to Romans, Corinthians, Galatians, and Thessalonians are not written from prison.

Even more noteworthy is Paul's attitude toward his imprisonments. While he could languish in discouragement, and the circumstances must have been difficult, he chooses to view his captivities as opportunities for furthering his mission. He thus sees his chains as a liberating means of furthering his ministry to the Gentiles (Eph 3:1; 4:1). While Paul is imprisoned, the word of God cannot be (2 Tim 1:8). Therefore, Paul writes to communities and individuals, transcending the bounds of time and space through the power of the written word. Involuntarily, he is also forced to exercise the ministry of absence. As long as Paul and the apostles are able to visit growing communities, their presence is compelling. However, given the limitations of their travels, the calling of the next generation of leadership is emboldened. Therefore, Paul mentions his helpers, such as Tychicus, Timothy, Epaphroditus, Epaphras, Aristarchus, Mark, Luke, Demas, Silvanus (Silas), Carpus, Crescens, Titus, Prisca (Priscilla) and Aquila, Erastus, Artemas, Zenas, Apollos, and Onesimus, as ones who are commissioned to spread the gospel on his behalf while he is in prison. Most robust is Paul's refusal to be confined by his chains, as declared in Philippians 3:13-14: " . . . but I do this one thing: I forget about the things behind me and reach out for the things ahead of me. The goal I pursue is the prize of God's upward call in Christ Jesus."

The Deprecation of Christ and the Gospel

In addition to dealing with Jewish factions promoting circumcision (Gal 2:12; 5:11-12; Phil 3:2; Col 2:11), Paul also must deal with advocates of other religions who deprecate Christ and the gospel. These teachings and practices are especially clear in Colossae, where travelers would come from all parts of the world to enjoy the hot springs and healing waters of Hierapolis, just a few miles away. Within this interreligious setting, circumcision and asceticism were seen in Hellenistic religions as means of overcoming the desires of the flesh by punishing the flesh and living in self-denying ways. Other religions also promised to enlighten flesh-bound humans with God's saving knowledge by means of intermediary angels. Paul, however, declares that it is in Christ that the treasures of wisdom and knowledge are hidden, and it is to fine-sounding arguments and philosophies that the gospel is an affront. Paul further argues that these religious prescriptions are of no help against indulging in selfish, immoral behavior. Rather, the only hope for personal transformation is to "live in Christ Jesus the Lord in the same way as you received him" (Col 2:6). Therefore, Paul challenges these competing religious views in an itemized way (Col 2:1-23).

False Beliefs and Practices in Colossae

- Vain philosophies and foolish deception, which conform to human traditions and the way the world thinks and acts rather than Christ

263

- Religious prescriptions such as eating or drinking or about a festival, a new moon observance, or Sabbaths

- Mysterious religious practices, such as harsh self-denial, angel worship, and reports of visions

- Ascetic rules and regulations: "Don't handle!" "Don't taste!" "Don't touch!"

In responding to these crises, Paul addresses them directly, and in doing so, his answers become the central thrusts of his letters. As a result, in reading Paul's letters, appreciating the context of each greatly enhances one's understanding of its meaning. A contextual reading of Paul's writings also helps one grasp an overall sense of his message, and one is aided likewise by noting the character of the material he uses.

II. Features of Paul's Shorter Epistles

While some of the features of Paul's shorter epistles are shared by Romans and the Corinthian correspondence, others are unique to these six letters. Especially the christological hymns and some of the materials he uses are distinctive here, and getting a sense of what he does with this material also assists in making sense of his message. At the outset, Paul's praying for his audiences both sets the tone for his communications and orients the audience to his concerns and message for each group.

Paul's Prayers for His Audiences

Nowhere is the typical structure of Paul's letters as clearly observed as in his shorter letters to churches. Beginning with greetings to Gentiles and Jews alike ("grace and peace . . . ") and prayers for his audiences, Paul then develops the main thrust of his message in each of the letters before concluding with final greetings. In addition to thanking God for their faith and commitment, Paul tells believers that he is praying for them, and he also requests their prayers for him. Indeed, Paul's desire for believers to be established in the faith is furthered by his prayers and illustrated in their content: "Be rooted and built up in him, be established in faith, and overflow with thanksgiving just as you were taught" (Col 2:7).

Paul's Prayers for the Churches

- Giving thanks for their faithfulness and praying that he might visit them (Rom 1:8-10)

- That they will pass the test and be complete in Christ (2 Cor 13:7-9)

- That they will be given "a spirit of wisdom and revelation that makes God known," and that the eyes of their hearts "will have enough light to see . . . the hope of God's call"—"the richness of God's glorious inheritance" and "the overwhelming greatness of God's power" at work among believers (Eph 1:17-19)

- That God will strengthen their inner selves and that Christ will live in their hearts—granting "the power to grasp love's width and length, height and depth" and knowing "the love of Christ that is beyond knowledge," so that they "will be filled entirely with the fullness of God" (Eph 3:13-21)

- That their love might become enriched with knowledge and insight, so that they "will be able to decide what really matters and . . . will be sincere and blameless on the day of Christ"—"filled with the fruit of righteousness, which comes from Jesus Christ, in order to give glory and praise to God" (Phil 1:9-11)

- That they be "filled with the knowledge of God's will, with all wisdom and spiritual understanding," so that they can live lives "worthy of the Lord and pleasing to him in every way"—"producing fruit in every good work and growing in the knowledge of God, . . . being strengthened through his glorious might," so that believers might "endure everything and have patience," enabling them to "take part in the inheritance . . . granted to God's holy people" (Col 1:9-12)

- To see them in person and to complete whatever their faith needs, causing them "to increase and enrich [their] love for each other and for everyone" and "to be blameless in holiness before our God" when the Lord Jesus returns (1 Thess 3:10-13)

- That God will make them "worthy of his calling," accomplishing "every good desire and faithful work by his power"—that "the name of our Lord Jesus will be honored" by them, and that they "will be honored by him" (2 Thess 1:11-12)

- That God will "encourage [their] hearts and give [them] strength in every good thing [they] do or say" (2 Thess 2:17)

- To see Timothy and thus to be filled with happiness—reminded of his "authentic faith" and reminding him "to revive God's gift that is in [him] through the laying on of [Paul's] hands" (2 Tim 1:3-6)

- That Philemon's "partnership in the faith might become effective by an understanding of all that is good among [believers] in Christ" (Phlm 1:6)

Note that Paul's sharing the content of his prayers with his audiences is often preceded by giving thanks for them and their lives. It is from gratitude and love that his ministry stems. In addition to praying for them, his asking them to be praying for him becomes a basis of mutuality in a common mission. Their prayers for him are as important in his ministry as are his prayers for them. In these requests, he asks them to be praying that he will have confidence to be faithful to his callings, and also that he might be able to visit them again.

Paul Requests Prayer

- That he will convey "a message that confidently makes this secret plan of the gospel known" (Eph 6:19)

- That he will be released through their prayers and "the help of the Spirit of Jesus Christ," hoping that he "won't be put to shame in anything" but seeking to magnify Christ whether he lives or dies (Phil 1:19-20)

- "That God would open a door for the word" to be preached clearly regarding the "secret plan of Christ" (Col 4:2-4)

- Praying continually, that "the Lord's message will spread quickly and be honored," and that Paul and others "will be rescued from inappropriate and evil people" who fail to respond with faith (1 Thess 5:17, 25; 2 Thess 3:1-2)

- "That requests, prayers, petitions, and thanksgiving be made for all people," praying for "kings and everyone in authority" so that believers can live quiet and peaceful lives "in complete godliness and dignity" (1 Tim 2:1-2)

- Paul hopes he will be released from prison because of Philemon's prayers (Phlm 1:22)

In Paul's prayers for believers and in his requests that they be praying for him, he acknowledges the central factor of mission—the workings of God in ways seen and unseen. The furthering of the gospel of grace and peace is itself finally a gift of grace as well.

Paul's Use of Traditional Material II (Hymns, Wisdom Material, Lists of Vices and Virtues)

In addition to his own content and message, Paul continues to make use of other forms of material that likely circulated beyond his personal ministry. These include christological hymns (see "Excursus IV"), wisdom sayings, exhortations (paraenetic material), and lists of vices and virtues. Some of this material may also have been familiar to Paul's audiences, if not in the particular, at least in the general forms involved. Most important, however, is the way Paul uses the material in relation to his rhetorical purposes.

Wisdom Sayings and Exhortation (Paraenetic) Material

In addition to preaching and worship material, Paul makes use of other sorts of materials. This would have included wisdom-oriented sayings, showing the connection between actions and consequences, and yet Paul also creates new associations, connecting familiar landmarks with points he desires to make. For instance, as the Romans held gladiator contests in Ephesus (and to this day there is a stone sculpture in that city, going back to Roman times, featuring a helmet, two swords, and a shield), Paul's yoking the imagery of armor to the warfare of the Spirit would have communicated clearly to his audiences.

Wisdom Sayings Used by Paul

- "The one who plants and the one who waters work together, but each one will receive their own reward for their own labor." (1 Cor 3:8)
- "Bad company corrupts good character." (1 Cor 15:33)

- "The one who sows a small number of seeds will also reap a small crop, and the one who sows a generous amount of seeds will also reap a generous crop." (2 Cor 9:6)

- "A little yeast works through the whole lump of dough." (Gal 5:9)

- "A person will harvest what they plant." (Gal 6:7)

- "If anyone doesn't want to work, they shouldn't eat." (2 Thess 3:10)

The function of wisdom sayings is to motivate good and bad behaviors positively and negatively. For instance, Paul indicates that industrious and responsible labor pays off, whereas carelessness and irresponsibility result in negative outcomes. Therefore, the audience is motivated to choose the positive path over the negative one. The *Didache*, a late-first-century manual of Christian discipleship, lays out a similar set of choices: the *way of life* over and against the *way of death*. The choice is clear for intended audiences; the life-producing path is superior to its alternatives. In building on other images familiar to his audiences, Paul's exhortation to put on the armor of God fills out the larger picture of how to prepare for the spiritual battle in which believers find themselves. As an allegory, or an extended set of metaphors, one can imagine each of these features being the subject of practical instruction, encouraging spiritual preparedness in the Christian walk.

The Armor of God (Eph 6:10-17)

- "Be strengthened by the Lord and his powerful strength," putting on God's armor, enabling "a stand against the tricks of the devil"

- The struggle is not "against human enemies but against rulers, authorities, forces of cosmic darkness, and spiritual powers of evil in the heavens"

- "Therefore pick up the full armor of God so that you can stand your ground on the evil day and after you have done everything possible to still stand," including:

  o "the belt of truth around your waist"

  o "justice as your breastplate"

- ○ "shoes on your feet," enabling the spreading of "the good news of peace"

- ○ "the shield of faith," which extinguishes "the flaming arrows of the evil one"

- ○ "the helmet of salvation"

- ○ "the sword of the Spirit, which is God's word"

Lists of Vices and Virtues

Paul continues the practical thrust of his letters by listing negative vices to avoid and positive virtues to embrace. Much in these lists would not be new information to his audiences; the particular items are divided clearly into categories of the deplorable and the commendable. In that sense, Paul is reminding them of what they know and is exhorting them to hold fast to upstanding ways of living, despite worldly pressures to do otherwise. The rhetorical crafting and uses of these types of lists were common in the Greco-Roman world, and in addition to Hellenistic cultural norms, they especially would have connected with respectable values rooted in Jewish faith and practice.

Among the lists of vices and virtues used by Paul, he tends to begin with the negative list and move on to the positive counterpart. This is understandable, as his goal is to finish strong with what he hopes people will do. In Paul's shorter letters, these lists also tend to appear toward the later parts of his letters, a slightly different pattern from Paul's operation in Romans and 1 Corinthians. Such a practice reflects Paul's exhortative thrust in these letters.

Lists of Vices

- The Gentiles are filled with injustice, wicked behavior, greed, evil behavior, jealousy, murder, fighting, deception, malice, gossip, slander, hatred of God, rudeness, pride, and bragging; they invent ways to be evil and are disobedient to parents; they are without understanding, loyalty, affection, and mercy (Rom 1:29-31).

- Worldly people are sexually immoral, greedy, swindlers, worshippers of false gods, abusive, and drunks (1 Cor 5:10-11).

- Those who will not inherit God's kingdom include the "sexually immoral, those who worship false gods, adulterers, participants in same-sex intercourse, thieves, the greedy, drunks, abusive people, and swindlers" (1 Cor 6:9-10).

- Selfish deeds of the flesh include "sexual immorality, moral corruption, doing whatever feels good, idolatry, drug use and casting spells, hate, fighting, obsession, losing one's temper, competitive opposition, conflict, selfishness, group rivalry, jealousy, drunkenness, partying, and other things like that" (Gal 5:19-21).

- That which is unfitting for holy persons includes: lying, stealing, bitterness, losing one's temper, anger, shouting, slander, sexual immorality, impurity, greed, obscene language, silly talk, and vulgar jokes (Eph 4:25–5:4).

- The wrath of God is against "sexual immorality, moral corruption, lust, evil desire, greed (which is idolatry), . . . anger, rage, malice, slander, . . . obscene language," and lying (Col 3:5-9).

While some of the items in Paul's lists of vices seem to be commonly assumed, his listing of virtues shows a bit more creativity. In laying out what believers should aspire to, he often describes their consequences in greater detail, developing further implications as a means of enhancing awareness of the difference their application will make.

Lists of Virtues

- "Love is patient, kind, not jealous, not bragging, not arrogant, not rude, not seeking one's own advantage, not irritable, not keeping a record of complaints, not happy with injustice but happy with the truth, putting up with all things, trusting in all things, hoping for all things, and enduring all things" (1 Cor 13:4-7).

- "The fruit of the Spirit is love, joy, peace, patience, kindness, goodness, faithfulness, gentleness, and self-control" (Gal 5:22-23).

- "Light produces fruit that consists of every sort of goodness, justice, and truth"—that which is "pleasing to the Lord" (Eph 5:9-10).

- "Don't get drunk on wine, which produces depravity," but "be filled with the Spirit in the following ways: speak to each other with psalms, hymns, and spiritual songs; sing and make music to the Lord in your hearts; always give thanks to God the

Father for everything in the name of our Lord Jesus Christ; and submit to each other out of respect for Christ" (Eph 5:18-21).

- "God's choice, holy and loved" people should "put on compassion, kindness, humility, gentleness, and patience," being tolerant with each other and forgiving each other, putting on "love, which is the perfect bond of unity," controlled by "the peace of Christ" and indwelt by "the word of Christ" (Col 3:12-16).

- "Respect those who are working with you"; "think of them highly with love because of their work"; "live in peace with each other"; "warn those who are disorderly"; "comfort the discouraged"; "help the weak"; "be patient with everyone"; "make sure no one repays a wrong with a wrong"; "always pursue the good for each other and everyone else"; "rejoice always"; "pray continually"; "give thanks in every situation"; "don't suppress the Spirit"; "don't brush off Spirit-inspired messages, but examine everything carefully and hang on to what is good"; "avoid every kind of evil" (1 Thess 5:12-22).

Especially in laying out the character of love, the fruit of the Spirit, and the character of transformed living, Paul proceeds with a double interest. On one hand, he simply wants believers in Jesus to embrace the moral norms of Judaism and to live in ways cohering with the faith and practice of the Mosaic Law. While disparaging religious markers of covenant faithfulness, Paul really does want people to live in ways that honor God's covenant with the children of Abraham. In addition, Paul also has an investment in showing that the inward, transformative power of the Holy Spirit has greater capacity to produce a changed life than the legalistic promulgation of an external code—an interest devoid of divine empowerment. This is why he emphasizes transformative features of the New Covenant, which are empowered by the Holy Spirit.

Sensitivity to the Contextual Situation

While critical scholars have questioned Paul's authorship of Colossians and Ephesians because they are somewhat different in their thrust from some of Paul's other letters, the problem is that they are also very Pauline overall, and the differences are more likely a factor of sensitivity to the contextual situations to which he was writing. For instance, in Paul's writing to the Philippians, a proud and royal Hellenistic city (the home of Alexander the Great, founded by his father, Philip II, the king of Macedonia), he makes almost no Jewish or scripture references. This is not because Paul was not the author; rather, he is sensitive to the audience, and he makes other context-aware connections—athleticism, rigor, positive attitude, and greetings from Roman officials and others in Rome. Likewise, Paul addresses the Day of the Lord in writing to the Thessalonians because he is aware they are dealing with a particular theological crisis along those lines. Therefore, the same can be said about Colossians and Ephesians, in that they address with great contextual sensitivity the sorts of issues that believers in Asia Minor would have been facing.

If that is the case, Colossians is probably written first, followed by a more expansive treatment of similar themes in Ephesians. As Romans reflects a later and more developed version of much of the content in Galatians, so the same can be said of Ephesians in relation to Colossians. In addressing believers in Asia Minor, however, Colossians appears to be addressed to one community—one that Paul had never visited but of which he was aware—while Ephesians is probably more of a circular, designed to be read and engaged among the churches in addition to believers in Ephesus. That would also account for the specific religious issues addressed by Colossians and the more general thrust of Ephesians.

III. The Message of Paul's Shorter Epistles

Much of Paul's message to the churches comes through in his addressing particular crises and contextual issues, bolstering his concerns by the material he uses. Therefore, in the challenge to Peter and the circumcision faction, the gospel is preserved: one need not become outwardly Jewish to be inwardly committed to Christ. Then again, following the way of Christ will involve repentance from some activities practiced by non-Jewish members of society, so aspects of idolatry and sexual immorality were to be left behind among recipients of the New Covenant. Regarding the delay of the *Parousia*, Paul advises believers to wait for the return of the Lord but also not to forfeit their means of subsistence. Though in prison, he celebrates his liberty in Christ, and Paul challenges the syncretism of his audiences with the all-sufficiency of the Lord Jesus Christ.

One in Christ Jesus

In addressing the many divisions between individuals and groups in the Mediterranean world, Paul argues that "there is neither Jew nor Greek; there

272

is neither slave nor free; nor is there male and female, for you are all one in Christ Jesus" (Gal 3:28). It is hard for audiences in later generations to appreciate the radical nature of this teaching. Socioeconomically, slaves and masters did not share fellowship with one another, but in Christ, there is no division between members of different social strata. Imagine the shock of those who observed Christians regarding one another as equals, despite some being rich and others being poor. Furthermore, in Christ there is no difference between male and female, as all share equally in the power and promise of the gospel. Even within a patriarchal society, male and female believers in Christ shouldered responsibilities together, including leadership within the church. And, in the extension of Abraham's promise to the Gentiles, who are enabled to become children of promise through faith, divisions between Jews and Gentiles are now overcome.

However, being one in Christ is not simply a matter of refusing to be subject to societal divisions or the privileging of diversity; its root lies in collective participation in the work of Christ for humanity, in that through his redeeming work, humans are reconciled to God, to themselves, and to others. While death came by one person, Adam, in one person, Christ, are all made alive. Therefore, to be *in Christ* is to be reconciled to God and to others through the transformative power of God's grace. Receiving the divine gift of grace, then, produces a new species of being as new creations, sharing in the reality of a new humanity, overcoming not only the penalty of sin but also its bondage. Being *in Christ* then leads to being assimilated into his character and likeness, through the work of the Holy Spirit, so that believers become ever more like him, immersed in his love. It is a union rooted in relationship but resulting in transformation, as the righteousness of God is not only received as an undeserved designation; it also is experienced as an empowering reality.

The Mysteries of God

Paul's shorter letters to churches are highly sacramental despite saying very little about rites most commonly associated with sacraments of the church—baptism and communion. The Latin word for something holy, *sacramentum* ("sacrament") is actually based upon the Greek word, *mystērion* ("mystery"), which interestingly enough is never directly associated with baptism or eucharist in the New Testament. Rather, the great mystery of God, according to Paul, is that in Christ Jesus, God has stepped in and changed human history, bridging the gaps between Jews and Gentiles, so that all humanity is granted the possibility of participating in God's blessing to Abraham and his offspring.

According to Ephesians 3:1-7, God's secret plan throughout the ages is to make the Gentiles "coheirs and parts of the same body" with the Jews through the work of Jesus Christ. This hidden secret of God is now revealed to the world, and Paul announces it as a herald of the gospel—the good news. This is why there is one Lord, one faith, and one baptism (Eph 4:5). The essential unity of the body of Christ as a spiritual reality transcends religious forms and practices, as well as other markers of distinction. The eschatological work of Christ does not supercede one religion with another; it supplants all that is of creaturely origin with a new creation, a reality brought about by the Spirit for all who believe.

Personal Transformation

In addition to the gift of personal transformation, effected by the work of the Holy Spirit in the life of the believer, Paul also proposes a way forward in the experience of the believer. Especially in his letter to the Philippians, "the New Testament letter of joy," Paul emphasizes rejoicing as a positive and buoyant approach to living, which not only changes one's perception of reality but also affects that reality. Paul exhorts believers to live lives of inward gratitude and expressive joy, acknowledging what God in Christ has done and continues to do in and through the lives of believers. Interestingly, given that Paul is able to be content whether he has much or little, he finds that God is able to supply people's needs according to divine riches in glory (Phil 4:12, 19). Earlier in that chapter, Paul also shares the secret of how one's life becomes transformed by a new perspective on things. Rather than being anxious, one should offer prayers and petitions to God, along with thanksgiving (Phil 4:6). And as persons become like the object of their focus, Paul shares the secret of inward transformation (Phil 4:8-9):

> From now on, brothers and sisters, if anything is excellent and if anything is admirable, focus your thoughts on these things: all that is true, all that is holy, all that is just, all that is pure, all that is lovely, and all that is worthy of praise. Practice these things: whatever you learned, received, heard, or saw in us. The God of peace will be with you.

Holy Living in a Diverse World

As the lists of virtues and vices discussed above suggest, one of Paul's primary concerns in his letters is to inspire his audiences to holy living, despite being residents in a diverse, multicultural world. Especially important to Paul is teaching and convincing Gentile believers in Jesus to adopt standards of personal morality in keeping with Jewish faith and practice. Salvation may be a gift to be received by grace through faith, but the truest sign of having received the righteousness of God is the way one's attitudes and actions conform to a lifestyle that is pleasing to God. While part of Paul's concern is to convince people that some aspects of worldly morality are wrong and ought to be avoided, Paul's larger concern is the transformation of individuals' character by the power of the Holy Spirit, bringing about the fruit of the Spirit—"love, joy, peace, patience, kindness, goodness, faithfulness, gentleness, and self-control" (Gal 5:22-23). Against such there can be no law, and the fruit of the Spirit are always more authentic measures of one's spiritual condition than gifts of the Spirit, or even outward adherence to the Law. Those features can be falsified, but the fruit of the Spirit cannot. Finally, holiness is the result of love—for God and for others. As Paul writes in his first letter to the Thessalonians (1 Thess 3:13), "May the love cause your hearts to be strengthened, to be blameless in holiness before our God and Father when our Lord Jesus comes with all his people. Amen."

IV. Engaging Paul's Shorter Epistles

As a means of engaging Paul's shorter epistles to churches, consider the contexts to which Paul was writing, and, making connections with contemporary settings, consider how Paul's message might be relevant for today.

First, note that Paul was probably considered a liberal by some Jewish and Christian leaders because he emphasized the core of Jewish faith and practice rather than their boundaries. How would one identify and champion the heart of the biblical message for today, and how would an understanding of Paul's advocacy for the new believers and his insistence on their being accorded full status within the community of faith be applied today?

Second, consider Paul's lists of vices and virtues; if Paul were writing today, would he include the same things, or would he add or delete some of the items? Whatever the case, how are the fruit of the Spirit cultivated in people's lives in later generations, and how does the transformative work of the Holy Spirit make a difference in believers' lives today?

Third, how does the unifying work of the Holy Spirit help believers in later settings transcend boundaries and divisions between groups of people? If the mystery of Christ's reconciling diverse peoples of the world, making no distinction between individuals and groups, were to take hold in contemporary society, which boundaries would be bridged today, and how would you contribute to believers being one in Christ—participants in a new reality—individually and corporately? In engaging these issues, the messages of Paul's shorter letters are readily taken to heart.

Chapter 10

Paul's Letters to Individuals: The Pastoral Letters and Philemon

Begin with the text. Read 1 and 2 Timothy, Titus, and Philemon, and note important themes and details that come to mind.

Author: Paul (although scholars question his direct authoring of the letters to Timothy and Titus)

Audiences: Timothy, Titus, and Philemon

Time: ca. 60–65 CE

Place: written from prison (in Ephesus—Philemon; in Rome—1 and 2 Timothy and Titus)

Message: The goal of instruction is love from a pure heart, a good conscience, and a sincere faith (1 Timothy); neglect not the gift that is within you from the laying on of my hands (2 Timothy); avoid stupid controversies, genealogies, and fights about the Law, because they are useless and worthless (Titus); receive Onesimus back as a brother (Philemon).

Paul's letters to individuals include two letters to Timothy, one to Titus, and another to Philemon. As the letters to Timothy and Titus are aimed at helping leaders of churches exercise and promote stable approaches to church leadership and organization, they are called the Pastoral Letters. While these letters possess a good number of traits shared with Paul's other epistles, they also show significant differences in terms of vocabulary, grammar, and emphasis, which leads many or most critical scholars to doubt Paul's being the primary author. Then again, it is a mistake to assume that a writer as versatile and creative as Paul would never adjust to a new situation. or that his letters to an individual would be identical in form and thrust to letters he wrote to churches, or that the use of different scribes would have no bearing on the syntax of different letters. Nonetheless, thoughtful readers should at least be aware of the fact that the Pauline authorship of these letters is questioned, whether or not Paul or an associate penned them. Paul's letter to Philemon

276

is unquestioned in its authorship, though, and it reflects Paul's attempt to convince a slave owner to receive back graciously his slave, Onesimus. Paul's characteristic rhetorical strategies are evident in this letter, and it reveals interesting dynamics between believers in the Asia Minor churches.

I. Crises and Contexts

Like the other epistles of the New Testament, the crises behind the Pauline correspondence with individuals are largely exposed in the communications themselves. Whereas the Corinthian correspondence alludes to letters that Paul has received from believers asking what they should do, those features are largely absent in Paul's other letters. In a mirror reading of the text, crises and contextual issues are inferred with some degree of accuracy, but not without some speculation. As companions of Paul, Timothy is mentioned over two dozen times in the New Testament (six times in Acts), and Titus is mentioned a dozen times. Therefore, they are important co-leaders in the Pauline mission beyond the twelve apostles, alongside Barnabas (mentioned thirty-one times), Silas/Silvanus (eighteen times), James (brother of Jesus, eight times), Mark (eight times), Priscilla/Prisca and Aquila (six times each), Ananias (six times), Tychicus (five times), Luke (three times), and others. As pastoral leaders at Ephesus and Crete, Paul provides them helpful counsel. Paul writes to Philemon about a particular crisis regarding Onesimus, his slave.

Slavery, Suspicion, and Reconciliation

Paul's letter to Philemon is written with regard to a particular crisis. Onesimus, Philemon's slave, is apparently estranged and under suspicion, and Paul writes to Philemon, urging him to receive Onesimus back in a reconciling way. Or it could simply be that Paul's engagement with Onesimus has led to his staying longer than planned and that Onesimus is worried that he will be in trouble for his delayed return to his master (Phlm 1:11-16). Few details are given as to what might have happened, but the setting is described as well as several clues. Philemon is apparently a wealthy believer in Colossae, whose home is used as a house church for worship. Paul greets him and others who meet in his house church, including Archippus and Apphia. The text is not clear about why Onesimus has gone missing or why he might be reluctant to return. Paul offers to make compensation if any harm has been done or debt is owed, but such infractions are not implied directly. What Paul does do is appeal to Philemon to forego any sort of retribution or punishment that might have been expected for a runaway slave. While Paul does not seek to abolish the institution of slavery, as Christians did later in the modern era, Paul does seek to reform relationships within the institution—calling for regarding a slave as a brother in Christ, to be treated fairly and humanely.

A bit more of the relationship between Paul and Onesimus might be interesting. First, in his letter to Colossians, Paul mentions sending Onesimus with Tychicus to Colossae with a letter; apparently he has been sent to Paul while in prison, probably in Ephesus, and in relation to that contact, Onesimus has become a believer (Col 4:7-9; Phlm 1:8-16). Second, Paul appears to have learned of the tension between the servant and the master from the visit of Onesimus, for which he is grateful. It could be that he has even sent this letter to Philemon via Onesimus, although such is only a conjecture. Third, Paul declares his love for Onesimus and regards him as a brother in Christ, challenging the social stratification integral to the institution of slavery. Paul declares Onesimus to be his beloved brother in Christ every bit as much as Philemon is, expecting him to do the same. Fourth, here we have a cluster of names associated with Paul's imprisonment in the region, which argues for Paul's Ephesian imprisonment as the origin of the letter.

In addition to Onesimus, Paul's associates mentioned both in Colossians and Philemon, as well as the Ephesian situation, include: Aristarchus (Acts 19:29; 20:4; Col 4:10; Phlm 1:24), Mark (Col 4:10; Phlm 1:24), Epaphras (Col 1:7; 4:12; Phlm 1:23), Luke (Col 4:14; Phlm 1:24), and Archippus (Col 4:17; Phlm 1:2). In making his appeal, Paul does so not just man to man; he does so from community to community. From those in prison with him and around him to Philemon and his household, Paul uses the plural form of "you" as a means of making a corporate appeal (Phlm 1:24): "May the grace of the Lord Jesus Christ be with *your* spirit." But more on Paul's rhetorical strategy will follow later.

The Waning of First-Generation Leadership and Its Challenges

Whether Paul or an associate wrote the Pastoral Letters, they reflect a threshold involving the changing of the guard. The first generation of apostolic leadership in the church is waning, and such leaders as Paul, Peter, and James will not be around in the future to guide the movement forward. Therefore, systems and procedures must be set up so as to move the church forward as a growing institution, tying responsibilities to offices and structures rather than keeping with looser, familial types of organization. As the movement grows, the need for reliable structures also grows, and the author of the Pastorals intends to establish the means by which order can be maintained in the church and its mission can be furthered. Regardless of authorship, either Paul or a helper, Timothy and Titus here receive instructions as to how to appoint leaders and how to further the work of the community by means of setting the framework for emerging generations of leadership. Here we see the routinization of charisma, which happens within most organizations as they grow, and the baton is thus passed to the next generation by the founders.

On this point, critics question Paul's role, given that he normally resorted to charisma and personal power, with relationships being key, while the Pastoral Letters resort to impersonal structures of leadership. However, even charismatic leaders do organizing work, especially if they desire their movements to advance beyond a single generation. If an apostle is in prison, in likely the last chapter of life, his or her interest will obviously seek to ensure that the movement continues from strength to strength—a development that is aided by serviceable structures being in place. Of course, these institution-building features are less pronounced in 2 Timothy, and they are still largely fluid even in 1 Timothy and Titus. They also are not entirely innovative, as they build on the appointing of *deacons* (servant-leaders) to care for the Greek believers in Acts 6:1-6, the appointing of *presbyters* (elders) in Asia Minor in Acts 14:23, the leadership of "the apostles and the elders" that is clear in Acts 15:2–16:4, Paul's instruction to Ephesian leaders to faithfully supervise the flock, and Paul's greeting the *bishops* (supervisors) and deacons in Philippians 1:1. The constructive work in 1 Timothy and Titus simply seeks to define the characteristics of leaders as a means of furthering those values as the movement grows and as the direct influence of first-generation leaders wanes. Further institutionalizing developments and leaders' foibles can be seen in 1 Peter 5:1-5, as motivations for seeking leadership positions are challenged. And, in 3 John 1:9-10, Diotrephes the primacy-lover excludes John's fellow believers from his church. Structural changes can help, but no structure is perfect.

Institutions, Charisma, and Values

In setting up institutional offices and roles, however, some of the assets of charisma are forfeited, and this seems somewhat unlike Paul's operation in his earlier ministry career. Then again, even young adults, realizing they might not be present in the future, will set up structures to carry forth a cause, and Paul here is no different. Note, however, that the values of leaders to be chosen are not those of intrepid courage and unflappable zeal. Rather, Paul calls for selecting leaders who are wise, judicious, beyond reproach, and trustworthy.

The bases for some of the desired features are explained by the author: if one cannot manage one's own family well, how will one do at managing a group; if one cannot be respected outside the church, how will one win people over to the movement as well as be a positive example within the church? Most of these attributes would have been shared within the larger society, and in that sense, Paul is simply concerned that leaders of the institution be exemplary and able to embody its values, whatever they may be.

On the willingness to sacrifice charisma for character, the modeling of family households poses a helpful example. In particular, to make being the husband of one wife or the wife of one husband (1 Tim 3:2, 12; 5:9; Titus 1:6) a basis for leadership forfeits a good number of assets. While this admonition could simply refer to marital faithfulness, it is more likely a challenge to polygamy—though rare in Greco-Roman society—or perhaps the garnering of concubines within a well-to-do household. Whatever the case, Paul clearly is willing to do without certain advantages for the sake of prioritizing example. If a leading citizen is not willing to be faithful to his wife, he cannot be a fitting moral example within the community of faith. Or if a wealthy man has extended his marital arrangement to include concubines or more than one wife, or is known for consorting with prostitutes, such cannot further Jewish-Christian values. Even if such a person would be able to contribute influence, wealth, and a robust volunteer pool to the service of the community, such assets are insufficient to offset the long-term corrosive impact upon the values of the community of faith. The lives of leaders will always set the moral tone for the character of institutions they serve, and unless they exemplify their communal values, the standards of the institutions will suffer.

Hardship in Prison: "Bring My Coat!" "Come before Winter!"

While it is difficult to know which of Paul's imprisonments are the bases for his various prison letters, it is especially clear in 2 Timothy that the circumstances are rough, and that he needs personal comfort and support. He mentions his suffering (2 Tim 1:12), and in addition to feeling embattled by false teachers, Paul also declares that he is being poured out as a sacrifice to God, and that the time of his death is near (2 Tim 4:6). He feels deserted, as Demas has fallen in love with worldly things and gone to Thessalonica. With Crescens off to Galatia and Titus to Dalmatia, only Luke is with him; so Paul asks that Timothy come and visit him, along with Mark, and that he bring the coat Paul left at Troas, as well as the scrolls and parchments to help him in his writing (2 Tim 4:9-13). Especially urgent is his final appeal, where he pleads with Timothy to come before winter (2 Tim 4:21). Again, these vulnerable details are not the sort of thing that someone feigning Paul's name would have concocted. They represent the personal appeal of a leader who feels he is at the end of his life, desiring human comfort and fellowship from those into whom he has poured his life and who will also carry forth their shared mission into the future.

II. Features of Philemon and the Pastoral Letters

The primary distinctive feature of Philemon and the Pastoral Letters of Paul is that they are written to individuals. That fact, of course, will affect the form of the communication, but will it also affect the content? In several ways, a personal letter is different from an epistle to a group and also from a circular to be read in several settings. A personal letter will often be concerned less with how something comes across, perhaps taking risks an epistle might not. For instance, liberty is taken with the letter to Titus, even throwing in a regional slur confirming the difficulty of dealing with those whose lifestyles are out of step with Jewish-Christian values (Titus 1:12): "Someone who is one of their own prophets said, 'People from Crete are always liars, wild animals, and lazy gluttons.'" Likewise, a letter emboldening a young leader to especially be on his guard regarding false teachers might expand lists of vices and virtues, and much of the distinctive vocabulary in the Pastoral Letters is related to those particulars—not necessarily a factor of different authorship. Still common with the other epistles of Paul, however, are the opening greetings, the general teachings, and the extension of personal greetings—the latter of which are missing in a circular, such as the one Paul claims to have sent with Tychicus to Ephesus (Eph 6:21; 2 Tim 4:12).

Rhetorical Persuasion

One of the key features of Paul's letter to Philemon is the way he uses persuasive rhetoric to convince Philemon to receive Onesimus back graciously. Such rhetorical persuasion can also be seen in his other writings, but it is especially pronounced in this brief "postcard" of a letter. Paul follows his usual pattern of beginning with a greeting and prayer and concluding with the extension of personal greetings. In between we see Paul's compelling persuasive power at work; no wonder he was so successful in his mission!

The Rhetorical Devices of Philemon

- *A veiled threat*—I could command you to do the right thing, but I appeal to you in love (1:8-9)

- *Garnering sympathy*—I appeal to you as an old man, a prisoner for Christ Jesus (1:9)

- *Family appeal*—Onesimus is like a child to me; I became his father in faith while in prison (1:10)

- *A play on words*—Onesimus (whose name means "useful") is useful to both of us (1:11)

- *Playing to emotions*—I'm sending you my very heart (1:12)

- *Transactional bargaining*—Okay, Onesimus has stayed longer than planned, but he really is doing so on your behalf; would you rather that he be in Colossae and you be here with me . . . in prison? (1:13)

- *Appeal to process*—Not wanting to do anything without your consent, of course (1:14)

- *Spiritualized value*—Perhaps all of this has happened so that you might value Onesimus all the more as a brother in the Lord (1:15-16)

- *Ambassadorial appointment*—Welcome Onesimus as welcoming me (1:17)

- *Managing indebtedness*—If he owes you anything, I'll repay it; speaking of debts, though, you owe me nothing less than *your life* (1:18-19)

- *Affirming the positive*—And, of course, I know you'll do much more than I ask (1:20-21)

- *Accountability is coming*—Prepare a guest room; I'm coming to check up on you, as an answer to your prayers, of course (1:22)

Trustworthy Sayings Deserving of Full Acceptance

One of the most distinctive features of the Pastoral Letters is that they contain five sayings that appear to be either authoritative quotations or trustworthy advice, introduced as "reliable sayings" (*pistos ho logos*). As Paul's other letters do not contain this particular form of attribution, this is one of the reasons his authorship is here questioned. And, the emphasis here seems to be upon appealing to "the trustworthy word of teaching" that supervisors are expected to follow as a means of combating false teachers (Titus 1:7-9). That seems a bit more formulaic than Paul has otherwise been; then again, the presentation of "reliable sayings" in the Pastorals is itself diverse and non-uniform.

First, adding the phrase "deserves full acceptance" to two of the sayings (1 Tim 1:15; 4:9) appears to be rephrasing in a sound bite what Paul has taught earlier (regarding the salvation of all humanity—Rom 1:16; 11:11-12; 1 Cor 1:21; 2 Cor 6:2; Eph 1:13-14—and regarding God's saving work coming into the world—Rom 5:12-21). Second, the aspiration to be a supervisor and pastoral leader is simply affirmed as a commendable interest, not a selfish one (1 Tim 3:1). Therefore, in cultivating new leaders, not only is the leadership of Timothy affirmed, but he is thereby emboldened to encourage others to consider their own callings to ministry and leadership. Third, a third christological hymn is cited in 2 Timothy 2:11-13, as is done in Philippians 2:5-11 and Colossians 1:15-20. Christ is the focus of Christian faith and practice, both by conviction and example. Fourth, a fuller statement is uttered as a rephrasing of the gospel message entirely characteristic of Paul's teachings elsewhere in his writings (Titus 3:4-8). God's saving work through Christ Jesus is certainly worth preaching and building upon in pastoral ministry.

Reliable Sayings

- "Christ Jesus came into the world to save sinners." (1 Tim 1:15)

- "If anyone has a goal to be a supervisor in the church, they want a good thing." (1 Tim 3:1)

- "Our hope is set on the living God, who is the savior of all people, especially those who believe." (1 Tim 4:9-10)

- "If we have died together, we will also live together.
    If we endure, we will also rule together.
    If we deny him, he will also deny us.
  If we are disloyal, he stays faithful." (2 Tim 2:11-13)

- "When God our savior's kindness and love appeared, he saved us because of his mercy, not because of righteous things we had done. He did it through the washing of new birth and the renewing by the Holy Spirit, which God poured out upon us generously through Jesus Christ our savior. So, since we have been made righteous by his grace, we can inherit the hope for eternal life." (Titus 3:4-8)

On the basis of form, critical scholars disparage these sayings as non-Pauline, but such is a critically flawed move. Whoever is sharing advice with Timothy and Titus, he is repackaging Pauline teaching, preaching, and wisdom. Thus, asserting that such a practice calls into question Paul's direct involvement assumes an overly narrow capacity of a resourceful and creative leader. Over and above matters of authorship, though, the function of these texts is clear. Pastoral leaders moving into the next generation are entrusted apostolic content to share with others. Here we see the transition from the preaching and teaching *of* the apostles to the tradition *about* the apostles' preaching and teaching—packaged in forms that others can use and build upon. As they are handed over to the primary pastoral leaders of the churches in Ephesus and Crete, those traditions likely continue to impact later generations of believers in ways commensurate with Paul's historic mission.

The Support and Selection of Qualified Leaders

In addition to affirming the leadership of Timothy and Titus, Paul gives them the tools to inspire and embolden the ministries of others. This leadership-development approach involves the ministry of multiplication. The solitary venture is insufficient; effective ministry happens by selecting, equipping, and supporting others in the good work. Paul affirms the ministry gifts of Timothy and Titus, reminding them of the laying on of hands and the Spirit's anointing (1 Tim 4:14; 2 Tim 1:6, 14; Titus 3:5), as well as their commissioned charges at Ephesus and Crete (1 Tim 1:3; Titus 1:5). Beyond that, though, he also asserts that pastoral elders and teachers should be supported well—doubly well—including financial and moral support. This is not to say that church leaders were "paid" in a salaried way; rather, they were to be released for ministry—liberated from dependence on gainful employment, so that they would be free to travel in ministry and to devote full energies to the upbuilding of the community of faith. Therefore, the ministries of pastors and teachers should be supported in all ways they deserve.

Elders should be well supported; they should (1 Tim 5:17-22) . . .

- be supported doubly well, "especially those who work with public speaking and teaching"

- not be accused unless "confirmed by two or three witnesses"

- not selected hastily, but with discernment

In addition to enjoining financial and moral support, Paul inserts a challenge to those who might resort to gossip in criticizing the leadership of pastoral elders. Unless allegations are confirmed by two or three witnesses, they deserve to be disregarded, as scripture wisely teaches (Deut 17:6; 19:15) and as earlier attested by Paul (2 Cor 13:1; cf. also Matt 18:15-17). As well as holding leaders accountable, Paul also defends their reputations. Paul advocates a discerning process by which church leaders are selected, and this should not be done hurriedly, but with prayer and deliberative process. While it is worthy for a believer to aspire to positions of leadership and service (1 Tim 3:1), there are qualifications that must be met before they are selected by the community (1Tim 3:1-13; Titus 1:5-9). Therefore, Paul lays out the qualifications for elders, servants, and supervisors as a means of ensuring that the chosen leaders of the churches will further their dearest values.

Elders, servants, and supervisors must be without fault; they should (1 Tim 3:1-13; Titus 1:5-9) . . .

- "be faithful to their spouse, sober, modest, and honest"— showing hospitality and being "skilled at teaching" (1 Tim 3:2)

- be without fault as God's managers—not "stubborn, irritable, addicted to alcohol," or bullies (Titus 1:7)

- be gentle, dignified, and peaceable—not greedy, two-faced, or given to gossip

- manage their own household well—seeing that "their children are obedient with complete respect" (1 Tim 3:4) and "can't be accused of self-indulgence or rebelliousness" (Titus 1:6)

- not be new believers—tested and holding onto the faith that has been revealed

- "have a good reputation with those outside the church" (1 Tim 3:7)—loving what is good, and being "reasonable, ethical, godly, and self-controlled" (Titus 1:8)

- "pay attention to the reliable message as it has been taught to them"—encouraging people with healthy instruction and refuting those who speak against it (Titus 1:9)

A word should be said here about the sorts of functions each of these roles seems to have played within the early church. While particular functions of each position would not have been exclusive, and while some responsibilities would have accompanied all three roles, some of the general features of each position are worthy of consideration. *Deacons* (servants) tended to carry out the maintenance work of the local meeting—organizing meals and fellowship gatherings as well as outreach ventures. *Presbyters* (elders) tended to gather as a group and to discern corporately the direction of the meeting, including the exercise of teaching and preaching ministries. *Overseers* (bishops, superintendents, supervisors) tended to provide pastoral oversight of the community or a cluster of communities in ways that provided nurture, support, admonition, and care. As the early church grew in number and expanse, these roles became more highly developed, although it is important not to impose a later, more advanced perspective upon the less formal and primitive situation of the first-century Christian movement.

Women, House Codes, and Cultural Sensitivity

While the Apostle Paul ministers alongside women and declares in Galatians 3:28 that in Christ there is neither Jew nor Greek, slave nor free, male nor female, here in 1 Timothy 2:8-15 he declares (vv. 11-12), "A wife should learn quietly with complete submission. I don't allow a wife to teach or to control her husband. Instead, she should be a quiet listener." He then justifies the claim by pointing out in verses 13-15 that Eve was deceived, not Adam, and that the woman will be kept safe through childbirth, provided she continues in faith, love, and holiness, combined with self-control. Some interpreters have read this passage as forbidding all females to teach males, but such a reading is problematic for several reasons.

First, Paul himself ministered alongside Lydia and Priscilla (Acts 16:14-15; 18:1-26), and he was quite happy for Priscilla and Aquila to have taught Apollos—a formidable Christian leader—setting him straight on a thing or two regarding his preaching and its content. Second, if Paul really has declared that in Christ there is neither male nor female, the issue cannot be a gender-based one but it is more likely related to culture-bound, contextual issues, such as the need for prophesying women in Corinth to cover their heads in worship (1 Cor 11:3-16), or to ask their husbands at home if they seek understanding rather than interrupt someone uttering a prophetic message (1 Cor 14:32-35). Thus, ministry preparedness and religious knowledge was more likely the issue rather than gender. Third, as Paul seeks to encourage women who are leaders in worship in their house-church settings throughout his writings, his counsel here cannot be taken as diminishing the role of women in Christian worship or leadership. Rather, it probably reflects something of a behind-the-scenes approach to the type of issue alluded to in 1 Corinthians 11 and 14, as a matter of appealing to conventional house codes rather than excluding women from ministry on the basis of their gender.

Ministering and Leading Women in the Pauline Mission

- Lydia and her household believe, and she offers Paul and his associates hospitality (Acts 16:14-15, 40)

- Paul's mission among leading women in Greco-Roman cities is successful (Acts 17:4, 12; including Damaris of Athens—Acts 17:34)

- Phoebe, a deaconess at Cenchreae, is a benefactor of Paul's ministry, by means of whom he sends his letter to the Romans (Rom 16:1-2)

- Prisca (Priscilla) and Aquila are co-laborers who risk their lives for Christ, holding also a house church in their home (Rom 16:3-5; 2 Tim 4:19)—schoolers of Apollos (Acts 18:1-26)

- Mary and Persis have worked hard for the Lord (Rom 16:6, 12)

- Junia is a prominent woman among the apostles (Rom 16:7)

- Tryphaena and Tryphosa are coworkers in the Lord (Rom 16:12)

- The mother of Rufus is also like a mother to Paul (Rom 16:13)

- Euodia and Syntyche are co-laboring women leaders in Philippi (Phil 4:2-3)

- Additional women lead house churches in their homes or in those of others (Chloe—1 Cor 1:11; Nympha—Col 4:15; Apphia—Phlm 1:2)
- Paul sends greetings from Claudia in Rome and to and from Prisca and Aquila in Rome and Ephesus (2 Tim 4:21; Rom 16:3; 1 Cor 16:19)

The point here is that not only did Jesus embrace women in his ministry, but Paul also ministered alongside women and encouraged their ministries. In Acts, Philip's four daughters were also involved in prophecy (Acts 21:8-9). What seems to be at work in 1 Timothy 2:1-15 and Titus 2:1–3:2 (as well as Eph 5:21–6:9, Col 3:18–4:1, and 1 Pet 2:16–3:9) is a set of house codes—standard domestic conventions of propriety—to which Paul and Peter call for adherence as a means of bolstering the reputation of the church and furthering the gospel. These domestic relationships expected rulers, masters, husbands, and parents to be loving and just, and they also expected citizens, slaves, wives, and children to be respectful and orderly. Paul calls for submission to the government in Romans 13:1-7 as a means of Christian witness, and he calls for wives to submit to husbands and children to be obedient to parents. However, he also emphasizes husbands loving their wives and children, and in Ephesians 5:21 Paul begins his counsel to husbands and wives with the admonition to be mutually submissive to each other. After all, headship is to be understood not as domination, but as the life-giving source for another. That being the case, neither in the Corinthian correspondence nor in the Pastoral Letters is Paul overriding his conviction that in Christ there is no difference between male or female, nor is he departing from his longstanding practice of encouraging women in ministry. Rather, he is calling for respect and propriety in social situations, not challenging social structures, but transforming them from within, in egalitarian and loving ways.

III. The Message of Philemon and the Pastoral Epistles

Again, much of the message of these letters is conveyed in the material that is featured, but coming back to central themes lifts the content beyond original contexts to its application in later ones. As these letters reflect also the later stages of Paul's ministry, they convey a matured and seasoned perspective on the core issues of his ministry and the life of the church. These cohere around relationships, faithfulness, perseverance, and keeping Christ at the center of faith and practice.

The Transformation of Societal Structures

In keeping with Paul's approach to house codes, Paul does not radically challenge social structures—the sort of thing that slavery abolitionists and feminists have done in later eras, also in the name of biblical teaching. While at times the Bible has been used to resist structural changes within society, I think Paul would approve of challenging oppressive structures, even though he did not do so some cases during his day. He certainly did with regard to Jew-and-Gentile divisions! Just as importantly, perhaps, he called for the transformation of relationships within societal structures. For Philemon, he called for treating Onesimus as his equal—his brother in Christ. This would mean that Onesimus should have nothing to fear in returning to his master, despite having run into irregularities along the way. Some four or five decades later, Ignatius of Antioch refers to a man named Onesimus who is bishop of the church at Ephesus (*Letter to the Ephesians* 1–2); whether this is the same person is impossible to say. What is the case, though, is that Paul comes across as a strong advocate for slaves, and he holds masters and other believers accountable for treating servants, slaves, and common workers in respectful and egalitarian ways. Paul's advice to Timothy advocates the respecting of domestic order, but he also encourages women prolifically as partners in ministry and equals before the Lord. In that sense, the Pastoral Letters do not depart much from the rest of Paul's example, although if they were crafted for public consumption, they might have been more nuanced.

Neglect Not the Gift That Is within You

Especially tender are Paul's personal appeals to Timothy, whom he urges to come and see him before the winter winds make sailing impossible. As a way of reminding him of the heart of his concern, Paul declares that the goal of his instruction is "love from a pure heart, a good conscience, and a sincere faith" (1 Tim 1:5)—the sort of thing developed likewise in his letters. Paul also reminds Timothy of their personal history together (Acts 16:1-5) and reminds him "to revive God's gift that is in you through the laying on of my hands" (2 Tim 1:6). It almost seems that Timothy lacks confidence in his own leadership, as Paul then asserts: "God didn't give us a spirit that is timid but one that is powerful, loving, and self-controlled" (v. 7). In seeking to bolster

Timothy's confidence, Paul also declares, "Preach the word. Be ready to do it whether it is convenient or inconvenient. Correct, confront, and encourage with patience and instruction . . . . Endure suffering, do the work of a preacher of the good news, and carry out your service fully" (2 Tim 4:2, 5). Paul regards Timothy as a son in his letter to the Philippians (2:22), and in his personal letters to Timothy, that intimacy of relationship is confirmed.

Resisting False Teachers and Their Ploys

By contrast, Paul seems less worried about Titus and his capacities to manage his situation. This could also reflect a lesser level of familiarity, but Paul encourages Titus to be faithful to his charge on Crete, and he simply exhorts him to resist false teachers and their ploys: "Avoid stupid controversies, genealogies, and fights about the Law, because they are useless and worthless. After a first and second warning, have nothing more to do with a person who causes conflict, because you know that someone like this is twisted and sinful—so they condemn themselves" (Titus 3:9-11). While some scholars see early gnostic teachings and practices as part and parcel of the adversaries to be resisted in the Pastoral Letters, such a move is unwarranted. The questionable morality of non-Jewish Gentiles in Ephesus and on Crete offers plenty of fodder for imagining the antitheses of the holy life to which believers in Christ are called (1 Tim 4:7b-16). Bringing to mind the lists of vices Paul levies in his other letters, Paul gives Timothy a digest of the sorts of behaviors to challenge in robust ways:

> We understand this: the Law isn't established for a righteous person but for people who live without laws and without obeying any authority. They are the ungodly and the sinners. They are people who are not spiritual, and nothing is sacred to them. They kill their fathers and mothers, and murder others. They are people who are sexually unfaithful, and people who have intercourse with the same sex. They are kidnappers, liars, individuals who give false testimonies in court, and those who do anything else that is opposed to sound teaching. Sound teaching agrees with the glorious gospel of the blessed God that has been trusted to me. (1 Tim 1:9-11)

As a means of combating false teachers, Paul encourages Timothy to stay true to the things he has learned from the beginning. He has known since childhood the holy scriptures, which make one "wise in a way that leads to salvation through faith that is in Christ Jesus" (2 Tim 3:15). After all, "Every scripture is inspired by God and is useful for teaching, for showing mistakes, for correcting, and for training character, so that the person who belongs to God can be equipped to do everything that is good" (2 Tim 3:16-17).

Remember Christ—His Work and Empowerment

Especially in the trustworthy sayings that Paul features as the backbone content of his letters to Timothy and Titus, the work and empowerment of Christ are key. Not only did Christ come into the world to save sinners (1 Tim 1:15), but this gift is available to all people (1 Tim 4:9-10). And the gospel is worth suffering for, because in dying together with Christ, believers also live together in him; those who endure also rule with him. Those who deny him will be denied by him, although he is also faithful even to the disloyal (2 Tim 2:11-13). Because the Savior's kindness is given out of mercy, not out of human deservedness, the new life experienced in him is made available through the Holy Spirit, making believers righteous by grace, granting the hope of eternal life in him (Titus 3:4-8). In these ways, Paul summarizes his understanding of the gospel in fresh ways, consolidating previous statements and expanding on others. In so doing, Paul provides the next generation of leadership a firm foundation on which to base their emerging ministries.

IV. Engaging the Pastoral Epistles and Philemon

In engaging the letters to Timothy, Titus, and Philemon, highly personal aspects of Paul's ministry and relationships are revealed. Again, many critical scholars find reason to doubt Paul's direct contribution here, but the personal features of these letters are worth noting whoever their author(s) might have been. And, because they display so many Pauline characteristics, they deserve consideration simply as questioned letters rather than secondary, or "deutero," ones. As the biblical text speaks with genuine clarity to later audiences on its own, some of the features worth pursuing involve the following questions.

First, what are your thoughts about the relationship between mentor and mentee in the letters to Timothy and Titus? How does Paul's reminding Timothy to recover the boldness that came as a result of Paul's earlier ministering to him become a source of strength for Timothy in later situations? And, how does Paul's urging Timothy to bring his coat and to visit him before winter suggest the mundane reality of Timothy's reciprocal ministry to Paul? Are there people in your life who have been of great support to you to whom you should express your gratitude, and are there ways you might feel called to offer back some form of ministry to those from whom you have received so much? The personal relationships in these letters continue to inspire and to speak in later generations.

Second, if you were to gather a list of "trustworthy sayings" that deserve to be accepted and remembered, what would they be? As one generation of leadership passes the baton to future generations of leadership, how can worthy articulations of the gospel message be conveyed in ways faithful and effective? And, how can leaders be formed today who will be able to lead in the future by their example and character, as well as their understanding and expression? Traditionalism may be the dead faith of living people, but tradition is the living faith of dead people. How can the best of tradition be preserved in ways that continue to speak to the condition of the world in the light of God's work and revelation in the Christ Events?

Third, how can structures and relationships be transformed by the love and truth of Christ in ways that preserve responsibility and accountability, while also being seasoned with equality and grace? Are there some societal structures that need a bit of revamping in the name of justice and reform, and if so, how might their transformation be envisioned? Or, if being entrusted with responsibilities requires structures of authority to be defined and instituted, how can structures serve the mission of the institution in ways that bolster community rather than diminish it? And, are there ways that being one in Christ might make all things new between persons and between and within groups, even if structures remain the same? If so, how might Paul's letter to Philemon pose a guide to mutuality, grace, and consideration in seeking to further reconciliation and equality in today's communities and organizations?

PART III

THE GENERAL EPISTLES AND REVELATION

In addition to letters attributed to Paul, the New Testament contains eight other letters written by different authors to different audiences. Two of these letters are written to particular churches and individuals (2 and 3 John), but the others were written to circulate among multiple audiences, and are therefore called "general" or "catholic" (universal) epistles. The New Testament concludes with an apocalypse, the Revelation of John, and as it declares the final victory of God at the end of the age, it makes a fitting ending not only of the Christian scriptures but also of the entirety of the Old and New Testaments. Just as Genesis begins with the beginning of the world, with God having the first word, followed by a river and the tree of life in a garden of paradise, Revelation concludes with the end of the world, with God's having the last word, accompanied by a river and the tree of life in the heavens, whose leaves become the healing of the nations. Pretty fine bookends!

The General Epistles tend to cluster around three groupings. Hebrews and James are on their own as individuated letters, although they also engage to some degree the Pauline writings and mission. The Petrine cluster includes two letters attributed to Peter and one by Jude, which is very much like 2 Peter. The three Johannine letters cohere with each other, although 3 John is most distinctive. In addition, Revelation possesses seven letters from Christ to churches in Asia Minor (Rev 2–3), and the ordering of its letters reflects the route of a circuit preacher, beginning at Ephesus, proceeding north to Smyrna and Pergamum, and then heading back east and south, through the other churches, culminating in Laodicea. Such an ordering also suggests the sort of traveling-ministry routes that apostles and their associates would have followed in conveying messages and greetings from other believers, both nearby and from afar. Some of the composition theories about these works are as follows.

Jewish-Christian Epistles

Hebrews and James reflect Jewish-Christian epistles, but they are very different in their purposes and thrusts. *Hebrews* is an apologetic composition, presenting multiple reasons that audiences should believe in Jesus as the Christ. Jesus fulfills the central typologies of Hebrew scripture, and he is superior to angels, high priests, the sacrificial system in Jerusalem, and even the temple. Because the temple is referred to as a current object of authority, the Epistle was composed before its destruction by the Romans in 70 CE, so a good guess as to its dating would be around 65 CE. As early as the second century, Clement of Alexandria identified its author as Paul (followed by the Latin Vulgate and the King James Bible), but most scholars in the modern era are convinced that it was not written by Paul. Thus, the author remains unknown, although good guesses might include Barnabas, who came from a priestly lineage, and Priscilla, who served as a theological instructor for Apollos at Paul's request. Might its being written by a woman account for its anonymity? It could be, but such can only be a guess, attractive though it may be to some interpreters. The strongest hypothesis, though, argued by Martin Luther, is that Hebrews was written by Apollos of Alexandria, whose ministry overlapped Paul's. Philo of Alexandria, whose writings were known throughout the Mediterranean world, worked with biblical texts symbolically and allegorically, and the writer of Hebrews certainly employs such a technique—including referring to God's creative and redemptive action through the divine Word, the *Logos*. The origin and destination of the writing are unknown, although the extension of greetings from those who are from Italy in the last few verses suggests that it was written to Jewish Christians in Rome. This "group from Italy" (Heb 13:24) may have been citizens displaced following the expulsion of the Jews by Emperor Claudius in 49 CE, but if Apollos ministered in Ephesus, Corinth, and elsewhere, any of those sites would be a reasonable guess for the letter's origin. Conversely, the Italy reference could also reflect being written from Rome to believers somewhere within the larger Christian mission.

James, however, is written to the twelve tribes scattered everywhere in the diaspora, probably from Jerusalem if it is indeed written by James the brother of Jesus—the traditional view. Other than the greeting, the rest of James has very little explicitly Christian content; it is pervasively Jewish, reflecting a rather early stage in the developing Christian movement. It refers to people in your *synagogue* (the Greek word for "meeting," Jas 2:2), and the reference to God as *kyriou Sabaōth* ("Lord of the Sabbath," 5:4) reflects the distinctively Jewish character of the Epistle. Some of its interest appears to be engaging the Pauline mission, in that it emphasizes that Abraham was justified by his obedience and works, not by his faith alone. If men came from James to Antioch, as reported in Galatians, might this epistle be seen as something of an anti-Pauline circular? Stranger things have been imagined, although James and Galatians are by no means at odds with each other in terms of the overall thrusts of their messages. James also emphasizes several practical aspects of faithful living and offers valuable wisdom for addressing everyday challenges.

The Petrine Cluster

The letters attributed to Peter seek to edify believers and to build them up in the faith. If they were written by Peter, they must be dated before his death at the hand of Nero, who persecuted Christians in Rome the last four years of his reign (64–68 CE). The connection with Rome is bolstered by the first letter's having been written "from Babylon" (associated also with Rome in Revelation) with the help of Silvanus (Silas) in the company also of Mark (1 Pet 5:12-13). The opening of 1 Peter declares that it is written to the churches in Asia Minor: "To God's chosen strangers in the world of the diaspora, who live in Pontus, Galatia, Cappadocia, Asia, and Bithynia." First Peter bears a number of features similar to Peter's preaching in Acts and to the Jesus tradition in the Gospels. Therefore, scholars are more willing to accept the apostolic authorship of the first of the Petrine Epistles than the second. It does emphasize hierarchy, authority, and structural leadership—the sorts of things associated with Peter's legacy.

By contrast to the first letter, 2 Peter does not mention an audience, a place of origin, or an amanuensis (scribe), and its style is considerably rougher than that of 1 Peter. It is also similar to the letter attributed to Jude, so scholars are wont to push 2 Peter later, attributing it to a different author. A further reason for doing so is that Paul's letters are described as being available, which would have taken some time, and "Some of his remarks are hard to understand, and people who are ignorant and whose faith is weak twist them to their own destruction, just as they do the other scriptures" (2 Pet 3:16). If this implies a reference to the compilation of all of Paul's letters, that would push it several decades later, and if the adversaries mentioned in 2 Peter and

295

in Jude reflect second-century Gnosticism, then it is impossible to assume Peter was the author.

However, several problems accompany such conjectures. First, the Petrine Epistles are more like each other than either is like any other part of the New Testament (excepting Jude, perhaps), and despite 2 Peter being rougher, this could be a factor of its not being written by an amanuensis. Second, not all of Paul's writings are implied, nor are they necessarily gathered; it is simply a plurality of letters that is mentioned, and it is unlikely, especially in Rome, that only one or two of Paul's letters would have been known a decade or more into his public ministry. Third, while the false teachers mentioned in 2 Peter and Jude bear some similarities with gnostic heresies in the second century, Gnostics were not the sole proprietors of distorted or problematic faith and practice. Paul's correspondence with Corinthian Christians in the 50s alone bears out that fact. And Jude need not have been an underlying source for 2 Peter; the reverse could also have been the case. Likewise, the similarities could simply reflect contacts between individuals or traditions, or even attendance at the same church conference, as believers gathered and shared concerns together. Therefore, while the authorship of 2 Peter is questioned, its alternative identity has not been established; likewise with Jude. In the light of second criticality, the authorship of the Petrines is questioned but not critically overturned.

1, 2, and 3 John

The authorship of the Johannine Epistles involves a variety of challenges for interpreters, but they clearly represent outreach within a cross-cultural setting, and the traditional view that they were written in Ephesus makes sense. As Ephesus was the heart of the Pauline mission to the Gentiles, the traditional view that John the apostle made his home there after the Roman destruction of Jerusalem in 70 CE seems plausible. Asia Minor was a thoroughfare of Christian missionary outreach and conventional travel, and both Jewish and Gentile members of society came to believe in Jesus as the Christ. According to second-century writers, though, there was not just one Christian leader in Ephesus named "John" but two—the Disciple and the Elder. They are reportedly buried in Ephesus, and their tombs are marked by the altarplace of the sixth-century Basilica of St. John, built by the Emperor Justinian, based on that ancient memory. While scholars share a variety of opinions on Johannine authorship, the most plausible inference is that John the Disciple wrote the bulk of the Fourth Gospel, while John the Elder wrote the Epistles and likely was the final editor and compiler of the witness of the beloved disciple, "whose testimony is true" (John 21:24).

The three Johannine letters, though, are different in their form. First John was written as a circular, to be distributed and read among churches of the area. It begins with a prologue regarding the Word, the light, and the life, and these features are very similar to the Gospel's prologue, which was probably added by the final editor as a worship piece. The second and third letters are written by "the Elder," addressed to the chosen lady and her children (2 John) and a leader named Gaius (3 John). In that sense, 2 John is an epistle to a particular church, perhaps involving a woman leader as its pastor. Another possibility is that the church itself is being referred to in a feminine way, as the Elder closes his letter by extending greetings from their "sister"—apparently a reference to his own community. Second John is most similar to 1 John, and it clearly is written by the same author, dealing with teachers called "antichrists," as are mentioned in 1 John (1 John 4:1-3; 2 John 1:7). Third John, however, is the most distinctive of the letters. It is also written by the Elder, who appeals to Gaius to continue extending hospitality despite its having been denied by Diotrephes, who loves to be first (3 John 1:9-10). Diotrephes, who loves primacy, has reportedly excluded Johannine ministers from his church and has threatened to expel any who take them in. If indeed church governance was an issue here, it makes sense that the Elder may also have added material to the Johannine Gospel dealing with church unity and Christ's leading believers through the Holy Spirit—available to all. Therefore, the Johannine Epistles were plausibly written between 85 and 95 CE, between the first and final editions of John's Gospel.

The Revelation of John

The Revelation of John ("apocalypse" means disclosure, or revelation) is also connected traditionally with Ephesus, and this is the only one of the five Johannine writings that actually features the name "John," naming him as the author. The problem, though, is that Revelation is the most distinctive among the Johannine writings from vocabulary and grammar standpoints, so in that sense, it shows the least evidence of being written by the same author as any of the other four. This, of course, could be a function of the genre—apocalyptic writing is inherently different from letters and narratives, so differences are to be expected. And, Revelation does share a number of themes with the other Johannine writings, so it cannot be considered non-Johannine. If the Gospel of John was finalized by the author of the Epistles, though, it could be that the underlying voice of John's Gospel narrative could have played a role also in the formation of the Johannine Apocalypse. It could also be that Revelation was also edited by an author other than its primary author, so even stylistic differences cannot negate particular contributions within the Johannine circle of Christian leaders. Probably we have here a "Johannine school" of early Christian leaders within the same sector of the movement, so several hands were likely involved in preaching, writing, collecting, and editing the five Johannine writings, even if particular aspects of composition are elusive. One theory embraced by some scholars is that several Christian leaders, influenced by John the Apostle (or even the Elder), are responsible for this corpus, explaining how his name came to be associated with them. Whatever the case, Revelation is the only work explicitly referencing the name "John" as the author.

More certain regarding the writing of Revelation are the time and place. Given that the seven letters of Christ to the churches (Rev 2–3) address the churches of Asia Minor around the time of Domitian, the production of Revelation between 95 and 100 CE is a strong guess.

A chronology of the second and third generations of the Christian movement looks something like this:

66–73 CE—The Roman invasion of Judea and the Jewish War

70 CE—The destruction of the Jerusalem temple, followed by the *fiscus Judaicus*—a tax is levied upon all Jews (two drachmas) to be paid to the temple of Jupiter in Rome

Ca. 70–80 CE—Jewish and Christian leaders to other sectors of the Christian movement:

—Andrew to Scythia (Bulgaria)

—Thomas to Parthia (India)—as early as 52 CE)

—Philip to Hieropolis (in Asia Minor)

—John to Ephesus (in Asia Minor)

81–96 CE—Under Domitian's reign emperor worship is once more required

Ca. 100 CE—John the apostle dies (according to Eusebius)

100–115 CE—Ignatius writes to churches in Asia Minor encouraging the appointment of one bishop in every church

Chapter 11

The Epistle to the Hebrews

Begin with the text. Read Hebrews, and note important themes and details that come to mind.

Author: unknown, but Apollos is a good guess

Audience: to Jewish and other communities open to embracing Jesus as the Messiah/Christ—possibly in Rome

Time: ca. 65 CE, likely before the destruction of the temple in Jerusalem in 70 CE

Place: from an unknown diaspora setting, possibly Antioch, Ephesus, Corinth, or Alexandria

Message: Christ is supreme!

Mistakenly referred to as the Epistle of Paul to the Hebrews in the Latin Bible (the Vulgate), the Epistle to the Hebrews has some overlap with Paul's ministry, but it is significantly different in terms of its language, vocabulary, and thrust. Whoever the author is, he is deeply concerned with demonstrating the ways that Jesus fulfills the ideals of Israel as a means of convincing audiences to receive him as the Messiah. He also exhorts believers to continue in the faith rather than fall away and calls for rigor and discipline in Christian living. In both outreach and exhortation the focus is placed on Christ, who establishes the New Covenant as the pioneer and perfecter of faith.

I. Crises and Contexts

Rather than crises, appreciating the contexts within which Hebrews was written is most illuminating for understanding the text. As the roles of Christ are compared to the Jerusalem priesthood, its sacrifices, and the temple, the writing of Hebrews is likely earlier than the Roman invasion of Judea in 67 CE, and certainly before the destruction of the temple in 70 CE. It reflects the perspective of diaspora Judaism in the first-century Mediterranean world, and it targets Jewish and God-fearing audiences of its day. Some contact with the Pauline and Johannine missions is apparent, at times reflecting parallel developments, as well.

The Idealization of Jewish Values in the Diaspora

For Jews able to travel to Jerusalem for any of the three pilgrimage festivals during the year, the temple and its festivities were of great significance. Likewise, the work of the priests and the sacrificial system in Jerusalem not only provided a meaningful means of strengthening the human-divine relationship but also created the social fabric needed for bolstering a sense of identity among Jewish populations within reach of Jerusalem. For Jewish communities outside of Palestine, though, travel to Jerusalem was more difficult. Therefore, in such settings as Babylon, Alexandria, Rome, and Sardis, Second-Temple Judaism came to value its Jewish heritage in ways other than depending on the sacrificial and priestly systems in Jerusalem.

First, the Jewish faithful would come together in synagogue meetings on the Sabbath, either in homes or in buildings dedicated to regular Jewish worship. In the weekly meeting for worship, scripture would be read and interpreted, hymns would be sung, and responsive readings would be recited. Second, various Pharisaic schools would interpret scripture, often under a leading rabbi, and they would articulate meanings of passages regulating Jewish life. Third, community events and schools would be organized around synagogues for the benefit of Jewish families' interests in training their children in ways Jewish. Coming together for special meals and celebrations would thus happen locally, even if trips to Jerusalem were less frequent than for Jews living in closer proximity. Fourth, as a result of Jewish interests abroad, the Septuagint translation of scripture into Greek made it possible for biblical education and exhortation to continue, and therefore Judaism prospered in the larger Hellenistic world beyond Judea and its environs. As a result, diaspora interpreters of Jewish history and worship life would often reframe Jerusalem-based values in typological ways, making the meaning transferrable to distant regions as well as geographically connected ones.

The Allegorizing Work of Philo of Alexandria

One of the greatest interpreters of Jewish scripture in the early part of the first century CE was Philo of Alexandria, a Greek-speaking philosopher and leader, who expounded upon the meanings of biblical texts in ways that connected their symbolic meanings with valued understandings of virtue rooted in Greek philosophy. Philo also led a delegation of Alexandrian Jewish leaders to meet with Caesar Gaius Caligula in 40 CE, complaining about the ways that Jews were being persecuted by Greeks in Egypt and opposing Caesar's plan to erect a statue of himself in the Jerusalem temple. As far as we know, Philo only visited Jerusalem once, but his allegorical method of biblical interpretation had an extensive impact upon Jewish thinkers of his day and also upon early Christian writers—arguably the authors of Hebrews and John. Notable in his approach to Jewish scripture is the high value placed on the role of Moses and the Law rather than David and the kingdom. Philo also used the Greek Septuagint as inspired scripture, as did most first-century Jews in the Mediterranean world.

Philo's allegorical method of biblical interpretation made extensive use of any number of symbolizing operations in seeking to develop expanded meanings of details in biblical texts. For instance, in his analysis of Genesis, Philo expounded upon the theological meanings of such details as the changing of the names of Abram to Abraham and Sarai to Sarah. Philo also allegorized the seven days of creation rather than seeing them as twenty-four-hour periods. He referred to manna from heaven as evidence that the Jewish synagogue schools were superior to the Greek encyclical schools of Alexandria; after all, divine instruction is better than its earth-bound counterparts. Perhaps most intriguing is his development of the *Logos* (Word) of God as the means by which the world was created, as well as the source of reason and human enlightenment. In doing this, Philo drew also from Stoic thought and the work of Heraclitus of Ephesus, a philosopher of the fifth century BCE, who explained the basis of order and rationality as being the divine *Logos*, a principle of truth accessible to every person and the source of human reason. Part of what we see in the book of Hebrews is a highly allegorical treatment of Jewish institutions and authorities, with their fulfilled meaning being centered in Jesus as the Christ. In addition, at least three of the christological hymns of the New Testament have interesting overlaps with Philo's *Logos* theology.

A Partner in the Jewish Mission to the Gentiles

Given that Apollos is described in Acts 18:24 as "a native of Alexandria" who was "well-educated and effective in his use of the scriptures," and that he traveled in his ministry through Ephesus, Corinth, and other sectors of the Gentile mission (perhaps even Crete—Titus 3:13), it is understandable that since the days of Martin Luther he has been associated with the authorship of Hebrews. After all, if Apollos hailed from Alexandria, and if Philo—probably the most influential Jewish thinker in Egypt at the time—had been appointed to head a delegation to Rome a decade or so earlier, it is hard to imagine that Philo's allegorical method of biblical interpretation would not have made an impact upon an early evangelist and teacher such as Apollos. It is also notable that Apollos is described by Paul in 1 Corinthians as ministering effectively, and it is not hard to imagine that Paul had Apollos in mind when he declared that "I didn't come preaching God's secrets to you like I was an expert in speech or wisdom" (1 Cor 2:1—i.e., as Apollos did). In other words, if the letter to the Hebrews represents the sort of preaching Apollos might have carried forth, it is perfectly understandable that some might have claimed to be his followers, competing with the missions of Peter and Paul, and that Paul might even have felt outclassed by some of his preaching ministry.

Whoever wrote Hebrews clearly aimed at connecting the person and work of Christ with the fulfillment of Israel's most treasured values. Therefore, in Hebrews Jesus not only fulfills Jewish scripture; he fulfills the leading typologies of Judaism itself—angels, the temple, the priesthood, the sacrificial system, the covenant (not on stone tablets, but on hearts of flesh), and the Law. In that sense, cohering with the references connecting Titus and Apollos (Titus 3:13) and the Hebrews author to Timothy (Heb 13:23), the author of Hebrews works alongside the Pauline mission in complementary ways. He emphasizes the sacrifice of Christ, the blessing of Abraham, the dwelling place of God, the role of faith in the lives of believers, the importance of leaving sin behind, the willingness to suffer for Christ, and the importance of extending loving hospitality to others. Therefore, among the New Testament letters we see several models of Jewish-Christian outreach, of which Hebrews is a leading example.

However, if engagement with the Pauline and other Christian missions is a reality for Hebrews, some disagreement and negative fallout is also apparent. Falling away is a theme addressed, and while some of that may simply be a factor of becoming lazy or enticed by the ways of the world (Heb 4:11-16; 5:11-14), it appears that religious debates with other Christians had a discouraging effect upon some. In Hebrews 6:1-12 the writer calls for pressing on into maturity of faith—not belaboring a foundation of "turning away from dead works, of faith in God, of teaching about ritual ways to wash with water, laying on of hands, the resurrection from the dead, and eternal judgment—all over again" (vv. 1-2). These seem to be the sort of things that were debated in partisan rivalries perhaps echoed in 1 Corinthians 1, although this can only be a guess. What the writer of Hebrews does say, though, is that it is "impossible to restore people to changed hearts and lives who turn away once they have seen the light, tasted the heavenly gift, become partners with the Holy Spirit, and tasted God's good word and the powers of the coming age" (vv. 4-5). Not only are they hard to bring back into the fold of believers, but "they are crucifying God's Son all over again and exposing him to public shame" (v. 6). Perhaps they are like the soil that receives the seed of the gospel, but whose growing seed is crowded out by thorns and thistles, harkening back to the teachings of Jesus in the Synoptics. To persevere in the faith, though, avoids the plight of spiritual laziness and sluggishness, inspired by those "who inherit the promises through faith and patience" (v. 12).

Four Groups in the Early Church

That being the case, the writer of Hebrews is easily seen as an adherent of the fourth of four groups within the larger Jewish-Christian mission to the Gentiles.[1] *Group One* believed in the full conversion of the Gentiles to Judaism, insisting upon faithful observance of religious customs and circumcision as well as Jewish practices and beliefs (the priests and Pharisees who came to believe in Jesus—Acts 6:7; 15:5); perhaps James, or at least those who "slipped in to spy on our freedom" and those who came from James (Gal 2:4, 12) would have been influenced by this group. *Group Two* adhered to most Jewish laws and customs, including circumcision and food laws; if John Mark felt that Paul's mission was getting too liberal, perhaps he and Peter might have represented this group, which is why Paul was upset with both of them (Acts 15:38; Gal 2:11-12). This group likely embraced "the teaching of the Lord to the Gentiles through the Twelve Apostles" (the *Didache*). *Group Three* did not insist on circumcision or the keeping of Jewish food laws, as they did not believe such was required for receiving the blessing to Abraham's children. Or, as Paul would say, "Everything is permitted, but everything isn't beneficial" (1 Cor 10:23; 6:12). *Group Four* saw no abiding significance in Jewish cults or feasts; they saw Christ as transcending them all. While I do not think that Jesus's references to "your law" and "their law" in John's narrative proves that John's sector of Christianity had individuated from Judaism (John 8:17; 10:34; 15:25), it does suggest the sort of perspective reflected in Hebrews, where Christ is superior to the temple, the priesthood, and its sacrificial systems. Therefore, on a scale of gradations emphasizing the most to the least outward observances of Jewish identity and religious customs,

---

1. The division of the four groups comes from Raymond E. Brown and John P. Meier, *Antioch and Rome: New Testament Cradles of Catholic Christianity* (Mahwah, NJ: Paulist Press, 1983), 2–8.

Hebrews and John (and perhaps Stephen) would be on the far end of the scale in spiritualizing directions.

II. Features of Hebrews

While Hebrews is considered an epistle, it is closer to a theological treatise, or an apologia for Jesus as the Jewish Messiah/Christ, than a letter. Intended for Jewish audiences and others in the larger Mediterranean world, the Epistle to the Hebrews seeks to show the supremacy of Christ in all ways, featuring how he fulfills the leading typologies of Israel and provides a new and living way into the sanctuary of God (Heb 10:20). Jesus establishes the New Covenant and Testament, fulfilling the Old (8:8; 9:15; 12:24)—extending the blessings of Abraham and Moses to the world, to be received by faith.

Typological Exegesis

With few exceptions, allegorical interpretation tends to function horizontally, finding various parallels with an earlier set of images, whereas typological interpretation tends to function vertically, showing various ways that an earlier source of authority is fulfilled in God's redemptive action hence. The typological approach of Hebrews thus operates to establish connections between great sources of authority in Hebrew scripture and the work of Jesus Christ as their culmination. In sketching these connections, we see the work of a master preacher-teacher, setting up three sets of three subjects fulfilled in their final object, Jesus.

Beginning with the *patriarchs*, the life-giving contribution of Abraham is now fulfilled in his descendant—Jesus, who is now a sibling of all who believe. Therefore, membership in the blessed family of Abraham is now accessible to all by faith, and the house of Moses is now a larger household, given that the Law is perfected in Christ Jesus. Believers thus now become the new household of God. Indeed, the Israelites entered into God's "rest" under the leadership of Joshua; therefore, the inheritance of the promised land is available to all, as the gift of God's Sabbath-rest is now received by those who believe. In these ways, Jesus Christ fulfills the typology of Israel's patriarchs.

The Patriarchs

- *Abraham*—the children of father Abraham are now siblings of Jesus (2:10-18)

- *Moses*—the house of Moses is now the larger household of Jesus (3:1-19)

- *Joshua*—the "rest" of the promised land is now a new Sabbath available to all (4:1-16)

In addition to the promise of the patriarchs, Christ also fulfills the typology of Israel's *priesthood* in Jesus's being a high priest, even of the order of Melchizedek. In earlier Jewish interpretation, Melchizedek plays an interesting set of roles. He is presented in Genesis 14:18 as the priest of God Most High, to whom Abram gives one tenth (a tithe) of all he has, but his origin and destiny are unmentioned. Jewish interpreters speculated that he might have been a transcendent figure—with no beginning or end. Thus, his priesthood might be considered an eternal priesthood, out-classing the human priesthoods of Aaron and Levi. His name means "king of righteousness" in Hebrew, and since he is called the "king of Salem" (*shalom* in Hebrew means "peace"), the author of Hebrews references Jesus as fulfilling the place and order of Melchizedek as the true "king of righteousness" and "king of peace"—a Son of God and a king forever, prefiguring the character of Jesus's priesthood (Heb 7:2-3). In developing this connection, Hebrews sketches further parallels with Psalm 110, which presents the Lord as making someone's enemies a footstool for his feet and restoring the global significance of Melchizedek. This is one of the most important psalms for early Christians, and when Jewish contemporaries envisioned a Messiah in the lineage of David, it is precisely this psalm of cosmic triumph they had in mind.

As a means of expanding that connection, Hebrews links the calling of Jesus as Son of God (Ps 2:7) with the calling of Aaron to be the priestly son of God; therefore, Jesus's priesthood fulfills that typology in cosmic perspective. In the gift of Abram's offering, he blessed Melchizedek, who in turn blessed Abram's descendants; therefore, Jesus as a priest forever—of the order of Melchizedek—issues in an eternal covenant of promise. Thus, the priesthood of Christ is above that of the priests in Jerusalem, who continue to offer sacrifices season by season and year by year. Christ's blood, however, is shed once and for all for the sins of the world. He is the perfect priest because he is the ultimate sacrifice. In these ways, Jesus Christ fulfills the typology of Israel's priesthood.

A Perfect Priesthood—Even to the Order of Melchizedek (Psalm 110), Jesus is . . .

- Called as Aaron was—yet as God's Son (5:4-5; 7:11)
- The final object of Abram's tribute—not just a tithe but a *promise* (6:13–7:10)

- Above the levitical priesthood—a priest forever, like Melchizedek, offering a once-and-for-all sacrifice—an enduring remedy to the world's need (5:6-10; 7:11-28)

In addition to fleshing out the implications of Psalm 110, the author of Hebrews also sees Jesus's coming as the Messiah/Christ as fulfilling God's First Covenant with Israel with a new and final covenant through Christ. Further, as *covenant* means "testament," the primary basis for calling the Christian scriptures "the New Testament" is the book of Hebrews, which sees the typology of God's Law given through Moses as being fulfilled according to Jeremiah 31:31-34 (developed twice: Heb 8:8-12; 10:16-17) by means of writing God's Law on hearts of flesh instead of tablets of stone. This inward transformation, however, takes place as a function of the dwelling place of God, also receiving a change of address. No longer is it in the tent of meeting in the wilderness, or even the temple in Jerusalem. Rather, God's dwelling place is now among his people and within them, including all who believe.

And, while sacrifices for the nation of Israel, and even for the high priest, must be offered annually at least, this shows that they are not ultimate in their value. In contrast, Jesus has no need of sacrifice on his own behalf (as he committed no sin), and his sacrifice is final because it is a once-and-for-all gift to the world. That is why the New Covenant fulfills and displaces the First Covenant. Despite the gift of the Law, people kept on sinning, which required atoning sacrifices to restore their relationships with God; therefore, it was imperfect. In the New Covenant, however, not only is the ultimate sacrifice offered for all, but God also takes up residence in human hearts, bringing about conformity to God's ways inwardly. Such indeed is the new and living Way, and Jesus Christ thus not only fulfills the typology of God's Covenant with Israel, he inaugurates a New Covenant with the entire world.

God's Covenants—Old and New (Jer 31:31-34)

- The First Tent of Meeting—and the *New Dwelling Place of God* (8:1–9:25)

- The First Sacrifice: the blood of bulls and goats—and the *Ultimate Sacrifice*: the blood of Jesus Christ (9:26–10:31)

- The First Covenant—and the *New Covenant* (8:6; 10:39; 12:22-24; 13:20-21)

Heroes of Faith

One of the most memorable features of Hebrews is the listing of heroes of faith in chapter 11. Like Stephen and Paul reciting the history of God's saving-revealing work in Israel in Acts 7 and Romans 10, the writer of Hebrews gives an overview of high points in Israel's history, so as to inspire future generations with examples of how people's exercise of faith in generations past might provide models and inspiration for the future. In doing so, he begins with a description of faith: "the reality of what we hope for, the proof of what we don't see" (11:1). It is by faith that God's creative work by God's word is received, and the elders of the past were approved precisely because they exercised this sort of faith (11:2-3). Note, however, that in all of these examples, exercising faith in God does involve works of faithfulness, while not involving dead works of religious observance. This issue will surface again when considering the Epistle of James, especially in relation to Galatians and Romans.

By Faith (Heb 11) . . .

- "*Abel* offered a better sacrifice to God than Cain"
- "*Enoch* was taken up so that he didn't see death"
- "*Noah* responded with godly fear when he was warned about events he hadn't seen yet"
- "*Abraham* obeyed when he was called to go out to a place that he was going to receive as an inheritance"
- "*Sarah* received the ability to have a child, though she herself was barren and past the age for having children"
- "*Abraham* offered Isaac when he was tested"
- "*Isaac* also blessed Jacob and Esau concerning their future"
- "*Jacob* blessed each of Joseph's sons as he was dying and *bowed in worship over the head of his staff*"
- "*Joseph* recalled the exodus of the Israelites at the end of his life, and gave instructions about burying his bones"
- "*Moses* was hidden by his parents for three months when he was born"
- "*Moses* refused to be called the son of Pharaoh's daughter when he was grown up"

- ○ "... he left Egypt without being afraid of the king's anger. He kept on going as if he could see what is invisible"

- ○ "... he kept the Passover and the sprinkling of blood, in order that the destroyer could not touch their firstborn children"

- ○ "... they crossed the Red Sea as if they were on dry land, but when the Egyptians tried it, they were drowned"

- ○ "... Jericho's walls fell after the people marched around them for seven days"

- *Rahab* the prostitute wasn't killed with the disobedient because she welcomed the spies in peace

- *Gideon, Barak, Samson, Jephthah, David, Samuel,* and *the prophets* through faith performed great feats, but "God provided something better for us so they wouldn't be made perfect without us"

The New Covenant and Testament

The central feature of the Epistle to the Hebrews is that it portrays typologically and allegorically the many ways in which Israel's promise is fulfilled in Christ Jesus. Typologically, the great institutions of Israel—the patriarchs, the priesthood, the temple, sacrifices, and the covenant—are all fulfilled in Christ. He embodies their highest ideals and provides an ultimate expression as a blessing to the world. Allegorically, the heroes of the faith provide models of how to live faithfully in relationship with God, and the author connects their example to the importance of trusting in Christ as the initiator of the New Covenant and honoring him in the world.

III. The Message of Hebrews

As clearly as any other book in the New Testament, the letter to the Hebrews moves from the indicative to the imperative. It declares what God has done, in the history of Israel and in the Christ Events, and it exhorts what people are to do in response. That being the case, the author of Hebrews calls people to consider Christ, to believe in him, and to live their lives in keeping with God's holy and peaceable standards.

Christ Is Supreme!

The overall thrust of showing Jesus as fulfilling the central typologies of Israel is to emphasize the supremacy of Christ in all ways Jewish. At the outset, Christ is supreme over *angels*. None of God's angels (messengers) were ever called God's "Son," nor were any of them invited to sit at the right hand of God while their enemies were made into a footstool for his feet (Heb 1:5-14). As God's firstborn, Christ receives worship from even the angels, and their message about him is authoritative. Their message is attested by the working of signs, miracles, and the gifts of the Holy Spirit. And yet, just as humans are lower than the angels, Jesus was made lower in order that he might taste death and thereby deliver humanity from it through his sacrifice. Therefore, he is crowned with glory and honor through his death as a means of humanity's experiencing the full grace of God (2:1-9).

Christ is also supreme over Jewish *priesthoods, sacrificial systems,* and the *Law*—as "the apostle and high priest of our confession" (3:1), Jesus empathizes with humans because he was tempted in all ways as they are, yet without sin (2:18; 4:14-15). Over and against the ineffective commandments of the Law, a better hope is offered through Christ because it comes with a pledge (7:19-21). As a result, the superior sacrifice of Jesus inaugurates a better covenant (7:22; 8:6). The heavenly realities are cleansed by means of Christ's better sacrifice (9:23), giving believers better and lasting possessions (10:34). Over and against even the heroes of the faith, God has provided something better for believers so that those heroes would not be perfected alone (11:40). Therefore, in the surpassing work of Jesus as the Christ, the Old Covenant is perfected in the New.

The Shadow and the Substance

In a fascinating treatment of typological realities and their physical manifestations, the author of Hebrews does something similar to Paul's argument in Colossians 2:17, where he claims that "These religious practices are only a shadow of what was coming—the body that cast the shadow is Christ." Rather than asserting that the body of Christ casts a shadow over religious forms, however, the writer of Hebrews emphasizes the divine and eternal realities, of which Jewish practices and religious forms are but a copy and a shadow, not the substance (Heb 8:5). Therefore, the eternal holy place of God is represented by the tent of meeting in the wilderness and the holy of holies in the Jerusalem temple, but the substance of that reality is Christ—that holy place in which humanity is now invited to meet with God. Likewise, the Mosaic Law "is a shadow of the good things that are coming, not the real things themselves" (10:1). That is because the Law does not perfect the individual, but transformation is now possible in Christ Jesus by the power of the Holy Spirit.

At this point, the writer of Hebrews makes some provocative claims that challenge not only the religious strongholds of Judaism, but also the value of religious forms within all religions, including Christianity. Put bluntly, God's saving-revealing work is never confined to religious forms; these are but a shadow of the substance—a time-bound copy of the eternal reality. In particular, "it's impossible for the blood of bulls and goats to take away sins" (10:4); rather, animal sacrifice is offered by God as a gift to humanity in order for people to glimpse the unimaginable—that their sins are forgiven despite their undeservedness. After all, in human ways of thinking, "there is no forgiveness without blood being shed" (9:22). Therefore, in establishing the New Covenant through the once-and-for-all sacrifice of Christ, rather than humans offering sacrifice for God's sake, God has become the final sacrifice for humanity's sake. Because Jesus "suffered outside the city gate to make the people holy with his own blood" (13:12), believers are now invited to join him in that new city whose architect and builder is God (11:10, 16). Nonetheless, God still welcomes the sacrifices of his people, but these are sacrifices—continually offered up and doing good—of praise and sharing with others in need (13:15-16). With these sacrifices God is indeed well pleased.

Personal Appeals

In addition to extolling the supremacy of Christ and describing the New Covenant, the writer of Hebrews issues personal exhortations, calling for a faithful response to the gospel message. These are direct appeals, exhorting people to action in life-giving ways. At the heart of the appeals is the call to embrace the message of Christ, not becoming stubborn or hardening one's heart as did the rebellious Israelites in the desert, but abiding in the confession of faith rather than falling into disobedience. In two of these appeals (4:11-16; 10:19-25) the author summarizes the message in ways that exhort the audience to action in several ways. Believers are also called to maturity—not simply dealing with the basics of the faith, but pressing on in action and discipline while resisting the pressures of the world. In this pursuit, Christ becomes the exemplary focus of the believer, enduring the cross and its shame, as the pioneer and perfecter of one's faith.

Calls to Action in Hebrews

- Pay attention to what you have heard—the Son's message—lest you drift from it (2:1)

- Today if you hear Christ's voice, do not harden your hearts as the Israelites did in the wilderness (3:7-9, 15-16; 4:7)

- "Let's make every effort to enter that rest so that no one will fall by following the same example of disobedience"; "let's hold on to the confession since we have a great high priest"—Jesus, God's Son; "let's draw near to the throne of favor with confidence so that we can receive mercy and find grace when we need help" (4:11-16)

- "Let's press on to maturity"—"moving on from the basics about Christ's word" and following "the example of the ones who inherit the promises through faith and patience" (6:1-12)

- "Let's draw near with a genuine heart with the certainty that our faith gives us"; "let's hold on to the confession of our hope without wavering"; let's consider each other carefully for the purpose of sparking love and good deeds, not failing to meet together with other believers and encouraging each other (10:19-25)

- "Let's also run the race that is laid out in front of us"—throwing off "any extra baggage, getting rid of the sin that trips us up, and fixing our eyes on Jesus, faith's pioneer and perfecter" (12:1-2)

In these ways, the Epistle to the Hebrews is not simply an outreach to potential believers; it also calls for actual believers to bolster their commitments and to move from the beginnings of Christian faith into maturity. In the light of Hebrews 6, where some have fallen away because of fruitless religious debates, the question arises as to whether it is possible to lose one's salvation in Christ. Likewise, in the light of Hebrews 12:14-17, one may miss out on one's birthright, like Esau, if distracted by a root of bitterness or sexual immorality. As peaceable demeanor and righteous living are both empowered by grace, the author of Hebrews reminds his audience: "Pursue the goal of peace along with everyone—and holiness as well, because no one will see the Lord without it. Make sure that no one misses out on God's grace" (12:14-15). Because God is a consuming fire, serving God with awe and gratitude is the only imaginable response to encountering God's glory and grace faithfully (12:18-29).

Consider Him—Tempted but without Sin

In addition to inviting his audiences to come to faith in Jesus as the Christ, the writer of Hebrews finally calls people to be faithful to their confessions and commitments. If indeed some followers of Christ had fallen away, perhaps disenchanted by such debates and divisions as those between followers of Apollos, Cephas, and Paul in 1 Corinthians, the writer of Hebrews brings the focus back on Christ, whose ministry and work on the cross are the sustenance of all who seek to live in ways pleasing to him. Just as Paul pointed to the gospel of Christ as the main focus of Christian living, so does the writer of Hebrews. He invites his audience to consider him who endured the cross—its suffering and shame, fixing our eyes on Christ Jesus as the focus of Christian living (12:1-3). Therefore, in struggling with the frustrations and challenges of life, Christ became an exemplary way forward; if he endured in faithfulness, so can his followers.

Here Jesus also becomes an empathic brother to believers, in that being fully human, he became a high priest who understands human weaknesses: he "was tempted in every way that we are, except without sin" (4:15). Therefore, what the Law could not produce in empowering people to rise above the grip of sin, the priestly work and example of Christ provide a potent way forward. In focusing on Christ and embracing the discipline of faith (12:1-13), the believer is liberated to live into God's Sabbath rest and the habitation promised to Abraham. The example of Christ, in his sinless humanity, thus becomes an invitation for all to "draw near to the throne of favor with confidence so that we can receive mercy and find grace when we need help" (4:16). For that is what it means to become an inhabitant of that eternal city whose architect and builder is the gracious God of Israel (11:9-10; 12:22-24).

IV. Engaging Hebrews

As you consider the ways that the Epistle to the Hebrews addressed the audiences of the first-century Mediterranean world, how might it speak to audiences in later settings? How might the revelatory and redemptive work of Jesus as the Christ bring about a New Covenant for those familiar with Judaism and also for those who might not be? If you were attempting to demonstrate the difference Christ makes for those who embrace his mission, how might you do so in the settings with which you are familiar? The following questions might facilitate that reflection.

First, read again the five passages in the New Testament that seem to reflect early Christian worship material, or christological hymns, and notice similarities and differences among them: John 1:1-18, Colossians 1:15-20, Philippians 2:5-11, 2 Timothy 2:11-13, and Hebrews 1:1-4. Taking it a bit further, what words and names are used to refer to Jesus as the Christ? Why were these terms used by early Christians? How did they understand God's saving work through Jesus as the Christ? And in that sense, what difference does the overall impression of early Christian worship material make for later generations of believers?

Second, consider the many ways that Jesus as the Christ fulfills the various typologies of Israel—the priesthood, the temple, the sacrificial system, and the First Covenant—and reflect on how the New Covenant is similar to and different from these. If Israel's religious forms and expressions are the copy and shadow of timeless and spiritual realities, how does that impact later understandings of Christian faith and practice seeking to actualize their substance and essence over and above their religious expressions? Then again, religious expressions of faith and practice are important, but how are their time-bound and culture-specific features crafted meaningfully without being mistaken for the transcendent realities they represent?

Third, in our struggles with trials, frustrations, and temptations, how does focusing on Christ and Israel's heroes of faith make a difference for us in later generations? Note that the ten heroes of faith named in 11:4-31 include women as well as men, and even a murder victim and a prostitute. Perhaps there's hope for the rest of us, too! As faith focuses on what is not yet seen, how do the examples of the faithful inspire the faithfulness of others? And finally, in fixing one's eyes on Christ, who was tempted in all ways that we are tempted—yet without sin—how does the object of one's focus empower believers in their own struggles and challenges? In that sense, what difference does the New Covenant make for people's lives today, personally and experientially?

The Christological Hymns of the New Testament

In the correspondence between Pliny the governor of Bythinia in Asia Minor and Emperor Trajan around 110 CE, Pliny describes the excuses of those who are accused of being Christians and thus are worthy of punishment by death. They denied being Christians—they only met with Christians on a certain day of the week, eating some ordinary food, and singing hymns to Christ as though he were a god (Pliny the Younger, *Letters* 10.96). These people were let off the hook and not charged, especially if they were willing to revere Caesar's image and bow down to the Empire. If early Christians made use of their own worship material, though, might some of it be contained in the New Testament writings themselves? In support of this possibility, several passages appear to represent such material. They are referred to as the christological hymns of the New Testament.

As a means of identifying this sort of hymnic material, several features make a passage a likely candidate. First, the unit represents worship material with Christ as the subject. Second, several tenets of faith are listed, one after the other, without elaboration—simply asserted.[1] Third, sometimes the material appears in a verse-like pattern, with a certain cadence to it—likely material to have been recited. Fourth, sometimes the first-person plural is used (as in John 1:1-18), reflecting a community's use of the material. Therefore, the four main passages identified as likely christological hymns include John 1:1-18, Philippians 2:5-11, Colossians 1:15-20, and Hebrews 1:1-4. Note, however, the distinctive features and functions of each.

---

1. Note, for instance the staccato phrases in 1 Tim 3:16: "Without question, the mystery of godliness is great: he was revealed as a human, declared righteous by the Spirit, seen by angels, preached throughout the nations, believed in around the world, and taken up in glory."

Philippians 2:5-11

One of the two hymns used by Paul in his letters is the humiliation-exaltation passage of Philippians 2, featuring Christ as a role model for serving one another. Believers are extolled not to think of themselves more highly than others but to pour themselves out in service, as that is the way of the Lord. After all, even though he was equal with God, he emptied himself, becoming a servant of all, and it is God that therefore has lifted him up. That is the sort of attitude that believers should also have, so Philippians 2:5-11 is an exemplary christological hymn (actually beginning in v. 6):

Adopt the attitude that was in Christ Jesus:
Though he was in the form of God,
   he did not consider being equal with God something to exploit.
But he emptied himself
   by taking the form of a slave
   and by becoming like human beings.
When he found himself in the form of a human,
   he humbled himself by becoming obedient to the point of death,
   even death on a cross.
Therefore, God highly honored him
   and gave him a name above all names,
so that at the name of Jesus everyone
   in heaven, on earth, and under the earth might bow
   and every tongue confess that Jesus Christ is Lord,
   to the glory of God the Father.

Colossians 1:15-20

The second christological hymn used by Paul functions to provide his audience a worthy focus of worship—a compelling alternative to competing religions. Rather than the mystery religions of Asia Minor, it is Christ who is the source of creation and also the means of God's redemption. Here the theme of preexistence comes into play, and yet the death of Jesus on the cross is also emphasized. Therefore, the Son not only reveals the invisible God but also holds all things together in himself, bringing peace to all humanity as the head of the body—the church. In that sense, this confession not only emboldens believers but also becomes a means of outreach to others:

The Son is the image of the invisible God,
  the one who is first over all creation,

Because all things were created by him:
  both in the heavens and on the earth,
  the things that are visible and the things that are invisible.
    Whether they are thrones or powers,
    or rulers or authorities,
  all things were created through him and for him.

He existed before all things,
  and all things are held together in him.

He is the head of the body, the church,
who is the beginning,
  the one who is firstborn from among the dead
  so that he might occupy the first place in everything.

Because all the fullness of God was pleased to live in him,
  and he reconciled all things to himself through him—
  whether things on earth or in the heavens.
    He brought peace through the blood of his cross.

Hebrews 1:1-4

In comparison to the other christological hymns, Hebrews 1:1-4 is most similar in content and thrust to John 1:1-18. In these two passages God's speaking through his "Word"—his Son, who is also the light—reveals God's love and character in world-changing ways. As the creative agency of God's redeeming work, Jesus conveys God's character and message to the world. The same God who has spoken at many times and in many ways now calls forth a believing response to God's saving-revealing Word. As with the beginning of John's Gospel, the prologue to Hebrews engages audiences experientially, drawing them into an encounter of worship before proceeding with the content of the letter:

In the past, God spoke through the prophets to our ancestors in many times and many ways. In these final days, though, he spoke to us through a Son.

316

God made his Son the heir of everything and created the world through him. The Son is the light of God's glory and the imprint of God's being. He maintains everything with his powerful message. After he carried out the cleansing of people from their sins, he sat down at the right side of the highest majesty. And so, the Son became so much greater than the other messengers, such as angels, that he received a more important title than theirs.

John 1:1-18

The christological hymn at the beginning of John's Gospel was likely patterned after the prologue of 1 John 1:1-4, bearing echoes of the Elder's claims regarding what "we have seen" and what "we have all received." That being the case, John 1:1-18 appears to be an affirmation of what has been learned from the Johannine story of Jesus, re-crafted into a new introduction. If the references to John the Baptist (vv. 6-8, 15) are seen as the original beginning of John's Gospel, with the *Logos* hymn woven around it, we find a fairly balanced rendering of three hymnic verses of similar length and cadence. Or, these verses could also have been added as a means of integrating the hymn with John's narrative plot. Whatever the case, the hymnic beginning of John's Gospel whets the appetite of new readers experientially, drawing them into the message of the gospel they are about to encounter.

In the beginning was the Word
    and the Word was with God
    and the Word was God.
The Word was with God in the beginning.
Everything came into being through the Word,
    and without the Word
    nothing came into being.
What came into being
    through the Word was life,
    and the life was the light for all people.
The light shines in the darkness,
    and the darkness doesn't extinguish the light.
. . . .
The true light that shines on all people
    was coming into the world.

The light was in the world,
>and the world came into being through the light,
>>but the world didn't recognize the light.

The light came to his own people,
>and his own people didn't welcome him.

But those who did welcome him,
>>those who believed in his name,
>he authorized to become God's children,
>>born not from blood
>>nor from human desire or passion,
>>but born from God.

The Word became flesh
>and made his home among us.

We have seen his glory,
>glory like that of a father's only son,
>>full of grace and truth.

. . . .

From his fullness we have all received grace upon grace;
>as the Law was given through Moses,
>so grace and truth came into being through Jesus Christ.

No one has ever seen God.
>God the only Son,
>>who is at the Father's side,
>>has made God known.

In reflecting on the character and content of these hymnic passages, several observations follow. First, references to human and mundane aspects of Jesus's ministry are missing; despite his presentation along these lines in the Gospels, he is not referenced here as Jesus of Nazareth, the Son of Man, or the prophet predicted by Moses (Deut 18). So, those christological terms are more likely rooted in historical memory than in theological development. These worship motifs, on the other hand, have their root primarily not in the actual ministry of the historical Jesus but in the worship life of his followers and should be understood in those terms.

Second, the main thrust of the worship material involves Christ's agency from the Father, perhaps rooted in Jesus's own sense of commissioning (cf. Deut 18:15-22 and other biblical passages). As a result, the mission of Jesus as the Christ is seen by later believers as effecting God's saving-revealing work and creating the basis for the New Covenant. Therefore, these units of material are crafted in such a way as to be serviceable in corporate meetings for worship, affirming Jesus's mission in terms accessible to Gentile audiences as well as Jewish ones.

Third, assuming some of these hymns were in use before Paul's writings were finalized, they would have been among the first of early Christian materials to be standardized—perhaps even in written form. Therefore, the assumption that understandings of Jesus went exclusively from earlier, low christological beliefs (featuring the humanity of Jesus) to later, high christological beliefs (featuring the divinity of Jesus) gets turned on its head. Of course they did to some degree, but some high christological material was even earlier than Paul's writings, and some emphases on Jesus's fleshly humanity (say, John 1:14 and 19:34-35) are clearly later.

Fourth, note the diversity of references to Jesus as the exalted Christ. There is little uniformity here in terms of particular titles and phrases, and that fact illustrates the exploratory and expansive character of early Christian beliefs about Jesus as the Christ. Later theological councils were forced to reconcile these and other christological statements in the New Testament, but these earlier definitions are more creative than ordered.

Fifth, these different confessions also served different functions. Whereas the Colossians hymn is designed to bolster solidarity with Jesus as the Christ, challenging his deprecation by other religious traditions, the Philippians hymn builds upon the kenotic (self-emptying) example of Jesus as a humble pattern for believers to emulate. That is how one's salvation is worked outwardly in the world (Phil 2:12). The Christ hymn of Hebrews sets the stage for Christ's superiority over sources of Jewish authority, and the Christ hymn of John prepares later audiences to receive the Gospel's message.

Sixth, these hymnic passages also communicate in cross-cultural ways. The christological hymns in John 1 and Hebrews 1 effectively translate the Jewish agency motif into terms that would have been welcomed among Jews and Gentiles in the larger Mediterranean world. They connect with the work of the fifth-century BCE philosopher from Ephesus, Heraclitus, who taught that it was the *Logos* of God that created order out of chaos—the spark of life and source of reason available to all humanity. Philo's *Logos* doctrine is also indebted to Heraclitus, whose work he also connects with God's creative-redemptive Word *in the beginning* (Gen 1:1).

Therefore, in reflecting on the christological hymns of the New Testament, one can detect a great deal of energy and creativity in believers' understanding of the saving-revealing mission of Jesus as the Christ. It also becomes clear how this material has made it into the worship life of the church, and in that sense, the form of the material continues to serve its functions well. As earlier meanings are considered in the light of later ones, new insights emerge as to what the worship life of early believers might have been like. In that sense, the exploratory character of earlier worship material informs and inspires the same in later generations, as well.

Chapter 12

The General Epistles: James–
2 Peter (and Jude)

Begin with the text. Read the Epistles of James, Peter, and Jude, and note important themes and details that come to mind.

Authors: traditionally, James the brother of Jesus (James); Peter (1 and 2 Peter, although some scholars question 2 Peter); Jude the brother of Jesus (Jude, although this view is questioned)

Audience: believers everywhere

Time: between 52 and 68 CE

Place: from Jerusalem (James and possibly Jude) and Rome (1 and 2 Peter)

Message: Embrace God's wisdom (James); live in ways pleasing to Christ (1 and 2 Peter); beware of false teachers (Jude).

The Epistles of James, 1 and 2 Peter, and Jude are written to believers everywhere, and this is why they are also called the General (or Catholic—as in universal) Epistles. In fact, James begins with a greeting to the twelve tribes scattered in the diaspora (Jas 1:1), and 1 Peter is written to "God's chosen strangers in the world of the diaspora, who live in Pontus, Galatia, Cappadocia, Asia, and Bithynia" (1 Pet 1:1). Like the Epistles of Ephesians, Hebrews, and 1 John, as well as the four Gospels, Acts, and Revelation, these writings were designed to be circulated among the churches, providing encouragement, instruction, and admonition as needed by believers. James and Jude are associated with the family of Jesus, perhaps written by his brothers, and the Petrine Epistles bear traits associated with Peter's ministry in Rome—written from "Babylon" (1 Pet 5:13). As such, they offer wisdom for Christian living in an increasingly hostile world, seeking to inspire and encourage their audiences toward faithfulness in Christ.

321

I. Crises and Contexts

While some of the crises named in these four letters imply hardships faced by believers in the world, they also reflect hardships experienced within the church. If men came from James, spying out the freedom of Paul and his mission, as mentioned in Galatians, what might James have said about the Pauline mission in his own writings? Pointedly, does the Epistle of James bear elements of being an anti-Pauline circular? And, if 2 Peter reflects concerns about "people who are ignorant and whose faith is weak [who] twist [Paul's words] to their own destruction, just as they do the other scriptures" (2 Pet 3:16), might we infer a bit of additional tension here with the Pauline mission—at least with associates of Paul? Whatever the case, 2 Peter and Jude confront with some vehemence false teachers, labeling them as the villainous "Balaam" and "Cain" from the Old Testament (false prophets and brother-killers), so here we see attempts to address concerns within the Christian movement as well as the problems of living as followers of Jesus in an adversarial world. Unrealistic are views of the early church that see it as trouble-free and unified on all accounts—even among apostles. Indeed, there was unity within the diversity, but there was also diversity within the unity.[1]

James and Paul—Missions in Conflict?

It is no accident that Galatians/Romans and James were hot points of contention between Martin Luther and officials in the Catholic Church in the early sixteenth century; those tensions were likely germane to Christian leaders in the first century, as well. As Luther challenged the works-righteousness of his day and the granting of indulgences (certificates assuring the forgiveness of sins) in exchange for monetary contributions, his contention was bolstered by the Pauline gospel of salvation, received freely as a gift of grace through faith (Rom 4:2-22; Gal 3:6-18). In response, James was used as a counterfoil by Catholic theologians. Faith without works is dead, they affirmed; and Abraham was justified not by faith alone but by his *works* (Jas 2:18-26). However, was this debate simply a factor of differing interpretations of scripture, or might it also reflect historical conflicts underlying the biblical texts themselves? A closer look at the context may help.

Given that the Jerusalem Council in Acts 15 was called as a means of reconciling several aspects of contention following the first Pauline mission,

---

1. See James D. G. Dunn, *Unity and Diversity in the New Testament: An Inquiry into the Character of Earliest Christianity*, 3rd ed. (London: SCM Press, 2006).

one wonders if aspects of those tensions might be reflected in the writings of Paul and James, two of the central figures at the Council. In particular, the contrastive parallels between the gospel-letters of Paul (Galatians and Romans) and the wisdom-letter of James seem to reflect a sustained dialogue. They debate whether the word of God is actualized by hearing or by doing, and they have different takes on Genesis 15:6 and Habakkuk 2:24.

James in a Corrective Dialogue with Paul and His Associates?

- Is God's word actualized by hearing or by doing?
  - (*Paul A*) "You irrational Galatians! . . . Did you receive the Spirit by doing the works of the Law or by *believing* what you heard?" (Gal 3:1-2; Rom 10:16-17)
  - (*James A*) "You must be *doers* of the word and not only hearers who mislead themselves." (Jas 1:22)
- Abraham and righteousness (joint citations yet differing interpretations of Gen 15:6)
  - (*Paul B*) "In the same way that Abraham *believed* God and it was credited to him as righteousness, those who *believe* are the children of Abraham." (Gal 3:6-7; Rom 4:3-22)
  - (*James B*) Wasn't Abraham "shown to be righteous through his *actions* when he offered his son Isaac on the altar? . . . Abraham believed God, and God regarded him as righteous." (Jas 2:21-23)
- Is righteous living by faith or by works? (joint citations of Hab 2:4)
  - (*Paul C*) "But since no one is made righteous by the Law as far as God is concerned, it is clear that the righteous one will live on the basis of *faith*." (Gal 3:11; Rom 1:17)
  - (*James C*) "So you see that a person is shown to be righteous through *faithful actions* and *not through faith alone*. . . . As the lifeless body is dead, so faith without actions is dead." (Jas 2:24-26)

On the face of it, James indeed seems to be engaged correctively with Paul's message of God's righteousness being established by grace through faith, not by works of the Law. Then again, on basic subjects, Paul and James agree. Both are critical of outward religiosity, although Paul refers to it as "works of the Law," while James challenges religious posturing that is devoid of charity. And both affirm the importance of trusting in God and the conviction that inward faith is expressed outwardly in terms of loving action. Therefore, it cannot be said that James and Paul disagree with each other on the basis of salvation as being faith or as being the importance of works as expressions of righteousness. After all, Paul declares in Romans 2:13: "It isn't the ones who hear the Law who are righteous in God's eyes. It is the ones who do what the Law says who will be treated as righteous." And according to James 5:15, "Prayer that comes from faith will heal the sick, for the Lord will restore them to health." Therefore, the thrusts of their messages also cohere.

Paul and James in Coherent Agreement on Faith and Works

- Both are critical of outward religiosity without inward authenticity

   o (*Paul A*) "We know that a person isn't made righteous by the works of the Law but rather through the *faithfulness* of Jesus Christ." (Gal 2:16)

   o (*James A*) "True *devotion*, the kind that is pure and faultless before God the Father, is this: to care for orphans and widows in their difficulties and to keep the world from contaminating us." (Jas 1:27)

- Both advocate trusting in God as the only way forward

   o (*Paul B*) "Don't think of yourself more highly than you ought to think. Instead be reasonable since God has measured out a portion of *faith* to each one of you." (Rom 12:3)

   o (*James B*) "Whoever asks shouldn't hesitate. They should ask in *faith*, without doubting. Whoever doubts is like the surf of the sea, tossed and turned by the wind." (Jas 1:6)

- Both call for charitable deeds as the true evidence of faith

   o (*Paul C*) "Being circumcised or not being circumcised doesn't matter in Christ Jesus, but *faith working through love* does matter." (Gal 5:6)

○ (*James C*) "Someone might claim, 'You have faith and I have action.' But how can I see your faith apart from your actions? Instead, I'll show you my faith by putting it into practice in *faithful action*." (Jas 2:18)

Despite overall agreement between the missions of James and Paul, however, first-century tensions still may have been real. Especially if the more conservative Jewish contingent of the Jesus movement was worried about Gentiles who came to faith without being expected to adhere to central aspects of Jewish faith and practice, one can appreciate the assertion that faith on its own is insufficient. Thus, one must appreciate the religiously conservative consternation over the success of the Pauline mission, especially if outward signs of Jewish orthodoxy were not apparent. Likewise, Paul pushed back with some energy against the influence of men who came from James, whom he calls the party of circumcision (group, not festival—Gal 2:12); he thus intensely opposes the Judaizing tendencies among critics of his mission, as grace is received by faith, not works of the Law. Therefore, these contextual tensions are certainly understandable, and reading James, Galatians, and Romans within that light is essential for grasping the intensity of their meanings.

Social-Status Tensions within the Church

Another set of tensions is also reflected in James, but the issue is one of socioeconomic status rather than religious practice. As a significant number among the Jerusalem priesthood are reported as joining the Jesus movement in Acts 6:7, this must have created a new set of challenges, as members of different societal strata were now faced with the challenge of creating community together. As Sadducees in Jerusalem would have been accustomed to asserting their political and economic influence in society at large, the tendency for members of the community on lower rungs of society would have been to seek to garner favor by showing them special treatment because of their wealth, status, and influence. This tendency toward favoritism is confronted by James, who regards all as equal before the Lord. If a man comes to meeting wearing a gold ring and fine clothes, James rebukes favoring him over the poor man in rags (Jas 2:1-4). He further reminds his audience that it is the poor who are the heirs of the kingdom, and that the wealthy are known for dragging people into court, implicitly over the repayment of debts (2:5-7). In such a challenge, James asserts that people are dishonoring the poor, and that the rich—even as believers—find it all too easy to dishonor the Lord if they fail to embrace his teachings on equality, humility, and generosity.

The Persecution of Christians in Rome

If the Petrine Epistles indeed were written in Rome, awareness of the political situation will help illumine their context. While a common inference is that the church in Rome was undergoing current persecution under Nero when these letters were written, they also may have been produced before the fire in Rome (64 CE), after which Nero's persecution of Christians escalated. Nonetheless, the reputation of Jesus followers (first called *Christianoi*—"Christians," or "Christ-niks"—in Antioch, Acts 11:26) in Rome was a problematic one. First, given that Caesar Claudius had expelled Jews from Rome in 49 CE over dissension regarding *"Chrestus,"* it is likely that Jesus followers were blamed by Jews and others for being divisive. This preceded Paul's visit by a decade or more, and one of Paul's main reasons for writing Romans was likely to assuage tensions between adherents of Jesus and Jewish members of Roman society. Second, the novel fact that Jesus followers worshipped together with slaves and masters, Jews and Gentiles, males and females—with upper- and lower-class members of society sharing table fellowship together—was likely puzzling to Rome's aristocracy. It must have seemed ludicrous to break down the established economic and social strata among long-time Roman citizens, calling into question the very sanity of Christians. Third, given that crucifixion was a penalty reserved for seditious criminals, Jesus's followers' worshipping a victim of crucifixion must have been hard to fathom. Further, with Jewish zealotry on the rise in the 40s and 50s, leading to Rome's cracking down on Judea from 66–73 CE, associations with Jewish insurrectionists must have posed an obstacle for Jesus adherents to overcome.

Therefore, it is not hard to imagine why Nero picked on Christians in 64 CE after his burning the city got out of hand, if not before. Within such a context, it is easy to appreciate how the stage was set for Christians to be blamed as scapegoats, leading even to their public humiliation and death by Nero and his forces. Indeed, 2 Peter is written from the perspective of the author's anticipated martyrdom (2 Pet 1:12-15), so it is from a situation ranging from the early-to-middle 60s CE that the Petrine Epistles were likely written.

False Teachers—Continued

In most of the New Testament epistles and letters, admonitions are given to stay away from sinful practices and to avoid false teachers and their instruction. Sometimes the concerns are specific; at other times they are general. While scholars have tended to view New Testament adversaries as reflecting early Gnosticism exposed in the mid-second century, it is naïve to think that the pre-gnostic mission to the Gentiles had no dissension on matters of faith and practice from day one. The opposite is far more likely. At every stage and incidence of Christian outreach to non-Jewish populations, the challenge was twofold: first, to help people understand the gift of God's grace received by faith in Jesus as the Christ—in contrast to prevalent myths and philosophies; second, to help people understand and commit to the heart of Jewish religious and lifestyle expectations, even if not all of its outward forms were embraced. This appeal to faith in Christ and the resultant change in behavior is explicit in 1 Peter 1:13-21.

In even sharper confrontations of false teachers who might advocate different doctrines and standards, 2 Peter and Jude share a common set of admonitions, bolstered by appeals to angels (2 Pet 2:4, 11; Jude 1:6) and woeful harkening back to the sinful residents of Sodom and Gomorrah and their punishments (2 Pet 2:6; Jude 1:7). Here an interesting confluence with concerns over distortions within the Pauline mission is apparent. What 2 Peter 3:11-16 describes as the twisting of Paul's teaching about holy living and godliness by unlearned men who likewise distort the scriptures, Jude 1:4 names more pointedly: "Godless people have slipped in among you. They turn the grace of our God into unrestrained immorality and deny our only master and Lord, Jesus Christ." Whether or not the same false teachers are here implied, common rhetoric is shared: Jude 1:18 quotes (or is quoted by) 2 Peter 3:2-4, which reminds people of the prediction that "in the last days scoffers will come, jeering, living by their own cravings, and saying, 'Where is the promise of his coming? After all, nothing has changed—not since the beginning of creation, nor even since the ancestors died.'" In the two letters a shared set of descriptions expose the character of false teachers along several lines of concern.

Characteristics of False Teachers

- Even angels were judged by God; so shall be the false teachers (2 Pet 2:4; Jude 1:6)

- They are "irrational animals, mere creatures of instinct" (2 Pet 2:12; Jude 1:10)

- They "enjoy unruly parties in broad daylight"—acting as seductive "blots and blemishes," corrupting your love feasts (2 Pet 2:13; Jude 1:12)

- "They are always looking for someone with whom to commit adultery"—"on the lookout for opportunities to sin" (2 Pet 2:14; Jude 1:7)

- They follow the way of Balaam, the false prophet who led others astray (2 Pet 2:15; Jude 1:11)

- Their condemnation is sure (2 Pet 2:3, 9, 17; Jude 1:7, 11, 13-15)

- They are grumblers and scoffers, living by their own desires (2 Pet 3:3; Jude 1:16, 18)

Therefore, the General Epistles display tellingly the sorts of issues faced within communities of faith and between them, as traveling ministers and prophetic teachers taught in ways that made sense to them, even if somewhat different from the ways of their more Jewish counterparts. Interestingly, anticipation of the Lord's return seems to have conveyed two effects. First, it promised a reward to the faithful: suffering for Christ in the present world is to be vindicated by being glorified with him in the next. Second, it leveraged accountability toward the unfaithful: warning that false teachers and immoral persons will be judged when the Lord returns and dispenses just rewards. Therefore, those who deny the second coming of Christ are exposed as problematic, not simply because they fail to embrace the conviction that he will return, but also because they take license to live according to their own desires and schemes rather than submitting to the life-producing ways of God.

II. Features of the General Epistles

Other than Hebrews, the General Epistles are all rather short—covering a modest number of themes, but calling overall for right belief and action. The letters attributed to James, Peter, and Jude are more notably Jewish in their perspective, perhaps two or three decades earlier than the more Gentile-oriented letters attributed to John. They also engage a distinctive set of traditions—some of them cohering with Jesus traditions embedded in the Gospels. They fit what is known of the ministries of Peter and James, although very little is known of Jude. While this does not prove aspects of authorship, it does offset some of the problems ascribed to traditional views.

Wisdom That Is from Above

One of the distinctive features of the Epistle of James is the way it emphasizes the value of wisdom. In James, wisdom is centrally connected to love; it bears direct implications regarding relationships with God and others. In relation to God, wisdom is a gift from God, to be sought and welcomed; it roots centrally in being able to see one's situation and condition from the perspective of divine understanding. When sufferings and hardships come, how should they be met? Rather than resented, they should be welcomed as opportunities for growth and the development of personal character. Therefore, the truly wise person will view trials and ordeals as occasions for joy. After all, those who stand firm in times of trial will be found worthy before the Lord, and in surviving an ordeal one is strengthened in ways that could not have happened otherwise (Jas 1:2-12).

Wisdom from above also enables one to embrace a humble and gracious lifestyle. The source of most conflicts in community is jealousy, selfish ambition, the craving of possessions, and selfish desires—ways of living and being that deny the truth (Jas 3:13–4:10). These lead to strife, contention, and disorder, but *wisdom from above* is "pure, and then peaceful, gentle, obedient, filled with mercy and good actions, fair, and genuine. Those who make peace sow the seeds of justice by their peaceful acts" (3:17-18). Not only does friendship with the world make one an enemy of God, but it also puts one at odds with other members of the community. The way of wisdom, however, is rooted in humility towards others—grounded in God's faithfulness and grace. As believers humble themselves, God will lift them up. Therefore, heavenly wisdom brings about reconciliation with persons as well as with God.

James and the Jesus of Matthew

Given that James represents the Jerusalem-based Jesus movement, it conveys a number of Jewish ideals that also resemble the teachings of Jesus—especially those preserved in the Gospel of Matthew. One can therefore understand why the Matthean tradition is thought to have developed for several decades within the Jerusalem community of believers before the Roman invasion between 66 and 73 CE scattered the movement to other Jewish centers, such as Antioch or Damascus. A particularly interesting feature of James is that it bears over a dozen similarities with the teachings of Jesus in the Sermon on the Mount. These connections are so pronounced that at least some sort of traditional contact is probable; it could even be that the teachings of Jesus influenced the ministry of James, or that the Matthean rendering of Jesus's teachings was influenced by James and other leaders within this particularly Jewish center of the early Jesus movement. Whatever the case, note these similarities.

Parallels between James and the Sermon on the Mount

- Consider it joy when you face challenges (Jas 1:2; Matt 5:11-12)

- Be complete and whole (Jas 1:4; 2:22; Matt 5:48)

- Those who ask, believing, will receive (Jas 1:5-12; Matt 7:7-11)

- Judge not, for you will be judged accordingly (Jas 1:12-13; 4:11-12; 5:9; Matt 7:1-5)

- God's ways involve humility, grieving/mourning, righteousness, mercy, peace, meekness, purity (Jas 1:9-10, 20-21, 27; 2:13; 3:17-18; 4:6-10; 5:11; Matt 5:3-10, 20; 6:33)

- Good gifts come from the Father (Jas 1:17; Matt 7:11)

- Anger is not God's way (Jas 1:19-20; Matt 5:22)

- Be doers of the word, and not hearers only (Jas 1:21-27; Matt 7:24-27)

- True devotion is authentic before God and charitable toward others (Jas 1:26-27; Matt 6:1-6)

- Loving one's neighbor is a good place to begin, but not the end (Jas 2:8-9; Matt 5:43-47)

- On keeping the Law entirely—adultery and murder (Jas 2:10-13; Matt 5:27-32)

- A tree is known by its fruit (Jas 3:12; Matt 7:15-20)

- Earthly treasures are short lived and finally of no avail (Jas 5:1-6; Matt 6:19-21)

- The prophets offer an example of steadfast patience (Jas 5:10; Matt 5:12)

- Swear not and do not make solemn pledges by heaven or earth (Jas 5:12; Matt 5:33-36)
- Let your "Yes" be yes and your "No" be no (Jas 5:12; Matt 5:37)

Petrine Testimonies to the Lord's Ministry

While modern scholars have been quick to challenge traditional views of New Testament authorship overall, and especially with reference to the Petrine Epistles, the fact is that a good number of features do cohere with themes associated with the Apostle Peter and his life as well as details resembling a Petrine memory of Jesus's ministry and teachings. While Peter's ministry and influence cannot be confined to the traditional material underlying Mark and that which is added by Matthew, the presentation of Peter in Acts combined with the Petrine Epistles and Jude demonstrate several features that cohere among these writings. Although Petrine authorship is impossible to prove or disprove, 1 and 2 Peter do indeed convey memorable testimonies to, and noteworthy features of, the Lord's ministry.

First, a set of scripture references associated with Peter and his ministry is notable in the Petrine cluster of letters, as the fulfillment of the prophets' words is now actualized in the mission of Christ and declared by the apostles (2 Kgs 17:23→Acts 3:18-26; 10:43; 1 Pet 1:10-12; 2 Pet 3:1-2; Jude 1:17). In contrast to their presentations in the Gospels and Acts, these scripture images are used in the Petrine Epistles as examples of what it means to follow Jesus in terms of faith and practice. In particular, five biblical themes all bear direct implications for Christian discipleship within the Petrine tradition.

Scripture Fulfillments in the Petrine Tradition

- The *suffering servant of Isaiah*, fulfilled in Jesus, becomes a calling for his followers to be willing to suffer likewise (Isa 53→Mark 8:31; Acts 3:13-26; 4:24-30; 1 Pet 2:19-25; 3:17–4:2; 4:16-19; 5:6-11; 2 Pet 1:1; Jude 1:1)
- Bearing *"the name"* of Christ may itself lead to suffering (Ps 79:9-13→Mark 13:13; Acts 5:41; 1 Pet 4:14)
- God's enemies are made *a footstool for the feet of God's anointed*—seated *at God's right hand*, inspiring boldness (Ps 110:1→Matt 5:35; Mark 12:36; Acts 2:34-35; 5:31; 1 Pet 3:22)

- Jesus's cross is called *"the wood"* or *"the tree"* (Deut 21:22-23➟Mark 14:43, 48; Acts 5:30; 10:39; 1 Pet 2:24—see also Gal 3:13), he bore the curse for humanity

- Jesus, *the stone the builders rejected,* is now the *cornerstone* (Ps 118:22➟Mark 12:10; Acts 4:11; 1 Pet 2:4-7)

A second feature of the Petrine letters is that they reference first-hand memory of Jesus's ministry and reflect upon his mission and words with intentionality. Of course, such features do not prove particulars of authorship, but they do cohere with the traditional connecting of Peter with these writings. For instance, 1 Peter 5:1 appeals to other church leaders "as a fellow elder and a witness of Christ's sufferings," and 2 Peter 1:16-18 harkens back to the encounter on the Mount of Transfiguration: "we witnessed his majesty with our own eyes. He received honor and glory from God the Father when a voice came to him from the magnificent glory, saying, 'This is my dearly loved Son, with whom I am well-pleased.' We ourselves heard this voice from heaven while we were with him on the holy mountain." References to Jesus's ministry also seem to be firsthand rather than secondhand reports, such as descriptions of Jesus's suffering on the cross (1 Pet 2:21-24). And, the significance of things observed is also conveyed (v. 23): "When he suffered, he did not threaten revenge. Instead, he entrusted himself to the one who judges justly."

A third feature worth noting is that much of the content in the Petrine letters coheres with themes and features associated with perceptions of Peter's personal contributions elsewhere in the New Testament. Presented as a bold personality in the Gospels and Acts, the author of 1 Peter calls for believers to be bold and steadfast in their faith, standing firm in times of trial (1 Pet 2:20; 5:9-12). Note also that Mark is mentioned as a companion (1 Pet 5:13), bolstering the likelihood that the first Gospel does indeed include some of Peter's memory of Jesus's ministry. Another Petrine theme is the anticipated return of Christ. If Peter's understanding of the kingdom's coming before the passing of the apostles is echoed in Mark 9:1 (as engaged correctively in John 21:18-23—pointing to Peter as the source of Mark's presentation), it is no surprise that emphases upon the Lord's imminent return would accompany Peter's continuing legacy (1 Pet 4:7; 5:4-10; 2 Pet 1:16-21; 2:9; 3:1-14; Jude 1:17-19). Likewise, appeals to submitting to authority are especially associated with Peter's personal impact—obeying God rather than humans (Acts 4:19; 5:29; 11:17; 1 Pet 2:4, 15-16; 4:1-6, 17) and calling for submission to authorities and honoring domestic codes (1 Pet 2:13–3:7). Therefore, it is not surprising that Peter's legacy is associated with institutional church leadership (Matt 16:17-19; Acts 1:15-26) and pastoral shepherding ministries (John 21:15-17; 1 Pet 5:1-4), as Christ's caring for his flock is continued by his followers and their followers (Mark 6:34; 14:27; John 10:1-16; Rev 7:17).

Fourth, much in the Petrine Letters is reminiscent of Jesus's teaching as represented in several gospels—including Mark and Matthew—but also echoed in the Johannine and Lukan writings. Again, whether or not this material goes back to the exact words of Jesus, it clearly reflects apostolic memory of his teachings delivered for the benefit of his followers several decades later. It is no surprise that having heard the teachings of the Lord in the form of admonitions and exhortations in the Petrine Letters, believers should have desired that the stories of the Lord's ministry be rendered in ways that would also be of benefit to the churches. If Peter's "son Mark" (1 Pet 5:13) were with him in Rome, it would not be surprising if the gospel narrative bearing his name should have sought to preserve some of that content in narrative form.

Jesus Tradition in the Petrine Letters

- People are called to follow Jesus (Mark 1:17; 2:14; 8:34; 10:21; John 21:19, 22; 1 Pet 2:21)

- Followers of Jesus should be on their guard and alert (Mark 13:9, 34-37; 2 Pet 3:17; 1 Pet 1:13; 5:8)

- People should not be anxious but should cast their cares upon God, who cares for them (Matt 6:25-30; 1 Pet 5:7)

- Those who humble themselves will be exalted by God (Luke 14:11; 1 Pet 5:6)

- The good works of the faithful bring glory and praise to God (Matt 5:16; 1 Pet 2:12)

- Followers of Jesus should not pay back evil with evil (Matt 5:39; 1 Pet 3:9)

- Those who suffer for Christ's sake are indeed blessed (Matt 5:11; 1 Pet 4:14)

- Silver and gold are not to receive primary value (Matt 10:9-10; Acts 3:6; 1 Pet 1:7, 18)

- The seed of the gospel grows in hidden ways (Mark 4:3-32; 1 Pet 1:22-23)

- The Lord wishes that none should perish (Matt 18:14; John 3:16; 2 Pet 3:9)

- Be prepared, as the Lord will return as a thief in the night (Matt 24:42-43; 2 Pet 3:10)

The vast number of similarities between the Petrine cluster of letters and the Gospels, including the presentation of Peter in Acts, shows a clear trajectory attributed to apostolic memory and delivery. While it cannot be proved that Mark's content included Peter's preaching (Eusebius, *Ecclesiastical History* 3.39), it also cannot be said that such a view is lacking in evidence. Of course, there were many developments and approaches within the early church, and they also influenced each other, but distinctive presentations of Jesus also were influenced by the ministries of those who furthered those traditions. From a cognitive-critical perspective, the dialogue between perception and experience among first- and second-generations of Christian leaders is here apparent. In addition to representing the teachings of Jesus, we also see here a robust proclamation of the Christ Events accompanied by implications for Christian living. Central within that association is the suffering servant.

The Suffering Servant Then and Now

The most frequently cited Old Testament verse in the New Testament is Psalm 110:1, and the most frequently cited Old Testament chapter in the New is Isaiah 53—featuring the suffering servant. Distinctive in the presentation of the suffering servant motif in 1 Peter is the way that the focus is not so much on the atoning work of Jesus on the cross—a central interest in Acts and Paul—as it is on the connection between the suffering of Jesus and that of his followers. In 1 Peter 2:11-25 the message is to live as strangers in the world, submitting to authorities and being willing to suffer, especially if it is unjust. Pointedly, Peter asks in verse 20, "But what praise comes from enduring patiently when you have sinned and are beaten for it? But if you endure steadfastly when you've done good and suffer for it, this is commendable before God." It is from this vantage point that Martin Luther King Jr. derived the basis for his nonviolent approach to civil disobedience—believing that unjust suffering in the name of truth and what is right will always be redemptive. After all, Jesus is the paradigmatic example of the redemptive suffering of the innocent (2:22-24). This also reveals the way the world is radically changed.

Therefore, Isaiah's faithful servant, Israel, typologically fulfilled in Christ, points the exemplary way forward in dealing with oppression and persecution in the world. It is essential that if suffering comes, it not be for doing evil or violence; such hardship is too easily justified as deserved punishment by those keeping the law. Rather, if suffering is to be undergone, it must be a result of doing what is right instead of for doing what is wrong (1 Pet 3:14–4:19). That is the basis for embracing house codes and submitting to elders and authorities; such is the basis for humble and compelling Christian witness, whereupon God indeed restores and empowers the faithful. As in the Pauline writings, appeals to domestic standards in the Petrine writings are not extended as a means of keeping people in their place or setting up divinely ordained hierarchies and institutions. Rather, they are cited as a call to live respectably within Greco-Roman society so as to be an effective witness to the work of Christ and his way. The gospel of God is radical enough; that will speak for itself. After all, his is the glory and the power forever; these do not belong to the forces of human empires and their means (5:5-11).

III. The Message of the General Epistles

The overall purpose of the General Epistles is edification—they seek to build up their audiences and to establish them in their faith. As circulars to be read among the churches, they were likely carried and read by ministers who were not the authors, but their being shared would have established and maintained contact with the authors as a means of extending apostolic and associated influence to those who might benefit from it. Several highlights of their message thus include the embracing of wisdom from above, affirming the new priesthood established by Jesus, and waiting expectantly for the Lord's return.

Consider It All Joy

Like 2 Corinthians and 1 Peter, James addresses the problem of human suffering and disappointment from a faith-based perspective. Rather than seeing trials as reasons for discouragement, they are "occasions for joy" (Jas 1:2). It is precisely because one cannot see the results of one's trials that one must exercise trust, which calls for wisdom—the capacity to envision mundane aspects of life from a transcendent perspective. And wisdom will be given to those who ask; therefore, one should not waver in doing so (1:3-8). It takes a good deal of faith to be grateful to God *despite* undesired trials; it takes a good deal more faith to thank God *for* them. And yet, when this is done, one affirms the fact that although one might not have wanted things to turn out the way they did, even disappointments allow new possibilities to emerge.

Along these lines, the poor actually are blessed with higher spiritual status, as they are forced to trust more profoundly and extensively, thus emboldening their faith in God (Jas 1:9-12). The wealthy, however, might not be honored by God, despite receiving honor within society. Their wealth may even become an obstacle in their capacity to sense their full reliance on God. Likewise, it is the humble stance that shows the way of wisdom—saying, "if the Lord wills," this or that will happen, rather than boasting on human planning and ingenuity (4:13-17). This is why intensive prayer and authentic confession also tend to make a difference; they become added opportunities to exercise one's faith (5:13-18). Thus, the eyes of faith enable one to glimpse the larger picture of what God might be doing in and through one's trials, rather than simply trying to avoid them. Faith produces human endurance, but it also envisions what God might be doing, beyond what is outwardly apparent.

You Are a Royal Priesthood

One of the ways 1 Peter seeks to encourage its audiences is to affirm their new identity as "a holy priesthood" and "a chosen race, a royal priesthood, a holy nation, a people who are God's own possession" (1 Pet 2:4-10). Whereas believers were often disparaged among religious and civic leaders in Asia Minor due to their challenging of Jewish convictions regarding the Law and opposition to other religions and their idolatries, 1 Peter seeks to edify. Despite Christ being the building block that was rejected, he is become the cornerstone of the whole new world. Therefore, his followers form a new and royal priesthood, connecting humanity with God. As a result, they should always be prepared to give an answer for the hope that is within them. This will allow those who malign believers to become convicted of their misjudgments, and it will force those who have disparaged believers to come under conviction as they are faced with the truth about the gospel and its representatives (1 Pet 3:13-17). In providing his audience a reasoned basis for their convictions, he also calls for exemplary living as a compelling witness.

Prepare for Christ's Return and Judgment

In that preparedness, believers also become readied for Christ's return, though no one knows the day or the hour. Reminding them of what he had written in his first letter, the author of 2 Peter admonishes his audience to recall in the present what had been foretold by the holy prophets, the Lord, and the apostles: in the last days a number of things will happen. While scoffers will question, "Where is the promise of his coming?" as though nothing ever changes (2 Pet 3:4), the Day of Judgment is indeed coming. While "a single day is like a thousand years and a thousand years are like a single day" unto the Lord (2 Pet 3:8), he is not slow in his coming. Indeed, he will appear like a thief in the night, and his followers will want to be found faithful on that day (vv. 9-10). As the present world will be destroyed, believers await a new heaven and a new earth, where righteousness is at home; that is why they should live into that reality in the here and now.

In anticipation of that new, heaven-on-earth reality, Christ's followers should "make every effort to be found by him in peace—pure and faultless" (2 Pet 3:14). This is the same message that "our dear friend and brother Paul wrote to you according to the wisdom given to him, speaking of these things in all his letters" (vv. 15-16). While some fail to grasp that message, Peter's audience is to be on its guard, growing in grace and knowledge of the Lord and savior Jesus Christ. It is to him that all glory belongs, and therefore this world is seen in new perspective from the vantage point of the next. That's what makes all the difference (2 Pet 3:1-18)!

IV. Engaging the General Epistles

In engaging the General Epistles, several themes surface as bearing special weight. First, in dealing with disappointment and suffering, how can the faithful exercise faith in ways that embrace the value of what may come from trials rather than resenting or becoming discouraged by them? Of course, a challenge calls forth boldness and courage, but when the outcome is not apparent, how can one trust in God's sovereignty and provision beyond what can be seen? That takes a special measure of faith. Regarding suffering, how does the example of Christ encourage his followers? Given that his suffering was undeserved, it bore with it redemptive possibilities. Therefore, all the more reason for living in blameless and upright ways; if one is deserving of punishment, that is simply a fair judgment. According to Martin Luther King Jr., who built his philosophy of nonviolent resistance upon the teaching of 1 Peter, undeserved suffering is always redemptive in its possibility. Therefore, Christ as the ultimate suffering servant not only died for the redemption of the world, but his example bears with it redemptive possibilities to emulate in every generation—then and now.

Second, despite the fact that those with wealth and influence might have greater capacity to reward those who treat them well than do the poor, God is no respecter of persons, and in Christ there is no distinction between societal groupings or stratifications. Therefore, treating all persons with benevolence and honor is the way to live, extending God's love and grace to all. Pure religion undefiled involves caring for widows and orphans; those with greatest need invite the greatest consideration. Right living is a direct reflection of one's spiritual faith, and it also makes a clear testimony in the world. After all, while God's grace is received alone by faith, faith without works is dead. Even one's loving works, though, are empowered by grace, and the capacity to discern and address the needs of others is also a gift from God.

Third, as in the first century, speculation may arise regarding the Lord's return or ways of envisioning the last days. Here Peter's counsel matches that of Paul in the Thessalonian letters: continue to anticipate the Lord's return, but do not allow that hope to detract from the present calling, which is to honor his already having come by one's faithful living in the here and now. While God's judgments will bring their rewards on the last day, making things right, Christ is indeed come, both on the shores of Galilee and through the sanctifying work of the Spirit (1 Pet 1:2), who spoke through the prophets (1:11) and continues to empower his followers (4:14) in all ways they need. Therefore, rather than give credence to speculation and guesswork, celebrating Christ's having already come in one's life is the best way to anticipate his final return at the end of the age—whenever that may be.

Chapter 13

The Johannine Epistles

Begin with the text. Read the three Johannine Epistles, and note important themes and details that come to mind.

Author: John the Elder

Audience: churches in the region (1 John), a particular church and its leader (2 John), Gaius (3 John)

Time: ca. 85 CE (1 John), ca. 90 CE (2 John), ca. 95 CE (3 John)

Place: traditionally, Ephesus

Message: Love one another (1 John), reject teachers who deny Jesus came in the flesh (2 John), extend hospitality to others despite its having been denied by Diotrephes (3 John).

While some scholars question whether the Johannine Epistles were written by the same author (given their differences) or in a different sequence, reasons for doing so are less than compelling. While 3 John is the most different from the others, and while its canonical acceptance was delayed into the third century, this does not imply a difference of authorship. Rather, as the Elder's concern shifts toward dealing with the withdrawal of hospitality from a local Christian hierarchical leader, this would involve a different set of issues and would explain the letter's delayed reception among other Christian leaders—especially hierarchical ones. Second John, though, is very similar to 1 John, as the appeal to love one another continues, as does the labeling of false teachers as "antichrists." The three antichristic passages in 1 and 2 John, however, reflect two different crises, rather than one, so considering the particular contexts and crises of the Johannine Epistles is essential to grasping their meaning. Their relation to the Gospel of John is also an important consideration, and in my view, rather than seeing them as written before or after the Johannine Gospel, the best answer is: *both*. Assuming the first and final editions of John were written around 80–85 and 100 CE, respectively, the Epistles were likely written between those two editions, with the Gospel being finalized by John the Elder after the death of John the beloved disciple (according to Eusebius, after 98 CE). Interestingly, the Epistles of John both affirm the content of the Gospel and illumine the context behind its later material (John 1:1-18; 6; 15–17; 21).

I. Crises and Contexts

Before considering the crises and contexts behind the Johannine Epistles, the reader would do well to review the crises and contexts behind the Johannine Gospel. Over several decades, Johannine Christianity faced a multiplicity of crises—sometimes more than one at the same time—and as new crises emerged, older ones did not disappear. Rather, they often lingered, and their effects continued to be felt, even as new and acute crises emerged. That is a more realistic approach to history and the real-life setting of early Christianity.

Therefore, the larger Johannine situation faced at least seven crises over seven decades, and the Johannine Epistles reflect four of those crises (the third through the sixth as described above in the chapter on John's Gospel) with defining clarity. Following the first period in Palestine (30–70 CE), the second period of the Johannine situation involved moving to one of the mission churches, such as Ephesus in Asia Minor (ca. 70–85 CE), where two crises became acute. First, while being welcomed within the local Jewish synagogue, believers soon found their commitment to Jesus as the Jewish Messiah and Son of God to be at odds with the local Jewish leadership. This led to followers of "the Nazarene" being disciplined, which led to a departure from the synagogue and the joining of Gentile believers in Jesus in their meetings for worship. Second, with the reign of Domitian (81–96 CE) came a new emphasis on emperor worship as a requirement for all subjects of the Empire, although Jews were granted a dispensation—expected to pay a special tax instead. This placed believers in a difficult situation, especially if they were distanced from the synagogue. If they did not worship Caesar—offering incense or saying "Caesar is Lord"—they were subject to punishment and even death.

The third period of the Johannine situation saw the transition to engaging other Christian communities and leaders within Asia Minor (ca. 85–100 CE), and again, two largely-sequential-yet-overlapping crises presented themselves. First, when faced with required emperor worship during the reign of Domitian, not all Christians felt this was a problem. Therefore, as traveling Christian ministers delivered their messages of encouragement, not all of their teachings were agreed upon by others. Teachers and ministers from non-Jewish backgrounds especially might have found it easier to advocate cultural assimilation and participation in emperor-laud (especially if outward only) than to stand against it. They defended their non-suffering view of discipleship with a non-suffering view of Jesus as totally divine (the heresy known as "Docetism"), and they are labeled "antichrists" by the Elder. A second crisis followed this one, in that "Diotrephes, who likes to put himself first" (3 John 1:9-10) had been excluding Johannine traveling ministers from his own community, willing also to expel his own church members who took them in. It could be that he thought Johannine Christians were heretical Docetists, but he was more likely threatened by their egalitarian and Spirit-based approach to church organization and leadership—an approach he felt was obsolete and ineffective, given church splits and further crises in the Johannine situation. That approach also probably threatened his appeal to structural hierarchy as a means of holding his own church together and establishing his own authority. While reflected also in the Gospel of John, these four crises thus receive further definition from the particulars of the Johannine Epistles.

Disagreements over What Is Sinful and Worldly

The first contextual issue that presents itself when reading the first two chapters of 1 John involves claims to be "without sin." While some scholars have seen this claim as a forerunner of second-century Gnosticism, this view is problematic. Indeed, later Gnostics claimed to have received secret knowledge from God, resulting in their enlightenment and achieving the status of perfection. They could do no wrong (in their view) and were thus incorrigible. Gnostics also tended to deny the humanity of Jesus as the Christ, as he was seen to be divine and thus immune to suffering and death. However, this view is problematic on several accounts.

First, rather than Gnosticism, the main issue in Ephesus and Asia Minor in the late first century had to do with pagan worship and associated practices, as the cults of Artemis and Aphrodite were prominent in the region. Remember that Paul had caused a riot in Ephesus three decades earlier, as Demetrius the silversmith accused Paul of destroying the Ephesians' relationship with their patron goddess, Artemis. As a result, thousands of citizens gathered in the amphitheater, shouting for two hours: "Great is Artemis of the Ephesians!" (Acts 19:28, 34). And, regionally, the nearby city of Aphrodite had its own cult of goddess worship to advocate; the promise of most pagan religions was prosperity and the good life, in exchange for sacrifices, offerings, and cultic loyalty. Therefore, pagan worship was of major civic and economic interest in the Greco-Roman world. Unlike Jewish worship, though, some forms of pagan worship attracted participants by appealing to materialism and eroticism, promising prosperity and fertility in return for patronage. Cultic prostitution, drunkenness at festivals, and gluttony at feasts were thus common factors of civic celebrations, and while Jewish believers would have been more likely to stand aside from such practices, Gentile believers took more time in transitioning from one set of cultural standards to another. So, claiming to be without sin in 1 John more likely represents disagreement over particular moral issues within the church rather than perfectionism proper.

Second, the Elder too argues for sinlessness, so perhaps the adversaries are simply quoting the Elder's rhetoric back to him: "We know that everyone born from God does not sin, but the ones born from God guard themselves, and the evil one cannot touch them" (1 John 5:18). It is doubtful that the Elder was a gnostic perfectionist. And, the reason for the Elder's writing is that his audience might *not sin*; although if they do, they "have an advocate with the Father" (2:1); he especially wants them to avoid a death-producing sin (5:15-17). The reason the Elder declares that any person born of God "does not sin" and that one who "remains in relationship to him does not sin" (1 John 3:6) is to motivate people to stop sinning in particular ways: "Any person who sins has not seen him or known him. Little children, make sure no one deceives you. . . . Those born from God don't practice sin because God's DNA remains in them. They can't sin because they are born from God" (3:6-7, 9). Therefore, his point is that if people are really born of God, they should not be sinning; it is a call to confession of sin and repentance from it.

Third, the intense discussions of "sin" probably have to do with the fact that members of Johannine Christianity were in heated disagreement over what was sinful and what wasn't. Insignificant sins were not the issue, but death-producing sins were. At this point, the last word is likely the first word of 1 John: "Little children, guard yourselves from *idols*!" (5:21, emphasis mine). In other words, those claiming to be without sin were not claiming to be perfect; they were claiming that it was not sinful to participate in civic festivals honoring the local deities and in pagan celebrations—including the rising tide of required emperor worship. This is likely what the Elder, along with Johannine Christians of Jewish background and convictions, was labeling as "a sin that results in death." One need not pray about that; it is totally wrong (5:15-17). Rather, Christ came to be the atoning sacrifice for the sins of the entire world (2:2; 4:10), so forgiveness is real, but it hinges also upon repentance and acknowledgment of sin—the very thing some believers were reluctant to do.

Finally, this explains why "loving the world" is identified as a problem. On one hand, all unrighteousness is sin (5:17), but if pagan celebrations yoked well-being and prosperity to participation in cultic practices and civic celebrations, and if they enticed people with festivals and appealed to sexual drives and prosperity, it is understandable that the Elder would draw a sharp line between loving the world and loving the Father. The problem is not that Johannine Christianity is sectarian (as some recent scholars have argued); the problem is that it is cosmopolitan. It is seeking to maintain Jewish standards of faith and practice among Gentile believers who are unevenly convinced about what is sinful and what is not. Therefore, the appeal to love not the world—if related to idolatry, local pagan festivals, and Gentile Christians' reluctance to embrace all Jewish standards—is perfectly understandable (2:15-17):

> Don't love the world or the things in the world. If anyone loves the world, the love of the Father is not in them. Everything that is in the world—the craving for whatever the body feels, the craving for whatever the eyes see and the arrogant pride in one's possessions—is not of the Father but is of the world. And the world and its cravings are passing away, but the person who does the will of God remains forever.

A Return to the Synagogue—An "Antichristic" Schism

Another set of misunderstandings deserves correction regarding the identity of the Johannine antichrists. Whereas modern scholarship has wrongly seen them as Gnostics, and fundamentalists have anachronistically seen them as Marxists, several biblical facts deserve a closer look. First, the term "antichrist" never occurs in Revelation; it only occurs in 1 and 2 John. Therefore, it might be related to "the Beast" and "666" in Revelation, but it is not necessarily the same threat being identified. Second, the three passages in 1 and 2 John describe the antichrists as plural, not a singular individual, and their action is both past and contemporary with the Elder's writing, not a futuristic prediction. Third, it appears that we have here two different movements of people in the late first century (one group leaving and the other coming) also espousing different theological investments (one group denying Jesus being the Messiah/Christ and the other denying he came in the flesh). They did not think of themselves as antichrists, but they are labeled as such by the Elder within his Christ-centered situation, seeking to diminish their appeal.

Therefore, the first antichristic crisis (1 John 2:18-25) involved a church split—a schism—in which fellow believers abandoned John's church and likely joined another religious group, probably the local synagogue from which they'd come (v. 19). They deny that Jesus is the Christ and thus deny the Father as well as the Son (v. 22). Therefore, the first antichristic threat likely involves Jewish believers abandoning John's community and returning to the religious and social security of the synagogue in a way that involved diminishing their belief that Jesus was the Messiah/Christ, the Son of God. Showing a bit of pained griefwork here, the Elder exclaims: "They went out from us, but they were not really part of us. If they had been part of us, they would have stayed with us. But by going out from us, they showed they all are not part of us" (1 John 2:19). So what happened here? A likely scenario goes something like this.

First, as Johannine and other Jews and Christians resettled among diaspora Jewish communities in Ephesus and elsewhere, the move toward greater adherence to the Law of Moses within Pharisaic Judaism came to emphasize Jewish monotheism and the *Shema* (Deut 6:4). Second, the adding and use of the *Birkat ha-Minim* to the twelfth of the Eighteen Benedictions in Jewish synagogue worship functioned to discipline Jesus adherents in their faith expressions. They were free to respect Jesus as a prophet, but not as the Messiah/Christ or as the Son of God. That was blasphemous (John 10:33). Some Jesus followers did acquiesce, and some of them (not necessarily in this setting) came to be known as Ebionite Christians—having a low Christology while still seeing themselves as believers in Jesus. Third, some, or perhaps most, of the Johannine Jesus adherents felt they had to leave the synagogue and began worshipping with Gentile believers on a regular basis. This created another set of crises, as they probably felt that Gentile believers were not Jewish enough—causing these Jewish believers to miss the benefits of synagogue membership and association. Fourth, having sought to discipline perceived ditheists rather than to expel them, some of those who left were apparently courted to return to the synagogue by its leaders. This is probably what is reflected by the first antichristic threat—a church split, whereby some abandoned their community and faith in Jesus as the Christ and Son of God and returned to the familiarity and socio-religious comfort of the Jewish synagogue.

In addressing this sort of problem, the Elder echoes the evangelist's insistence that the Son and the Father are one; to deny the Son is to lose the Father precisely because the Father sent the Son, who represents him faithfully. In Jewish agency theology, following Deuteronomy 18:15-22, the prophetic agent is in all ways like the one who sent him. Therefore, in leaving the community of the Son, schismatics would be forfeiting the very thing they sought to regain in rejoining the synagogue—the pleasure of *the Father*. The Elder thus continues to admonish others not to defect, but to abide in Jesus and the teaching about Jesus as the Christ that they had heard from the beginning (2 John 1:9). This solidarity is described as the Lord's old and new commandment—to love one another (1 John 3:11, 23-24; 4:7-21; 2 John 1:5). Therefore, if one really loves God, one will not abandon one's brothers and sisters, who share loving fellowship with the Father and the Son.

Docetizing Preachers—The Threat of "Antichristic" Assimilation

While the first antichristic crisis in the Johannine situation involved a church split, the second crisis labeled antichristic by the Elder involves anticipated church visits by "false prophets" traveling in ministry, teaching that Jesus did not come in the flesh (1 John 4:1-3; 2 John 1:7). The heresy here referenced is known as Docetism (not Gnosticism), and it might even be the case that the refusal to acknowledge the suffering humanity and death of Jesus was *not* the main tenet in these teachers' public ministries. Rather, if they were teaching a distorted view of grace versus works (cf. the distortions of Paul's teachings, 2 Peter 3:15-16; Jude 1:4), it could be that these were simply Gentile Christian preachers, traveling in ministry, who embraced a more liberal stance toward assimilation than Jewish-Christian leaders would have desired. Therefore, the Elder applies a litmus test to their orthodoxy: if they are unwilling to acknowledge the suffering humanity of Jesus—especially its implications, that his followers must also be willing to suffer if required by the truth—then they are to be regarded as "antichrists" and denied access to believers' communities. It is often the practical implications of a doctrine that make it attractive to some but also dangerous in the minds of others. Therefore, the attraction of docetic teachings regarding a non-suffering Jesus lies in its implications for non-costly discipleship and cheap grace.

The cost of discipleship increased substantially when Domitian added the expectation of emperor worship to civic festivals and local celebrations during his reign (81–96 CE). As he required even his officers to regard him as *dominus et deus* ("Lord and God"), the penalty for not participating in the imperial cult within the Roman Empire would have been costly. Here the correspondence between Pliny the governor of Bithynia (in northeast Turkey, more than two hundred miles from Ephesus) and Emperor Trajan (around 110 CE) is telling. It seems that the new governor is seeking counsel as to whether existing policies (likely going back to the days of Domitian, two decades earlier) regarding penalties aimed at Christians refusing to worship Caesar publicly should be continued. After all, the Jesus movement was not only becoming prevalent in the major cities but was also taking root in the villages and towns—nearly putting pagan worship cults out of business. Within his letter, Pliny makes the following inquiries and statements:

Pliny's Letter to Emperor Trajan (*Letters* 10:96)

- I don't know what to do concerning the trials of Christians:
  - Should young and old, male and female, upper and lower class be punished the same?
  - Is there room for pardon if they repent, denying Christianity and reverencing your idol?
  - Are they guilty simply for bearing "the name" if they have committed no other crimes?
  - Increasingly, anonymous lists are being circulated with names of accused; what should I do with those?
- Here's what I've done regarding those who recant:
  - I give all the accused a threefold warning, intermixed with beatings, that if they do not deny Christianity they will be executed; fanatics who still refuse but are Roman citizens I send to Rome for trial
  - Some of these denied ever being Christians; others said they used to be—between three and twenty years ago—but no longer were; they simply had a practice of:
    - meeting together on a given day of the week before dawn
    - partaking of ordinary food and singing a hymn to Christ as though he were a god
    - promising not to commit theft, murder, adultery, or dishonesty
  - Their innocence was proven by the fact that they:
    - denied being Christians
    - worshipped Caesar's image and the images of our gods—partaking of frankincense and wine
    - cursed Christ

- o We know that such persons *cannot* be Christians and are innocent of bearing "the name"
- o I therefore outlawed Christian assemblies, and pagan worship cults are now making a comeback
- However, some do not recant, which poses a problem:
  - o Two young women Christian ministers were brought up for trial; the truth about their practices was exacted by means of torture
  - o All they were guilty of, however, was being a part of this ludicrous superstition
  - o Therefore, I have suspended such trials, awaiting instructions as to whether the standard procedures should continue to be followed

From Pliny's letter, several standard procedures are clear. By the time of his writing, it had become a crime to simply bear the name "Christian," as followers of Christ had garnered a reputation for being strong-willed in their refusal to participate in emperor worship. This was seen as sedition, punishable by torture or death. However, if people accused of such a crime were willing to recant—denying being Christians, sacrificing to Caesar and other gods, and cursing Christ—they were eligible for being pardoned. Further, in the mind of Pliny and others, those who had denied Christ in such public ways could not be considered guilty of bearing the name "Christian," so they were to be declared innocent of such a crime. The trial and torture (and perhaps execution) of two upstanding Christian women ministers, though, has given Pliny pause. As their only crime was being a part of a fanatical cult, should he really keep punishing otherwise upstanding citizens such as these?

Emperor Trajan's Response to Pliny (*Letters* 10:97)

- You have done the right thing in checking into allegations regarding these "Christians," although no single rule applies in all cases; here, though, is how to proceed:
  - o Do not seek out Christians to persecute them, and do not give credence to anonymous lists

        ○ However, if an accusation is made against someone and he is guilty of the charge of being a Christian, he must be punished

        ○ If, though, he denies being a Christian and proves it by worshipping idols, he should be acquitted despite earlier suspicions

Note, however, Trajan's response and its implications. On one hand, Christians should not be hunted down; therefore, it is wrong to think that Romans programmatically persecuted all Christians across the Empire (although widespread persecution did take place during the second half of the third century CE between the reigns of Decius and Diocletian). On the other hand, the law remained in place, charging that those refusing to worship Caesar or to deny being Christians should be put to death—having been duly warned. While such codes were uneven in their enforcement, it cannot be said that Christian discipleship was a cost-free venture. On this score, some claims of recent scholars are overly simplistic or naïve. Given that Ignatius, Bishop of Antioch, was marched off to his death in Rome around 115 CE as a means of making examples of Christians who refused to bow down to Caesar, it is understandable that traveling Christian prophets and ministers might have found it all too easy to legitimate costless discipleship with a non-suffering Jesus. This is why the second antichristic crisis was identified as a threat by the Johannine Elder, as it relates directly to those who claim their assimilation with worldly ways is not sinful. The water and the blood (and the Spirit) testify to the human suffering of Jesus (John 19:34-35; 1 John 5:6-8), and this testimony empowers the authentic believer to overcome the world.

The Rejection of "the Friends" by Diotrephes the Primacy-Lover

In addition to dealing with fellow Christian prophets and traveling ministers teaching assimilation and easy discipleship, the third period of the Johannine situation involved dealing with other tensions within the early Christian movement. For whatever reason, a local Christian leader named Diotrephes has been rejecting Johannine Christians from coming to his church, and he is even willing to expel members of his own community if they extend them hospitality (3 John 1:9-10). While the details do not make it clear what issues were involved, the Elder mentions the following actions:

Actions by Diotrephes

- He does not welcome us—the brothers and the sisters

- Makes wicked accusations against us

- Forbids others to extend hospitality to Johannine Christians and throws them out of the church if they do so

While some scholars have seen Diotrephes as a charismatic egomaniac (loving to be first implies egoism), his being an early church bishop interested in preserving his structural authority is a stronger inference. If Diotrephes is willing to expel members of his own church who welcome Johannine Christians, that fact suggests that he is exercising a considerable degree of hierarchical authority there, perhaps putting into place a structural approach to maintaining Christian unity as championed by Ignatius of Antioch around this time period. As Ignatius advocated appointing a single bishop in every church as a means of addressing docetizing and Judaizing threats, especially among churches facing Roman persecution, one can appreciate that his being accused of being a "primacy lover" (*ho philoprōteuōn*—in Greek, the lover of "first-ness") bears a strong resemblance to emerging hierarchical leadership in the third Christian generation. As Simon Peter is called "first" among the disciples in Matthew (cf. Matt 10:2—*prōtos*) the Elder's labeling Diotrephes as the primacy-lover suggests that he is perceived as viewing his positional authority to be based upon Matthew 16:17-19, where Peter (and those following in his wake) receive the keys to the kingdom and the authority to make binding judgments. The actions of the Elder confirm such an inference.

Actions by the Elder

- He writes to "the church" complaining about Diotrephes's behavior

- He promises to visit, holding Diotrephes accountable in person

- He encourages Gaius to extend hospitality to others, despite its having been denied him and others

Now it could be that "the church" the Elder has written to is the local community where Diotrephes is serving, but if he is willing to expel his own members who cross him, that seems unlikely. Therefore, "the church" to which the Elder has written more likely represents an emerging Christian center (likely Antioch), whence Diotrephes has derived his authority. Note also that in planning to visit Diotrephes personally, the Elder seems to be following the Matthean structure of accountability (Matt 18:15-17) as a means of adhering to proper process. This also explains why the Elder finalizes the testimony of the beloved disciple (whose testimony is *true*) regarding Jesus's leading through the Holy Spirit—to whom all believers (not just Diotrephes) have equal access. In that later gospel-material, Peter is portrayed as affirming Jesus's sole authority (John 6:68-69), the Spirit of Christ leads people into all truth (John 15–16), and Peter is commanded to feed and nurture the sheep if he really loves the Lord (John 21:15-17).

II. Features of the Johannine Epistles

Conspicuous among the Johannine Epistles are their similarities to the Johannine Gospel. Clearly they represent the same sector of Christianity, although they also possess considerable differences. For instance, while the Gospel writer holds truth in tension—embracing the humanity and divinity of Jesus, present and future eschatology, embellished and existential views of miracles, and universal and particular presentations of salvation through Christ, the letters are somewhat devoid of tension. If one does not embrace Jesus as the Messiah/Christ, that person is the antichrist; if one does not acknowledge Jesus's having come in the flesh, that person is the antichrist; if one does not love one's brother, one does not love God; while God loved the world, the believer cannot. These sorts of either-or approaches to aspects of faith and practice differ from a both-and dialectical approach. The evangelist's thought is more characteristic of a first-order, original thinker; the Elder's seems more like a second-generation leader, committed to what has been heard from the beginning as a set of right answers versus their alternatives. Put otherwise, the evangelist calls for abiding *in* Christ (John 15:1-8); the writer of the Epistles calls for abiding in the teaching *about* Christ (2 John 1:9). Therefore, we probably have here the work of more than one Christian leader in the Johannine situation, whose works reinforce each other.

Echoes between the Gospel and the Epistles

One of the great Johannine riddles involves the relation of the Gospel to the Epistles. Were the Epistles written before the Gospel or after? Debates have raged over this question, and the fact is that a good deal of evidence supports both sides of the issue. If, however, the composition of the Gospel involved at least two editions, with (most plausibly) such material as the prologue (John 1:1-18), John 6 (the feeding of the five thousand, the sea-crossing, the Bread-of-Life discourse, and Peter's confession), John 15–17 (a second round of last-discourse material), and John 21 (the great catch of fish and the recommissioning of the disciples after the first ending in 20:31) were added a decade or two later, following the death of the beloved disciple (John 21:22-24), it is likely that the Johannine Epistles were written before *and* after the Johannine Gospel—between its two editions. One cannot, of course, be certain about such a history of composition, but it might also explain how the influence seems to go both ways.

Especially in 1 John we find a number of echoes from the Johannine Gospel; it is as though the Elder is affirming familiar content and applying it to the audiences in writing his letters. At the outset, he affirms the Johannine theme of testifying to "what we have seen and heard" (1 John 1:3; Acts 4:20; John 3:32) as a witness to first-hand encounter with the subject—the word of life. It could be that John the Elder was also an eyewitness to the ministry of Jesus; at the very least, he stands with the eyewitnesses, appealing to first-hand encounter with Christ as a direct spiritual experience. Many of the Gospel's themes are here applied to aspects of Christian discipleship, and perhaps this what the Elder means when he announces "the eternal life that was with the Father and was revealed unto us" (1 John 1:2). Note, therefore, a number of themes in the Johannine Gospel that are also developed in the Johannine Epistles.

Johannine Gospel Themes Echoed in the Epistles

- God's love for the world leads to the sending of the Son, who also loves his own (John 3:16➠1 John 4:9-11)

- The representative link between the Father and the Son is featured as essential (John 3:35; 5:19-21; 8:28➠1 John 2:22-24; 4:14; 2 John 1:3, 9)

- Jesus has come as the light of the world (John 1:9; 8:12; 9:5; 12:46➠1 John 1:5-7), yet the world loves darkness rather than light; therefore, believers are called to love neither the world nor its ways (John 3:19➠1 John 2:15; 3:1)

- The "new commandment" brought by Jesus is now the "old commandment," which has been heard from the beginning

351

(John 13:34-35➡1 John 2:7; 2 John 1:4-6)—"Love one another!"

- The Holy Spirit, through anointing believers, will teach them all things (John 14:26➡1 John 2:27)

- As the Son is the first advocate with the Father, he will also send another advocate—the Holy Spirit—who will be with his followers and in them (John 14:16-17➡1 John 2:1)

While these themes are part and parcel of the Gospel's first edition (ca. 80–85 CE), the evangelist probably continues to preach and write during the time that the Epistles are written by the Elder. In that sense, some of the Epistles' themes also seem to be echoed in the Gospel's later material. Given community defections, false prophets deying Jesus's coming in the flesh, inhospitable treatment by Diotrephes and his kin, and the worshipping of Christ the word of life in the Epistles, it is not surprising that in the Gospel's later material we find Jesus's prayer for unity, an emphasis upon his fleshly suffering and death, his promise to lead his followers through the Holy Spirit—available to all—and for a fuller worship hymn to Christ the *Logos*. Just as the Elder writes in order that the joy of his audiences may be complete as they share fellowship with the Father and the Son through the workings of the Spirit (1 John 1:4; 2 John 1:12; 3 John 1:4), these themes are also emphasized by the Johannine Jesus in the Gospel's later material (John 15:11; 16:24; 17:13).

Issues in the Johannine Epistles Echoed in the Gospel's Material

- The Spirit of Truth guides people into all truth (John 15:26; 16:13 ⬅1 John 4:6)

- As the Son laid down his life for his friends, so ought believers to do for one another (John 15:13 ⬅1 John 3:16)

- Despite the church schism in the Johannine situation, Jesus prays that his followers will be one, in order that the world will know that he is sent from the Father (John 17:21-23 ⬅ 1 John 2:19)

- The anti-imperial confession of Thomas, "My Lord and my God!" connects with the final admonition of the first Epistle: Stay away from idols! (John 20:28 ⬅1 John 5:21)

- Against the false teachings of the Docetists, Jesus really did come in the flesh, and the eyewitness saw that water and blood came forth from his side; even apostles will suffer and die (John 1:14; 6:51-58; 19:34-35; 21:18-24 ◀▥1 John 4:1-3; 5:6-8; 2 John 1:7)

- Faith in Christ is the victory that overcomes the world . . . because he has (John 16:33 ◀▥1 John 4:4; 5:4)

However the Johannine Gospel and Epistles were composed, we still have a confluence of themes and issues between them. Whether or not it was the Elder who bound up the witness of the beloved disciple after his death and circulated it among the churches, declaring that his testimony is true (John 19:35; 21:24; 3 John 1:12), this endeavor fits the distinctively Johannine claim about the one who is the way, the truth, and the life (John 14:6). After all, Jesus promises to lead his followers into truth, and truth itself is always liberating (John 8:31-32).

Engagements with Internal Adversaries

In addition to addressing external threats, the Johannine Elder also engages internal threats by setting up a variety of if-then statements designed to challenge the problematic views and actions, seeking to outline more profitable ways forward. In two sets of claims and two sets of corrective responses, the Elder engages the beliefs and practices of his opponents, although there may have been more than one set of concerns. For instance, the claims of those he seeks to correct in 1 John 1:6–2:11 might not represent the views of the secessionists in 2:18-25, and these clearly do not coincide with the teachings of the false prophets addressed in 4:1-3, despite both groups being labeled "antichrists." They probably, however, relate to issues regarding trivial and serious sins in 5:16-21, as the particulars of what is sin and what isn't are the main concern.

The first set of quoted claims highlights the incongruity between claiming to have fellowship with Christ while also living in sin—probably the sort of behaviors that Jewish believers were trying to convince Gentile believers to leave behind. Here the Elder pits one's claims to have fellowship with God against one's actions that are not pleasing to God. Living that way is self-deception, and if one does not acknowledge one's sinfulness, even God is made a liar; as Paul would say, "all have sinned and fall short of God's glory" (Rom 3:23).

If we claim . . .

- "'We have fellowship with him,' and live in the darkness, we are lying and do not act truthfully." (1 John 1:6)

- "'We don't have any sin,' we deceive ourselves and the truth is not in us." (1 John 1:8)

- "'We have never sinned,' we make him a liar and his word is not in us." (1 John 1:10)

Having exposed the incongruity of those who claim not to be sinning with three if-then challenges, the Elder poses three if-then ways forward. The goal here is not theological—getting people to accept a theory of the atonement; it is ethical—convincing people to repent if they have really received Christ's cleansing from sin. Therefore, the Elder's reason for writing is to convince people not to sin, although if they do sin, they still have an advocate with the Father (1 John 2:1).

But if we . . .

- "live in the light in the same way as he is in the light, we have fellowship with each other, and the blood of Jesus, his Son, cleanses us from every sin." (1 John 1:7)

- "confess our sins, he is faithful and just to forgive us our sins and cleanse us from everything we've done wrong." (1 John 1:9)

- "do sin, we have an advocate with the Father, Jesus Christ the righteous one. He is God's way of dealing with our sins, not only ours but the sins of the whole world. This is how we know that we know him: if we keep his commandments." (1 John 2:1-3)

After the first pair of three-fold syllogisms, the Elder then constructs another pair, again challenging what people might be claiming. Claiming to know and abide in Christ implies Christlike behaviors; if not, something has to give.

The one who claims . . .

- "'I know him,' while not keeping his commandments, is a liar, and the truth is not in this person." (1 John 2:4)

- "to remain in him ought to live in the same way as he lived." (1 John 2:6)

- "to be in the light while hating a brother or sister is in the darkness even now." (1 John 2:9)

As with the earlier set of challenges, here again the Elder also poses a threefold way forward. The Elder brings love into the picture and couches his ethical concerns in terms of the larger picture—right action is a reflection of loving God and loving one another.

But . . .

- "the love of God is truly perfected in whoever keeps his word. This is how we know we are in him." (1 John 2:5)

- "I am writing a new commandment to you, which is true in him and in you, because the darkness is passing away and the true light already shines." (1 John 2:8)

- "the person loving a brother and sister stays in the light, and there is nothing in the light that causes a person to stumble." (1 John 2:10)

In these rhetorical constructions, the Elder's primary goal is to call people within the community of faith to acknowledge sinful behavior for what it is, to confess it repentantly, and to live in ways that do not fracture the community or dishonor the ways of God. In pursuing this goal, he highlights the incongruity of those who claim to have fellowship with God and believers while not living by righteous standards, arguing that one cannot have it both ways. He further motivates right action as a call to love one another, seeking to live in such a way as not to be divisive and not to deny the values of Jewish-Christian faith and practice. Also of concern is simply caring for the physical needs of one's brothers and sisters (1 John 3:17). To fail to care for them is to remain in darkness and to hate one's brothers and sisters in the Lord.

Resorting to Labeling

An idiosyncratic rhetorical approach used by the Elder involves resorting to labeling, using invective and derogatory terms to villainize his opponents and to discourage others who might be tempted to follow their unfavorable examples. The fact that some of these targets are outside of John's community—either having abandoned it or intending to visit it—might account for the strong language used. These labels, however, are not terms used by the adversaries themselves. Rather, within this truth-oriented, Christ-centered, sibling- and God-loving community, such terms as "liar," "antichrist," "brother-killer," and "primacy-lover" are intended to disturb.

The Elder's Invective Slams

- "The one who claims, 'I know him,' while not keeping his commandments, is a *liar*, and the truth is not in this person." (1 John 2:4)

- Those who left us, who deny Jesus is the Messiah/Christ, never really were a part of us; they are *antichrists* and *liars*—denying the Father and the Son. (1 John 2:18-23)

- Those who do not love one another in community are *brother-killers—the party of Cain*. (1 John 3:12)

- False prophets who refuse to acknowledge Jesus's coming in the flesh are also the *antichrists*. (1 John 4:1-3; 2 John 1:7)

- "If anyone says, I love God, and hates a brother or sister, he is a *liar*." (1 John 4:20)

- "I wrote something to the church, but Diotrephes, who likes to put himself first, doesn't welcome us." (3 John 1:9)

Again, these invective slams are targeted to offset the effects of several crises in the Johannine situation. Those who are liars and brother-killers are those who refuse to live by the moral standards of this Jewish-Christian community, fracturing communities because of their moral indifference and example. The antichristic schismatics have likely broken off and returned to their familiar religious certainty, failing to acknowledge Jesus as the Christ, the Son of the Father; whereas the docetizing traveling ministers are labeled as false prophets and antichrists because they deny the suffering humanity of Jesus and its implications for costly discipleship. The primacy-loving Diotrephes has not really embraced the servant-leadership example of Jesus, and while the Elder might not oppose structural hierarchies in themselves, effective Christian leadership must facilitate the leadership of Christ through the Holy Spirit, which is always a function of truth and carried out in love.

An Appeal to Identity

Just as the Elder challenges the incongruity between what people claim and what they do, he levies a special charge against those who claim to love God but do not act lovingly toward other members of the community. While the charge of not loving one's brothers and sisters is used rhetorically to call people to confess and abandon sinful behaviors, not to leave the community of faith, and not to receive false teachers, it also relates to caring for the physical and social needs of less advantaged members of the community.

> This is how we know love: Jesus laid down his life for us, and we ought to lay down our lives for our brothers and sisters. But if a person has material possessions and sees a brother or sister in need and that person doesn't care—how can the love of God remain in him? Little children, let's not love with words or speech but with action and truth. This is how we will know that we belong to the truth and reassure our hearts in God's presence. (1 John 3:16-19)

In calling believers to love one another, the Elder roots such actions in the love of God. If one does not meet the physical needs of brothers and sisters, how can that person claim to love God (1 John 3:17)? And, if one claims to love the Father, whom one has not seen, how can one not love one's brothers and sisters, whom one has seen (4:20)? Therefore, to love God is to love one's brothers and sisters, and not to love one's brothers and sisters discredits one's love for God (4:7-21). Therefore, in seeking to maintain group solidarity and communal unity, the Elder appeals to the love of God and one another as its basis. One cannot claim the former without demonstrating the latter—it is an appeal to integrity and identity, and such is the thrust of its rhetorical power.

III. The Message of the Johannine Epistles

The Johannine Elder follows the example of the beloved disciple in declaring explicitly why he is writing. Taken at face value, he is writing in order that their joy might be full (1 John 1:4), in order that they might not sin (2:1), to offer a new commandment (2:8), because they know the truth

(2:21), because people are trying to deceive them (2:26), and in order that they may know they have eternal life (5:13). In addition, the Elder lists two sets of reasons he is writing to three groups of people: to little children, to parents, and to young adults, specifying particular concerns that speak to their condition. For children in the faith, he emphasizes receiving forgiveness in Jesus's name and a close relationship with the Father; for parents, he affirms their long-term knowing of the one who has existed from the beginning; for young people, he assures them of their victory over the evil one because of their embracing of the word of God within (1 John 2:12-14).

Here the Elder shows his awareness of people's needs at various stages of their faith development. The faith-development need of children is to be assured of their eternal destiny and the divine embrace. The faith-development need of mature adults, wrestling with the complexities of life, is to remain rooted in the human-divine relationship despite the changing of circumstances. The faith-development need of young adults is to develop a support group among the faithful and also to establish their autonomy within diverse and even hostile environments. And these needs continue to be addressed in the Elder's overall message.

Live in the Light

As one of the Elder's primary goals is to call his audiences away from sinning (1 John 2:1), one of his primary means of furthering that goal is to develop sets of dichotomies—life-producing options to be chosen versus death-producing venues to be rejected. In this he follows the motivational dualism of the Dead Sea Scrolls, which set the Children of Light over and against the Children of Darkness (in both cases fellow Jews), also represented in the sketching of "the two ways" in the *Didache* (a manual of discipline for early Christians), outlining "the way of life" versus "the way of death." In contrast to the explanatory dualism of the Johannine Gospel (accounting for why some stayed in the dark rather than embrace the light—John 3:18-21), the dualism of 1 John calls for adherence to the way of light, love, truth, goodness, righteousness—the way of God and Christ versus its diametric alternatives. After all, if "God is light and there is no darkness in him at all," one cannot maintain fellowship with God while living in darkness; but living "in the light in the same way as he is in the light" is the only way to enjoy true fellowship and the gift of life (1 John 1:5-7). Note these leveraged dichotomies as means of motivating righteous choices over their alternatives.

The Motivational Dualism of 1 John

- Live in the light rather than darkness (1 John 1:5-7; 2:8-11)

- Chose the way of life over the way of death (1 John 1:1-2; 2:25; 3:14-16; 5:11-21)

- Embrace love versus hatred (1 John 2:9-11; 3:13-18; 4:19-21)

- Adhere to the good and the righteous one versus evil and the evil one (1 John 2:1, 13-14, 29; 3:7, 12; 5:18-19; 2 John 1:11; 3 John 1:11), rejecting sin and lawlessness (1 John 1:7–2:2; 3:4-9; 5:16-18)

- Abide in the truth and not with those who are liars and deceivers (1 John 1:6-8; 2:4, 8, 21-22, 26-27; 3:7, 18-19; 4:1, 6; 5:6, 10, 20; 2 John 1:1-4; 3 John 1:3-4, 8, 10, 12)

- Choose the side of God the Father and his Son Jesus Christ (1 John 1:2-7; 2:1, 5, 14-17, 22-24; 3:1, 8-10, 20-23; 4:1-16, 20-21; 5:1-20; 2 John 1:3-4, 9; 3 John 1:6-7, 11) instead of aligning oneself with the devil, Satan, or the evil one (1 John 2:13-14; 3:8-12; 5:18-19)

"Love One Another!"—The Old and New Commandment

What Jesus gave as a new commandment in John 13:34-35, that his followers should love one another, the Elder propounds as "an old commandment that you had from the beginning" (1 John 2:7; 2 John 1:4-6). Keeping Christ's commandments shows that one really knows and loves him (John 14:15, 21; 1 John 2:3-6; 5:2-4), and those who keep Christ's commandments and affirm his will and pleasure receive whatever they ask (John 14:12-14; 1 John 3:22). To abide in Jesus's love is to keep his commandments, and his commandments involve believing in him and loving one another, just as he abides in the Father's love and displays that love to others (John 15:9-17; 1 John 3:23-24; 4:7-21). Of course, the command to love one another is not exclusive to the Johannine tradition, as Paul and Peter call for believers to do the same (Rom 12:10; 13:8-10; 1 Thess 4:9; 1 Pet 1:22), but the "new commandment" issued by the Elder involves loving one another by means of distinguishing light from darkness and discerning truth versus error. The love command thus relates to extramural threats as well as intramural considerations.

Test the Spirits—A Call to Discernment

Because the command to love one another serves as a general means of addressing particular concerns, it is likely uneven in its effectiveness. While there may have been disagreement over what is sinful and what is not, the Elder's appeals to love not the world, to walk in the light rather than darkness, and to love one another instead of being brother-killers finally give way to specificity in the last verse of 1 John—*stay away from idols!* Sometimes the lack of specificity, though, is ineffective in the long run, as a general admonition might not be pointed enough to challenge a threat sufficiently. This may explain why Johannine Christianity faced defections from within and distortions from without. It may also account for the attraction of structural hierarchies of leadership in the third Christian generation, as older familial forms of organization seemed ineffective in combating Judaizing, docetizing, and assimilative threats. Therefore, the Elder calls his audiences to test the spirits, to see if they are from God or not (1 John 4:1).

In addressing the four prevalent crises facing the Johannine situation when the Epistles were written, the Elder's call for discernment is actually reflected in the ways he addresses the various crises. First, as Jewish members of the community might be tempted to abandon the fledgling Jesus movement and return to the religious certainty of the synagogue, the Elder reminds people that to abandon the Son is to forfeit the Father (1 John 2:22-23). After all, their fellowship is with the Father and the Son (1 John 1:3; 2 John 1:3), and to receive the Son is to embrace the Father (1 John 2:24; 4:15; 2 John 1:9), as the Son was sent by the Father to be the savior of the world (1 John 4:14).

Second, in addressing the challenges regarding increasing pressures to participate in emperor worship, the Elder calls for staying away from idols and challenging such practices as death-producing sins (1 John 5:16-21). Whereas a stone monument to the Greek goddess, *Nikē* (meaning "victory") adorns the entrance to Domitian's temple in Ephesus, reminding subjects of their dominated status, Johannine audiences are exhorted to have no fear, because fear is overcome by perfect love (1 John 4:18). Indeed, faith in Christ is the *victory* that overcomes the world (1 John 5:4).

Third, in engaging the ministries of traveling teachers, a special level of discernment must be exercised. While their teachings might sound acceptable, if they advocate assimilation with the world in ways that raise consternation, bolstered by a non-suffering Jesus, they should be rejected as reflecting the spirit of the antichrist, departing from the teaching about Christ (1 John 4:1-3; 2 John 1:7-9). The Spirit, the water, and the blood testify to the price

Jesus paid on the cross; that is what is also expected of his followers (John 19:34; 1 John 5:6-8; later manuscripts added a trinitarian formula here).

Fourth, in dealing with emerging hierarchical leaders who also reject Johannine Christians from their churches (3 John 1:9-10), the Elder calls Gaius and others to imitate not that which is evil, but that which is good (v. 11). As friends of Jesus, partnership with him extends beyond structures and status; it involves embracing a spiritual anointing and following him in dynamic and faithful ways.

Extend Hospitality—Despite Its Having Been Denied

As a personal letter to Gaius, one can understand why 3 John was one of the last of the New Testament writings to be canonized. After all, why should personal correspondence be preserved for general use among the churches—especially when this one is critical of an emerging church leader? Then again, its being connected with John the apostle and John the Elder made the difference, and it has stayed within the Christian canon since the end of the third century CE. While the inhospitable behavior of Diotrephes is the occasion for the letter, its main message is to encourage Gaius to show hospitality, despite its having been denied by others. While it is not clear what the role of Demetrius is, it appears that the Elder is encouraging Gaius to be willing to extend him hospitality, speaking highly of him on all accounts (3 John 1:12). Therefore, Gaius is exhorted to imitate not what is evil, but what is good (v. 11); in doing so, he will be a partner with the Lord.

IV. Engaging the Johannine Epistles

As the context of the Johannine Epistles exposes several issues at stake, engaging them in later generations involves identifying parallels and applying the content accordingly. First, how do Christians make meaningful determinations as to what is wrong and right within later, ambiguous contexts? If death-producing sins are especially weightier than others, how do believers in different settings garner a sense of what preserves essential Christian values, as well as what threatens them in terms of faith and practice? And how does one effectively encourage others to consider taking particular issues more seriously than they might, if they really love God and one another?

Second, how does one apply the Elder's warnings against the antichrists to oneself? After all, the two antichristic threats in the Johannine Epistles represent different groups of early Christians, who felt they were justified in the actions they took—one group leaving John's community in the name of religious certainty, and the other traveling in ministry teaching an easy path of discipleship. A living faith might forfeit dogmatic certainty, but the Elder believes this is exactly what commitment to the Son whom the Father sent involves. And, authentic faith might involve suffering and a costly commitment to the truth, but such is the only way to experience the fellowship of the faithful. In both cases, commitment to Jesus as the Christ is the answer, but that includes embracing his divine agency and suffering humanity.

And what about effective Christian leadership? Is it rooted in structure and calling the shots from a hierarchical position of authority, or does it root in the truth and its power to convince? After all, abiding in Christ involves the confirming presence of the Spirit (1 John 3:24; 4:13), and the Spirit testifies to the truth if believers will but attend (1 John 5:6-8). Of course, the best combination is official leaders who are also spiritually attentive and able to garner a corporate sense of truth and the Spirit's leading. When that happens, people are enabled to walk in the truth (2 John 1:4; 3 John 1:3-4), and truth itself testifies in ways that are confirming (3 John 1:12) as Jesus's followers partner with him and one another in furthering the truth (3 John 1:8).

Chapter 14

The Revelation of John

Begin with the text. Read Revelation, and note important themes and details that come to mind.

Author: "John" (Rev 1:1, 2, 4, 9; 22:8)

Audience: the seven churches in Asia Minor

Time: 95–100 CE

Place: from Patmos and Ephesus

Message: Hang on; be faithful; God wins!

The word for Revelation in Greek is *Apocalypsis*, which means "opening" or "disclosure"—a revelation from God as to what has been, what is, and what is yet to come (Rev 1:4, 8; 4:8; 17:8). The Revelation of John fits into a genre of Jewish literature known as apocalyptic literature, and without an awareness of the ways that apocalyptic literature functions, mistakes of interpretation easily follow. For instance, interpreters who are unaware of the first-century context might see Revelation as being futuristic, pertaining only to the end of the world—thus seeing it as a timetable for the end times, when it is not. Most of its rhetorical thrust is aimed at the contemporary situation of its author and his audiences in the late first century CE, so interpreting Revelation is greatly aided by understanding its original context. On the other hand, some might interpret Revelation as only being invested in first-century realities, when it also portrays the endgame of history, the final victory of Christ and his bride—the church—and what God is doing in the meantime. Much of the book's content is symbolic; the question is what its symbolism conveyed to its original audiences within their contexts. In that sense, understanding the literary forms and functions of the Johannine Apocalypse in its first-century setting enables one to identify relevant meanings in every generation since.

I. Crises and Contexts

As part of the Johannine corpus, Revelation faces the same four crises in the second and third periods of the Johannine situation in Asia Minor between 70 and 100 CE. External to the Christian movement, we see dialogues with Jewish members of society (those who claim to be Jews but are not, Rev 2:9; 3:9) and especially the Roman imperial presence ("where Satan's throne is," Rev 2:13). Internally, debates over morality and assimilation continue (versus the actions of the Nicolaitans and the teachings of the prophetess "Jezebel," Rev 2:6, 15, 20), and it is Christ who holds "the keys of Death and the Grave" (rather than Peter or his successors, Rev 1:18). Among these contextual issues, the most dominant crises involved the welfare of Christians under the reign of Domitian (81–96 CE), who re-instituted emperor worship as a means of asserting control and influence over the nations within the Empire. The main message of Revelation is that "God wins," but the particulars of that good news are informed by a more detailed consideration of its crises and contexts.

The Function of Jewish Apocalyptic Literature and Its Backgrounds

The character and function of Jewish apocalyptic literature is that it discloses, uncovers, and reveals what God is doing in the world despite apparent failures of God's protection, values, and reign. In that sense, apocalyptic literature speaks most powerfully to those who are suffering persecution and hardship, while still believing in the rightness of their cause and the ultimate power of God. Within such settings, believing in the ultimate triumph of good over evil and the righteous over the unrighteous, apocalyptic literature conveys images of God's action—both vindicating and avenging—within the larger scope of cosmic events. It draws on familiar historic and literary images and applies them to contemporary political realities, bending meanings and associations in ways that provide hope to the faithful and assurance of God's final victory and rewards.

The book of Revelation thus does not come out of a vacuum; its imagery is rife with literary, political, and religious associations. From a literary standpoint, much of its imagery incorporates precedents from the biblical books of Daniel, Ezekiel, Nehemiah, Isaiah, Psalms, and even Genesis. First-century Jewish audiences would have recognized many of the links, seeing them as fulfilling or echoing prophecies from long ago. In addition, much of the intertestamental Jewish literature is also apocalyptic. The books of Enoch and Baruch, Gabriel's Vision, and the apocalypses of Lamech, Moses, and

Sedrach, among others, represent Jewish apocalyptic works around or before the first century CE. Likewise, a number of Christian pseudepigraphal apocalyptic texts were written after Revelation between the second and fourth centuries CE, including apocalypses attributed to Adam, Peter, Paul, James, Thomas, and Elijah. Therefore, a fuller understanding of the literary background of John's Revelation helps modern readers appreciate the range of meanings and associations that would have been understood in its original setting.

When interpreting the meaning of particular symbols and images in Revelation, it thus serves the reader well to consider the use of that imagery in earlier and contemporary Jewish and Christian literature. For instance, the four beasts and creatures in Daniel and in Ezekiel are now seen differently, as are the four horses of Zechariah; the seven trumpet blasts of Joshua not only bring down the walls of Jericho, but they now open up new epochs in the cosmos; the two olive trees and seven lamps of Zechariah now connect with two witnesses and seven churches; the adversarial serpent and the paradise of the garden in Genesis are defeated and restored, respectively; the one who is pierced in Zechariah and the one coming from the heavens in Daniel are both victorious; the ten horns of Daniel, and Gog and Magog of Ezekiel, are seen as nations that make war against God's people, and yet Israel's God is on the throne, and the angel Michael will garner God's victory, as envisioned in Isaiah and Daniel.

Biblical Imagery Employed by Revelation

- God's agent coming on clouds from heaven (Dan 7➠Rev 1)
- The one who is pierced (Zech 12➠Rev 1)
- A river and the tree of life (Gen 2–3➠Rev 2; 22)
- The Lord on the throne (Isa 6➠Rev 4–8; 19–21)
- Two olive trees and witnesses (Zech 4➠Rev 11)
- Seven lamps (Exod 25; Zech 4➠Rev 1)
- Four beasts and creatures (Dan 7; Ezek 1; 10➠Rev 4–7; 14–15; 19)
- Seven eyes (Zech 4➠Rev 5)
- The Lamb that was slain (Isa 53➠Rev 5–7; 12–15; 17; 19; 21–22)

- Four corners of the earth (Isa 11➞Rev 7, 20)
- Seven trumpets (Josh 6➞Rev 8)
- Four horses (Zech 1, 6➞Rev 6)
- Michael, the angel of war (Dan 10➞Rev 12)
- The serpent (Gen 3➞Rev 12; 20)
- Ten horns (Dan 7➞Rev 12–13; 17)
- Fallen Babylon (Isa 21; Jer 51➞Rev 14; 18)
- The Lord's trampling the wine press (Lam 1➞Rev 19)
- Gog and Magog (Ezek 38➞Rev 20)
- A thousand years (Ps 90:4➞Rev 20)
- Twelve stones (Exod 28; 39; 1 Kgs 18➞Rev 21)

Again, this biblical imagery conveys several meanings within its apocalyptic settings. First, God is portrayed as being in control, despite how dismal things might seem. Second, the treachery of the powerful and their wickedness is portrayed in grotesque ways, evoking disgust with intentionality. Third, God's impending judgment is heralded as a means of challenging the powerful and emboldening the faithful. Fourth, connections are made regarding signs of the times, fulfilling earlier images and predictions, giving a sense of divine irruption into human history. Fifth, the endgame, where God and God's powers win, provides hope for the afflicted, encouragement to the faithful, and a restored heaven and earth for all. This material spoke to its original audiences in these ways in the late first century, and it continues to speak to the oppressed likewise in every generation since.

The Whole World Is Deceived and Following the Beast—Living under the Empire

Reminiscent of the hopeless exclamation of 1 John 5:19, that "the whole world lies in the power of the evil one," the author of Revelation continues in that same vein, as the "whole world" is being deceived and bowing down to the Beast (Rev 12:9; 16:14). Some modern interpreters find plenty of room here for application, but usually wrongly. If an adversary is detested, he must be doing the work of the ancient serpent; if an adversary is widely popular, that shows that he must be "the Beast," after whom the entire world is following. Such references in the Bible, however, are not futuristic in their thrust; they are aimed at contemporary, first-century targets, calling for the faithful not to bow down to the Beast, even if all others seem to be doing so.

While some recent scholarship has helpfully clarified that the persecution of Christians in the late first century was by no means as programmatic and widespread as it became a century and a half later, this is not to say that it was not experienced as real by Johannine Christians. Indeed, Ephesus was vying with Pergamum to the north for *neokoros* (temple-keeper) status as the leading imperial worship site in the region. The privilege of that status would involve huge imperial favors—building municipal roads, marketplaces, and public baths and featuring festivals in celebration of the emperor's birthday and regional events. Such celebrations would involve wearing garlands in procession, offering sacrifices (ranging from incense to fatted bulls) to Caesar and other local deities (such as Artemis), and carrying on for several days in the marketplace—eating the food offered to idols and enjoying the merriment of the festival. While Jews were given a dispensation and not required to worship the emperor, Gentiles did not have such a dispensation, and if they did not participate in the festivities—especially as leading citizens—this could jeopardize the political and economic status of the city and the region. Therefore, not only was there pressure from local Roman authorities; there was also considerable societal pressure for all citizens to support the city's status and welfare by making a good showing for Rome when the festivities were on.

Yoking festivals and religious celebrations to imperial domination, of course, was not a Roman innovation. The attempt to subjugate Jewish populations by such means over two centuries earlier by Antiochus Epiphanes of Syria is described graphically in 2 Maccabees, albeit in somewhat embellished terms. While features of the following paragraph were not necessarily in play in Jerusalem or within every major imperial city, some of the strategies employed by dominating forces seeking to control a region bear remarkable similarities with what is addressed in Revelation. Given that the most powerful means of resistance and loyalty are always religious, when the Seleucid (Syrian) stewards of the Greek empire attempted to control Galilee, Samaria, and Judea, they compelled Jews to forsake Jewish laws and to worship the Greek god, Zeus. They then issued a decree to other Hellenistic cities, requiring the same of their Jewish subjects—on pain of death if they refused.

Imperial Domination from Antiochus Epiphanes to Domitian (2 Macc 6:1-9 NRSV)

Not long after this, the king sent an Athenian senator to compel the Jews to forsake the laws of their ancestors and no longer to live by the laws of God; also to pollute the temple in Jerusalem and to call it the temple of Olympian Zeus, and to call the one in Gerizim the temple of Zeus-the-Friend-of-Strangers, as did the people who lived in that place. Harsh and utterly grievous was the onslaught of evil. For the temple was filled with debauchery and reveling by the Gentiles, who dallied with prostitutes and had intercourse with women within the sacred precincts, and besides brought in things for sacrifice that were unfit. The altar was covered with abominable offerings that were forbidden by the laws. People could neither keep the sabbath, nor observe the festivals of their ancestors, nor so much as confess themselves to be Jews. On the monthly celebration of the king's birthday, the Jews were taken, under bitter constraint, to partake of the sacrifices; and when a festival of Dionysus was celebrated, they were compelled to wear wreathes of ivy and to walk in the procession in honor of Dionysus. At the suggestion of the people of Ptolemais a decree was issued to the neighboring Greek cities that they should adopt the same policy toward the Jews and make them partake of the sacrifices, and should kill those who did not choose to change over to Greek customs. One could see, therefore, the misery that had come upon them.

Under Roman rule, one or more deals were worked out with the Jews so that they could pay a special tax to Rome and be excused from having to participate in Roman imperial worship, but under Domitian things changed. As emperor worship was required for subjects of the Roman Empire to enjoy its benefits, both negative and positive incentives were used to motivate public support of the imperial presence in such places as Asia Minor. Thus here was virtually no sector of society that was not affected by the pressure to express loyalty and devotion to Rome. Domitian's temple in Ephesus was completed in 89 CE, and despite being in ruins now, at its entrance is still displayed a marble carving of the winged goddess *Nikē*—which means "Victory"—the point being that the Romans were the victors, and inhabitants of the region were subjects. Just down the street was the brothel, and a carving in the marble pavement showed visitors the way to one's heart's desires. This shows the domination strategy of linking sexual drives to economic prosperity to religious traditions to civic pride—and all of these to imperial loyalty. Therefore, it is no accident that a multiplicity of issues is addressed in the Johannine Epistles and Apocalypse; the pressures were real, and the issues were interwoven on multiple levels.

If the emperor's birthday was celebrated monthly, or even annually—sometimes for days on end—one can appreciate the political pressures under which Gentile believers in Christ must have felt themselves. Marble carvings in Ephesus and throughout the region show many instances of small loyal subjects making endorsed offerings before larger Roman soldiers and officials—displaying the right way to perform. Likewise, citizens and sacrificial animals wearing garlands are shown in procession, parading their support for the Empire and its benefits. In the Ephesus museum, a large sculpture of Domitian's head with an adjacent clenched fist and forearm can be seen today; the original full statue served to remind people of who was in charge.

Domitian's reintroducing the imperial cult to the Roman Empire, however, was not the only problem with his reign. Domitian was also known for killing his own guests at dinners in Rome, for the entertainment of those present (and likewise those who refused an invitation to attend), and even Roman historians report him as a wicked megalomaniac. In his own temple in Ephesus, where a description of his legacy was carved in the mantelpiece of the altar, spike-holes can be seen embedded across the entire area. This reflects *damnatio memoriae*—the damnation of his memory by following Roman officials, seeking to blot out his name and memory—as a bronze plaque was affixed, covering the writing. Indeed, it must have seemed that "the whole world" had gone after "the Beast" for Christians of the late first century CE, which is why visions of what God might yet be doing in the heavens provided hope for the earthbound.

The Number of the Beast: 666 (or Is It 616?)

A good deal of speculation has accompanied interpretations of 666 as the number of the Beast in Revelation 13:18 (although some ancient manuscripts list it as 616), but the exegetical question is what it meant to its original author and audiences—literally. Was it a mystery, or was it a code for something they would have understood back then? Assuming the latter, first-century understandings would have excluded identifying the number's meaning as a reference to Pope Paul VI, "Ronald Wilson Reagan" (three names with six characters each), the building owned by Donald Trump's son-in-law (address: 666 Fifth Avenue, New York), or 111 short of a three-fold perfect 777. Such speculation has nothing to do with a literal, exegetical reading of the text, despite being embraced by so-called "conservative" interpreters. Rather, the use of numbers to signify Hebrew letters as secret code-work for spelling out the names of adversaries is called *gematria*. Given that Hebrew language had no numbers, letters of the alphabet were used to signify numbers, with the first ten letters of the Hebrew alphabet signifying 1-10, the second ten letters signifying 20-100, and the next five letters signifying 200-500. And as the Hebrew alphabet consists only of consonants, vowels in Greek names would have been omitted from such designations. Thus, the numeric total in Hebrew of the letters N-R-N C-S-R (for *Neron Caesar*) is six hundred and sixty-six. As the value of the Hebrew letter *nun* is 50, deleting the second "n" from the name (to make it *Nero Caesar*) comes to 616, explaining how that number came to be used in some manuscripts instead of 666.

Therefore, 666 probably originated as a Jewish-Christian code referring to Nero and his henchmen during the persecution of Christians in Rome between 64 and 68 CE. Thus, Nero is likely the one referred to in Revelation 13 as the first Beast; coming up out of the sea referenced boats sailing from Rome. The healed head wound may refer to the legend that Nero would come back to life again, but more telling is the Beast's speaking blasphemies against God and being granted authority "to make war on the saints and to gain victory over them" (Rev 13:7). The hopeless plight of the faithful is reflected in the dictum: "If any are to be taken captive, then into captivity they will go. If any are to be killed by the sword, then by the sword they will be killed," calling for "endurance and faithfulness on the part of the saints" (Rev 13:10). Here the three and a half years of Nero's persecution of Christians in Rome is reminiscent of roughly the same time period that Antiochus Epiphanes afflicted the residents of Jerusalem with the abomination of desolation in the temple (Dan 11:31; 12:11; cf. also Mark 13:14). And, Caligula's attempt to erect a statue of himself in the Jerusalem temple in 40 CE, as well as Titus's destruction of the temple in 70 CE, must have brought back anguished memories of Babylonian and Greek desacrations.

In Revelation 13:11-18, however, the second Beast coming out of the earth probably refers to a traveling imperial entourage, perhaps making a circuit in the region. The second Beast is given the full authority of the first Beast, even setting up policies that would "cause anyone who didn't worship the beast's image to be put to death. It forces everyone—small and great, rich and poor, free and slave—to have a mark put on their right hand or on their forehead. It will not allow anyone to make a purchase or sell anything unless the person has the mark with the beast's name or the number of its name" (Rev 13:15-17). While there is no independent evidence as to what the mark of the Beast might have been, it suggests an outward sign of Empire-compliance as a basis for being a full commercial member of society, reflecting political and economic realities of Domitian's reign. Yoking professional guilds and regional governments to the Empire ensured broad compliance. Therefore, the woman who rides on the Beast reflects Mother Rome and the imperial cult, and the kings who commit blasphemy and adultery with her allude to ways that local kingdoms were drawn into doing Rome's bidding (Rev 17–18). Her being drunk with the blood of the saints thus reflects Christians' awareness of those who had suffered by not acquiescing to the Empire.

Further connecting the second Beast with Domitian is the fact that the seven heads of the Beast represent the seven hills of Rome-as-Babylon, and they also signify seven administrations going back to Caesar Augustus, which lead up to the eighth—following the brief administration of Titus—that of Domitian (Rev 17:9–11). Finally, Roman coins of the time feature baby Domitian surrounded by seven stars (planets), conveying his divine status. This is matched by John's vision in Revelation 1:16, 20 of Christ holding seven stars in his right hand—a direct challenge to Domitian's authority. As these seven stars are said to represent the seven lampstands and churches of Asia Minor, among whom Christ walks, one gets the sense that Revelation was performed among these churches during or shortly after the reign of Domitian.

A Circuit among the Seven Churches of Asia Minor

In Christ's letters to the churches of Asia Minor, we have a depiction of a preaching circuit that traveling ministers likely took, as they ministered in one church community for several days and then in another. The seven letters to the churches (Rev 2–3) were likely added as a unit to the larger collection of oracles and visions contained in the rest of Revelation, and an interesting feature is that each of them reflects particular knowledge of that community and its situation, applying then a prophetic message calling for repentance as well as delivering a word of encouragement.

II. Features of Revelation

While the book of Revelation was probably finalized and circulated between 95 and 100 CE, it contains earlier material that was either written or preached over an extended period of time. Such likelihood is supported by the fact that the composition includes many sets of visions (bowls, trumpets, and seals) opening up into a new set of images when coming to the end of a particular set. Many visions of things that are "at hand" were delivered as prophetic sermons among the churches of Asia Minor, and if there is some truth to the tradition that John was exiled to the island of Patmos by Domitian, several visions and messages were likely circulated among the mainland churches over a period of years before being gathered into a final form. As apocalyptic preaching and writing, one can imagine sets of sermons expanding on seven trumpets, seven bowls, or seven seals, each making a point in calling for repentance or for courage during hard times. These appear to have been strung together into a larger sequence later, encompassing what has happened, what is, and what is to come.

In terms of composition and progression, Revelation has several beginnings and several endings. Near the beginning, the seven seals are introduced by the throne scene (Rev 4), which is preceded by seven letters to seven churches (Rev 2–3), which are set in the context of John's vision on the Lord's day (1:9-20). This vision is introduced by declaring John's writing to the seven churches in Asia, drawing in Paul's "grace and peace" greeting and 1 Peter's royal priesthood affirmation (1:4-8). Reflecting an earlier edition, a final editor introduces the letter as Christ's revelation to his servant John, encouraging people to read it among the churches to their benefit (1:1-3). The endings of Revelation wind things up in a variety of ways. After a vision of Babylon's fall (Rev 18), there will be celebrations in heaven as the Beast is defeated (Rev 19) and Satan is bound (Rev 20). Then, the new heavens and earth are followed by a vision of the New Jerusalem, wherein the union of Christ and his bride—the church—is celebrated in cosmic glory (Rev 21). This is followed by John's vision of paradise restored, a reminder of the Lord's imminent return, and a climactic word from the angel to worship God and to live faithfully (22:1-17). In the final conclusion, the final editor adds his own admonition to respond faithfully to the words of "this scroll." If any add or detract from John's Revelation—beware! God will add to their accounts the plagues described therein (22:18-21).

As a larger composition, particular features of John's revelation include visions he claims to have seen, Christ's letters to the churches, descriptions of hardships faced by the faithful at the hands of the powers of Babylon and her subjects, the final victory of Christ, and the honoring of the saints. While some of the imagery is clear to its audiences, some of it is intentionally obscure, and for two primary reasons. First, as code language for resisting the Roman Empire and its collaborators, references to nations and leaders are veiled so as to protect authors and audiences alike. Second, as the imagery is suggestive, it allows itself to be applied in many directions, not just one or two, and this explains how John's Revelation continues to speak to the oppressed faithful during times of hardship from setting to setting and from generation to generation. In that sense, later audiences continue to find meanings that speak also to their own situations in ways timely; such is the imaginative power of apocalyptic.

Visions of John

In the opening scene, John claims to have had a vision of Christ—a Christophany—from which he catches glimpses of what is happening and what is to come. As with the callings of the prophets in the Old Testament, and even with Paul's Christophany on the road to Damascus, several features follow. First, a transformative spiritual encounter occurs—neither deserved nor expected. Christ simply appears to John, speaking with a megaphone voice (Greek: *phōnēn megalēn*), and John turns around and "sees" the voice. Second, his reaction is to fall down as though dead—smitten with awe at the divine encounter. Third, he is restored by Christ's right hand, and fourth, he is then given a message to write to the churches (1:10-20). While the literary features of John's apocalyptic visions are clear, it must be acknowledged that he claims to have been shown a set of images and messages by the Lord and his messengers, and in that sense, he is simply conveying that which he has received from on high.

Whether literally or figuratively, John claims "I saw" nearly three dozen times in Revelation, and after the opening-vision scenario, three times he is given an image of what is and will take place by a divine messenger who says "I will show you" what is and is to come (4:1; 17:1; 21:9). The first vision involves an encounter with one like the Son of Man portrayed in Daniel 7: "He wore a robe that stretched down to his feet, and he had a gold sash around his chest. His head and hair were white as white wool—like snow—and his eyes were like a fiery flame. His feet were like fine brass that has been purified in a furnace, and his voice sounded like rushing water" (Rev 1:13-15). He walks among the seven lampstands, and from his mouth comes a two-edged sword. As he holds the keys to both Death and Hades in his hand, it is his judgment that is to be feared rather than those with only worldly power and means. At his instruction, the letters to the seven churches are written.

The second vision is of a heavenly throne on which the Lord God is seated. This throne scene is of immense significance politically; it declares that, despite imperial powers and regional governors, there is only one eternal kingdom, and that belongs to God alone. From a heavenly perspective, all rulers and powers will eventually bow down to the Lord God of Israel, and the twenty-four elders attending the throne represent twelve tribes of Israel and the twelve apostles of Christ. They cast their crowns before the throne and cry out that the Lord God alone is worthy to receive glory, honor, and power (4:11). God has a scroll in his right hand, and the Lamb alone is worthy to open the seals of the scroll. When he opens the seals, they prefigure horses and riders bringing war, calamity, famine, and celestial torment. Nonetheless, 144,000—a faithful remnant of twelve thousand from each of the twelve tribes—will be spared destruction (7:1-17). At the opening of the seventh seal there is silence in heaven, and then seven trumpets begin their sequence of announcing plagues and horrors (8:2–11:19).

Three signs then follow. First, a woman gives birth to a son (reminiscent of Christ, but obscure in meaning), who is then opposed by a second sign involving the dragon-serpent, Satan. He makes war against the woman and the child and is engaged by the warrior-angel Michael (12:7-12), whereby the woman escapes into the desert and the son is snatched up to God. Outraged at his defeat, the dragon seeks to make war against those who hold firmly to the witness of Jesus; he thus gives power to the Beast coming out of the sea and the second Beast coming by land, whose number is 666 (13:1-18). Despite this tribulation, 144,000 triumph over the onslaught and possess on their foreheads the mark of Christ and God rather than that of the Beast (14:1–15:4). Following this, seven bowls of God's wrath are poured out upon the earth, declaring his judgment against its rulers (15:5–16:21). Until now, the realities typified in Revelation cover what has recently happened and what is impending, seeking to convince audiences to be faithful to Christ and not to give in to the Empire and its worldly demands. Each of the sequences grows with intensity, until things really get critical in numbers 5, 6, and 7. The goal, of course, is to lead audiences to repentance, not knowing when the final seal, trumpet, or bowl might be broken, sounded, or outpoured.

The third vision, however, signals a turn. No longer is the primary thrust one of warnings and impending catastrophe, but it heralds the victory of God—the defeat of the Beast and the fall of Babylon are at hand (17:1–18:24). This brings about celebrations in heaven (19:1-10), as the Beast is defeated by Christ and Satan is bound for a thousand years (19:11–20:15). The saints will thus reign over the earth as its judges, and the tables will be turned not only on the reign of Domitian, but on the entire Roman Empire. In Revelation 17:9-11 comes an indication of the time span over which the content of Revelation is given. When John says, "Five kings have fallen, the one is, and the other hasn't yet come," this suggests that some of this material was written during the days of Vespasian, after Nero's reign. As Titus reigned only for two years, his legacy is referenced by John's saying, "When that king comes, he must remain for only a short time." Domitian's subsequent reign is then apparently referenced thusly: "As for the beast that was and is not, it is itself an eighth king that belongs to the seven, and it is going to destruction." As the seven administrations since Caesar Augustus preceded the reign of Domitian, connecting his regime with the eighth, which is to be destroyed, would certainly have given hope to audiences between 81–96 CE.

Eight Administrations (Kings)

1. Augustus (27 BCE–14 CE)—allowed the worship of Julius Caesar

2. Tiberius (14–37 CE)—refused divine honors for himself

3. Caligula (37–41 CE)—insisted on divine honors [but did not persecute Christians]

4. Claudius (41–54 CE)—sought to reverse emperor worship [expelled Jews/Christians from Rome]

5. Nero (54–68 CE)—persecuted Christians as scapegoats after 64 CE [did not expect emperor worship; followed by the short reigns of Galba, Otho, Vitellius]

6. Vespasian (69–79 CE)—"the one [who] is" [the first of the three Flavian emperors]

7. Titus (79–81 CE)—the one who "hasn't yet come" but "must remain for only a short time"

8. Domitian (81–96 CE)—"the beast that was and is not, . . . an eighth king that belongs to the seven, and it is going to destruction" [required emperor worship]

John's fourth vision is the briefest (21:9–22:5), but it also heralds the greatest hope for believers. A new heaven and a new earth will be inaugurated by the New Jerusalem, the holy City of God, wherein every tear will be wiped dry, and death itself will receive a final deathblow. God's presence will now forever be with his people, and Christ is now united with his spotless bride— the church. On the gates of the City are written the names of the twelve tribes of Israel, and the twelve foundation stones bear the names of the twelve apostles. The measure of the City is given, and it is composed of the most precious jewels and materials imaginable. No uncleanliness will be a part of that

City, and the Lamb will be its light. Restoring the original image of paradise, a river of life runs through the City, and the leaves of the Tree of Life within it become the healing of the nations. In that sense, Revelation's last chapter not only concludes its own composition fittingly, but in canonical perspective, it fulfills the vision of God's design for humanity in Genesis 1–3.

The Four Visions of John in Revelation

- Christ's Message to the Churches (1:9–3:22)
  - John's opening Christophany (1:12-20)
  - Seven letters to seven churches (2:1–3:22)
- The Throne Scene (4:1–16:21)
  - The Lamb opens the scroll and its seven seals (5:1–8:1)
  - The seven trumpets—plagues and horrors (8:2–11:19)
  - Signs in heaven—the woman and child, the dragon, seven plagues (12:1–16:21)
- The Fall of Babylon and the Judgment of the Beast (17:1–21:8)
  - The woman who rides on the Beast (17:1-18)
  - The fall of Babylon (18:1-24)
  - The victory of the Lamb (19:1-21)
  - Satan's defeat and the ruling of the saints (20:1–21:8)
- The New Jerusalem and the Marriage of the Lamb and His Bride—the Church (21:9–22:5)
  - The twelve tribes as gates and the twelve apostles as foundations (21:9-21)
  - The Lamb as the City's light (21:22-27)
  - The river of life and the tree of life, whose leaves are the healing of the nations (22:1-5)

Christ's Letters to the Churches

Christ's letters to the churches of Asia Minor follow a basically similar form, and in conveying their messages to the churches, they communicate awareness of the issues faced in each situation, followed by admonitions to repent and words of encouragement. Sometimes plays on words are used; sometimes aspects of local pride and identity are drawn into the message as a means of making a point. Clearly, the delivery of such messages would elicit knowing responses from original audiences, and awareness of those connections also helps present-day readers appreciate the content of each letter.

A Common Pattern of the Letters of Christ to the Churches (Rev 2–3)

a) Introductory instructions: "Write this to the angel of the church in . . ."

b) Description of the situation that is "known" by Christ, the head of the church

c) An admonition, exhortation, and call to action is given (the core message)

d) . . . followed by promise of a greater reward than that offered by false means to fulfillment

e) Concluding admonition: "If you can hear, listen to what the Spirit is saying to the churches"

While the visions in the rest of Revelation offer general admonitions only (stay faithful to Christ and do not give in to worldly powers and pressures), the letters of Christ to the churches are pointed and direct. Among the issues addressed are the following. First, do not be lethargic, but recover your first love and first deeds (Ephesus, Sardis) in overcoming the challenges of the world. As deeply felt love hinges upon an awareness of one's being completed by the other, the key to recovering one's first love for Christ begins with an awareness of one's need before God and humble dependence on the divine other. Second, stand firm in what you are about to suffer (Smyrna and Pergamum). In 155 CE Polycarp, Bishop of Smyrna, would be burned alive for refusing to deny Christ or to worship Caesar, and according to tradition, Antipas, bishop of Pergamum ("where Satan's throne is") was cooked to death in a bronze kettle in 92 CE. Third, find a way to deal with the resistance offered by unconvinced Jews (Smyrna and Philadelphia)—those who "say they are Jews" but are not (labeled "Satan's synagogue" as an inflammatory slam). These three admonitions address hardships from without.

In addition, there are several challenges from within that the letters of Christ to the churches address directly. First, you must reject the teachings of the licentious Nicolaitans (Ephesus, Pergamum); according to some traditions, Nicolaus showed his overcoming the sin of jealousy by offering his beautiful wife to others and showing no anger. That must have led to other problems. Second, the false teachings of a woman labeled "Jezebel" are apparently leading some not only to eat food offered to idols but also to commit sexual immorality (Pergamum, Thyatira). The letter to Thyatira calls for repentance and warns of her demise. Third, some communities have grown confident in their own wealth and sufficiency (Sardis, Laodicea), and they are confronted with the charge to be zealous for Christ. In Laodicea, just a few miles from the hot springs in Hieropolis, hot water from the springs was rather tepid by the time it flowed in pipes across the valley; and cold-water therapy pools no longer served their purpose if they became lukewarm. Either hot or cold waters can be therapeutic, but Laodicea is neither. They must repent if they hope to be effective at extending the healing work of Christ in their contextual environment. In each of these letters, note the connections between the contextual realities of the audiences and the message delivered from the Lord.

The Letters of Christ to the Churches in Revelation

- *Ephesus* (2:1-7): the leading city of the Roman province of Asia; Paul stayed here for two years on his third missionary journey; the heart of the Gentile mission—with many traveling ministers coming through

  - *Situation:* I know your deeds; you have done well to hate the Nicolaitans and to reject false apostles, but you have left your first love

  - *Message:* "Change your hearts and lives and do the things you did at first. . . . I will move your lampstand from its place if you don't." (2:5)

- *Smyrna* (2:8-11): the main port on the west coast of Turkey; the church embraced some poorer members of society as well as merchants; Polycarp was later martyred there by the Romans for refusing to deny Christ or confess Caesar (ca. 155 CE)

  - *Situation:* I know the hurtful things that have been said about you by those who say they are Jews but are not (these are really Satan's synagogue)

- *Message:* "Don't be afraid of what you are going to suffer.
  . . . Be faithful even to the point of death, and I will give
  you the crown of life." (2:10)

- *Pergamum* (2:12-17): official center of emperor worship
  ("where Satan's throne is," v. 13) in Asia; also the home of Ga-
  len's medical school; Bishop Antipas was reportedly martyred
  here (roasted to death in a bronze kettle)

  - *Situation:* some there follow Balaam's teaching (eating
    food sacrificed to idols and committing sexual immoral-
    ity) and others follow the Nicolaitans' teaching

  - *Message:* Repent and "I will give those who emerge victori-
    ous some of the hidden manna to eat," as well as "a white
    stone with a new name written on it, which no one knows
    except the one who receives it." (2:17)

- *Thyatira* (2:18-29): military outpost and center of various
  crafts-makers' industries with their own professional guilds
  (Lydia, the Christian merchant of purple cloth, was from this
  city; Acts 16:14); acceptance into a guild was confirmed by
  being given a white stone

  - *Situation:* you put up with that self-appointed prophet Jeze-
    bel and allow her to mislead believers into eating food
    sacrificed to idols and committing sexual immorality

  - *Message:* "I am casting those who have committed adultery
    with her into terrible hardship—if they don't change their
    hearts" and lives; "to those who emerge victorious, I will
    give authority over the nations." (2:22, 26)

- *Sardis* (3:1-6): the capital of the ancient kingdom of Lydia;
  before the Romans, the Persians captured the city, surprising
  the king in the middle of the night—rather than die, he welcomed them unopposed; it boasted a major synagogue and a
  Greek gymnasium

  - *Situation:* the church at Sardis is lax in its faith; beware,
    Christ is coming as a thief in the night

  - *Message:* Wake up! Remember what you have received and
    obey it!

- *Philadelphia* (3:7-13): the "city of brotherly love" and of agricultural and commercial prominence; the gateway to the Lycus Valley; and home of kings Attalus II and Eumenes II; the "Synagogue of Satan" refers to persecuting Jews

  o *Situation:* Facing "Satan's Synagogue," this church has nonetheless overcome and not denied Christ's name

  o *Message:* "I have set in front of you an open door that no one can shut"; "hold on to what you have so that no one takes your crown." (3:8, 11)

- *Laodicea* (3:14-22): a wealthy city with a medical school and therapeutic waters—both cold and hot—also a textile center with much trade

  o *Situation:* "Because you are . . . neither hot nor cold, I'm about to spit you out of my mouth"; "you say, 'I'm rich, and I've grown wealthy, and I don't need a thing.' You don't realize that you are miserable, pathetic, poor, blind, and naked." (3:16-17)

  o *Message:* "Buy gold from me that has been purified by fire so that you may be rich, and white clothing to wear so that your nakedness won't be shamefully exposed, and ointment to put on your eyes so that you may see." (3:18)

Seven-Fold Warnings—Seals and Trumpets and Bowls—Oh My!

One of the interesting things about Revelation is its use of numbers. The number seven, for instance, conveys completeness, as do the numbers three, four, ten, twelve, forty, and one hundred forty-four thousand. By far the most common number is seven (used over fifty times), and its use especially denotes the completeness of a particular sequence moving toward a climax. Therefore, seven seals lead into seven trumpets, which lead into seven bowls of plagues and afflictions. The number four is used especially with reference to the four creatures and the four corners of the earth, while such fractions as a third and a fourth often denote what is destroyed. Ten refers to the kings that have succumbed to the Beast, and twelve refers to both the tribes of Israel and the apostles—making their combination (twenty-four) a means of favoring both

Jewish and Christian leaders. A hundred and forty-four thousand is a way of assuring audiences that no matter how bad the persecution gets, a remnant will survive among all the groups of faithful in the world. Therefore, the use of numbers in Revelation is highly symbolic.

Symbolic Numbers of Revelation

- *Two*—witnesses, olive trees, lampstands, beasts
- *Three*—angels, plagues, foul spirits, gates of the city on each side
- *Four*—living creatures, corners and winds of the earth, horns of the golden altar
- *Seven*—churches, angels, lampstands, stars, spirits, seals, horns, eyes, trumpets, thunders, heads, plagues, bowls, hills, thousands
- *Ten*—horns, kings
- *Twelve*—stars, gates, angels, tribes, apostles, foundations, pearls, names, kinds of fruit, thousands
- *Twenty-four*—elders, thrones
- *One hundred forty-four thousand*—twelve times twelve thousand: a robust remnant from each tribe

The Lamb's War and the Bride of the Lamb—A Vision of God's Endgame

The main thrust of Revelation is to affirm the victory of God against worldly adversaries and apparent setbacks to God's reign. This victory, however, is not garnered by means of human force or violence; rather, it is the Lamb's War that defeats the enemies of God—paradoxically, by laying down its life as a pure and unblemished offering. Because of this victory, the robes of the martyrs are made white by being washed in the blood of the Lamb, and Michael's victory over the dragon is garnered because of the sacrifice of the Lamb. While the kings of the earth make war against the Lamb, they will not succeed, and Babylon itself will fall. Significant here is the theological emphasis not only upon the cosmic power of the atonement but especially on the political means by which God's victory is achieved. The victory of the Lamb and Christ's followers is not won by resorting to evil means or to violence; rather, it is won by faithfulness and the willingness to lay down one's life rather than deny the truth. Therefore, the Lamb's War is one of trust and the willingness to suffer for the truth if required.

The victory of the Lamb, then, is celebrated by the marriage of Christ to his church—a spotless bride who has come through the tribulation in faithfulness and resolve. As the bride of Christ is joined with him in a cosmic celebration, the new heavens and the new earth are actualized. Further, that new relationship becomes the place where God's presence abides on earth, and by means of this new epoch-changing relationship, the victory of God is completed. The wedding celebration of the Lamb and the church thus provides a vision of God's endgame as a means of encouraging believers during dismal times of hardship and persecution. In keeping an eye on the future, the present and past are also thereby transformed.

III. The Message of Revelation

The message of Revelation assures believers that God will finally be victorious, thereby calling them to be faithful in the here and now. Despite tendencies of interpreters to see it as a predictive timeline of unfolding history, it was never intended to be taken that way. The main thrust was always contemporary and direct—challenging first-century audiences to be faithful to Christ and to the ethos of his followers living under imperial domination and within societies that only partially embraced Jewish-Christian concerns. That being the case, the message of Revelation speaks clearly to every generation since—calling believers to be faithful to Christ and his loving challenges to the world, assured also that the final victory, in the end, will be God's.

I Know Your Situation and Deeds . . . Repent!

In reflection, Christ's letters to the seven churches of Asia Minor might just as well have been written to all Christian traditions. One need not live in Asia Minor (modern-day Turkey) to be challenged to recover one's first love, to resist the teachings of those who compromise on morality and ethics, to reject the dichotomies of idolatrous empires today—submit to value X lest you experience consequence Y. On one hand, strong Jewish-Christian values are argued for each of the churches, and simply applying those values in later situations works well. In all things, adhering to Christ is the answer: in the face of Jewish religious certainty, hold to Christ—a dynamic approach to faith and practice. In the face of empire and its economic and political appeals, hold to Christ—his reign will abide at the end of the age. In the face of assimilative tendencies among indiscriminant teachers, stay focused on Christ—the purity of the Lamb calls for a spotless bride. These messages are worthy of application in every generation. On the other hand, a powerful thrust of the church-letters is the reminder that the situation of every church is known by Christ. Therefore, the Spirit's leadings can be appropriated as needed most in any situation—and that calls for discernment.

Behold, I Am Coming Soon . . . Hold On!

Another powerful message of Revelation is the call for the faithful to hold on, anticipating the coming of Christ at any moment. While early Christians sustained a diversity of views on the Lord's return—some believing that he would return before the generation of the eyewitnesses passed, yet facing disappointment when that apparently did not happen—an abiding hope in Christ's appearing continued. Therefore, the providing of hope for those suffering affliction for their faith is a powerful thrust of Revelation's impact. Christian martyrs in every generation have found consolation and empowerment in Revelation's message, and believing that the faithful—those whose names are written in the Lamb's book of life—will be exonerated on the last day emboldens those who resist affixing their signatures to worldly memberships that compromise their faith. Another feature of the Lord's coming is the promise that it also happens spiritually. Whether in clouds from the skies or in a half hour of heavenly silence, a genuine foretaste of the Lord's coming is granted to those who join the spiritual fellowship of those gathered around the Throne, abiding in faithful worship and living in the world.

Despite Calamities and Martyrdoms, God Wins!

The calling of believers is not to be successful; it is to be faithful, and this is one of the most enduring aspects of Revelation's message. No matter how bad things get in terms of plagues, calamity, and persecution, God and God's ways will finally win out in the end. So this vision of God's cosmic endgame empowers the faithful to reconceive lost battles in the light of the final victory and to reorient one's priorities along the lines of one's Ultimate Concern. As well as providing hope, a vision of the final outcome emboldens the faithful to resist taking shortcuts of integrity and demeanor that may jeopardize the furthering of God's work by abandoning the way of Christ. The reign of God can never be advanced by going against the character of the kingdom; this was the teaching of Jesus, and his ministry and life testified to that conviction.

Therefore, the way of the cross involves a paradox. The only way to gain one's life is to release it, whereas seeking to save one's life may actually involve its forfeiture in spiritual terms. In that sense, Revelation furthers the paradoxical way of Christ as represented elsewhere in the New Testament, and it does so in apocalyptic terms. With the assurance that God wins in the end, risks can be taken in the here and now, and apparent successes and failures may be regarded as the impostors they are, in the light of the New Jerusalem, which emanates from the Lamb.

Water Down the Message and Beware of the Plagues!

The book of Revelation closes with a warning to interpreters then and now: any who add to or detract from the words in "this scroll" will have added to them the plagues therein, and they will forfeit their share in the bounty of the tree of life and the blessing of the Holy City (22:18-19). Despite the views of some, this is not a defense of the King James Version of the Bible against more recent translations, nor is it a defense of the twenty-seven books of the New Testament against the adding of, say, the Gospel of Thomas. The thrust of this passage defends the book of Revelation against those who might be tempted to water down its message in the late-first-century situation—ignoring its hard sayings or adding easier ones. And, it could be that the final editor was aware of readers who had skipped over some of the more unsavory parts of the text as it was delivered and performed among the churches in Asia Minor. But who might have been tempted to water down the message? Most likely, such an inclination would have been attractive for Gentile believers living under the hegemony of the Roman Empire, seeking to legitimate compromises and avoid the way of the cross.

That being the case, this hard word indeed speaks to interpreters in all generations regarding Revelation and also the rest of the canon. Deal with the hard message first, exegetically, and then seek to appreciate its meanings and implications for authentic faith and practice. And in that sense, the end of the Apocalypse concludes with a response to the invitation at the finale of Christ's message to the churches. As Christ invites the church of Laodicea, "Look! I'm standing at the door and knocking. If any hear my voice and open the door, I will come in to be with them, and will have dinner with them, and they will have dinner with me" (3:20), the community of the Apocalypse declares at the end of the book: "Amen. Come, Lord Jesus!" (22:20). And, from beginning to end, the basis for Revelation's message is the gift of grace and peace (1:4; 22:21).

IV. Engaging Revelation

In considering the character of Jewish-Christian apocalyptic literature in general, and the message of Revelation in particular, consider the following questions for engagement. First, take note of some of the Old Testament imagery used in the Johannine Apocalypse, and consider earlier meanings in Daniel, Zechariah, and Isaiah (for instance) and note how the imagery is used in Revelation. Is it used in similar ways or in different ways? And, how would original audiences have understood the meanings of these appropriations of Jewish biblical themes within the late-first-century Mediterranean world? Do any new insights emerge from considering these images intertextually? If so, how so, and how does appreciating the biblical and apocalyptic background of Revelation help one discern its literary associations?

Second, consider how the message of Revelation spoke to believers living under the Roman Empire and occupation in the late-first-century situation, and reflect upon how the content of the message would have been both a challenge and an encouragement to its audiences. How did the letters of Christ to the churches challenge their original audiences, and how did the images presented in the rest of the Apocalypse call believers to faithfulness? And, what implications would such messages have for the would-be faithful in later generations and situations?

Third, why does Revelation seem most relevant to audiences who feel powerless, and how does its envisioning of God's breaking into human history embolden its audiences to persevere amidst the adversities they face? In facing the challenges of injustice and domination in the world, how does Revelation's presentation of the Lamb's War foster a sense of new possibilities for the faithful? And given an envisioning of God's final victory at the end of the age, how are God's people emboldened in their faithfulness while living as aliens in a strange land? In the words of the nineteen-year-old Quaker martyr in the seventeenth century, James Parnell, writing to family and friends before his death: "Be willing that self shall suffer for the truth, and not the truth for self." With that counsel, John would certainly concur.

AFTERWORD

The Jewish psychologist, Viktor Frankl, founded the third Vienna School of Psychotherapy as Logotherapy—the human quest for meaning. In contrast to the views of Freud and Adler, Frankl taught that the essential human drive was neither sex nor power but the quest for meaning in life. If one finds meaning, one can transcend the most excruciating pain and overcome the most difficult of circumstances; a sense of purpose makes that possible.[1] In reading the New Testament contextually, though, the goal is not simply to better understand its content in its original settings; it is also to connect those understandings with contemporary contexts—to find meaning in ways that engage the reader's life, experience, and worldview.

In doing so, new insights inevitably emerge. In particular, a fuller understanding of why something was reported or written gives one a more acute sense of its significance and meaning back then. This understanding thus informs the exegetical process—understanding what a biblical passage meant to its first authors and audiences yields insights, then, for later readers and their settings. Therefore, from one context to another, a contextual reading of the New Testament moves from particular meanings to general understandings, which then lead back to particular meanings for the reader. Thereby the hermeneutical process yields its fruit, as new understandings give way to new meanings and applications among contemporary readers.

On one hand, biblical interpreters are cautioned to let the text speak for itself—reading with a distanced and objective stance, rather than bending the text to go along with what the reader thinks it ought to say. Let the odd and unfamiliar content and expression stand; then do the work of sorting out its relevance for later settings. Then again, in reading the New Testament as scripture, one must be open to engagement, personally and subjectively. Further, discerning how a passage speaks to one personally and existentially is the fullest measure of any classic text, including the Bible. That being the

---

1. Viktor E. Frankl, *Man's Search for Meaning*, rev. ed. (New York: Simon and Schuster, 1962).

case, the counsel of Walter Wink and others well deserves to be heeded.[2] A transformative reading of the biblical text always involves "taking it personally"—engaging the meaning of the text subjectively. Or, put in the terms of 2 Timothy 3:16, how can the inspired writing of the text be honored by inspired readings of the text? That involves reflecting on its meaning personally and existentially.

The subject of the New Testament, however, is not simply the story of Jesus and the early Christian movement, laced with encouraging letters and visions from a transcendent perspective; no. The subject of the New Testament is centrally the story of God's interaction with humanity, making all things new through God's saving-revealing actions, breaking into human history in ways transformative, redemptive, and healing. In that sense, there is neither a single first meaning nor a single final meaning of the biblical text, as authors, audiences, and readers are all involved in the making of meaning. In engaging the content of the New Testament in the light of its original contexts, though, readers get a fuller sense of what things likely meant to original authors and audiences in the interest of making fuller sense of their meanings today. However, reader beware! In so doing, we not only read about the larger story of the divine initiative and human response in ancient times, but we become a part of that story in the here and now. Thus, within a contextual reading of the New Testament, we find ourselves moving from crisis to Christ . . . and back again.

---

2. Walter Wink, *The Bible in Human Transformation: Toward a New Paradigm in Bible Study*, 2nd ed. (Minneapolis: Fortress Press, 2010); cf. also Janice Capel Anderson and Jeffrey L. Staley, eds., *Taking It Personally: Autobiographical Biblical Criticism, Semeia* 72 (Atlanta: Scholars Press, 1995).

RESOURCES

Rather than list significant monographs or leading commentaries on each of the books of the New Testament, the reader is encouraged to research particular books and essays related to the particular subjects and passages of interest. Bibliographies are also available online and elsewhere, and visiting any decent library will acquaint the student with leading commentaries on every book of the New Testament as well as other reference works. Therefore, this list of resources is designed to inform the student of the sorts of resources that should be procured for one's library, or at least consulted within the course of one's introductory graduate or undergraduate studies. A number of fine website resources are also becoming available, so a few of the best of these will also be listed. Therefore, additional resources for studying the New Testament include the following types of works.

Translations and Study Bibles: recommended to be used with this text is *The CEB Study Bible* (Abingdon, 2013); other first-rate study Bibles include *The New Interpreter's Study Bible: NRSV with the Apocrypha* (Abingdon, 2003); *The HarperCollins Study Bible* (NRSV, rev. ed.; HarperOne, 2006); *NRSV New Oxford Annotated Bible with Apocrypha* (4th ed.; Oxford University Press, 2010); *The NIV Study Bible* (Zondervan, 2012); *The NIV Archaeological Study Bible* (Zondervan, 2006); *The Catholic Study Bible* (NAB, 2nd ed.; Oxford, 2011); and *The New Jerusalem Bible* (Image, 1985).

Concordances and Reference Works: in order to look up words and themes, make use of a good concordance such as *Young's Analytical Concordance to the New Testament* (Hendrickson, 1985); *The New Strong's Expanded Exhaustive Concordance to the Bible* (Thomas Nelson, 2010); and *The New Englishman's Greek Concordance and Lexicon* (Hendrickson, 1986). Also useful are such side-by-side comparison texts as *Synopsis of the Four Gospels, Revised Standard Version* (American Bible Society, 2010) and *Synopsis of the Pauline Letters in Greek and English* (Baker, 2010).

Contemporary Primary Literature: really important primary writings include *The Dead Sea Scrolls: A New Translation* (HarperSanFrancisco, 2005); *The Works of Philo* (Hendrickson, 1993); *Josephus: The Complete*

Works (Thomas Nelson, 2003); *The Apostolic Fathers: Greek Texts and English Translations* (Baker, 2007); and *Eusebius' Ecclesiastical History: Complete and Unabridged* (Hendrickson, 1998). The works of the Apocrypha are also extremely important for understanding the New Testament, and these can be found in many of the study Bibles above.

Bible Dictionaries and Encyclopedias: excellent one-volume works include *HarperCollins Bible Dictionary* (rev. ed.; HarperOne, 2011); *The New Bible Dictionary* (3rd ed.; IVP, 1996); *Zondervan Illustrated Bible Dictionary* (Zondervan, 2011); *Catholic Bible Dictionary* (Image, 2009); *The IVP Dictionary of the New Testament* (IVP, 2004); and *CEB Bible Dictionary* (Abingdon, 2011). Leading multivolume sets include *The Interpreter's Dictionary of the Bible* (Abingdon, 1962 and 1976); *The New Interpreter's Dictionary of the Bible* (Abingdon, 2009); *The Anchor Bible Dictionary* (Doubleday, 1992); and *The IVP New Testament Dictionary Set*, 4 vols. (IVP, 1993–2013). The best word-study New Testament dictionaries include *Theological Dictionary of the New Testament* (Eerdmans, 1964); *Dictionary of New Testament Theology* (Zondervan, 1986); and *The New International Dictionary of New Testament Theology and Exegesis* (Zondervan, 2014).

Commentary Series: individual commentaries can be found on particular books of the New Testament, but valuable series for introductory reading include the *New Bible Commentary* (IVP, 1994); *Zondervan Bible Commentary* (Zondervan, 2007); and Daily Study Bible and the New Daily Study Bible (Westminster John Knox Press). Commentaries for pastors include The New Interpreter's Bible (Abingdon); Interpretation (Westminster John Knox Press); and NIV Application Commentary (Zondervan). More academic commentary series include the New International Commentary on the New Testament (Eerdmans); the Word Biblical Commentary (Thomas Nelson); Anchor Yale Bible Commentary (Yale University Press); Tyndale New Testament Commentary (Eerdmans); and Hermeneia (Fortress).

New Testament Studies Websites: websites continue to develop, and some helpful ones include Bible Odyssey: People, Places, and Passages (http://www.bibleodyssey.org/); The New Testament Gateway (www.ntgateway.com); Electronic New Testament Educational Resources (http://catholic-resources.org/Bible/); The Johannine Literature Web (http://catholic-resources.org/John/); Early Christian Writings (http://www.earlychristianwritings.com/); Resource Pages for Biblical Studies (http://torreys.org/bible/); and Into His Own: Perspective on the World of Jesus (http://virtualreligion.net/iho/).

20197613R00251

Made in the USA
San Bernardino, CA
26 December 2018